FILM NOIR
PROTOTYPES

Other Applause Books/Limelight Editions by the same Authors

More Things Than Are Dreamt Of (1994)
What Ever Happened to Robert Aldrich? (1995)
Film Noir Reader (1996)
Film Noir Reader 2 (1999)
Horror Film Reader (2000)
Film Noir Reader 3 (with Robert Porfirio, 2002)
Film Noir Reader 4 (2004)
Gangster Film Reader (2007)
The Vampire Film from Nosferatu to True Blood (2011)
Film Noir The Directors (2012)
The Zombie Film (2014)
American Neo-Noir (2015)
Film Noir Compendium (2016)
Film Noir Light and Shadow (2017)

Other Books

David Lean and His Films (1974)
The Noir Style (1999)
Film Noir (Taschen Film Series, 2004)
L.A. Noir The City as Character (2005)
Roger Corman: Metaphysics on a Shoestring (2006)
Film Noir The Encyclopedia (4th Edition, 2010)
Film Noir Graphics: Where Danger Lives (2012)
The Film Noir Jigsaw: Critical Perspectives on the Classic Period (2016)

Also by Alain Silver

Robert Aldrich: a guide to references and resources (with Elizabeth Ward, 1979)
The Film Director's Team (with Elizabeth Ward, 1983)
Raymond Chandler's Los Angeles (with Elizabeth Ward, 1987)
The Samurai Film (3rd Edition, 2005)
James Wong Howe The Camera Eye (2010)

Also by James Ursini

The Fabulous Life and Times of Preston Sturges, An American Dreamer (1976)
The Modern Amazons: Warrior Women on Screen (with Dominique Mainon, 2006)
Cinema of Obsession (with Dominique Mainon, 2007)
Femme Fatale (with Dominique Mainon, 2009)
Directors on the Edge (2011)

FILM NOIR PROTOTYPES

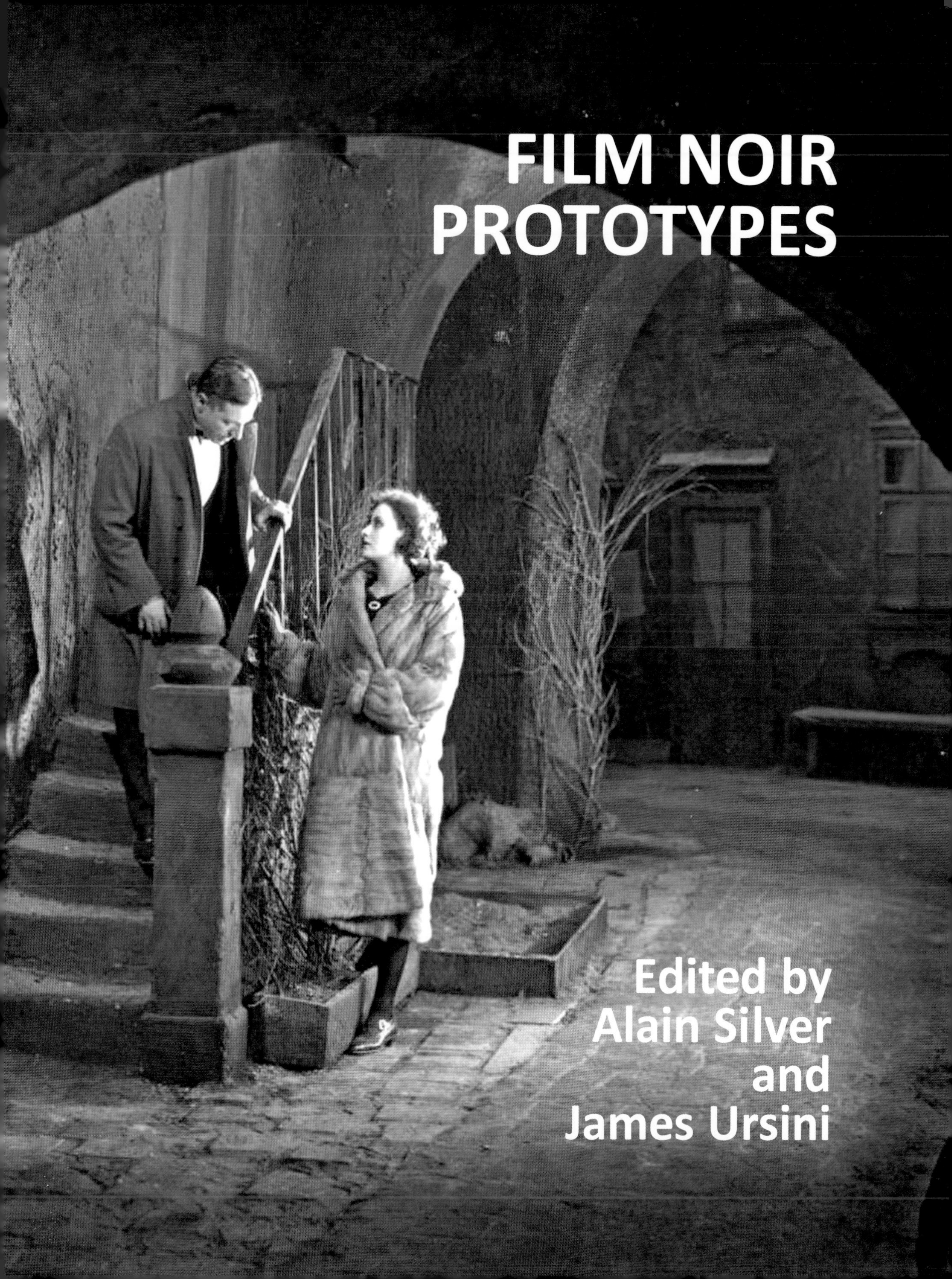

Edited by
Alain Silver
and
James Ursini

Published in 2018 by Applause Theatre and Cinema Books
An Imprint of Hal Leonard LLC.
7777 West Bluemound Road
Milwaukee, WI 53213

Trade Book Division Editorial Offices
33 Plymouth St., Montclair, NJ 07042

Permissions, sources and earlier copyright details may be found in the Acknowledgments, on page 7.

Printed in the United States of America.

Book and cover design by Alain Silver.

Library of Congress Cataloging-in-Publication Data

Names: Silver, Alain, 1947- editor. | Ursini, James editor.
Title: Film noir prototypes : origins of the movement / edited by Alain Silver and James Ursini.
Description: Milwaukee, WI : Applause Theatre & Cinema Books, 2018. |
  Includes bibliographical references.
Identifiers: LCCN 2017058777 | ISBN 9781495092749 (pbk.)
Subjects: LCSH: Film noir--History and criticism.
Classification: LCC PN1995.9.F54 F565 2018 | DDC 791.43/655--dc23
LC record available at https://lccn.loc.gov/2017058777

www.applausebooks.com

Front cover: *Pandora's Box*.

Back cover: clockwise from top left, director Josef von Sternberg with the cast of *Crime and Punishment*, Peter Lorre, Marian Marsh, Tala Birell, and Douglas Dumbrille; *Sabotage*, Alfred Hitchcock with Oscar Homolka; John Ford directs Victor McLaglen in *The Informer*; Cecil B. DeMille (seated) with Director of Photography Karl Struss directs Fredric March and Elissa Landi in *The Sign of the Cross*.

Frontispiece: *The Joyless Street* with Greta Garbo and Asta Nielsen.

Contents

Acknowledgments

Most of the twenty essays in this anthology are published for the first time. Reprint details are below. Most of the illustrations are from the collection of the editors, which was originally assembled with Robert Porfirio, Elizabeth Ward, and Carl Macek for *Film Noir: An Encyclopedic Reference to the American Style.* Others are from the Robert Porfirio Collection at Brigham Young University administered by James D'Arc, Lee Sanders, James Paris, and Timothy Otto. Some images were also provided by the individual contributors: Todd Erickson and James V. D'Arc, Julie Grossman, Robert Miklitsch, Jesse Schlotterbeck, and Tony Williams.

Stills and graphics are reproduced courtesy of Allied Artists, Associated British, Columbia, Continental, MGM, New World, Paramount, RKO, Selznick, 20th Century Fox, UFA, United Artists, Universal, and Warner Bros.

Special thanks must go to our frequent collaborators Elizabeth Ward and Linda Brookover for comments and suggestions on this volume. Mel Zerman, who started Limelight Editions, made the entire *Reader* series possible. With regards to this most recent volume John Cerullo, Carol Flannery, Marybeth Keating, Clare Cerullo, and Lindsay Wagner lent editorial support from Applause Theatre & Cinema Books/Hal Leonard.

Original publication information for selected articles; all are Reprinted by Permission:

"German Expressionism and Film Noir" by Robert G. Porfirio is adapted from *The Dark Age of American Film: A Study of American Film Noir (1940-1960)* by Robert G. Porfirio, a doctoral dissertation, Yale University: 1979.

"Looking Back—Victorinoir: Modern Women and the Fatal(e) Progeny of Victorian Representations" by Julie Grossman was first published in *Rethinking the Femme Fatale in Film Noir* by Julie Grossman, London: Palgrave MacMillan, 2009, pages 93-131.

"Proto-noir—DeMille Style" by Alain Silver and James Ursini is adapted from "The Moral Extravagance of C.B. DeMille" in *The UCLA Daily Bruin*, November 4, 1970, pages 8-10.

"Film noir, American painting and photography: a question of influence?" by Tom Ryall was first published in *A Companion to Film Noir*, edited by Andrew Spicer and Helen Hanson. Hoboken: Wiley-Blackwell, 2013, pages 158-174.

"Film Noir Graphics: Origins" by Alain Silver and James Ursini is adapted from the Introduction to *Film Noir Graphics: Where Danger Lives*, Santa Monica: Pendragon, 2012, pages 4-13.

"The Gangster in Film Noir" by Alain Silver derives partially from "The Gangster and Film Noir" in *Film Noir Light and Shadow*, Milwaukee: Applause, 2017, pages 26-63, which was itself revised and reprinted from "The Gangster and Film Noir: Themes and Styles," in *Gangster Film Reader*, Pompton Plains: Limelight Editions, 2007, pages 290-322.

"Women and Film Noir: Pulp Fiction and the Woman's Picture" by Julie Grossman was first published in *Kiss the Blood Off My Hands*, edited by Robert Miklitsch. Urbana: University of Illinois Press, 2014, pages 37-61.

Proto-noir from the hardboiled school:
Satan Met a Lady (1936).

Introduction

Alain Silver

As readers familiar with our previous work already know, we believe that film noir defines itself, as an individual film and as a film movement, by its style. As we recently noted in *Film Noir Light and Shadow*, two decades from our first published embrace in 1979 of the proposition initially articulated by Raymond Durgnat, Robert Porfirio, Janey Place and Lowell Peterson, and Paul Schrader to our "coffee-table book" and visual study of *The Noir Style* in 1999. As *Film Noir Light and Shadow* with its 750 high-quality images demonstrated, technological advances since 1999 now permit every survey of film noir to be richly illustrated.

The opening chapter of *The Noir Style*, "Out of the Past," contained our first extended analysis of some of the prototypes in film, art, photography and even the covers of hard-boiled literature that antedated and influenced the classic period of film noir. While we then focused on the noir films themselves, in sidebars on the work of photo-journalist Arthur Fellig aka WeeGee and German Expressionism our colleagues Linda Brookover and Robert Porfirio extended the discussion of prototypes even further. This volume continues that process. We are fortunate to have enthusiastic participation from many of those who contributed to our past anthologies, most of whom have also written or edited their own studies of the noir movement.

Film Noir Prototypes opens with a pointed discussion of crossover motifs from German expressionism to film noir adapted from the dissertation of our frequent collaborator, the late Robert Porfirio. In two essays Julie Grossman first considers the progression from how women were depicted in the Victorian era to film noir then elaborates on this further in a second piece which considers pulp fiction by women writers such as Vera Caspary and Dorothy Hughes that developed into film noir foundation texts, *Laura* and *In a Lonely Place*. Sheri Chinen Biesen also makes two contributions, first writing about noir pre-cursors adapted from Gothic literature, such as *Gaslight, Rebecca* and *Jane Eyre*, then providing a case study of émigré Fred Zinnemann's social-realist noir *Act of Violence*. Robert Miklitsch also considers the influences and evolution of character type, specifically the Rogue Cop, within the heart of the noir cycle.

James Ursini and I look to influences in earlier genre and filmmakers and write about the dystopian sci-fi *Metropolis*, horror films, gangster films, and the work of two directors seldom associated with noir, John Ford and Cecil B. DeMille. Homer Pettey probes for prototypes in silent and early sound projects which he dubs "paleo-noir"; Richard Edwards in the 1930s spy films of Alfred Hitchcock; James V. D'Arc and Todd Erickson in the work of early émigré director Robert Florey, in particular *The Face Behind the Mask*; and Tony Williams in the French wartime films that evolved from poetic realism. Discussion of literary antecedents is taken up by Marlisa Santos with novelist Cornell Woolrich, James Ursini with Dostoevsky's *Crime and Punishment*, and Jesse Schlotterbeck with the novella and real-life events that became *Double Indemnity*. Tom Ryall explores the visual influences on noir from both American painting and photography; and James Ursini and I recap how the covers of crime magazines and hard-boiled novels and gangster movie posters anticipate the iconography of the noir movement.

As always we hope that the cogency of the writing and the accompanying illustrations will lead the reader to view (or review) the films themselves.

German Expressionism and Film Noir

Robert G. Porfirio

In *The Street* (1913, opposite page) Ernst Kirchner—once a member of the seminal group of expressionist painters centered in Dresden and known as The Bridge—departs completely from naturalistic rendering of color and anatomy and recomposes the broad avenues of Berlin for his own purposes which, according to art historian John Canaday, involved using "hectic, slashing patterns to express the tension, the neurasthenic agitation, the sinister viciousness, of the city."[1] A similar nightmare vision of Berlin informs Karl Grune's *The Street* (*Die Straße*, 1923), an early "street film" whose sets, appropriately enough, were designed by expressionist painter Ludwig Neidner. Even more evocative in its use of ersatz studio streets and back alleys (designed by Mans Sohnle and Otto Erdman) is the "Vienna" of *The Joyless Street* (*Die Freudlose Gasse*, 1925) directed by G.W. Pabst. The surface shoddiness of this street's settings reflect the meager existence of its inhabitants (Figure 1 on next page) waiting in

The Cabinet of Dr. Calgari: Werner Krauss (left) as the titled Doctor and Conrad Veidt as Cesare.

1.

3.

2.

line to be exploited by the local butcher.

While these denizens are the victims of inflation and the cruel manipulations of financiers, the economic contrasts of a similar studio "street film" of the noir cycle directed by Fritz Lang, *Scarlet Street* (1945, Figure 2), are not so severe. Yet the existence of its hero, Chris Cross (Edward C. Robinson), is no less constrained by an unloving wife (Rosalind Ivan) who disparages his artistic abilities, a femme fatale (Joan Bennett) who takes advantage of his love and generosity, and a "benevolent" boss (Russell Hicks) who rewards twenty-five years of employment as an honest cashier with a pocket watch. His "joyless" life in contemporary New York, relieved only by the Sunday afternoons he spends painting, is reflected in the urban settings which have been recreated at the Universal lot. In the frame cited here, for example, Chris' melancholia as he waits for a bus with a co-worker is reinforced by the lighting and the use of rain. The three previous illustrations might usefully be compared with the last (Figure 3), which is taken from the semi-documentary film noir, *He Walked by Night* (1948, directed by Alfred Werker and Anthony Mann). Here the expressive photography of John Alton adeptly converts actual Los Angeles' locales, such as the one presented here, into what critic Robert Warshaw has described as "the dark, sad city of the imagination."

Chiaroscuro Effects

The combination of the partially sensitive orthochromatic film stock and bright arc lights that typified most of the Expressionist cycle produced startling chiaroscuro effects, as evidenced in this famous shot from F. W. Murnau's *Nosferatu* (1922, opposite, photographed by Fritz Wagner). When these effects were assimilated by the American horror film the use of panchromatic film stock, incandescent lighting, and the general constraints of the "studio look" subdued the harsh contrasts into what might best be described as a "balanced" low key style. During the noir period, when harsh, undiffused, and even arc lighting was resumed in conjunction with the new realism of depth-staging, something approximating the harsh contrasts of the Expressionist cycle began to reappear, though modified somewhat by the use of high-speed panchromatic stock. Such severe con-

trasts are in evidence in the example (Figure 4) from one
of the concluding sequences of *Scarlet Street*. The effect
here is understandably less expressionistic than the previous example, but the use of shadow is no less pronounced. Here however the figure of Chris Cross (Edward
G. Robinson) is hardly the index of evil that Nosferatu is,
though in conjunction with the semi-diegetic voices of
the two people—Kitty and Johnny— for whose deaths
Chris feels responsible, it is a fitting symbol of his own
tormented spirit.

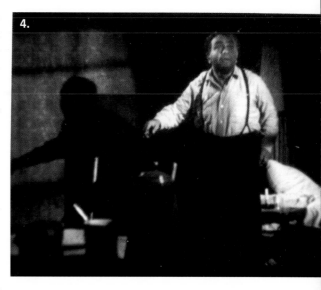

4.

Stimmung

Stimmung means literally "mood" and it can be either
gay or melancholy; the latter variety however seemed to
fit best the needs of the expressionists who wished to
express the "inner vibrations of the soul," a goal that was
partly psychological, partly metaphysical. As far as the
Expressionist cycle is concerned, this stimmung is most
often the province of the Kammerspielfilm, where the intimate atmosphere of social relationships can
use such devices as lighting to evoke a melancholy mood, as suggested in the example of *Alraune*
(Figure 5 on next page). The emphasis here is psychological rather than metaphysical, whence it is easily transformed into those "Germanic" tonalities of the American film noir, most often associated with
wet city streets, blinking lights, and rain-drenched windows, as in the specific example from *The
Possessed* (1947, directed by Kurt Bernhardt, Figure 6 on next page), a close shot of Joan Crawford
visually imprisoned behind the dark muntin bars and wet glass.

Faces and Gestures

Opposed to the "externalization" of naturalism and impressionism, painterly expressionism relies on stylization to reveal one's inner state, a state often marked by anxiety or worse. This tendency goes back at least to Edvard Munch, and is well represented here in Erich Heckel's *Portrait of a Man* (1919, at left), a woodcut in which the pale green of the face and hands plays off against a background of blue and brown. These unusual colors, together with the black, angular lines of the block print, suggest an apprehension bordering on neurosis. The nearest equivalent to such mannerism in the German cinema was the stylized performances of certain of its actors, an expressionist "school" of acting whose source was ironically the theater of Max Reinhardt; among the most adept at this rhetorical, exaggerated style of acting were Werner Krauss, Fritz Kortner, and Conrad Veidt. Shown here is Conrad Veldt in *The Hands of Orlac* (on page 16) performing a gesture quite representative of this school. Such expressionistic acting was not very compatible with the American naturalistic style, so the film

An early example of the legendarily expressive face of Greta Garbo in *The Joyless Street*.

noir was forced to rely on conventions of lighting and Hollywood's skill at typage (essentially type-casting to face and feature), making use of more subtle gestures to suggest inner "states." The success of the film noir in achieving this can be measured in the two final illustrations: the first relies more on camera placement and lighting to enhance actor Jack Lambert's features in *The Killers* (Figure 7 below); the second depends more on the plasticity of actor Richard Widmark's face in *Night and the City* (Figure 8 below).

7.

8.

Décor: The Staircase

In *The Haunted Screen*, Lotte Eisner mentions the atmospheric potential of stairwells and corridors but she describes the Germanic fixation with them in almost metaphysical terms. Actually, their most immediate source for the Expressionistic cycle is probably the Jessnertrappe, an unusual deployment of steps which was already a theatrical trademark of the outstanding German director, Leopold Jessner, in the teens. Macabre, deformed staircases can be seen in such classical entries as *The Cabinet of Dr. Caligari* (1919, below) and *The Golem* (1920, right); but they are more commonly used for atmospheric purposes within the "psychological realism" of the kammerspielefilm and the "street film," where their use can be detected as early as *Backstairs*, directed by Paul Leni and Jessner himself. For example, near the conclusion of G. W. Pabst's *Pandora's Box* (1928)—adapted from the same two Wedekind plays which became the basis of Alban Berg's opera *Lulu*—the stairwell adds something more than atmosphere since its diagonal lines serve to connect Lulu with Jack the Ripper (Figure 9 on next page), whom she welcomes back into her apartment with a rare gesture of kindness that proves to be her ironic undoing. While the more graphically unreal stairwells of early Expressionism made their way into the American horror cycle (begin-

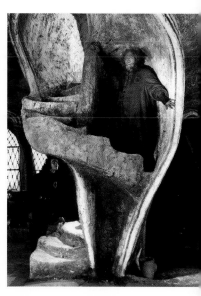

9.

ning probably with Paul Leni's *The Cat and the Canary* (1927, right) it was the second and sore "realistic" usage that was characteristic of the film noir, culminating in the labyrinthine corridors of *Kiss Me Deadly* (1955, Figure 10 below). Yet already in *Criss Cross* (1949) a similar deployment of downtown Los Angeles' settings was heightened by the use of interior stairwells (Figure 11 below). Appropriately enough, this film was directed by émigré Robert Siodmak, whose American career was crowned by *The Spiral Staircase*, a singularly Germanic conjunction of stairwell and psychological states illustrated elsewhere.

Décor: Middle-class Motifs

Pabst's *The Joyless Street* is one of the most famous examples of the third or "street film" phase of German Expressionism. Typical of the street films, it depicts the breakdown of the middle class world, although unlike later instances of this phase this one was entirely studio bound, and demonstrates the strong, lingering influence of an earlier Expressionism. In the frame illustrated here (Figure 12, opposite) the unkempt, naturalistic decor reveals the influence of the mid-twenties Neue Sachlichkeit (new objectivity) but the manner in which the diffused light emanates from half-closed

11.

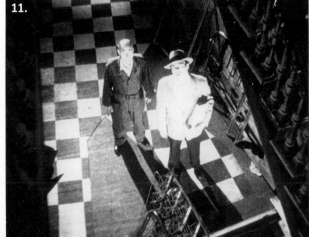

10.

Venetian blinds, rendering the young woman's corpse slightly imprecise and impersonal, evokes the atmospheric remoteness of an older style. Such Venetian blind "effects," heightened still further would become a veritable trademark of the American film noir. The example presented here from *Criss Cross* (Figure 13) lacks the traditional Venetian blinds yet creates stimmung quite efficiently with the play of lights on the film's major femme fatale (Yvonne de Carlo) and the inclusion of the elevated streetcar "outside" the window. In fact the scenario (by proletarian writer Dan Fuchs from the novel by Don Tracy), by centering attention on the chaotic lives of the petty bourgeoisie who dwell in the vicinity of Los Angeles' Bunker Hill district, is very reminiscent of the German "street films." And like many of the earlier street films, *Criss Cross* shrewdly blends location exteriors with a majority of studio interiors. In the illustrated sequence for example the "angel car" in the background is actually back-projected on a studio set. It is rather appropriate that this American "street film" was directed by Robert Siodmak and photographed by Franz Planer.

The "Demoniac Bourgeois"

The Expressionistic cycle's preoccupation with the "demoniac bourgeois," epitomized by figures like Dr. Mabuse who possess almost preternatural powers, has led to a good deal of speculation regarding their socio-political ramifications by Siegfried Kracauer and his followers. In *The Haunted Screen*, however, Lotte Eisner is content to point out that the demoniac preternatural connotations do not have to involve the diabolic and that its origins in Romantic literature descends immediately from the fiction of Ernst Hoffman. Despite the fact that *Dr. Mabuse, the Gambler* (1922) lacks the supernatural aura of classical Expressionism, the title character of Fritz Lang's film is clearly diabolic. In the illustrated scene (Figure 14, right) Lang relies rather obviously on the effect of surface decor to heighten this association. In her controversial essay, "Raising Kane," Pauline Kael asserts that a good deal of what Orson Welles imparted to *Citizen Kane* was drawn from the American film *Mad Love*, directed by émigré Karl Freund and adapted from the earlier German classic *The Hands of Orlac* (1924). Her assertion rests primarily on Welles' stylized performance and makeup as the elder Kane, and the associations she makes with *Mad Love*. Miss Kael's

hypothesis becomes less tenuous if one views Welles' treatment of Charles Foster Kane as simply the start of a series of demoniac characterizations—Col. Haki in *Journey into Fear*; Franz Kindler in *The Stranger*; Harry Lime in *The Third Man*; Gregory Arkadin in *Mr. Arkadin*; Hank Quinlan in *Touch of Evil*; Hastler in *The Trial*—where a stylized performance and mannered visuals heighten ambiguity and suggest a debt to German Expressionism that goes back at least to Welles' exposure to the German classics at the Museum of Modern Art just prior to his work on *Citizen Kane*. The image at left is from the concluding sequence of *The Stranger* (l946, directed by Welles and photographed by Russell Metty) during which the disguised, former Nazi leader Franz Kindler (Orson Welles) is impaled by one of the moving figures of an antique clock. The manner of Kindler's death and the stylized decor are well within an earlier tradition of expressionism.

The Studio Set

Fritz Lang's *Dr. Mabuse, the Gambler* forsakes the fantasy-like milieu of such earlier films as *Destiny* in favor of a contemporary urban environment that is visually heightened by the art nouveau inspired sets of Otto Hunte and Stahl-Urach. "Realism" of setting however did not lead Lang out to actual locales and he afforded himself of the controls provided by studio production. Thus the perilous atmosphere of the modern city was recreated on the lot as in Figure 15 where the German expertise in lighting (photographed by Carl Hoffmann) reinforces the effect of the luminous surfaces of the sets. The studio recreation of urban exteriors in a manner designed to heighten a perilous and oppressive atmosphere is also characteristic of the noir cycle's "studio" period, represented here by a frame from *The Lodger* (Figure 16). One of the Victorian "thrillers" typical of the early portion of the cycle, *The Lodger* (1944) was directed by émigré John Brahm and photographed by Lucian Ballard entirely on the Fox lot.

15.

16.

Sexual Debasement

The theme of sexual debasement is a common expressionistic motif, evidence of a debt to a fin-de-siecle Romanticism. In the Expressionist cycle this theme often takes the form of a femme fatale. Perhaps Lorelei would be a better figurative term here, the female sprite who lured those navigating the Rhine into a rocky shipwreck in the manner of a Homeric siren.[2] The Expressionist Lorelei has charms to ensnare a reputable member of the bourgeoisie or petty bourgeoisie and frequently reduce him to acts of public humiliation. One could, of course, read in this the conventional moral of the "wages of sin," but at the same time it is quite consistent with the expressionistic interest in the heightened emotional states associated with both the libido and guilt. The first image (right) is taken from the American edition of Hanns Ewers' *Airaune* illustrated by Mahlon Blaine, whose own life appears to have been tainted by the same decadent Romanticism from which he drew his artistic inspiration. In the illustration at right the heartless, artificial woman Airaune is seen "conquering" a wealthy state official. Below and right, the film versions.

Two adaptations of *Alraune* (1928 and 1930) featured Brigitte Helm (left), fresh from her dual role in Fritz Lang's *Metropolis*, as the first incarnation of the genetically enhanced, proto-femme fatale. Below, Hildegard Neff as the artificial seductress and Erich von Stroheim as creator of the soulless Alraune.

 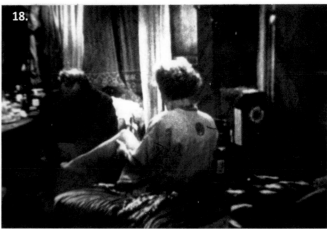

Less heartless but equally destructive is Frank Wedekind's *Lulu*. In the accompanying frame from Pabst's film, *Pandora's Box* (1928, Figure 17) Lulu, portrayed by American actress Louise Brooks, is seen after having triumphantly maneuvered Dr. Peter Schoen (Fritz Kortner) into a compromising situation before the eyes of his son and his fiancée.

Josef von Sternberg's *The Blue Angel* (1930) is a film that stands on the very edge of the Expressionist cycle but is the locus classicus for "Lorelei" figures in the American cinema. In the illustration (Figure 18) Lola (Marlene Dietrich) can be seen "allowing" the fallen Professor Rath (Emil Jannings) to put on her silk stockings for her.

From the expressionist prototype comes a classic period repetition of this action, the loose-living Kitty in *Scarlet Street* responds to the request of amateur artist Chris Cross that he be allowed to paint her by permitting him to lacquer her toenails (opposite). With subtler effect, Phyllis Dietrichsen (Barbara Stanwyck) arguably the ultimate femme fatale, uses "a honey of an anklet" to bring cynical Walter Neff (Fred MacMurray) to his emotional knees.

The ritualistic overtones of such acts of debasement, as those pictured here, suggest the coincidence of Freudianism and expressionism in their conjunction of sex, sadism, and fetish that fully carried over into the noir movement.

Notes

1. In *Metropolitan Seminars in Art, Portfolio 3: Expressionism* (New York: Metropolitan Museum of Art, 1958)
2. Perhaps best-known from the 1824 Heinrich Heine poem, "Die Lorelei," or the more recent 1913 "La Loreley" by Cubist poet Guillaume Apollinaire, the fatal female was actually created by Clemens Wenzeslaus Brentano in 1801 in "Zu Bacharach am Rheine."

A pose that typifies noir's depiction of female power and complex female identity: Lana Turner as Cora Smith in *The Postman Always Rings Twice*, about whom MGM declared, "She Gets Into Men's Blood.... And Stays There!"

Looking Back—Victorinoir: Modern Women and the Fatal(e) Progeny of Victorian Representations

Julie Grossman

Many film noir movies lend subjectivity to the independent women called femme fatales, depicting the psychological motives for becoming, or acting the role of, the "femme fatale." Contrary to popular culture's and film criticism's insistence that the deadly seductress figure defines American film noir, most noir movies suggest that women are forced into performing the role of "femme fatale" to escape social traps, thus offering a critique of the construction of the "femme fatale" on two levels. First, we see how women are forced to use their bodies and language to gain an upper hand in a society that habitually denies them freedom and culturally sanctioned opportunities. Second, many of these films expose the process by which the idea of the "femme fatale" is devised as a means of projecting male fear and anxiety onto the woman herself. The movies reflect how men in the culture project the idea of "femme fatale" as a label onto particular women in order to divide women into two easily regulated categories: "femme fatales" and "angels in the house."

These latter categories are, of course, familiar to us from our knowledge of the representation of gender in Victorian literature and culture, and indeed, I want to argue that Victorian narrative provides important parallels for understanding these projections. Victorian novels struggling with issues of female power can usefully be seen as precursors to film noir, which inherits yet extends Victorian narrative's investigation of categorical representations of women as angel/whore, as "good girl"/"femme fatale." Film noir's critique of binary representations of women, suggesting multiple portraits of strong, vulnerable women who resist simple categorization, is also anticipated in Victorian narrative.

Late-Victorian fiction and original cycle film noir register the crosscurrents, challenges, and anxieties of the modern period, and this historical link between Victorian narrative and Hollywood noir suggests some very interesting influences and continuities in representation. Certainly, to be culturally literate in modern America, one had to be familiar with British literature and culture. As Henry James, T. S. Eliot, and Raymond Chandler exemplify, modern American writers were often anglophiles, if not expatriates. To make the point from the perspective of American film history, Mark Glancy's book *When Hollywood Loved Britain* argues for the profound influence of Britain on American film of the 1930s and 1940s. While Glancy's focus is on issues of patriotism, the extensive list of films adapting Victorian novels (*The Mill on the Floss, David Copperfield, Great Expectations, Wuthering Heights, Jane Eyre, Dr. Jekyll and Mr. Hyde*, to name just a few) or featuring British talent (such as popular noir director Hitchcock, actors George Sanders and Laird Cregar, and noir screenwriter Joan Harrison) further demonstrates the important connections between Victorian culture and American film of the 1930s and 1940s.

More pointedly still, Guy Barefoot's book *Gaslight Melodrama: from Victorian London to 1940s Hollywood* repeatedly argues that Victorian London is a crucial source for film noir and 1940s Hollywood melodrama. While it's clear enough that "gaslight" noir films such as *Hangover Square, The Suspect,* and *The Spiral Staircase* invoke a nineteenth-century British context, Barefoot's analysis (along with Glancy's, Martha Vicinus's, and Helen Hanson's work drawing links between Victorian Gothic and 1940s melodrama) paves the way for understanding Victorian narrative as an important context for understanding film noir. Emphasizing connections between the Victorian gaslight city and the way Hollywood of the 1940s rehearsed this setting, Barefoot's book seeks to "investigate the often-conflicting attitudes evoked by the legacy of Victorianism and Victoriana traceable in Hollywood films, in films made in Britain, and in a wider cultural context" (12). Barefoot thus advances the possibility of pursuing these links with attention to gender, for which his focus on the evil lurking within the dark city has important implications.

My interest is in the extent to which Victorian narrative provides important parallels for understanding the representations of women and gender in film noir in the context of rapid cultural change and the advent of modernism. Engaged as it was with gender anxieties produced by changing social roles, Victorian fiction presented a ready model for early filmmakers. More specifically, representations of gendered time and space in late-Victorian novels offered, indeed, a "pre-history" for film noir: an avenue of investigation that noir films would be influenced by and would revisit repeatedly.

The "femme fatale" can be usefully redefined as sharing identity with the femme moderne who haunted nineteenth-century texts and then resurfaced as the "vamp" in silent film before the flourishing of film noir in the 1940s. These "fatal women" represent, on the one hand, the efforts of women to better position themselves and, on the other, the cultural opposition to formulations of modern female independence. My aim in introducing the Victorian period into a discussion of film noir is to broaden the cultural context from which film noir's "femme fatale" emerges in order to encourage finer readings of film noir movies and to expose the troubling reproduction and repetition of certain kinds of patterns in our ways of reading women, female agency, and narratives about powerful women.

Theda Bara's classic publicity pose for her portrayal of a "vamp" in *A Fool There Was* (1914)

The New Woman and "The Hidden Army" of World War II

Late 19th-century changes in gender roles were embraced and at the same time violently resisted. These shifts produced, in the late Victorian period, what Richardson and Willis call "the polyphonic nature of the debates around femininity at this time" that included public discourse that was at times "harmful and disparaging" (11, 13). Starting from the middle of the nineteenth century, there was, as Richardson and Willis recount, a dramatic increase of women in the work force; a gradual opening up of opportunities in education; a reevaluation and legislative reinvention of marriage, divorce, and property laws; and an increasing attention to the sexual double standard (see Richardson and Willis, 5–7). These substantive alterations in the lives and attitudes of women and men produced what Ella Hepworth Dixon called amazing changes in the social life of women (Ledger and Luckhurst, 86). While debates surrounding women's rights varied across issues such as sexuality, marriage, maternity, suffrage, and labor, the "New Women" agreed that a reinterpretation of women's social role was necessary for women to achieve greater independence and fulfillment:

> What the New Women did share was a rejection of the culturally defined feminine role and a desire for increased educational and career opportunities that would allow them to be economically self-sufficient. (Nelson, x)

Some New Women writers, such as M. Eastwood, were alert to the inflammatory language of empowerment invoked in popular commentary on the New Woman. In her 1894 essay "The New Woman in Fiction and in Fact," Eastwood hails the New Woman, as she parodies popular images of her, the "flashing, dashing, ripping, tripping creation," (Ledger and Luckhurst, 90).

The New Woman was appropriated not only by feminist activists but also by men and women rejecting new conceptions of female independence. About suffrage, many middle-class women, such as Mary Ward, insisted on women's lack of "sound judgment" (Ledger and Luckhurst, 93) and decried, in 1889, the case for suffrage as a "total misconception of women's true dignity and special mission" (94). Boyd Winchester's article on "The Eternal Feminine," published in *Arena* in 1902, finds women's genius in their "sentiment," "imaginative sympathy," and "moral susceptibility," insisting that

> every one who cherishes the slightest regard for the rare virtues and qualities of sweet womanhood must resent and abhor the too manifest tendency of modern social industrial, and educational innovations to unsex and abase our young women. (Nelson, 177)

Hyperbolic language in support and in defiance of the New Woman pervaded popular commentary. For Eastwood, the New Woman was "the weirdly bewitching, the soulful, the mysterious, the tricksy, the tragic, the electrifying, the intensely-intense, and utterly unfathomable new one" (90). Eastwood's participation in the invention of the legendary New Woman energized readers, while some commentary, like the critical attention later paid to the "electrifying" women in film noir, contributed to a sense of woman as "Other" and to increasingly bewildered responses to female social advancement.

A striking example of such negative mythifying is (the anti-New Woman) Ouida's reversal of conventional discussions of women of the period, an instance of backlash in 1894 that presages the postwar transposition of the independent woman into a "dangerous dame":

> The error of the New Woman (as of many an old one) lies in speaking of women as the victims of men, and entirely ignoring the frequency with which men are the victims of women. In nine cases out of ten the first to corrupt the youth is the woman. In nine cases out of ten also she becomes corrupt herself because she likes it. (Nelson, 157)

The passage suggests the extent to which the "bad women" become an effective vehicle for diverting energy for social change into forms of social hysteria, reflecting the generalized anxiety surrounding gender roles during times of transition. Susan Bordo notes, for example, that "the second half of the nineteenth century, concurrent with the first feminist wave...saw a virtual flood of artistic and literary images of the dark, dangerous, and evil female" (161). Bordo rightly observes that this is a recurring habit of representation "during periods when women are becoming independent and are asserting themselves politically and socially" (161).

The literature of the late-Victorian period certainly explored and tried to navigate these anxieties and contradictions, in part by constructing "angels in the house"[1] and by anticipating a continual resurgence of the "femme fatale" figure. Like many noir films, many nineteenth-century texts expose the "femme fatale" as a projection of male fears about the rise of independent women, the New Woman of both late Victorian England and postwar America. As Bram Dijkstra has said about the turn-of-the-century "femme fatale" figure as she is represented in art of the period,

> [l]iving under clouds and surf that seem like steam rising from the boiling cauldron of the elemental sea, these women represent that unabashed independence and elemental sense of freedom that men of 1900 feared, and found most fascinating, in the viragoes of their day. In the very directness of their passion and strength, these women embodied the paradox of the self-possessed and therefore hated, yet so very delectable and admirable New Woman, she who had thrown off the trappings of the household nun and had toppled her weak and fainting mother's pedestal. (265)

The repetition of "elemental" in the passage correctly identifies the force of ideation surrounding the female threat to established norms and conventions. Indeed, Rebecca Stott has observed that the presence of the "femme fatale" figure in late Victorian culture and literature "takes her place amongst degeneration anxieties, the rise of invasion scares, anxieties about 'sexuality' and 'race,' and concerns about cultural 'virility' and fitness" (22), just as, I would add, film noir explores anxieties about changed social and sexual roles of women in post-World War II America. As Stott claims, "the constitution of the femme-fatale-as-sign depends upon what else (besides Woman) is considered to be culturally invasive or culturally and politically Other at any historical point" (44).

For the women who had experienced independence and new forms of self-sufficiency in wartime America, the alienation caused by postwar changes in attitude was palpable. Film noir's sociocultural setting is one characterized by extreme gender anxiety, as men coming home from the war wondered what their wives had been doing when they were away and as women were driven back into the domestic sphere to resume functions as wives and mothers after a period of independence and new experiences as part of the work force during the war. When women entered the workforce—18 million women, six million for the first time—they discovered a venue for female desire, ambition, and for enhanced recognition of the contributions women could make to society and in the mar-

Left, an authentic dangerous "New Woman" of the Victorian Era, feminist and president of the National Union of Women's Suffrage Societies, Millicent Garrett Fawcett.

ketplace. According to Frank, joining the work force "markedly affected women's personal sense of themselves" (Frank, 17). Frank recounts myriad stories of the women who took pride in their contributions to the war effort, as well as their new and increased salaries. Lola Weixel comments, for example, on the changed perceptions of women welders:

> We were going to get in on the ground floor and be welders for ever and ever. It was almost an art, as well as a skill. It was a very beautiful kind of work. At the end of the day I always felt I had accomplished something. There was a product. There was something to be seen. (17)

While these women had experienced a dramatic movement from the margins to the center of social production, after the war, many of these women were fired or laid off: "As dramatically as they had come into the war plants," Deslippe explains, "they left or, in most cases, were fired":

> By the spring [of 1945], over 300,000 women had been laid off; that figure climbed to over 3,000,000 by the next year. In Detroit, the proportion of women in the automobile industry work force fell to 7.5 percent from 25 percent; in Los Angeles only 14 percent of the women who had worked in aircraft plants during the war still held their jobs in mid-1946. Nationally, women's share of employment in durable goods industries plummeted 50%. Many of these workers had considerable difficulty securing new jobs. A survey of 20,000 women workers in Detroit revealed that 72 percent of them had not yet found new jobs weeks after being released, despite their efforts. A note of desperation marked their search for work. "I was looking around madly for something to do because I didn't have that much money to last very long," one divorced woman with children reported. Those fortunate to secure employment took severe pay cuts: women who had earned an average of 85 to 90 cents an hour were now accepting jobs that paid only 45 to 50 cents an hour. (Deslippe, 13)

Government and industry began its dismantling of "the hidden army," one wartime government film's designation for wartime female employment (Frank, 19). One riveter, Edna Artman, recalls,

> [w]hen the war was over, they tried their darndest to get rid of the women. They said women were unstable, that we'd been absent too much, that we had our kids to look after. In my case they said I was too fat! Ford went from 18,000 to 2,000 women after they'd hired back in '46. (Frank, 20)

In her *Feminist Lives in Victorian England*, Philippa Levine devotes a chapter to the subject of women "Invading the Public Sphere" (126), as they discovered self-sufficiency and new venues for female agency in the second half of the nineteenth century. So, too, American women in the 1940s marched into the public sphere, having new social roles to play. This produced a cultural discourse and popular representations characterized both by meaningful change and by backlash.

Literature, Film, and Gender Invasion

Victorian narrative and film noir—both products of modern culture—are thus not only mutually informing, but also indicative of the continual problems we have in representing and in analyzing and understanding the complex experience of women in the social world. Like the cultural preoccupation with the "femme fatale" figure in film noir, the New Woman functioned as both a symbol of female power and an opportunity for dominant cultural voices to categorize and subordinate threatening calls for female agency. As Richardson and Willis note,

> the late nineteenth-century media reduction of the New Women to stereotypes might be considered a strategy of control, aimed at containing the threat they posed to the status quo. The bicycling Amazon and ugly bluestocking of caricature are more immediately accessible and memorable figures than woman concerned with social political change and thus were often used as a way of obscuring the latter's goals. (28)

In 1887, Rider Haggard warned of female incursions in his immensely popular novel *She*, an adventure tale about a male journey to the African Kor, where the dominant, powerful, and immortal Ayesha,

"She Who Must Be Obeyed," resides and rules the Amahaggar people. We know from early in the novel that "women among the Amahaggar live upon conditions of perfect equality with the men, and are not held to them by any binding ties" (63). As its preoccupation with female power suggests, the novel was, according to Elaine Showalter, a "complicated response to female literary dominance, as well as to British imperialism and fears of manly decline in the face of female power" (83). Showalter links the Amahaggar women directly to late nineteenth-century New Women: "Like the New Women novelists, they have renounced their dependencies on men" (85). Further suggesting the topical concerns about female social advancement, Showalter observes that it is no coincidence that the novel's main narrator, Holly, is a Cambridge don, since "the year when [Holly's and Leo's] quest begins, 1881, is also the year women were first admitted to the Cambridge examinations, and when, symbolically, the strongholds of male knowledge begin to fall" (85). The novel registers contemporary questions surrounding female independence and social advancement, questions that included a baffled wondering about the fate of (or "fatal" end to) male control over social institutions.

If *She* articulates anxiety about gender invasion and inversion ("Evidently the terrible She had determined to go to England, and it made me shudder to think what would be the result of her arrival there" [192–3]), parallel backlash concerns were echoed in 1945 in a *New York Times* story about women's growing influence in Hollywood. The article, "Hollywood Bows to the Ladies," offers the following: "Picture-making, like everything else, is coming more and more under feminine influence. The ladies, no longer content with being just glamorous, are invading in increasing numbers the production field, a sphere hitherto almost entirely masculine" (qtd. in Biesen, 127). The invasion language, as in *She*, registers the threat of female autonomy, independence, and passage into social spheres of influence: "This woman," says Holly, *She*'s narrator, "had confounded and almost destroyed my moral sense, as indeed she must confound all who looked upon her superhuman loveliness" (173). This "[confounding]" and admixture is echoed in the vampiric language invoked in publicity materials for

Early incarnations of "She/Ayesha" on film: below left, the 1925 British/German silent with a vampish Betty Blythe, whose costume recalls Bara's Cleopatra as She and Carlyle Blackwell as Leo Vincy/Kallikrates; right Helen Gahagan (before her political career) as a not particularly "Fatale" Ayesha in 1935 and Randolph Scott as Leo.

The Postman Always Rings Twice (1946). About Lana Turner's Cora Smith, MGM declared, "Her name is Cora.... She Gets Into Men's Blood.... And Stays There!" (qtd. in Biesen, 123).

Like *She* (as well as *Dracula*, which I'll discuss later), many film noir movies reveal, and yet also critique, destructive fantasies about female power that elide complex female identity. In most film noir movies, however, despite cultural preoccupations with the "femme fatale" figure, sympathy for the independence and struggles of women emerges. It is thus of great interest that these women's stories are then suppressed by critics, who reduce represented complex female experience to the simple role of the "femme fatale"—a role that then is codified and solidified as a defining feature of film noir.

Something similar is forewarned in readings of nineteenth-century fiction—in, for example, the reception of "cold" Estella, "frigid" Sue Bridehead, or most tellingly, readings of *Tess of the D'Urbervilles*. While some critics of Thomas Hardy's 1891 novel judge Tess's seductiveness (i.e., "she asked for it"), Rebecca Stott has rightly observed the strangeness of this pattern in Hardy criticism "which often assumes a male audience who know about the wiles of women" [172]). Similarly, Ann Ardis argues that by devaluing New Women fiction, late-Victorian male critics "produced a male image of culture and history" (57). Psychosocial assumptions and desires have, in these cases, resulted in canonized readings of film and literature that marginalize the stories of women and gender that are so central to nineteenth and twentieth-century narrative. Such projections of gender characteristics, like the contemporary (recent) male critical responses to film noir should be noted as points on a historical continuum on which gender categories are continually reasserted. My concern is that

Graphic depictions of *She*: below, Maurice Greiffenhegen's pre-Rapahelite vision for the 1912 edition. Right, sketch by G.C. Wilmshurst for "Heroines of the Modern Novel" in the *Illustrated London News*, 1908.

because we are so preoccupied with the category of the "femme fatale," we are blind to the stories of the women in film noir and to the varied historical backdrops that inform these stories.

Divided Realms

The representation of women in noir, as in Victorian literature, seems powerfully linked to divisions of space and time, a compartmentalization of experience that is, I would argue, critiqued by the logic of the texts in which the phenomenon appears. The drive to rigidly oppose realms—notably public versus private worlds; past versus present; city versus country—is expressed in Victorian fiction and in film noir at the same time as these spaces are identified in terms of gender. These oppositions, and our responses to them, have profound consequences for the cultural mediation of gender roles, in representation and in society, since these categories mold experience (as Foucault has taught us) into sharply regulated and often deeply oppressive spheres of influence. Indeed, I would argue along with Rebecca Stott that the "femme fatale" is a deeply Foucauldian concept: "In Foucauldian terms what we are witnessing is a process engaged not in stamping out the illicit and the anomalous but producing and regulating it" (25). I would add to Stott's commentary on late Victorian imbrications of the "femme fatale" that the construct, unleashed and expressed in order to be institutionalized, is alive and well in contemporary culture. The "femme fatale" is a product of dualistic thinking about women,

Below, *Great Expectations,* Charles Dickens' femme fatale Estella, bred to"break hearts" by Miss Havisham. Left, Valerie Hobson as Estella and John MIlls as Pip in David Lean's 1947 film. Right, the characters drawn by Harry Fraser for a 1910 edition.

but I hope that my discussion of the recurrence of these patterns helps to support my larger claim that there is a kind of urgency in the need to continue to put pressure on this category. The persistent projection onto women of mutually exclusive categories of being in the world often has tragic implications for women who stray from their roles or want to break down the oppositions that bind them.

Victorian narrative provides an important source for film noir in its preoccupation with the public and private dualism. Nineteenth-century literature very familiarly rehearses a dichotomy between the corrupt public realm and sacred domesticity. For example, in *Great Expectations*, Dickens calls Wemmick's home his private "Castle" world, and each day when he walks to work at "Little Britain," his face literally changes: "Wemmick got dryer and harder as we went along, and his mouth tightened into a post-office" (232). Wemmick becomes literally schizophrenic. In the following passage, Jaggers discovers that Wemmick has a meaningful private domestic life, which collides with the office world of Little Britain:

> "What's all this?" said Mr. Jaggers. "You with an old father, and you with pleasant and playful ways?"
>
> "Well!" returned Wemmick. "If I don't bring 'em here, what does it matter?"
>
> [Later, Jaggers repeats,] "You with a pleasant home?" (424)

Here Dickens gestures toward a critique of the compartmentalizing of experience, a division of space that enforces repression and impedes human contact, as Wemmick's transformation on the walk to work exemplifies. While Dickens's treatment of Wemmick's double life is treated comically, it also constitutes a kind of Victorinoir, a representation of ostensibly efficient social systems ready to break down or explode if provoked. Victorinoir threatens social stability. In this case, Wemmick's domestic castle and Aged P., seemingly protected by an artificial moat from the corrupting influences of London, are less a safe haven than a sign of impending rupture; as Pip observes after the revelation, "I had never seen [Wemmick and Jaggers] on such ill terms; for generally they got on very well indeed together" (426). Pip's commentary on this scene reveals the implications of failing to keep public and private worlds separate, itself indicative of the fragility of the boundaries that divide these realms.

Male Ideation and Women Fighting Back

Film noir not only rehearses these dichotomies but shows the dangers of crossing from one side of an opposition to the other. Because these boundaries that structure the noir and Victorian worlds are gendered, when women cross these lines, they become a threat to dominant male culture, as Rita Hayworth's Gilda does when she vamps for male audiences at the same time as she elicits sympathy for becoming increasingly victimized by Ballen's and Johnny's tyranny.

Gilda provides a good example of the problem with generalizing about representations of women in film noir. In 1956, Jacques Siclier wrote about "the relentless misogyny" in film noir, noting about Rita Hayworth that her role was to "Be beautiful and keep silent...she has nothing to say" (Palmer, 70). In fact, Hayworth's "crime" in Gilda may be that she speaks up. Gilda reveals that what's fatal in the "femme fatale" is the persistent ideation surrounding women. She calls attention to the victimization of women: first, through her several performances of "Put the Blame on Mame" (one, plaintively; one, humming; one, aggressively, as a part of her striptease); second, through her use of language as a weapon. Gilda in fact silences Johnny when she implicitly refers to the sexual meaning of "dancing," and disarms Johnny when she feminizes him by repeatedly referring to him as "pretty." Gilda's wit and her performances constitute a rebellion against Ballen's and Johnny's narrow construction of her identity, a misogynist representation of women within the film that is not—as a result of Gilda's power, intelligence, and invitation to sympathize with her—endorsed by the film.

The New Woman mounted a similar rebellion, a point Ann Ardis makes in connection to New Women fiction: "In some of these novels the convention of omniscience is also dismantled by female characters who assert their autonomy from a male narrator—thereby turning what Mikhail Bakhtin terms the 'monologic' structuring of realistic narrative into a polyphonic form" (3). Ardis's insight is analogous to Karen Hollinger's discussion of *Gilda*. For Hollinger, Gilda demonstrates female resistance to male-controlled narrative in the form of voice-over. Gilda's striptease "[dismantles]" Johnny's hold on her, at the same time as it expresses her frustration and anger.

Gilda's charismatic performances, like her wit, disrupt male voice-over, narration, and control, substituting female autonomy for male ideation. One thinks here of Simone de Beauvoir's comments about Brigitte Bardot, that "her eroticism is not magical, but aggressive": "But the male feels uncomfortable, if, instead of a doll of flesh and blood, he holds in his arms a conscious being who is sizing him up" (115). This is a useful gloss on Gilda's deflation of Johnny, her "sizing up" of him, at one point suggesting to him that "[a]ny psychiatrist would tell you that your thought associations are very revealing."

Rita Hayworth's famed "Put the Blame on Mame" number contributed to Rita Hayworth's status as pin-up, which, according to Maria Elena Buszek, reflected female agency in important ways. At the end of her chapter "New Frontiers: Sex, Women, and World War II," Buszek says,

> [t]he pin-up provided an outlet through which women might assert that their unconventional sexuality could coexist with conventional ideals of professionalism, patriotism, decency, and desireability—in other words suggesting that a woman's sexuality could be expressed as part of her whole being. (231)

Buszek's use of the term "decency" is interesting, given Gilda's first lines in *Gilda*, which play on a double meaning of "decent." Ballen calls to Gilda's bedroom, "Gilda, are you decent?" to which she replies, "Me? Sure, I'm decent." This is another instance of Gilda's manipulation of language, the gendered jockeying over the word "decent" reflecting female self-awareness and power to control discourse and meaning. In the context of the pin-up, as explored by Buszek, it is easy to see how the role of Gilda quickly was reduced to the "femme fatale." About the most popular pin-up, the famed "Varga Girl," Buszek says:

> The Varga Girl's strange ideal clarifies how, like the government-shaped ideal of home-front womanhood, this World War II pin-up was an ambitious composite of contradictory feminine ideals that, once embodied, presented a new and monstrous beauty. (186)

Rita Hayworth's image, like the other pin-ups who were "neither domestic nor submissive" (Buszek, 186), would eclipse Hayworth's life and properly nuanced readings of Gilda, as a result of cultural obsessions with the "femme fatale" figure.

The Victorian era had its own Gildas. If there were no pin-ups per se, there were strong female characters in Victorian fiction who rebelled against male control and stereotypes of female submissiveness. Authors like Dickens, the Brontës, Thomas Hardy, George Eliot, and Henry James forced a mediation between extreme conceptions of gender, whereby rebellions are repressed, and compromises are, in the end, achieved. As the "tamed" Estella (*Great Expectations*), Jane and Rochester (in *Jane Eyre*), Cathy II and Hareton (in *Wuthering Heights*), Bathsheba (*Far From the Madding Crowd*), Dorothea (in *Middlemarch*), and Isabel Archer (*Portrait of a Lady*) exemplify, the extent to which a character compromises with an opposing force (the city, sexuality, the class system, and society in general) measures his/her success as a character.[2] In noir, we see the same issues, the same relegation of women to the "natural" domestic realm, the eternal realm, but these dichotomies are troubled in such a way as to call attention to the ideological contradictions in dominant culture—to the fact, for example, that it's not so easy to keep women from contesting their oppressively circumscribed social roles.

In film noir, male violence against women often highlights this difficulty. The more powerful women are imagined to be, often, the more violent is the male reply. In Nicholas Ray's *In a Lonely Place* (1950), Dix Steele's temper (as embodied in his name) reflects anxiety about the loss of control

Rita Hayworth in a pin-up pose wearing the bare midriff Jean Louis gown from *Gilda*.

over changing conceptions of gender, a force of the narrative submerged in the story of a romantic idealist whose desire to control is upset. A common noir trope, the woman (here, Laurel Gray) is the signal of male loss of mastery, as the couple fall in love while Laurel becomes increasingly concerned about Dix's controlling demeanor and violent temper. Details and scenes in the film additionally reflect repressed sex and gender troubles: Laurel's relationship with massage therapist Martha ("she beats me black and blue"); Mel's dysfunctional devotion to Dix, featured as "feminine" submissiveness; and the suggestion that screenwriter Dix sublimates his violent tendencies into Hollywood scripts about murder.

At left, one scene in particular highlights the film's interest in gender inversions. Dix Steele (played by Humphrey Bogart) is placed in a female realm, the kitchen, and bends a grapefruit knife back into shape, since he is ignorant of its proper use. As Laurel's concerns about Dix's violent temper mount in the film, this moment suggests the crossing of gender boundaries and evokes a threat of violence. In response to *In a Lonely Place* and Dix Steele's volatile temper, Dana Polan says that "*In a Lonely Place* shows a violence installed within the heart of the dominant culture, ready to break out at any moment" (46).

As to the homme fatale I do want to reemphasize throughout this project the difficulty we have as readers and viewers in wresting control of the narrative from the psychotic men that people film noir. Close reading of many film noir movies shows such men struggling with the failure of their ideals concerning women to obtain in the actual world.

Male Passivity

At the other end of this extreme violence is the passive and powerless male, who similarly reflects anxiety about female independence and rebellion. Such is the case for Thomas Hardy's male protagonist Jocelyn Pierston, whose name inverts the masculine threat of a character like "Dix Steele." Pierston appears in Thomas Hardy's last-published novel, *The Well-Beloved*, published in 1897, though written five years earlier. In his search for "the well-beloved," evanescent images of male notions of female perfection articulated in schematic narrative terms, Pierston feels helpless in his attempts to escape the cycle of idealization and disillusionment; the empowerment of woman as image clashes with the image's incapacity to obtain persistent gratification for male observers. This process of ideation is forewarned in the concern of Holly in Haggard's novel that once She has died, "elsewhere we may find her, and, as I believe, shall find her, but not here." The idea of (and the incipience of) the desired but inaccessible woman permeates the atmosphere, reflecting cultural ambivalence about the enticing independent woman and anxiety about male power to control her.

The pattern also repeats itself throughout film noir, exemplified in Scotty's obsessive ideation surrounding Madeleine in *Vertigo* (1958), or even Jeff Markham's initial vision of Kathy Moffett in *Out of the Past* (1947), which inevitably gives way to his own abandonment of agency ("Baby I don't care") and then disillusionment when she ceases to serve his ideal. At that point, like many male protagonists in late-Victorian literature and film noir, Markham becomes wholly passive to his fate. As Hardy's Pierston says about the "Well-Beloved," "I grew so accustomed to these exits and entrances that I resigned myself to them quite passively" (39). In *She*, Holly is also rendered passive with regard to female power: "We could no more have left her [She] than a moth can leave the light that destroys it" (182). In late-Victorian narrative and in film noir, the failure to come to terms with female agency is reflected in a pattern of representation in which male protagonists are unwilling to take responsibility for trauma and disruption. While these texts seem preoccupied with male impotence and passivity, such attention to men's helplessness masks the scapegoating of female desire and ambition as fatal.

Repression and Outing the Past

Gender trauma, as I've been arguing, strongly links film noir and Victorian narrative, which are both modernist reflections of disruptions of sex and gender roles. Often these disruptions are figured as hidden; often as violent eruptions. Dana Polan's reading of *In A Lonely Place*, for example, touches on the closeness of such violence to the surface of things, the proximity of criminality to "normal" domesticity (as is figured in the bent-back grapefruit knife) and conventional divisions of space and time. This latter organization of experience, dividing past from present, becomes a major source of anxiety for characters in Victorian fiction and film noir. Further, the anguished relation to the past is often figured in terms of deep unease about sex and gender. The heroes of *Out of the Past, In A Lonely Place*, and *The Blue Dahlia*, like so many noir protagonists, ambivalently repress the past, in effect "criminalizing" the troubled Victorian longing to achieve a continuity between past and present. As Maggie Tulliver says in *The Mill on the Floss*, "If the past is not to bind us, where can duty lie? We should have no law but the inclination of the moment" (475).

The endings of some noir films are deceiving in this respect. *Gilda, Johnny Guitar*, and *The Big Heat* end happily on the surface—Johnny and Gilda reunite, as do Johnny Guitar and Vienna, and Dave Bannion has reclaimed his position as detective-hero. But the violence and despair associated with the past throughout these films suggests that the violence and retribution will continue, a notion echoed by McArthur at the end of his reading of *The Big Heat*. Although Bannion is back on the job, his earlier domestic life has been demolished. The poster in his office—"Give blood—now!"—ironically comments on the jaded heroism of the work of police detectives: "the bleak cycle has begun once more" (78). In *Gilda*, we see a rebellion against the Victorian straining to resolve the breaks between the past and the present. As Johnny Farrell viscerally and contemptuously dismisses Gilda's overtures to discuss their former relationship, the film shows how ineffectual Johnny's attempt is to repress the past and to suppress Gilda, whose intelligence and wit, as well as her sexuality and anger, frustrate him in scene after scene.

In film noir there is very often a tension between a central lesson of the movie, which is that the past must be revisited or redressed, and the fatalistic insistence on the part of the male protagonist that he repress or escape from the past, a past that is usually characterized by his having been entrapped by sexuality (via the "femme fatale") and/or violence (fighting criminals, engaging in criminal activity, or soldiering in a war). The past thus functions as a fatal other, allied with the threat of the woman.

In *Out of the Past*, Jeff Markham/Bailey must inevitably renounce his dream of running his gas station and marrying his angelic and

A pastiche from *Vertigo*: the obsessed Scottie Ferguson (James Stewart) attacks Madeleine Ulster (Kim Novak), while her alter ego Judy (also Novak) watches.

passive country girlfriend Ann in the sleepy town of Bridgeport, California. In an inevitable return of the repressed, his past relations with the "femme fatale" Kathie Moffett (Jane Greer) and the corrupt Whit Sterling (Kirk Douglas) resurface; Jeff's repressed past life as a cynical private investigator who fell in love with a deadly seductress proves, in the end, fatal. Although the woman is identified within the film and in critical discourse as the single source of desolation in the film, it is the male protagonist's failure of vision, his failure to interpret experience, that dooms him in *Out of the Past*. Kathy Moffett herself points this out when she says to Jeff, "I never pretended to be anything but what I was. You just didn't see it. That's why I left you."[3] In its associations between the dangerous woman and the past, film noir recalls representation of "She" and of Dracula and the female vampires that attend Dracula, as atavistic regressive forces threatening to pull stalwart men back in time, back to a different social order of things.

One thinks, for example, of Lucy Westenra in Stoker's *Dracula,* who becomes a "femme fatale" because of her desires, desires that violate sexual and social taboos. Carol A. Senf comments that Bram Stoker was "so horrified at sexual openness that he chooses the female vampire as a shocking metaphor of the new liberated woman" (64).[4] Stott notes that "it is perhaps no coincidence that 1897, the year of the publication of *Dracula*, saw the amalgamation of the different suffrage societies into the National Union of Women's Suffrage Societies" (73). And indeed *Dracula* plays out its conservatism by insisting on maintaining all of the cultural oppositions it represents: public/private, city/country, past/present. In addition to showing a violation of space (Dracula, the sexual Eastern

Frances Dade as Lucy Weston (Westenra) more flapper than femme fatale in the 1931 film version of *Dracula*.

other, invades the space of stalwart Western domestic stability), the novel makes possible a critique of the arbitrary division of past and present. Further, in its tortured presentation of the demarcation of cultural spaces, Victorian anxiety about changing gender roles frames an important narrative model for film noir.

In his fascinating essay about the haunting of Victorian conceptions of character in the modern period, Ronald R. Thomas sees Dracula not as a figure of the past but a force of the future. For Thomas, Dracula's role as a modern force of transformation is often expressed in the cinematic effects associated with adaptations of Stoker's novel. Dracula is a "spectre" of the fantastic technologies of incipient modernism.

Thomas argues that the novel takes on "the real" in ways that make the prestidigitation of film a perfect medium for superseding "the two principal orthodoxies of the nineteenth-century novel: the myth of historical progress and the fantasy of the authentic self" (305). Stoker's novel came "on the scene" around the same time as did cinema, Lumiere's cinematographic wonders premiering in 1895, two years before *Dracula* was published. Dracula is, thus, like the New Woman, and, indeed, like cinema, a shape-shifting force whose powers threaten the status quo (the perceived "real").

Dracula is more an agent of the liberating, subversive powers of modernity than he is of the power of the past. Those older forces, and the ideologies of the self they embodied, were more properly represented by the Victorian century that was reeling into the past as the novel was being published and the cinema was being born. (307)

The perspective Thomas brings to bear is important not only because it reinforces the significance of Victorian culture and ideology to modern representation—"'the movies,'" says Thomas, "have become the principal medium through which the Victorian novel, and even Victorian culture, has maintained its ghostly afterlife in modern society" (289)—but also because it underscores the interplay between threatening new forces and the backlash conservatism that these new powers give rise to. Thomas explains the nostalgia initiated by late-nineteenth-century transformations as "phantom shadows of the Victorian characters we can no longer be" (306).

The seductions of Dracula thus figure paradoxically as the prestidigitations of a new and modern world and as a forced eruption of the past that is itself alternately a safe sociocultural haven and a nest of uncivilized histories. In this way, Dracula does the cultural work of the so-called femme fatale, evoking a frightening future and a seemingly innocent but secretly guilty past.

Film noir conjures up the independent and imminent New Woman, and the Victorian novel haunts film noir like the undead. The visitation of the past resonates profoundly in film noir's representation of repressed histories, whether such failed forgetting is about violence experienced during the war; male friendships forged during the war lost to postwar resumption of conventional sexual and social roles; Johnny's and Gilda's unrevealed failed romance from the past; or various other traumas or formative histories reverberating, often obliquely, in the lives of male and female characters in noir.

The horror novels of the Victorian period in particular look forward to film noir. These novels problematize the Victorian inheritance of romantic confidence that a meaningful link can be established between the past and the present. They call into question this romantic assumption about the forward progress of history. Stoker's *Dracula*, for example, is about the sexualized savage beast wreaking havoc on western civilization. Similarly, *Dr. Jekyll and Mr. Hyde* and *The Picture of Dorian Gray* are explicitly about the violent consequences of repressing the past, whether in the form of (uncivilized) bestial sexuality in Stoker and Stevenson or in the form of the aging process (immortal youth repressing mortality) in Wilde's novel. If, as in mainstream Victorian fiction, the continuities between past and present are manageable, Victorian culture values making the connection between past and present, since the past provides a meaningful context in which to understand the present. In Victorian horror, however, we see the limits of Victorian faith in the ability to forge these links. This doubt becomes the Victorinoir underbelly of nineteenth-century fiction.

On the one hand, in *Dracula*'s bizarre postscript, Stoker gestures toward resolution through repression. At the novel's conclusion, years after the men and Mina destroy Dracula, when Jonathan and Mina go to Transylvania, we are told that "[e]very trace of all that had been was blotted out" (382). On the other hand, the final enforcement of Victorian repression of the dark side does little to ameliorate the story's emphasis on the violent consequences of compartmentalizing "the Other"—all that Dracula represents (sexuality, the East, and an uncivilized past) and the inevitable failure of this repression.

Interestingly, the exhortation to repress, to "blot out" past suffering, is, in one noir film, explicitly made from father John Forbes to his son Tommy (right) in Andre de Toth's *Pitfall* (1948): Tommy asks, "Daddy, what makes a dream?" Forbes answers, "The mind is like a very wonderful camera...evidently, from the day we're born, the mind takes pictures and stores them away. Now and then one of those pictures comes loose in our sleep and that becomes a dream; so the trick is, take only good pictures and have only good dreams." At one level, in psy-

Posed as a femme fatale, a gun-toting Mona Stevens (Lizabeth Scott) looms over her "psychotic stalker" J.B. MacDonald (Raymond Burr) in *Pitfall*.

chological terms, repression and projection surely drive this narrative. The Forbes family insists on restoring a repressed middle-class existence after John Forbes has an affair with Mona and kills Smiley, all of which redounds on Mona. However, there are severe social inequities (and iniquities) resulting from gender and class that are represented in *Pitfall*: Mona is the voice of critical commentary in the film (much like Gloria Grahame's Debby Marsh in *The Big Heat*, another misunderstood and ill-treated non-domestic woman in noir). She gets, as Eddie Muller says,

> the rawest deal. She's arrested for the murder of MacDonald. And the last Forbes sees of her, she's being swallowed into the maw of the injustice system. He can't even muster a "Tough luck, kid...." While John Forbes stewed over his indiscretion, Mona Stevens had to cope with the fixation of a horny married man, the return of a vengeful ex-con, and the obsessions of a psychotic stalker. (*Dark City*, 95)

This film, which presents a sympathetic non-domestic woman and shows her being scapegoated, bears some resemblance to Lucy Westenra's non-domesticity. "Why can't they let a girl marry three men?" Lucy asks; unsurprisingly, she is cursed and her sexuality transposed into evil (68). With a "voluptuous" and "wanton" smile, Lucy casts "a spell" on Arthur, who kills the "femme fatale" "like a figure of Thor" to restore the idea of pure Lucy that had come under attack (222).[5] Like Dracula, film noir movies represent cultural fears concerning the loss of old sources of power and fear of the new sources of power: "Women," says Bram Dijkstra, "who wanted to usurp part of man's place [in creation] were going against nature, becoming mock-men themselves, caricatures of masculinity, viragoes" (211).

Film noir reworks the Victorinoir cultural logic that seeks alternately to express and contain these anxieties by representing desperate women facing the challenges of modern existence. While film noir's tone is often defined in terms of male despair and entrapment (evoked poetically by Jeff Bailey's "I'm caught in a frame and all I can see is the frame" in *Out of the Past*, or Brad's "I'm backed up in a dark corner and I don't know who's hitting me" in *The Dark Corner* [1946]), these films also articulate the traps laid for women. One recalls Susan's evocative line in *The Big Combo* (1955): "I live in a maze, Mr. Diamond, a strange blind and blackened maze and all of the twisting paths lead back to Mr. Brown." The evocation here, however, bespeaks the helplessness of desiring modern women confined by social rules enforced by men that govern female activity. Far more often than is acknowledged, these women aren't evil "femme fatales" but are femmes modernes, only interpreted as "femme fatales" diagetically by unreliable male characters, then by viewers and critics unable to resist the seductiveness of reading women as wicked. The coding of these women as "femme fatales" casts female assertion of authority as "fatal"; female agency is then appropriated by male protagonists who are themselves deeply violent (hommes fatales). There is, for example, Humphrey Bogart's Dix Steele, as discussed above, or many of Robert Ryan's men. These men act violently to restore conventional power relations, exemplifying transmutations of the patterns in Victorinoir.

Victorinoir expresses repressed cultural rage at female rebellion. This is best illustrated in the persecution of female vampires: the killing of Lucy in *Dracula*; the men's execution of Carmilla in Le Fanu's story.[6] Female vampire energy, symbolic of women going against social norms, is appropriated by male culture, mythified anew, "[figures] of Thor" acting violently to restore the "proper" power differential in the regulation of sex and gender identities.

The extremity of repression and projection displayed in movies like *Pitfall* speaks to persistent obsessions with maintaining clearly demarcated cultural spaces, a way of representing experience which Victorian narrative and film noir reproduce at the same time as their stories reveal the destructiveness of the effort. The destabilization of social orders certainly generates much of the drive in Victorian horror, which anticipates, as I've suggested above, film noir's concern with repression and its ultimate portrayal of the return of the repressed. This failure of repression, according to film noir and Victorian horror texts like *Dracula, Dr. Jekyll and Mr. Hyde*, and *The Picture of Dorian Gray*, thus manifests itself as Victorian energy turned to hate. The violence that had, in short, represented the underbelly of the system in Victorian culture becomes the dominant mode in modern culture and film noir.

The City

The dangers of imagining experience in terms of strict opposition and the failure to resolve these dichotomies are also played out in film noir's interest in the motif of city versus country (or "the natural" world), a rearticulated version of the battle between the domestic angel and non-domestic woman. Again, the noir fictional world recalls, on the surface, Victorian representations of the city as tainted and corrupt. For example, Pip's arrival at Barnard's Inn in London constitutes the first in a series of disappointments to his great expectations: "I thought it had the most dismal trees in it, and the most dismal sparrows, and the most dismal cats, and the most dismal houses (in number half a dozen or so), that I had ever seen" (196). In noir, the city's role is paradoxically antagonistic and an expression of the characters' own inner conflicts: as paranoid nightmare, for example, in Jules Dassin's *Night and the City*, reflecting HUAC witch hunts taking place in America in the late 1940s and early 1950s.

Years later, as film noir flourishes in the 1970s, in *Klute* (1971), Donald Sutherland plays John Klute, whose origins and residence in the Pennsylvania suburbs highlight Bree Daniel's excessively urban lifestyle as a psychologically conflicted call girl. She says to him, "Did we get you a little, Klute, the sin and glitter of the big city?" He replies, "Oh that's so pathetic."

This kind of pitting of city against country, where the "femme fatale" resides unnaturally in an urban den of iniquity is emphatically portrayed in John Dahl's *The Last Seduction* (1994), in which Manhattan's Bridget Gregory stands so counter to the small town of Beston, New York (where she's on the lam) that she hides in her car to avoid the relentless assault of "Good Morning!"s from Beston's cheerful inhabitants. Bridget puts out a cigarette in a cake she finds in Mike's refrigerator that has

Below, left, C.A. Vanderhoof's sketch of Barnard's Inn, London in 1891. Right, *Klute*: an unkempt New York City street traversed by Bree Daniels (Jane Fonda) and investigator John Klute (Donald Sutherland).

written on it "Love, Grandma." She is so clearly an emanation of the dark, cynical city that she takes as a pseudonym "Wendy Kroy," a version of "New York" spelled backward. As Judith Walkowitz has said about women entering the public world in late nineteenth-century London, the city, for the New Woman of the late Victorian period and, I would add, film noir existed as both "a place of danger and of possibility" for women (80). The fascination of these female portraits emerges out of the agonistic relationship between the femme moderne and her environment, a struggle between women's desires and ambitions and the psychosocial traumas and conquests that follow such determination.

Case Study: *Bleak House* (1852; 1920)

The Victorinoir link between a dangerous past, a tainted city, and the femme moderne can be seen in Maurice Elvey's fascinating silent film adaptation of Dickens's *Bleak House* (which first appeared in series installments in 1852). Elvey's 1920 film, written for the screen by William J. Elliot, looks back to the high Victorian critique of social hypocrisy, class oppression, the violently brutal conditions of the poor in the city, but does so through the lens of a noir style and point of view, emphasizing death and the failure of social institutions to address human need and desire.

This adaptation of *Bleak House* interestingly isolates and focuses on the story of Lady Dedlock, the mysterious and suspicious dark lady of the novel. Contemporary reviewers of the film were surprised, as the following comment by *The Bioscope* suggests, by Elvey's and Elliot's choice to foreground the story of Lady Dedlock:

> Though one reads "Bleak House" to renew acquaintance with such delightful people as Mr. Turveydrop and Mr. Chadband, Mr. Skimpole, and Mrs. Jellyby, Cadby or Grandfather Smallweed, and cares very little about Lady Dedlock's early love affair or Mr. Tulkinghorne's investigations, there is no doubt whatever that the investigations which lead up to the murder of the solicitor are sufficient to form the basis of an excellent film drama. (February 26, 1920)

The review observes, as the comment suggests, the story's emphasis on the anonymity, distress, and alienation of outsider figures in the social world. Indeed, the film focuses on the victims of modern social institutions, Lady Dedlock, Captain Hawdon (existentially renamed "Nemo" in the novel, Latin for "Nobody), and the desperate and doomed young street urchin Jo. Lady Dedlock is the central of these Victorinoir figures. Like the hard-boiled women in film noir, she is punished for her expression of desire by inflexible social conventions and the men around her, notably Mr. Tulkinghorne, Sir Leiscester Dedlock's solicitor, who personifies the callous and dehumanizing social institutions that characterize the modern world for Dickens.

In the novel, Dickens's language makes clear the threat of the lurking and hulking Mr. Tulkinghorn (with an "e" in the film), who is motivated by the desire to acquire power through the exploitation of other people's secrets. Tulkinghorn "wears his usual expressionless mask—if it be a mask—and carries family secrets in every limb of his body, and every crease of his dress" (151). Paralleling the perverse and corrupt male power brokers in film noir such as *Chinatown*'s Noah Cross and *Gilda*'s Ballen, Tulkinghorn is defined by his vampirish manipulation of the vulnerability of others. He lies in wait to impose threat and menace on those around him: "More impenetrable than ever, he sits, and drinks, and mellows as it were, in secrecy; pondering, at that twilight hour, on all the mysteries he knows" (284).

In Elvey's adaption, Tulkinghorne similarly exploits Lady Dedlock's secret—that she has had an affair with Captain Hawdon before she marries Sir Leicester, although she was told that the child of that romance, Esther Summerston, died in birth. While the film lacks Dickens's mythifying descriptions of Tulkinghorn, the solicitor in the film is similarly menacing in his devotion to rule and convention. For Tulkinghorne, "the honour of the Dedlocks is a religion," and thus he immediately grows suspicious of Lady Dedlock's dramatic reaction to the letter whose handwriting she recognizes as that of her (thought to be dead) lover from 18 years earlier, Captain Hawdon (now known as Nemo,

"Nobody," "ragged, foul and filthy" [Elvey]).

The film shows Lady Dedlock to be victimized by Tulkinghorne's merciless devotion to "hon-our" at all costs, showing her role as "cold and haughty leader of society" to be the direct result of a brutal past. Although this is the extent of Elvey's reference to Lady Dedlock's coldness and mysteri-ousness (the rest of her story is cast very sympathetically in terms of Tulkinghorne's "hunting down" of her secret to expose her), Dickens outlines Lady Dedlock's anomie in more recognizably noir terms. She lives "in the desolation of Boredom and the clutch of Giant Despair" (143), and the contradiction of hopelessness, cynicism and desire characterizes her affect, as it does most of film noir's leading characters. Her life is "detestable monotony," (13), and yet she carries some dark energy, becoming "restless, very restless" (202).

The novel also suggests a continuity among the interminable and arbitrary workings of Chancery, the ruthless victimization of the innocent (notably illustrated in the story of Jo), the foggy impenetrable and morally degenerated noir city, and the cruel fate of Lady Dedlock, whose experi-ence, like that of the impotent Chancery, is of "a deadened world" (7):

> My Lady Dedlock's place has been extremely dreary. The weather, for many a day and night, has been so wet that the trees seem wet through...the vases on the stone terrace in the foreground catch the rain all day: and the heavy drops fall drip, drip, drip upon the broad flagged pavement, called, from old time, the Ghost's Walk, all night. (8)

Defined by the rainy noir setting that surrounds her, and haunted by the past, Dickens's hard-boiled Lady Dedlock "supposes herself to be an inscrutable Being, quite out of reach and ken of ordinary mortals" (11). Lady Dedlock's alienation is characterized by an affect symbiotically in keeping with her environment.

Elvey intermittently uses what we would now identify as strikingly noir visual terms in his adaptation, and the style highlights in particular the trauma of Lady Dedlock's femme moderne. Elvey's mise-en-scène is most striking in three noir sequences. The first serves as a refrain for the film. In a shot repeated three times, Elvey first marks Hawdon's death by framing the gated bars leading into the graveyard with an arch whose lamp hangs from its center. This lovely noir image, clearly derived directly from the drawings of Phiz, Dickens's illustrator, is invoked again when Lady Dedlock comes here with Jo; however, this time, Elvey then cuts to a shot of Lady Dedlock and Jo from the graveside, the characters seemingly now locked behind the bars they look through. The scene looks forward to the many shots in film noir of bars and gates symbolizing characters trapped and fated.[7] In Elvey's shot, there is no context or color, only darkness, outside the iris capturing the bars.

Consecrated ground.

Elvey once more invokes the graveside shot at the end of the film, when Lady Dedlock falls at the steps of the arched gates, clinging to

At left, "Consecrated Ground" 1853 illustration by Phiz (aka Hablot K. Browne).

the bars. Elvey gives us first an establishing shot, then cuts in closer to Lady Dedlock holding on to the gate. The final shot of the film is here, with Lady Dedlock at the graveyard steps and Esther praying by her mother's side with bars behind her.

The graveyard scenes prefigure a noir style while framing the story of a woman victimized by unbending gender and class laws, as does the murder scene, in which George goes to see Tulkinghorne at his flat to inquire about Hawdon. In this scene, George waits for Tulkinghorne to answer (he is not at home) and stands at the right side of a shot of a stairwell framed by an arch. While George's shadow cuts diagonally across Tulkinghorne's door, a veiled woman in black sneaks up the stairs and hides in the shadows on the left across the hall from Tulkinghorne's door (we think the woman could be Lady Dedlock but learn later it is Hortense, the embittered French maid Lady Dedlock earlier fired for spying on her). After George leaves, the lawyer does return to his flat, and walks up the stairs, as the woman again slips into the shadows. Tulkinghorne enters his room, with the door behind him presumably still open, and the film cuts to an iris shot of a hand firing a gun into the lit room. We see Tulkinghorne drop, then the killer shuts the door and descends the chiaroscuro-lit stairwell. Elvey prefigures the noir style, using shadows and iconic emphases on figures of murder and mystery ("the gun") to capture the desperation of individuals caught in the moral and social webs of modern existence.

The film highlights gender and class as the site of social misery, drawing out this Victorinoir aspect of Dickens's novel. That Lady Dedlock and Hortense share a possible role as murderer establishes a structural link between these women seemingly belied by their class differences and the hatred between them. However, both women are manipulated by Tulkinghorne and both feel trapped and are trying to better position themselves. Like Lady Dedlock, Hortense is treated with contempt by Mr. Tulkinghorne, who throws her a coin after she brings him the note hidden by Lady Dedlock about Jo's friendship with Nemo (Captain Hawdon). Later in the film, Detective Bucket discovers Jo and arranges a performance in Tulkinghorne's office to try to discover the truth about Lady Dedlock. Detective Bucket and Tulkinghorne dress Hortense up in Lady Dedlock's black clothes, the film again establishing a link between these two women marked—their reputations "blackened"—by their desires. Jo is asked to identify the woman in black, whom he escorted to Hawdon's gravesite. First he says that Hortense is that woman, but then he corrects himself. Jo has been educated by living on the city streets to notice visual details; here, he observes that Hortense doesn't wear the rings that Jo remembers "the veiled Lady in black" wearing ("she 'ad rings on wot sparkled"). As Jo makes his declaration, he is flanked by the representatives of the law and its enforcement—on the right, Detective Bucket, and on the left, a perversely jubilant Tulkinghorne shaking with glee, rubbing his hands together in an appetitive gesture of dominance, success, and knowledge. In the background stands Hortense, the black-dressed silent evidentiary pawn standing behind Jo. The mise-en-scène foreshadows Hortense's marginalization—although here she moves up to take Jo's place. Later in the film, when Hortense, "out of work and desperate, presses Mr. Tulkinghorne for more money," he ignores her. She says, "You use me as a tool! You fling me aside! I will be avenged!"

The film's emphasis on the story of these women brings into relief the femme moderne's story, a Victorinoir dramatization, filtered from Dickens's as, once again, the most interesting ("For this picture," the titles begin, "we have chosen the most dramatic of all the tales embedded in the book— the story of the hunting down of Lady Dedlock, and the discovery of her secret"). Elvey's film highlights Lady Dedlock's noir story of failed female desire in the context of modernity's rigid social scripts. Further, if Dickens "dreamed" the cinema, as Grahame Smith argues in his book about Dickens's anticipation of film, the dreaming—as interested as it was in criminality, the labyrinthine dangers of the city, and the haunting psychosocial effects of class and gender—took a distinctly noir cast.

Hardy and Victorinoir

Thomas Hardy continues this Victorian dreaming of film noir's social conflicts and embattled gender identities. There is no better example of the tragic consequences for women and culture of rigid psychosocial gender expectations than is seen in Thomas Hardy's *Tess of the D'Urbervilles* (1891). The novel systematically posits and then criticizes the imagining of woman, alternately, as angel or "femme fatale." Hardy reveals Angel Clare's failure to see Tess beyond images; when he finds out that Tess has been raped and exploited by Alec D'Urberville, Angel remarks, "You were one woman and now you are another" (298). Tess internalizes this unmerciful reading of her self when she says, "She you love is not my real self but one in my image; the one I might have been" (281). Tess is caught and bound by those awful projections, as is Judy

Barton in Hitchcock's noir film *Vertigo*. Judy is literally remade into the fictional Madeleine, first by Gavin Elster then by Scotty Ferguson—at left Judy approaches Scottie's room almost completely transformed, now a blonde in a gray suit but with her hair still down. Although Scotty cruelly and absurdly repeats to Judy, "It can't matter to you," viewers maintain an identification with him because he is initially duped (though primarily by Elster and not the woman) and because he is played by James Stewart, whose star text promises virtue and middle-class morality. Despite Scotty's psychotic insistence on projecting an idea of woman onto Judy herself ("Couldn't you like me just the way I am?" Judy asks Scotty), the audience identifies with him. This identification signifies the perverse stubbornness of ideation about women and gender that appears within these texts, but that also extends to readers and viewers whose repetition of the controlling projection of the idea of the femme onto complex representations of female experience stymies their ability to read and interpret these texts well. The representation of women's stories and female autonomy is often submerged in discussions of the "femme fatale."

Hardy's interest in the gender problems resulting from the projection of narrow categories on offer is continued in *Jude the Obscure*, published four years after *Tess of the D'Urbervilles*. In this novel, Sue Bridehead's vexed psychological state and social condition are repeatedly made clear to Jude, but he insists that her behavior is not "natural." Just as Jeff Bailey refuses to acknowledge the real hard-boiled Kathy Moffett (in favor of a fantasy of her) in *Out of the Past*, Jude can't accept Sue's measured responses (Sue says, "I care for you as for anybody I ever met" [160]). Jude's difficulty accepting Sue's ambivalence recalls Pip's relation to Estella, the "femme fatale" figure in *Great Expectations*. Estella's schematic role in the novel as a projection of Pip's desires is conveyed in her warning to Pip that he is in love with an idea and not her self:

"I have tried to warn you of this; now, have I not?"

I said in a miserable manner, "Yes."

"Yes. But you would not be warned, for you thought I did not mean it. Now, did you not think so?"

"I thought and hoped you could not mean it. You, so young, untried, and beautiful, Estella! Surely it is not in Nature."

"It is in my nature," she returned. (376)

Hardy's Jude Fawley shows similar blindness with regard to the woman he claims to love. That Sue rebels against female social roles Jude respects as an intellectual point, but when Sue refuses to be feminine and sexually available (such refusal coded in the novel as "capriciousness" and "inconsistency," just as in film noir movies), Jude falls back on cultural stereotypes about deceitful and harmful woman:

> Or was Sue simply so perverse that she willfully gave herself and him pain for the odd and mournful luxury of practicing long-suffering in her own person, and of being touched with tender pity for him at having made him practice it? ...Possibly she would go on inflicting such pains again and again, and grieving for the sufferer again and again, in all her colossal inconsistency. (189)

Although *Great Expectations* is clearly less interested in and enlightened about gender politics than are Hardy's novels, the logic of *Great Expectations* and *Jude the Obscure* makes available a feminist insight into the substitution of male fantasy for complex psychic and social female experience. This is why female characters in these novels seem to take the place of the free-floating desires of the male protagonists. Estella is an embodiment of Pip's illusory expectations, a surrogate representation of money and class; Sue Bridehead is a surrogate for Christminster, the apogee of higher education to which Jude aspires. Jude, we are told, "[parts] his lips" as he addresses the Christminster wind: "'You,' he said, addressing the breeze caressingly, 'were in Christminster city between one and two hours ago, floating along the streets, pulling round the weather-cocks, touching Mr. Phillotson's face, being breathed by him; and now you are here breathed by me—you, the very same '" (19). One could argue that Sue is in fact an irrelevance, given the way the beginning of the passage posits the wind as a means of trafficking desire between the two male intellects—surely Sue's complex character interrupts and frustrates the flow of such desire. While Sue Bridehead becomes Jude's ostensible object of desire, Jude continues to express his erotic attachment to Christminster: "[Jude] was getting so romantically attached to Christminster that, like a young lover alluding to his mistress, he felt bashful at mentioning its name again" (20). Indeed, Jude's desires are cast in terms of his failure to measure up to other men, who have resources he lacks; Jude is "elbowed off the pavement by the millionaires' sons" (161). A noir sentiment, both in its suggestion of competition among men and the idealist's turn to cynicism, the comment might well describe *Double Indemnity*'s Walter Neff. Like Jude, Walter Neff is seduced not just by a woman, Phyllis Dietrichson as the "femme fatale," but also by the homosocial fantasy that he can compete with Keyes ("I was trying to think with your brain, Keyes"; "It's something I had been thinking about for years").

James Naremore has explored the intriguing thesis that "the 'original' film noirs can be explained in terms of a tense, contradictory assimilation of high modernism into the American culture industry as a whole" (7). Modernist literature and film noir certainly share an interest in style (in Paul Schrader's words, "artistic solutions to sociological problems" [*Noir Reader 1*, 63]). They also both inherit some major Victorian conflicts about the representation of class and gender. As Philip Kemp has argued, class in noir is "no joke. It functions as an instrument of oppression, a cause of hatred and violence." Using *The Locket* as an example (another film in which a woman's psychological illness represents social disorder), Kemp notes the way that the *The Locket* "furnishes a mordant parable of the wealth-based class system, and the moral and psychological distortion inflicted on those who live in it" (82). In *Double Indemnity*, from Neff's point-of-view shot of a production-line office layout at the "Pacific All-Risk" company, to Neff's admission to Keyes that the murder/get-rich-quick scheme was something he'd been thinking about "for a long time," to the elevator operator's comment that he couldn't get insurance because of "something loose in the heart," the film repeatedly paints a portrait of modern life as a classist society that traps people in meaningless jobs so that their lives are drained of meaningful social interaction. It is notable that the "lovable" character in this film charms Wilder's audiences by showing what a slave to actuarial charts he is.

Walter Neff's homosocial desire, as is the case for Hardy's Jude, is activated by the awareness of an oppressive setting: for Jude, the limited possibilities on offer in rural Marygreen; for Neff, modern conformity, characterized by actuarial charts and cubicle office space. For both of these modern characters, idealism and desire frustrate them quite literally to death.

The Vamp

In the years intervening between Victorian representations of "bad women" and film noir's "femme fatales," silent film reconfigured the vampire as the cinema vamp, a shadow image of the femme moderne flapper figure. In the films of Theda Bara, for example, woman was presented as a sorceress who stole men's power to determine the fate of the self and community. As Janet Staiger has said about the representation of "bad women" in early American film, "[t]he vampire or spider image of sucking away the man's blood was a powerful metaphor for the threat she represented" (150).

As in the earlier literary medium and the later film noir explorations of gender distress in changing social periods, bad-women silent films such as *Traffic in Souls* (1913), *A Fool There Was* (1915), and *The Cheat* (1915), Staiger rightly says, "insist upon the value of a new independent, intelligent, and aggressive woman, even a desiring woman. Thus, the films are not simple instances of patriarchal repression of women" (xvi–xvii). Indeed these films present women cast as vampires and spiders subverting social norms and conventions designed to subdue and control them. In *A Fool There Was* (Frank Powell, 1915), we see a direct link between Victorian regulation of gender identities and Hollywood film, since the film was adapted from a play by Porter Emerson Browne inspired, first, by the Philip Burne-Jones painting "The Vampire," (below left) on view in 1897 (the year of Stoker's publication of *Dracula*) and second, by the Rudyard Kipling poem "The Vampire" that was also inspired by the painting. Kipling's poem begins with the line "A FOOL there was," which Browne and the 1915 movie used for their titles.

Apart from an earlier film adaptation inspired by the painting and Kipling poem (Kalem's *The Vampire* [1913]), *A Fool There Was*, as James Card notes, was the most influential film to initiate an on-screen projection of the deadly seductress figure.

The Vampire.

Like the sexualized Victorian literary heroines such as Lucy Westenra, Tess, and Estella, cast darkly to simplify gender politics, sexualized women in early film were similarly portrayed, in order to highlight the convention of Victorian female purity: "Early film," Card suggests, "inherited the heroines of the Victorian theatre. Their essential quality was purity. They were the noble women whom men were expected to place on pedestals and court only with poetry and romantic protestations of eternal devotion" (181). In contrast, in 1923, the fan magazine *Classic* called Bara the "red enemy of man...daughter of the new world...peasant...goddess...eternal woman" (Card, 189). Dawn Sova discusses how Theda Bara "slithered across pre-1920 screens in forty movies between 1916–1919 as 'The Vamp,' short for 'vampire'" (Sova, 21). And yet, as in Victorian literary representations of the "femme fatale" figure, the contexts of these representations often showed these characters to be feminist, or part of a feminist rebellion against conventional gender identities.

In *A Fool There Was*, the New Woman Elinor articulates a reasonable and sympathetic critique of the double standard that regulates gender roles: "You men shield each other's shameful sins. But were it a woman at fault, how quick you'd be to expose and condemn her." Elinor's feminist remark is paralleled in Geschwitz's defense of Lulu at the end of the court scene in *Pandora's Box* (1929), when Geschwitz attacks the smug prosecuting attorney: "Counselor, do you know what would have happened to your wife if, as a child, she'd had to spend her nights in cheap cafes?" While popular readings of Lulu cast her as a quintessential "femme fatale," the film shows the men to be the more dangerous source of violence. Schoen, with his menacing and intermittently shadowed gaze; the exploitative Marquis Casti-Piani; Roderigo; Lulu's "father" Schigolch; Alwa, the weak cohort; then, famously, Jack the Ripper—are brutes, killers, exploiters, and fools, and Lulu, a femme moderne who really just wants to have fun, is trafficked among the men, until she's finally stabbed to death by Jack the Ripper. As Martin Esslin has said, "Lulu is a character of pristine innocence; it is society which is sick" (qtd. in Davidson, 47).

The packaging of these films about vamps prefigures the marketing of film noir "femme fatales." Speaking of cultural representations of women in the Weimar period, Patrice Petro says that, "[t]o a certain extent, the representation of the modern woman was a projection of male anxieties and fears—anxieties and fears emanating from various phenomena of modernity that were recast and reconstructed in terms of an uncontrollable and destructive female sexuality" (34).

Sheri Chinen Biesen similarly catalogs the publicity advertisements that capitalized on the craving of American viewers for treacherous women. The publicity for *Murder My Sweet* (Edward Dmytryk, 1944) reads, "Don't fall for that feeling.... She kills like she kisses!" (Beisen, 115), and advertising for *The Postman Always Rings Twice* takes on the imagined perspective of a version of Garfield's character, overwhelmed by desire, announcing, "You must be a she-devil...you couldn't make me feel like this if you weren't" (Biesen, 122). Out-of-control men are repeatedly overshadowed by the demonized powerful and competent woman. Indeed, as Beisen notes in her discussion of *Gilda* (Charles Vidor, 1946), "[p]ublicity for *Gilda* reproaches strong, independent women as responsible for violent male behavior" (152). Petro's account of this phenomenon in the context of German culture suggests modernity, and particularly the modern city, figured as a seductive female: "this tendency to exaggerate in representing Berlin as a woman reveals less about women in Weimar than it does about a male desire that simultaneously elevates and represses woman as object of allure and as harbinger of danger" (43).

Jackie Stacey has written extensively about the complicated forms of identification produced between female spectators and Hollywood stars. Her book *Star Gazing: Hollywood Cinema and Female Spectatorship* devotes several chapters to analyzing the processes that governed female spectatorship in Britain during the 1940s and 1950s. In her discussion of the "reproduction of feminine identities in relation to cultural ideals" (227), Stacey points to the subversiveness inherent in female viewers' identification with on-screen actresses:

> The processes, and practices, which involve reproducing similarity seem to be those extra-cinematic identifications, which take place in the spectator's more familiar domestic context, where the star's identity is selectively reworked and incorporated into the spectator's new identity. Even in these cases, identification involves not simply the passive reproduction of existing femininities, but rather an active engagement and production of changing identities. (171)

Stacey's research and her extensive interviews with wartime and postwar female viewers reveal that these women experienced empowerment, as they saw dynamic versions of themselves on-screen. The processes of identification between female viewers and Hollywood stars can provide multiple and progressive opportunities for women to reimagine themselves:

> [T]he qualities of confidence and power are remembered as offering female spectators the pleasure of participation in qualities they themselves lacked and desired.... Hollywood stars can thus be seen as offering more than simple role models of sexual attractiveness (though clearly they offered this too!). However, they were also remembered as offering female spectators a source of fantasy of a more powerful and confident self. (158)

Stacey's analysis of the forging of "the spectator's new identity"—the prospect of "changing identities" during a time of gender instability and rapid social change—sheds light on the projection of fatality onto roles associated with female desire. If it is the case that, as Stacey says, "many forms of identification involve processes of transformation and production of new identities, combining the spectators' existing identity with her desired identity and her reading of the star's identity" (172), then surely it is in the perceived best interests of men and the status quo to control that reading. Projecting a categorical label such as the "femme fatale" onto female images of desire short-circuits the transformation Stacey implies is inherent in female spectators' relationship to these images.

Richard Dyer is also interested in spectator identification. In his fascinating discussion of the relationship between the spectator and the impact of star image on role and character, Dyer suggests the role of sympathy in contemporary viewer responses to Lana Turner, a point that complements my suggestion that Cora Smith is more of a subject in *The Postman Always Rings Twice* than critical and popular discussions of that film usually allow for: "the film is about Cora at least as much as it is about Frank" (Dyer, "Lana," 418). Dyer notes Cora Smith's impulsiveness, but also her entrapment and her ambition, complicating a simple view of Cora as the means of Frank's destruction:

> Thus if in terms of the relationship between the motivational and star image levels, Turner serves to mask the contradictions of the femme fatale type (a type, of course, that reflects the male construction—and fear of—the female), in terms of the relationship between the structural and star levels, Turner serves to open up the tension between what women are for men and what that means for women as women. (I am not positing here any brilliance on Turner's part—though I would never wish to denigrate her performing abilities—or an untutored feminist sensibility on the part of the director, writer, or whoever; it is rather that in the relationship between her life/films and women audiences, a certain registering and defining of the female experience in this society was possible and that this happens in *Postman* simply because she is in it.) (418)

Stacey's and Dyer's research and insights suggest a context for understanding the psychosocial associations that viewers draw between the Hollywood star and the desires of female viewers, which further helps to explain the tone of fascination and danger (as well as an intermittent cultural hysteria) that has circulated around cinematic images of strong women.

Louise Brooks's portrayal of Lulu fits squarely in the habitual pattern of projection and mystification, mythified as Brooks has been by critics. Adou Kyrou in *Amour-Erotisme et Cinema* wrote that "Louise is the perfect apparition, the dream woman without whom the cinema would be a poor thing. She is much more than a myth, she is a magical presence, a real phantom, the magnetism of the cinema" (qtd. in Card, 205). The mythifying of the female image carries with it the danger of objectifying powerful women as animalistically other, as in Sova's referencing of Theda Bara as having "slithered across pre-1920 screens." In the case of *Pandora's Box*, indeed, the predisposition has been to see the luminous portrayal of Lulu by Louise Brooks and Pabst's claustrophobic yet radiant close-ups of Brooks as contributing to Lulu's narcissism and an unsettling and inexplicable seductiveness, her "cool, enigmatic charm" (Davidson, 33). However, *Pandora's Box* invites us not to share in the violent projection of lack and failure on the part of the men in the film onto Lulu but to criticize their failures and respond to Lulu's vivacity and beauty. Indeed, Patrice Petro provides a context for Lulu's vitality as a positive marker of female agency in popular German images of the modern woman: "when we turn to the magazines and films that made their appeal explicitly to women, it is indisputable that the representation of the modern woman did address women's experiences of modernity—their dissatisfactions with traditionally defined gender roles and their desire for a transformation of those roles" (36).

While Lulu isn't herself a feminist character, her story, in its disregard for the social script written by patriarchy and enforced by the men around her, is indeed feminist. Changing roles constantly,

Louise Brooks as Lulu in *Pandora's Box*.

as Karin Littau suggests, Lulu is utterly transgressive. And because Lulu's agency is utterly untethered to social convention, it must, according to cultural norms, be destroyed diagetically and then extra-diagetically contained by means of bestial imagery, as is seen in Lotte Eisner's striking comments on Lulu:

> [Lulu's] face is so voluptuously animal that it seems almost deprived of individuality. In the scene with Jack the Ripper, this face, a smooth mirror-like disc slanting across the screen, is so shaded out and toned down that the camera seems to be looking down at some lunar landscape. (Is this still a human being—a woman—at all? Is it not rather the flower of some poisonous plant?) (qtd. in Doane, 153).

Somehow, placed in proximity to iconic serial killer Jack the Ripper, Lulu, for Eisner, is the "poisonous" one.

Louise Brooks herself rebelled against the control of her director Pabst (as she did against Hollywood, leaving films altogether in 1937). The oft-quoted chilling exchange between Brooks and Pabst toward the end of the filming of *Pandora's Box* is recorded in Brooks's autobiography and by Elsaesser: "'Your life is exactly like Lulu's,' [Pabst] said, 'and you will end the same way.' At that time, knowing so little of what he meant by 'Lulu,' I just sat sullenly glaring at him, trying not to listen. Fifteen years later, in Hollywood, with all his predictions closing in on me, I heard his words again—hissing back to me" (qtd. in Elsaesser, 34). Interestingly, the snake imagery here is appropriated by Brooks to signify the venomous treatment of her by Hollywood—a telling contrast to sexist fantasies about the vamp, a personified "slithering" Theda Bara, both Eve and the snake.

If there seems to Pabst and to others some cruel logic in spirited women being brutally killed, it shouldn't be a surprise that representations of women that subvert conventional authority structures elicit simplistic responses and labeling, such as branding them as "femme fatales." In Hollywood, studio executives exploited publicity stunts to mythify Theda Bara, reportedly calling in phrenologists to confirm, "[n]ever in all my experience as a professional character reader have I gazed into a face portraying such wickedness and evil—such characteristics of the vampire and the sorceress" (Golden, 63). Such virulent responses surely justify the reading by actresses who have played "vamps" and "femme fatales" of their roles as complex, psychological, and social—and, explicitly in the case of Theda Bara, as feminist. Said Bara in 1915, "The vampire that I play is the vengeance of my sex upon its exploiters. You see ...I have the face of a vampire, perhaps, but the heart of a 'feministe'" (qtd. in Staiger, 160).

Bara's comment reveals the politics of silent-cinema's vamp, who was, as Buszek argues, "symbolic of not just feminism's potential power to destroy the family and society,

Theda Bara.

but also the ways in which it might positively introduce new ideas about both women's passion and men's frailty as gender roles fluctuated not independently, but in relation to one another" (161).

The culmination of the late-Victorian vampire, who became the vamp of silent cinema, is film noir's "femme fatale." Sheri Chinen Beisen alludes to a Press book publicity image of *The Postman Always Rings Twice*, part of whose tagline I quoted earlier. Here it is in its entirety: "A caricature of a huge hand cleaves a butcher knife above the tagline: 'Her name is Cora.... She Gets Into Men's Blood.... And Stays There! His name is Frank... His Savage Boldness Will Thrill the Women!'" (123). Parasitic images of excess, blood-sucking, and contamination are apt vehicles for expressing contemporary anxieties about female power and transgression, resurfacing metaphors, as we have seen, that derive from Victorian vampire narrative. As women gain validation as part of the working population and the sexuality of women is expressed outside the strictly circumscribed spheres of prostitution and domesticity, fiction and film work to articulate, grapple with, and in some cases contain female power and independence. As Biesen says, "The representation of independent, transgressive 'femme fatales' and complex career women coincided with a wartime female labor force, nationally and inside the film industry" (125).

By offering strong and vital modern women, familiarly called femme fatales, who often gain our sympathy through their struggle to assume independence, film noir destabilizes gender categories, as did silent cinema's vamp, and allows us to see more clearly the reception of Victorian conceptions of class and gender in present-day popular culture and academic discourse, as well as the ongoing force of binary oppositions in the presentation and understanding of gender in contemporary culture. Such analysis exposes the extent to which we may be repressing film noir's past and helps us to come to a greater understanding of how cultural ideation about women informs our reading of, as well as writing about and filming, their experience, then and now.

Her authentic experience trumped by gender myths, Rita Hayworth once famously claimed that "[e]very man I knew went to bed with Gilda...and woke up with me." In her discussion of "Shakespeare's Sister" in *A Room of One's Own* (1929), Virginia Woolf gave voice to the phantom women elided by biased social conventions. Woolf wished to adumbrate, give outline to, the talented women who had not been acknowledged in canonical narratives. Analysis of misreadings of women in noir and a fuller understanding of the historical backdrops that inform our reception of them helps us similarly to outline the missing sisters of Gilda.

Notes

1. In Coventry Patmore's "The Angel in the House" (Ricks, 321-22), the speaker's "sadness [is] banish'd far" by the workings of the domestic female angel. This poem became increasingly popular after its initial publication in 1854. Martha Vicinus has noted the high stakes of maintaining the angel's prominent role: "Rigid social rules ensured the safety of the bourgeois family; within the home, women were assigned a special position as caretakers of morality and religion, for their unique sensibility made them alone capable of child care and domestic responsibilities" (2).

2. The virtue of compromise (and accommodation) is hailed throughout Victorian fiction. In the face of the hard rigors of "the real," Pip eventually compromises his "great expectations"; Rochester, in the end a "caged eagle" (439), sacrifices his "will" and passion to live "happily" in an isolated forest denizen with Jane. In *Far From the Madding Crowd*, Bathsheba progresses from her rash and undisciplined romance with Troy to settle with the sturdy Gabriel Oak. Isabel Archer accepts the limits of her desires in mature recognition of the failure of her marriage to Gilbert; Hareton and Cathy II take up "normal" domestic life, shorn of the passion and chaotic desire that characterized the relationship between Heathcliff and Catherine; and finally, in a wistful but bracing allusion to past models of heroic action (past venues, I should add, defined by myths of force and mastery), George Eliot says the following: "the medium in which their *ardent deeds* took shape is for ever gone" (766).

3. In "From Passionate Attachments to Dis-Identification," Zizek attempts to recover the contemporary (postmodern) "femme fatale" because of the way she "brutally [destroys] the spectral aura of 'feminine mystery,' by acting as a cold manipulating subject interested only in raw sex...." Zizek interestingly contends that the new "femme fatale"'s "strategy is the one of deceiving the male protagonist by openly telling the truth. The male partner is unable to accept this, and so, he desperately clings to the conviction that, behind the cold manipulative surface, there must be a heart of gold to be saved, a person of warm human feeling" (para 10). As my reading of Kathy Moffett and women in noir generally suggests, this pattern is already present in original-cycle film noir. Something similar is happening in Travis Bickle's obsession with Iris's "heart of gold" in *Taxi Driver*.

4. In her intriguing essay about Sheridan Le Fanu's *Carmilla* (1872), Tamar Heller writes about the female vampire's expression of nineteenth-century cultural anxiety about female desire. Heller discusses how female desire is interpreted by medical discourse as hysterical, as in the theories of Weir Mitchell (that figured so prominently in Gilman's "The Yellow Wallpaper"). The "appetite" of Le Fanu's vampire is particularly transgressive insofar as Carmilla is linked sexually to Laura:

> ...since female homoeroticism excludes men and eludes control, to figure female sexuality as lesbianism underscores the threat that women's desire poses to male authority—a threat that would become increasingly pronounced in the decades to follow Le Fanu's story, as feminist agitation further politicized bonds between women. (79)

5. The idea of scapegoating unconventional women to maintain purity and clearly demarcated gender boundaries has cultural resonance in contemporary popular culture, in, for example, the broad success of the novel and stage musical *Wicked*. The novel by Gregory Maguire, *Wicked: The Life and Times of the Wicked Witch of the West*, reimagines the iconic moral poles of *The Wizard of Oz*, as does the book

D.H. Friston's drawing: as a hooded Carmilla reaches for Laura, the General rushes in with his sword.

Strangers on a Train.

Wicked by Winnie Holzman, brought to life on stage first in 2003 with music and lyrics by Stephen Schwartz. *Wicked* (which became a touchstone for "Ugly Betty" in the television series of the same name) addresses the cultural habit of scapegoating to unify the population—"something bad is happening in Oz."

6. "Carmilla's execution suggests a feminized version of castration; moreover, the stake driven through the body of the lesbian vampire whose biting had mimicked the act of penetration is a raw assertion of phallic power. Yet, in the light of the tale's thematics of female knowledge, it is also telling that Carmilla is decapitated, and that her head, site of knowledge and of voice, is struck off" (Heller, 90).

7. Recall Dave Bannion at the auto yard in *The Big Heat* and Guy Haines talking (in *Strangers on a Train*) from behind the grate, symbolically taking on Bruno's criminality after Bruno tells him he has killed Guy's wife (above).

Works Cited

Ardis, Ann. *New Women, New Novels: Feminism and Early Modernism* (New Brunswick, NJ: Rutgers University Press, 1990)

Barefoot, Guy. *Gaslight Melodrama: From Victorian London to 1940s Hollywood* (London; New York: Continuum, 2001).

Biesen, Sheri Chinen. *Blackout: World War II and the Origins of Film Noir*. Baltimore: Johns Hopkins University Press, 2005.

"Bleak House" (review). *The Bioscope* (February 26, 1920): 56.

Bordo, Susan. *Unbearable Weight: Feminism, Western Culture, and the Body*. Berkeley: University of California Press, 1993.

Brontë, Emily. *Wuthering Heights*. Ed. Linda Peterson. New York: Bedford Books, 1992.

Brontë, Charlotte. *Jane Eyre*. Harmondsworth, Middlesex, England; New York, NY, USA: Penguin, 1997.

Buszek, Maria Elena. *Pin-Up Grrrls: Feminism, Sexuality, Popular Culture*. Durham, NC: Duke University Press, 2006.

Card, James. *Seductive Cinema: The Art of Silent Film*. 1st ed. New York: Knopf, 1994.

Davidson, David. "From Virgin to Dynamo: the 'Amoral Woman' in European Cinema." *Cinema Journal* 21.1 (Fall 1981): 31-58.

De Beauvoir, Simone. "From Brigitte Bardot and the Lolita Syndrome," *Women and the Cinema: A Critical Anthology*. Ed. Karyn Kay and Gerald Peary. New York: E. P. Dutton, 1977. 112–16.

Deslippe, Dennis A. *"Rights, Not Roses": Unions and the Rise of Working-Class Feminism*, 1945–1980. Urbana and Chicago: University of Illinois Press, 2000.

Dickens, Charles. *Bleak House*. Harmondsworth: Penguin, 1971.

_____. *Great Expectations*. London, New York: Penguin Books, 1965.

Dijkstra, Bram. *Idols of Perversity: Fantasies of Feminine Evil in Fin-De-Siècle Culture*. New York: Oxford University Press, 1986.

Doane, Mary Ann. *Femmes Fatales: Feminism, Film Theory, and Psychoanalysis*. New York: Routledge, 1991.

Dyer, Richard. "Lana: Four Films of Lana Turner," *Imitation of Life: A Reader on Film and Television Melodrama*. Ed. Marcia Landy. Wayne State University Press, 1991. 409–28.

Eliot, George. *The Mill on the Floss*. Oxford: Oxford University Press, 1981.

_____. *Middlemarch*. New York: Bantam, 1985.

Elsaesser, Thomas. "Lulu and the Meter Man: Louise Brooks, Pabst, and 'Pandora's Box,'" *Screen* 24.4–5 (1983). 4–36.

Frank, Miriam, Marilyn Ziebarth, and Connie Field. *The Life and Times of Rosie the Riveter: The Story of Three Million Working Women during World War II*. Emeryville, CA: Clarity Educational Productions, 1982.

Glancy, Mark. *When Hollywood Loved Britain: The Hollywood "British" Film 1939–1945*. Manchester; New York: Manchester University Press; Distributed exclusively in the USA by St. Martin's Press, 1999.

Golden, Eve. *Vamp: The Rise and Fall of Theda Bara*. Vestal, NY: Emprise Pub., 1996.

Haggard, H. Rider. *Three Adventure Novels*. New York: Dover Publications, 1951.

Hanson, Helen. *Hollywood Heroines: Women in Film Noir and the Female Gothic Film*. London: I. B. Tauris, 2007.

Hardy, Thomas. *Tess of the D'Urbervilles*. London; New York: Penguin Books, 1978.

_____. *The Well-Beloved*. Oxford; New York: Oxford University Press, 1986.

_____. *Far from the Madding Crowd*. New Wessex ed. New York: St. Martin's Press, 1977.

_____. *Jude the Obscure*. 2001 Modern Library pbk. ed. New York: Modern Library, 2001.

Heller, Tamar. "The Vampire in the House: Hysteria, Female Sexuality, and Female Knowledge in Le Fanu's 'Carmilla' (1872)," *The New Nineteenth Century: Feminist Readings of Underread Victorian Fiction*. Ed. Barbara Leah Harman and Susan Meyer. New York and London: Garland Publishing, 1996. 77–95.

Hollinger, Karen. "Film Noir, Voice-Over, and the Femme Fatale," in Silver and Ursini, *Film Noir Reader*, 242–59.

James, Henry. *The Turn of the Screw*. New York and London: W. W. Norton and Company, 1966.

_____. *The Portrait of a Lady*. New York: Modern Library, 1951.

Kemp, Philip. "From the Nightmare Factory: HUAC and the Politics of Noir," *The Big Book of Noir*. Ed. Edward Gorman, Lee Server, and Martin Harry Greenberg. New York: Carrol and Graf, 1998.

Ledger, Sally and Roger Luckhurst, (ed.) *The Fin De Siecle: A Reader in Cultural History c. 1880–1900*. Oxford and New York: Oxford University Press, 2000.

Levine, Philippa. *Feminist Lives in Victorian England: Private Roles and Public Commitment*. Oxford: Basil Blackwell, 1990.

Littau, Karin. "Refractions of the Feminine: The Monstrous Transformations of Lulu" *MLN* - Volume 110, Number 4, September 1995 (Comparative Literature Issue), pp. 888-912.

Maguire, Gregory. *Wicked: The Life and Times of the Wicked Witch of the West*. New York: HarperCollins, 1995.

McArthur, Colin. *The Big Heat*. London: BFI Pub., 1992.

Muller, Eddie. *Dark City: The Lost World of Film Noir*. 1st St. Martin's ed. New York: St. Martin's Griffin, 1998.

Naremore, James. *More than Night: Film Noir in its Contexts*. Berkeley: University of California Press, 1998.

Nelson, Carolyn Christensen, (ed.) *A New Woman Reader*. Toronto: Broadview Press, 2001.

Palmer, R. Barton. *Perspectives on Film Noir*. New York; London: G. K. Hall; Prentice Hall International, 1996.

Petro, Patrice. *Joyless Streets: Women and Melodramatic Representation in Weimar Germany*. Princeton, NJ: Princeton University Press, 1989.

Polan, Dana B. *In a Lonely Place*. London: BFI Publishing, 1993.

Richardson, Angelique, and Chris Willis, *The New Woman in Fiction and in Fact* (*New* York: Palgrave Macmillan, 2002).

Ricks, Christopher B. *The New Oxford Book of Victorian Verse*. Oxford; New York: Oxford University Press, 1987.

Riquelme, John Paul. "Shalom/Solomon/Salome. Modernism and Wilde's Aesthetic Politics," *The Centennial Review* 39 (1995). 575–619.

Senf, Carol A. *The Vampire in Nineteenth-Century English Literature*. Bowling Green State University Popular Press, 1988.

Server, Lee, Edward Gorman, and Martin Harry Greenberg. *The Big Book of Noir*. 1st Carroll & Graf ed. New York: Carroll & Graf Publishers, 1998.

Showalter, Elaine. *Sexual Anarchy: Gender and Culture at the Fin De Siecle*. New York: Penguin, 1990.

Silver, Alain, and James Ursini, eds. *Film Noir Reader*. New York: Limelight Editions, 1996.

Sova, Dawn B. *Women in Hollywood: From Vamp to Studio Head*. 1st Fromm International ed. New York: Fromm International, 1998.

Stacey, Jackie. *Star-Gazing: Hollywood Cinema and Female Spectatorship*. London; New York: Routledge, 1994.

Staiger, Janet. *Bad Women: Regulating Sexuality in Early American Cinema*. Minneapolis: University of Minnesota Press, 1995.

Stoker, Bram and Leonard Wolf. *Dracula*. New York: Signet Classic, 1992.

Stott, Rebecca. *The Fabrication of the Late-Victorian Femme Fatale: The Kiss of Death*. Basingstoke: Palgrave Macmillan, 1992.

Thomas, Ronald R. ""Specters of the Novel: Dracula and the Cinematic Afterlife of the Victorian Novel,"." *Victorian Afterlife*. Ed. John Kucich, John and Diane Sadoff. Minneapolis/London: University of Minnesota Press, 2000.

Vicinus, Martha. *Independent Women: Work and Community for Single Women*, 1850–1920. Chicago and London: University of Chicago Press, 1985.

Walkowitz, Judith R. *City of Dreadful Delight: Narratives of Sexual Danger in Late-Victorian London*. Chicago: University of Chicago Press, 1992.

Woolf, Virginia. *A Room of One's Own*. New York: Harcourt Brace Jovanovich, 1981.

Zizek, Slavoj. "From 'Passionate Attachments' to Dis-Identification." <http://www.gsa.buffalo.edu/lacan/zizekidentity.htm>.

Brigitte Helm as the seductive "False Maria" in *Metropolis*.

Proto-noir motifs in *Metropolis*

Alain Silver

1. An Indulgence in Effects

Metropolis begins very "loudly." The first shot after the series of dissolves which introduce the city is of steam whistles announcing a change in the workers' shift. The white blasts fill the screen, until they reach a point where the viewer is almost forced to "hear" their shrill scream. The whistles set the mood for the entire film, for the ensuing contrast between the relentless press of workers and the idyllic, peacock infested pleasure garden of "the Sons of the masters of the city" [Frame 1 on next page]. Their image reappears several times, most forcefully when the robot or false Maria incites the workers towards the destruction of the city, like the whistles shrilly urging them on to a new task. The staging and framing of the uniformed workers controlled by the whistles is clearly adapted from the oppressive treatment of men in prison that would often be depicted in noir most typically in the Hellinger/ Brooks/Dassin *Brute Force* (1947).

A list of Lang's other physical motifs—the giant clock, the gong in the workers' city and the like—would illustrate the versatility of the production design and little else. Any number of directors could have borrowed some expressionistic sets from a local theater and simply photographed his actors moving around in them, an impression that *The Cabinet of Dr. Caligari* (1920) may give the viewer. But the movie is an early example of a genre that can justify a certain amount of indulgence in effects for their own sake. As a result, some of the most enduring (and important in the sense of being adopted or adapted by others) prototypes in *Metropolis* are what

Right and below, the factory whistles that sound loudly to control the movements of the workers. The volume is "raised" when more of them blow steam.

the filmmakers devised for expressionistic effect that evolved into standard usages for a dystopian fantasy and later film noir.[1]

The most complex of these was the Schüfftan process—named for cinematographer Eugen Schüfftan, who devised it while in charge of special effects on *Metropolis*—involved the use of mirrors placed directly in front of the lens. In one variation a portion of the surface was scraped away to reveal a full-scale set within which performers went on with their prescribed actions. The other portion reflected a miniature that was modeled in the style of the full-scale set and appended it. Alternatively the mirrors were set at 45° with a miniature and actors positioned at the proper distance and so that their reflections were superimposed. It was a necessarily precise operation, much more so than a glass shot which usually joined a set and miniature along a definite, fairly straight line, for it actually placed the actors within the model. Thus Lang was able to "place" his workers in immense rooms [2] filled with gigantic machines. Without the aid of matte work or optical printing, this was a major accomplishment for 1927.[2] The process was to be employed by many other directors, such as Hitchcock in his proto-noirs *Blackmail* (1929) and *The 39 Steps* (1935).

Lang's other innovations were less spectacular but also important. The "videophone" sequence [4] was one of the first back projections and Lang's cameraman had to work out a system of pulleys to keep the camera and projector synchronized.[3] For the shots of the city with the cars and bi-planes (the tiny models are one of the few effects that have not worn well with time) weaving through the skyscrapers, a scale model was shot in frame-by-frame stop motion.[4] And the arcs of electricity passing over the robot during its transformation were spinning pieces of tinfoil shot on a black background and superimposed.[5] The

city/Tower of Babel at night [3] with the light diffusing out of the windows was accomplished with the aid of animation, another part of Lang's tool box that anticipates the matte work, miniatures and/or full-size set of a mechanism that evoke the urban underworld in numerous film noir, as in particular the opening of director John Farrow's *The Big Clock* (1948).

In terms of dramatic impact, Lang's most spectacular scenes were accomplished without these innovations. The pillar of water [5] crashing up out of the pavement and the subsequent flooding of the under ground city was shot on a full scale set and exploited by Lang to the utmost by intercutting between the shots of Maria sounding the gong and the children rushing out of their houses and fleeing through the streets. The water jet becomes an image of contrast to the steam factory whistles, just as the frightened children's haste contrasts with their fathers' mechanical lethargy. Finally, with the chaos of the malfunctioning machinery reaching its peak, Lang closes with a shot of all the children in the square, their arms reaching up towards the figure of Maria who is clutching the lever of the now silent gong, an image (below) which Kracauer describes as "ornamental despair."[6]

Lang also made dramatic use of the camera in a subjective manner: in the destruction of the elevators, for example, where the frightened Maria stands mutely witnessing them fall one after the other to the bottom of the shafts, until huge clouds of smoke billow out almost engulfing her. In the scene where one of the monstrous engines exploded, the camera tracked in slowly and then as the

Workers at the Machine. Far right, it transforms into "Moloch" inside of which masked Egyptian-style overseers await the entrance of slaves from an earlier era.

MOLOCH!

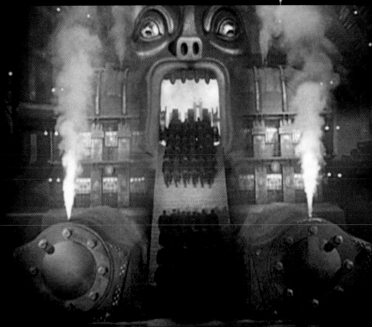

Prisoners at work in *Brute Force*. Inset at right: the shift changes in *Metropolis*.

Above, aftermath of the prison revolt in *Brute Force.* Center, Freder in prison-like worker garb. Bottom, underground work site in *Metropolis.*

Rioters assault their environment in *Brute Force* (above) and *Metropolis* (opposite). Below, the False Maria and the Foreman incite the workers into revolt.

machine burst, back quickly simulating an abrupt recoil from the concussion. He accentuated this effect ever further, later, when he mounted the camera on a pendulum-like device to convey the tremorous sensation as the workers' city collapses. All of this was years before Hitchcock's first use of cross-cut traveling shots that alternate between characters and their POVs and other examples from the classic period.

The aesthetic values of Lang's film cannot be weighed solely on the basis of his innovative visual usages, however. Indeed some of the most striking sequences and shots—the flashlight pursuit through the maze of tunnels (anticipating analogous scenes in films such as *He Walked by Night* (1948) or *The Third Man* (1949); the false Maria's malevolent, spidery shadow as she scurries up a ladder; or Rotwang's test of his robot by having her perform for a group of businessmen, followed by a montage of faces and excited eyes, as "she" passes with titillation to spare (left and right below)—are not the products of special camerawork but of Lang's imaginative mise-en-scène.

2. Biblical Imagery and the Law of the Master

One of the most striking aspects of *Metropolis* is its complex, interwoven allusions to mythic, religious symbolism. These have been liberally integrated throughout the picture, and several major archetypes can be easily distinguished: John Fredersen, the father, is the stern God; his son, Freder (whose name is derived from the father's, much as the second person of a divine trinity is, in theological terms, a reflection, a product of the Father's self-perception) is a form of the Messiah; Maria, the virgin; the workers, the chosen people and her disciples; Rotwang, the devilish schemer who deceives the righteous, etc.

6.

Fredersen is, perhaps, the least complete of the figures. He is never a benevolent, forgiving deity, but the harsh God of the Old Testament, the Master whose law commands unreasoned obedience. It is Fredersen, who inflicts the tenth plague of Egypt, the killing of the children (the first born) and who remarks "Tomorrow thousands will ask in anguish, where is my son?" This reference, at least, is fairly explicit. Subsequently, his bearded informant, who appears early in the picture via videophone, will become a sort of Moses, the one who will bring the populace to their senses after their orgy of violence (and worship of a "Golden Calf"—see [6] opposite page of the False Maria posed like an idol). Not until the very end, when he kneels, agonizing in a circle of light as his son wrestles with Rotwang on the cathedral roof, is Fredersen softened. After this figurative sacrifice of his son, his harshness is dissipated and a Biblical millennium[7] beckons.

It is Freder who goes out in search of knowledge of his "brethren," after Maria's intrusion into his personal Eden. With visual bravura, Lang uses simile and transforms a huge machine breaking down before his (and our) eyes into a fiery idol of "Moloch."

And they have built the high places of Baal which are in the valley of the son of Hinnom, to offer up their sons and their daughters to Moloch.[8]

By opposing falsegods to whom children are offered in human sacrifice, Freder assumes the guise of an Old-Testament Prophet or Christ figure. Unlike the rich young man in search of salvation (Matthew 19:20-22[9]), he does abandon his worldly possessions. Lang's images are extremely precise: the dark figure of Freder, arms outstretched, "crucified" by a vague, clocklike machine, cries out, "Father, father, I did not know that ten hours could be torture" clearly recalling the first of Christ's last words.[10]

Opposite, Rotwang (Rudolph Klein-Rogge) gestures defiantly at Fredersen (Alfred Abel) with his artifical hand. Below, a messianic Freder takes over the Clock.

The Pentagram counterposed with Rotwang's robot that he will transform into the False Maria.

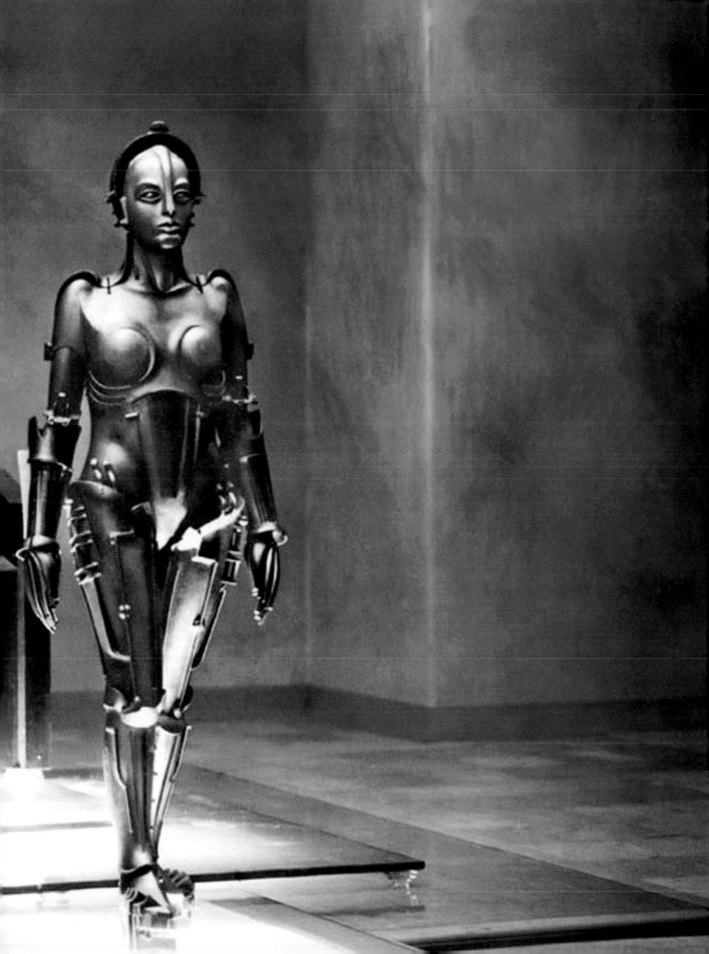

Ritual sacrifice and destruction: Maria with the children (above). The False Maria "burned up in fire" (below). The eyes of the False Maria (bottom).

With Maria—Mary, the virgin redemptress—Lang's allusions are again clear. The followers flock to her through catacombs reminiscent of early Rome and beat their breasts as if in litanical chanting. She, who stands on an altar flanked by a dozen expressionistic crosses, is the most consciously mystical of all the characters. From her first, enigmatic appearance she is the one who calls men brothers. She is also the one who relates the story of Babel, which Lang applies analogously to the Metropolis—the intercutting of aristocratic planners contemplating the tower with superimposed endless lines of slave workers is obviously a variant of the first few scenes. One might even say that Lang gets a little carried away, as the compositions become almost prophetic in tone. In a shot that frames the fair-haired Master (silhouetted in long shot) between a trio of bare-headed slaves (medium close in the foreground), Lang has each in turn raise a defiant fist then descend out of camera range. After a beat, suddenly hundreds of men rush up the distant steps towards their enemy on the horizon. The next shot—the tower in ruins—foreshadows the outcome of the workers' revolt.

By opposing Maria, Rotwang and his diabolical invention become Apocalyptic anti-Christs:

> And the beast hid great iron teeth, eating and breaking in pieces and treading down the rest...and had ten horns.[11]

With just a slight stretch of her angular metal protrusions, this description could apply to the female automaton (Rotwang himself has an artificial hand), whose initial "human" features are Satanic, almost sensual, eyes. Add to this the supernatural power of transmorgrification with which Rotwang, in a variant of the Galatea myth, imbues her; and she becomes a succubus, Lilith leading the city fathers, the first men, to damnation. Here, to represent forces both primitive and evil, Lang's symbols are classically derived. The doors of Rotwang's house, which open and close mysteriously behind the trapped Freder, are all inscribed with the pentagram, the five-pointed star, which is the mark of infernal incantation and the brand of Medieval conjurors whose tradition the scientist follows. His alchemic creation, the robot Maria, rises up before the wealthy Lords of Metropolis like Venus from the sea by Botticelli or Moreau (opposite). Her seductive dance and her dark, heavily made-up eyes (the only feature which distinguishes her from the real Maria and which are that way from the first close shot when she "dissolves" from steel into flesh) mark her as the painted whore of Babylon, who is also the "the mother of harlots and abominations of the earth."[12] Such a bifurcation anticipates the good/evil dichotomy of the femme fatales portrayed by Joan Bennett in Lang's own noir films *The Women in the Window* (1944) and *Scarlet Street* (1945). True to type, Maria's fate is the same as her Biblical antecedent:

> ...waters that thou saw where the harlot sits are the people and nations and tongues. And the ten horns that thou saw, and the beast, these will hate the harlot and will make her desolate and naked, and will eat her flesh, and will burn her up in fire.[13]

In these contexts, the inundation of the underground city is not the calamity of Noah, but the flood of revelations, the upheaval before judgment where the virgin will supersede the harlot:

> For the flood gates from on high are opened and the foundation of the earth are shaken.[14]

Although the patterns in this final instance are not as absolutely applicable as before, the conclusion reaffirms all of Lang's allegorical implications. It is after the defeat of the beast and the false prophet, when they have been relegated to the flames and fallen back into the abyss: the Lord (Fredersen), no longer a ravenous Moloch or oppressive Caesar, reestablishes the covenant with his people, and together they look metaphorically forward to the thousand years of peace.

3. Social Consciousness and Its Consequences

At one point Lang himself became disenchanted with his film: "I don't like *Metropolis*. It's false, the conclusion is false; I had already rejected it while I was still making the picture."[15] If there is a failing in this movie is not Lang's theme of the city oppressing the workers or the conflict between them and the "bosses" but his manner of exposition, his didactic insistence on some points. Very early with his weary lines of workers docilely marching to and from giant freight elevators, Lang appears to be creating a study of how the city of the future may imprison its populace and bend them to its will. But after Freder abandons his love play and acquires a "cause," *Metropolis* reverts to an episodic structure where characters often function without concern for any other. When they are suddenly all rejoined

for the chase across the cathedral rooftops, Lang is satisfied with merely letting the sequence run its course. The chase itself is somewhat anticlimactic after the energy and power of the workers' riot and the flood; and for the first time, the sets really look like sets. And after it is over, realistically the motivations for Fredersen's change of heart in abrupt fashion are not strong enough to be convincing.

Kracauer contends that the ending of the picture is actually a justification or apology for certain National Socialist preachings—i.e. a sort of benign despotism, that the people need to be guided onto the true path with or without their consent—that "the pictorial structure of the final scene confirms the analogy between the industrialist and Goebbels."[16] And if Fredersen does represent the godhead or possessor of absolute power, he is, by extension, a kind of dictator. However, the frequently recounted story of how Lang was summoned by Goebbels in 1933 to be offered a job as head of German film production and his flight into France the same day[17] makes it clear that if a reference to Goebbels or Hitler was intended, it was probably slipped past the unsuspecting Lang by scenarist Thea Von Harbou.[18] The difficulty remains that, irrespective of who put it there or what the Nazis saw in it, the ending is blatantly artificial. After Rotwang has as expected fallen to his death, the sudden union of the upper and lower classes ("There can be no understanding between the hand and the brain unless the heart acts as mediator") is indeed a "false conclusion"; it is "a sham alliance between labor and capitol."[19] As Freder and Maria gaze lovingly at each other (above), the city, the Metropolis, still looms behind, threatening like Gog and Magog to erupt once more in strife. Arthur Conan Doyle described this movie as "beyond the wildest dreams."[20] It is complex, allegorical, occasionally heavy-handed, and not without flaws. What dreams of the characters and their desire bring is another matter.

Notes

1. According to Lang, the vision of the city was inspired by his first view of the New York skyline at night. This was reaffirmed to the Author during an interview at Lang's home on August 12, 1972.
2. Fritz Lang, "La Nuit Viennoise," *Cahiers du Cinéma*, 179 (June, 1966), p. 57.
3. Ibid., p. 58.
4. Ibid., p. 57: this forty seconds of screen time took six days to record in this laborious fashion, and the first take was ruined at the processing laboratory.

Publicity poses with a figure and clock face: the 10-hour one below and Charles Laughton for *The Big Clock (right)* twenty years later.

Lang's expressionistic eye montage (above right) also antedates Salvador Dali's effect for Hitchcock's *Spellbound* (above left) by almost twenty years.

5. Ibid., p. 58.

6. Siegfried Kracauer, *From Caligari to Hitler* (Princeton: Princeton University Press, 1947), p. 376.

7. Revelations, 20:2. He seized the dragon, the ancient serpent who is the devil and Satan, and bound him for a thousand years. 3. And he threw him into the Abyss, shut it, and sealed it over him, so that he could not deceive the nations until the thousand years were complete.

8. Jeremiah, 32:35.

9. "20. 'All these I have kept,' the young man said. 'What do I still lack?' 21. Jesus answered, 'If you want to be perfect, go, sell your possessions and give to the poor, and you will have treasure in heaven. Then come, follow me.' 22. When the young man heard this, he went away sad, because he had great wealth." *New International Bible* (Colorado Springs: Biblica, 2011).

10. Luke 23:34, "Father, forgive them, for they know not what they do."

11. Daniel, 7:6-7.

12. Revelations, 17:5.

13. Revelations, 17:15-16.

14. Isaias, 25:18.

15. Fritz Lang, *Cahiers du Cinéma*, 99 (September, 1959), p. 2.

16. Kracauer, p. 164.

17. Most recently by Peter Bogdanovich, *Fritz Lang in America* (London: Studio Vista, 1967), p. 128.

18. As Lang affirms in Bogdanovich, p. 124

19. Kracauer, p. 376.

20. Lang, *Cahiers* 179, p. 58.

Below, triptych: evolution of costume for the femme fatale. Left, Theda Bara in *Cleopatra*. Center, remarkably similar garb for Brigitte Helm in *Metropolis*. Right, quite staid by comparison (thanks to the Motion Picture Code), Joan Bennett in a peignoir for Lang's *Scarlet Street*.

A very early femme fatale: Musidora (Jeanne Roques) in *Les Vampires*.

Paleo-Noir

Homer B. Pettey

Film scholars often trace stylistic influences for film noir to German Expressionism of the silent era, such as Robert Wiene's *The Cabinet of Dr. Caligari* (1920) and F. W. Murnau's *The Last Laugh* (1924). The fantastic plots, yet realistic settings of Louis Feuillade's serials *Fantômas* (1913-14), *Les Vampires* (1915-16), and *Judex* (1916) greatly influenced crime melodrama by providing cinematic thrills, overt feminine sexuality, and amoral gangsters. Poetic Realism of the 1930s in France, such as Julien Duvivier's *Pépé le Moko* (1937) and Jean Renoir's *La Bête Humaine* (1938), also had profound effects on the narratives and moods of film noir. European directors in Hollywood who fled fascism in the 1930s made films that had recognizable noir traits, such as Fritz Lang's *Fury* (1936). The best classification for the Poetic Realism films and the 1930s crime films, including gangster films such as William Wellman's *Public Enemy* (1931), would be proto-noir, that distinctive, yet not fully developed form of noir. This proto-noir period extended from 1930 until 1941 with the release of John Huston's *The Maltese Falcon*, which followed two proto-noir adaptations of Dashiell Hammett's novel, *The Maltese Falcon* (1931) and *Satan Met a Lady* (1936). The film noir period extends from *Double Indemnity* (1944) and *Murder, My Sweet* (1944) well into the mid-1960s, since the arbitrary date of 1959 for *Odds Against Tomorrow* does not account for numerous noirs, such as *Blast of Silence* (1961) and *Experiment in Terror* (1962), among others. Still, a number of silent and early sound films reside outside the general classifications of film noir history, even though they are sometimes included in lists as being noir-like. These films reveal visual experiments, often stylistic use of camera angles, provocative chiaroscuro lighting, strategic use of shadows and silhouettes, real world locations, and melodramatic crime-based narratives with doomed, psychotic, or imperiled protagonists—all standard designations for the visual style and plots of noirs. Examples of American paleo-noirs include D. W. Griffith's *The Musketeers of Pig Alley* (1912), Josef von Sternberg's *Underworld* (1927), and Roland West's *Alibi* (1929), all of which reveal stark, morally compromised urban worlds of violence, sexuality, and corruption. Paleo-noir seems an appropriate term of these early noirs in cinema history, especially with the advent of neo-noir from the New Hollywood period of the late 1960s to the present day. These paleo-noirs experimented with cinematic techniques later associated with film noir in order to create an aesthetic that appealed to audience's desires for spectacle and the forbidden. Moreover, their success at the box office, especially *Underworld* and *Alibi,* convinced studios to take on more violent, sexualized outré spectacles in the 1930s, thereby leading to the proto-noir period.

Paleo-noir designates both the earliest examples of the noir genre and field of study that examines how these early aesthetic, narrative, and thematic experiments evolved into the periods of noir (proto-noir, film noir, and neo-noir). Due to the loss estimated between 80-90% for all films before 1930, paleo-noir, akin to other early-cinema studies, also relies upon film archaeology of archival, commercial, technological, and industry materials to reveal points of coherence between these early films and later experiments with this particular genre. Similar to other paleo-fields, paleo-noir entails uncovering the social and economic environments that produced these early films, discovering audience, critical, and studio responses to these early films, analyzing aesthetic connections and interactions among these early cinematic experiments, and speculating on the adaptive processes by which paleo-noir developed into later forms of the genre. In particular, close reading of paleo-

LATER

The Little Lady meets Snapper Kid, the chief of the Musketeers

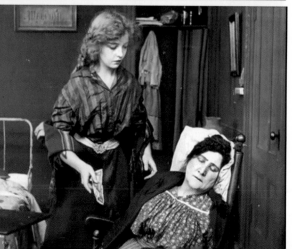

noir aesthetics enables patterns of convergences and divergences in the cinematic print record to emerge that reveal the complex artistic evolutionary chronology of film noir.

D. W. Griffith's *The Musketeers of Pig Alley* stands out as the first American film devoted to organized crime and the first film to employ shot framing and camera angles to express ulterior motives, criminal sensibilities, and violent intentions. Even though the name "Pig Alley" may refer to the lower East Side of Manhattan, Griffith might well have imagined Quartier Pigalle in Paris as inspiration, that district below Montmartre known for criminals, the Grand Guignol, and decadent artists, whores, and lower-class forms of vice. While using the Fort Lee, New Jersey studio for most of the film's interior scenes, Griffith also took his camera outside to the real world locales of the lower East Side of New York city, as the numerous entrances to and exits from the tenement and adjoining saloon in the film depict. This tale of innocence saved from the underworld Griffith casts in his typical melodramatic formula of the imperiled woman and a nefarious triangle of desire. Wife (Lillian Gish) of a poor musician (Walter Miller) encounters the loitering Musketeer chief, the Snapper Kid (Elmer Booth) in the stairway of the tenement. The Snapper Kid accosts the wife and tries to exact a kiss from her but is pushed away by a slap and a chest punch (frame above left). After the shock wears off, the Snapper Kid claims to his thug underling that the wife is his kind of woman, and with a jaunty cock of his hat, he proceeds from center frame diagonally to vanish extreme left foreground. This type of oblique angle created by physical movement before a centrally-placed stationary camera will characterize the mood and illicit intent of the criminals throughout this 17-minute film. Here, Griffith, much like film language decades later in film noir, provides a cinematic signature to evoke emotions, to portray psychological states, and to reveal sexual feelings of the male, criminal class.

The wife returns to her apartment only to discover her mother-in-law dead (left), an odd detail that never finds a resolution within the narrative. Griffith then cuts to Pig Alley populated with small children, men drinking beer out a bucket, women with laundry following an S-line to weave through the crowd as men engage with street women, all presented with a stationary camera in a long shot framed by brick walls left and right and with brick tenement wall backdrop. From the mid-center right side of the frame emerge the Snapper Kid and his cohort, who lean against the wall in the extreme right foreground. Again, Griffith has created a visual diagonal arrangement of bodies without moving the

camera. The arrival of the musician, now flush with funds, attracts the Snapper Kid's attention. The musician moves from center frame past the camera to right, all the while the Snapper Kid's eyes follow him with criminal intent. He nudges his underling and they depart along the wall, producing an oblique angle of movement. Emerging from the saloon next to the tenement stairway, the Snapper Kid wields a blackjack on the unsuspecting musician and steals his wallet: the action follows a line of diagonal movement from extreme right to center frame for the assault and reverse that angle of physical movement for the escape from the scene.

Crawling to his doorway, the musician makes his way inside with the help of his wife, which Griffith has conveyed through a few quick parallel-cuts. As the inter-title proclaims, the musician remains determined to retrieve his money and he departs, with a wistful wife looking out the door. A friend comes to cheer up the wife and takes her off to a local ball. Like the crowded Pig Alley shot,

Right, *Musketeers of Pig Alley*: the "Little Lady" (Lillian Gish) avoids eye contact as she walks down a crowded street after her encounter. Above, the celebrated walk forward during "the gangsters' feudal war" into a cropped close-up: Elmer Booth as the Snapper Kid has an intimidating stare while criminal cohort has his back.

Below, one might expect the "Little Lady" to say "I cannot go, my mother-in-law just died"; but she doesn't. At the Gansters' Ball, a puff of smoke telegraphs the entrance of the Snapper Kid.

Griffith places the camera in center of the frame and has the Snapper Kid and cohort arrive from mid-right and proceed to the foreground. Along with her friend, the "Little Lady" (wife) enters the "Gangster Ball," according to the inter-title, where she is introduced to a gangster in a straw boater (Alfred Paget) before her friend dances off with another man; all the while, seated in the left foreground, the Snapper Kid observes them. The boater gangster invites the wife into the barroom behind the curtains and there, he offers her a seat at a small round table. Cut to the Snapper Kid moving diagonally from left foreground to mid-center right in order to find out the boater's intentions. A waiter has brought them a tray of drinks. The boater hands the wife a photograph, leans over her drink to point out a detail in the photo, thereby obscuring her view, but not the audience's, of him slipping something into her drink.

Observing as well is the Snapper Kid, who enters, violently takes the drink from the wife's hand, tosses it behind him, and in the same movement threatens to strike the boater. The wife departs the Grand Dance of the Jolly Three, as do, a short time later, the Snapper Kid and his henchmen. The boater collects his cohorts and the Snapper Kid collects his own back at the tenement saloon. Griffith cross-cuts between the boater gang departing and the Kid's in the saloon. The Kid, fidgeting with his pistol in his coat pocket, stands leaning against the bar in a visual line that nearly matches the gang leaning against the tenement wall in Pig Alley. They exit the saloon and again Griffith sets up the stationary camera so that their movement past it creates another signature extreme oblique angle in relationship to the camera. To distinguish the two groups of gangsters, Griffith has the boater's crew depart the Jolly Three by descending below camera level in the center of the frame, relying upon the iconographic visual depiction of a descent into the underworld.

The camera then cuts to a tall wooden fence creating an extreme diagonal on the right side of the frame. A hand opens the gate and the shadow of the Kid appears as he skulks into Pig Alley with his crew. They depart along a now familiar angle from mid-center to extreme right foreground, but Griffith has the shot set so that their figures are in large close-up with their shoulders almost hitting the camera. This movement signals to the audience their violent state of mind. The boater's crew arrives at the saloon. In Pig Alley, the musician, in center foreground, mournfully examines his empty pants pocket before he departs. From the back of Pig Alley, the Kid emerges from the right, as the boater leaves the saloon with his crew, with Griffith using the same extreme close-up angle of departure past the camera as in the previous wooden wall scene. Again, a visual signal to the audience of the physical threat and murderous intent by both gangs.

Back in Pig Alley, a Chinese man accidentally bumps into the Kid, who reacts by viciously grabbing his pistol in his pocket. The Kid laughs, but immediately changes his expression to hatred. His gang now leaves Pig Alley, again creating that threatening physical angle in relationship to the camera. The boater's crew emerges from the right background of Pig Alley, obviously following the same route as the Kid's gang, and they, too, leave by making that same ominous close-up angle. The inter-title announces what the audience already apprehends visually: "The Gangsters' Feudal War."

The scene cuts to the wooden wall with the boater's crew. Cross-cut to the Kid and his gang creeping along the brick wall. Cut to the retreating boater. Cut back to the Kid moving along the wall at the extreme right, but now, Griffith has the camera at face level so that Kid's menacing glare fills the right portion of the frame. The boater's crew re-enters Pig Alley where they spread out and take cover behind beer barrels strewn in the alley. Along the brick wall on the right, the Kid's gang moves cautiously into Pig Alley. The visual line now forms an extreme angle from right foreground to left background, as the audience anticipates the ensuing gunfight. The moment that all of the Kid's gang occupy the foreground right of the frame, from the left middle ground pops up a crew member and Pig Alley soon fills with gun smoke (below left). The musician returns to Pig Alley via the doorway, but halts because of the violence before him. Cut back to the Kid and his gang in the foreground under siege by bullets. The Kid seeks shelter in the doorway, where a frightened musician looks on. The musician steals back his wallet from an unsuspecting Kid and flees Pig Alley. The shot now depicts the battleground as New York City cops invade from all sides. Cut to the Kid fighting off a cop and then fleeing Pig Alley the same way as the musician. The musician returns to his wife, they rejoice over the recovery of the money, but the Kid barges in on them with the cop in hot pursuit. The inter-title reads: "One Good Turn Deserves Another." The wife establishes the Kid's alibi (below right) and all works out in a real world, not necessarily an ethical morality. Like later noirs, *The Musketeers of Pig Alley* concludes with a private code resolving the narrative, not the accepted or expected social codes.

Left, presumably the title figure(s) in *The Perils of Our Girl Reporters* could improve their dangerous situations by packing a gun.

Two years later, Continental Feature's *The Gangsters of New York* (1914) would use the plot of *The Musketeers of Pig Alley* with its lower East Side dance and shoot-out among rival gangs with "gunmen hiding behind buildings and telephone poles."[1] In fact, the latter part of the 1910s includes numerous films about gangsters and criminals. For 1916 alone, nearly two or three times each month, film companies released underworld films or criminal serials. Some of these underworld films included: Universal's "underworld thriller" *Alias Jane Jones*; The two-reel Bison production *The Cage Man*; "The Social Pirates" episode of *The Disappearance of Helen Mintern*; Triangle Film Corporation's *The Dividend*; Universal's *The Heart of New York*; General Film Company's three-reeler In *House of the Chief*; Pathé's gangster serial *The Grip of Evil*; Biograph's two-reeler *The Science of Crime*; and, American Film Company's *A Dream or Two Ago*. Vitagraph Blue Ribbon Features advertised *The Lights of New York* (1916) as "A human interest drama of contrasts—picturing the shadows in the dim half light of the city's underworld, against a background of fashionable society in the full glare of the city's white lights."[2] Violence and sexuality dominated many of these films' narratives. General Film Company's three-reeler *From the Deep* (1916) examined the "repellent phases of life" with a "grafting detective" who "reaps the wages of sin."[3] General Film Company also released a two-reeler *The Better Instinct* (1916), about which *The Moving Picture World* commented: "The film is not as wholesome as it might be, for one of its characters is a representative of white slavers, and two others are procurers."[4]

Many of these silent paleo-noirs developed plots that focused upon the role of women as fatales, victims, and social avengers. Metro Pictures Corporation's Francis X. Bushman vehicle *The Great Secret* included Lillian Sullivan as a female detective. Mutual Film Corporation's advertised its fifteen-episode serial *The Perils of Our Girl Reporters* as populated with "Suave social blackmailers—crafty international spies—shrewd Chinese opium smugglers—terrified murderers—crooked politicians—rich society debutantes—police court habitues—" from the "underworld of a great city."[5] Private Feature Films offered a six-reeler *Ignorance* about a young woman's fall into the arms of underworld heel, a story "around the need of insistent watchfulness in the home of every young girl."[6] Commentary in the trade journals often noted the aesthetic experiments and camera work in these films. Yorke-Metro's *Pidgin Island* (1916) included fifty members of the Los Angeles police department as well as "25 real types of the underworld" to make a realistic portrayal of criminality, especially a mob melee that had "three cameras...stationed in different angles while the big fight scene was in action."[7] By the early 1920s, violent and sexually suggestive paleo-noirs attained such popularity among audiences that local boards and city fathers campaigned to censor them. Surprisingly enough, in Chicago of all places censors dismissed underworld pictures, which "The Real Censor Spirit" of *The Motion Picture World* reported among their list of "Pictures To Be Eliminated Entirely."[8] Of course, censorship hardly deterred studios, since underworld films continued to be produced throughout the 1920s, because they made money for production companies, distributors, and exhibitors nationwide.

The culmination of this silent paleo-noir period remains Josef von Sternberg's *Underworld*. This film opens with an ominous title card: "A great city in the dead of night ...streets lonely, moon-flooded ...buildings empty as the cliff-dwellings of a forgotten age ..." The mood of somber darkness pervades a doomed urban world, evoked in this inter-title with its allusion to James Thomson's pessimistic poem, "The City of Dreadful Night." The title card also alludes to the great novel of Chicago, Henry Fuller's *The Cliff-Dwellers*, the first paragraph of which—the novel's "Introduction"—aligns remarkably with the materialistic and violent modern existence depicted in *Underworld*:

> Each of these cañons is closed in by a long frontage of towering cliffs, and these searing walls of brick and limestone and granite rise higher and higher with each succeeding year, according as the work of erosion at their bases goes onward—the work of that seething flood of carts, carriages, omnibuses, cabs, cars, messengers, shoppers, clerks, and capitalists, which surges with increasing violence for every passing day.[9]

Ben Hecht, who received the first Academy Award for Original Screenplay, wrote the film's scenario *Underworld*—an original story of Chicago, which began a similar view of Chicago: "The huge tossing mechanism of steel, smoke and stone; of windows, of lusts, derbies, despairs and hallelujahs identified on the maps as Chicago was getting up steam for another day.... Something happened that blew the city's hat off and left it suddenly standing wild and looking at itself with terror."[10] Hecht wanted the film to begin with The Killer's escape from the county jail before he could be hanged, but Sternberg reordered that plot to conclude with the escape and the manhunt. Sternberg did keep the temporal symbolism of the hour ordained for the hanging by using the clock face in the first shot. A superimposed clock face reading 2 o'clock hovers over a modernist, tripartite skyscraper with its central shaft extending to a clock tower. Two o'clock foreshadows the hour awaiting the hanging of "Bull" Weed (George Bancroft). The sequence pulls back from the superimposed image to reveal in the foreground construction cranes on the left, empty, steel-frames of new building's skeleton on the right, and in the background the cityscape with the clock towered building still center frame.

Cut a Duesenberg shot diagonally positioned left to right in front of a large stone building, then cut to drunk rounding the corner and weaving along the empty street, shot diagonally right to left with only the sidewalk illuminated with a shaft of light from a street lamp. A quick cut reveals the bank building's first-floor windows exploding. The drunk stumbles in the next shot and looks toward the entrance. A man with a large suitcase under his arm emerges in the next shot. Now in a medium shot, the drunk, whom Bull later befriends and nicknames "Rolls Royce" Wensel (Clive Brook), smiles and offers sarcastically, "The great Bull Weed—closing another bank account." Bull grabs the drunk by the collar and forces him into the Duesenberg, which speeds off right of frame. Cut to a policeman running, whistling, and then firing his gun, as another policeman slides to the ground next to him, firing his weapon. Cut to the Duesenberg climbing the sidewalk to take out the corner in order to avoid the spray of bullets. Sternberg includes quickly paced shots of police procedures: manning the switchboard at headquarters, and then, cut to center-framed garage doorway with doors open as a police vehicle races through its entrance, followed by another, a motorcycle,

Underworld: prelude to a "violent conclusion" has "Feathers" (Evelyn Brent) with "Bull" Weed (George Bancroft) at his hide-out.

and another motorcycle. This exciting opening sequence contains just fifteen shots and lasts only one minute and twenty-three seconds. That quick pacing establishes how Sternberg visually tells this story, in fragmented, yet coordinated cuts that move the narrative apace. Additionally, this intricate scene employs numerous lighting, camera work, and urban elements that would become staples of film noir.

The second major scene of the Dreamland Café sexualizes the femme fatale and provides the elements for two triangles of desire that dominate the film's plot, one of burgeoning love and the other of sadistic sexual assault. This sequence begins with a shot of a building front above the awning with the sign Dreamland Café. Cut to large room of the speak-easy filled with tables and an upper-tier smaller, railed off space reached by a staircase. Waiters in black ties and long white aprons neatly bisect the room from a kitchen door located left background. Back to street level with a large cat pursuing a smaller cat left to right of frame among barrels and debris. The camera pans quickly right to left to reveal a small white cat ascending the steps of a building. Here, the triangle of desire plays out in a visual metaphor. Cut now to the entrance of Feathers (Evelyn Brent). She wears a flapper's outfit, with a gaudy Oriental-patterned silk knee-length jacket with ostrich feathers at the cuffs and neck, a silver satin dress with sequin mesh from belly button to the knees, silver shoes with black ribbons, and a bejeweled coche. Feathers stands in the entrance and provocatively adjusts her stockings. The camera then follows a feather from her coat descending to a kneeling man (Rolls Royce) sweeping up debris, who catches the floating feather and looks up. This symbolic connection foreshadows the love affair between Rolls Royce and Feathers that precipitates Bull's homicidal jealousy, his escape from County Jail, and the shoot-out with the police at the end of the film. Cut from Rolls Royce looking at the object of desire to Feathers standing at the entrance when Bull Weed enters, takes Feathers' arm, and they descend. Cut to their descent to the barroom main floor, where the proprietor greets them.

Evelyn Brent as the sultry "Feathers" in *Underworld*.

Inset above and below, the triangle: "Feathers" ponders her situation as Bull is passed out at a party. Later with the dapper if dissolute "Rolls Royce" Wensel (Clive Brook).

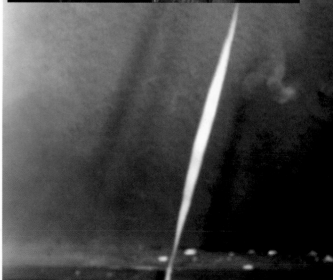

As Feathers moves among the crowded tables, Bull notices a newspaper clipping about his nighttime bank robberies. Newspaper headline reads: "Police Hunt Bank Bandits. Arrests Near In Last Week's Daring Robbery." Bull guffaws! As she makes quick remarks to friends, Buck Mulligan (Fred Kohler) wantonly eyes Feathers, who completely ignores him. Mulligan's girl (Helen Lynch) scolds him: "Keep your eyes off her! What do you think I'm here for?" Undaunted, Mulligan wants to show off his disdain for money in order to entice Feathers: "Watch me show that dame what I think of money." Here, the second sexual triangle plot emerges, only this time, violence characterizes the male desire. Only when Mulligan's attention turns toward Rolls Royce does Feathers take notice of him: "Buck Mulligan's looking for trouble." Mulligan asks Rolls Royce if he would like ten bucks, then wads it up and tosses into a spittoon. The camera pans diagonally from Rolls Royce's face down to the spittoon and back up again. Rolls Royce ignores the now-filthy ten spot, as Mulligan's pals jeer at him. Furious at his impotency, Mulligan demands that Rolls Royce pick up the ten spot, but again, Mulligan is ignored. In a stunning bit of camerawork, Sternberg shoots a close-up of Mulligan slugging Rolls Royce as the camera quickly tilts up to give the sensation of Rolls Royce collapsing to the floor. This POV technique to suggest the disorientation from violence occurs later in *The Lady in the Lake* (1947), when corrupt and homicidal cop Lt. DeGamot (Lloyd Nolan) decks the smart-mouthed Philip Marlowe (Robert Montgomery). In *Dark Passage* (1947), Delmer Daves turns this POV violence technique around by having just-escaped San Quentin prisoner, Vince Parry (Humphrey Bogart), beat unconscious an overly curious motorist, Baker (Clifton Young), in order to elude capture. Samuel Fuller's *The*

Wensel wants Feathers to make a choice between him and Weed.

Naked Kiss (1964) opens with prostitute Kelly (Constance Towers) beating a john unconscious, with the camera jerking with each punch that she lands, so forcefully that her wig falls off to reveal her bald head.

Mulligan threatens Rolls Royce: "Pick it up or I'll send you to the morgue!" Mulligan's explosion of violence Sternberg captures with the entire speak-easy erupting in confusion as the clientele flee up the stairs, as the camera quickly pans left to right across the barroom to the staircase, then tilts up to more fleeing customers running out, then pans sharply to the left, before cutting back to Bull. Mulligan's crew watches anxiously as large shadows of the fleeing customers parade across the back wall. Bull Weed steps in between Mulligan and the cowering Rolls Royce, whom he escorts over to his table. Again, Mulligan's face registers his fury and impotency. Rolls Royce courteously bows to Feathers as he takes his seat. Mulligan's crew restrains him: "Give me that gun!" Bull, shot in profile, faces Mulligan's direction, surreptitiously removes a gat from his coat and conceals it in the towel that had surrounded the champagne bottle in the bucket on the table. Bull smiles and pours Rolls Royce a drink, who has been looking at Feathers. Mulligan makes the introduction: "Rolls Royce, meet Feathers—my girl." Rolls Royce stands and toasts Feathers. Feathers with a half-blank, half-amused expression mocks him: Title: "How long since you had the body washed and polished, Rolls Royce?" Bull guffaws: "If you don't want Mulligan to bump you off, Professor, you'd better stick with me." Rolls Royce nods and shrugs: "With pleasure, sir." Bull guffaws again and repeats Rolls Royce's pleasantry. Cut to extreme close-up of a seething Mulligan, as his moll runs her little finger round his ear.

At Bull's table, Feathers gets to her feet: "Come on, let's drift!" Audiences and critics found the dialogue of the inter-titles so experimental and refreshing for using the conventional argot of the underworld. Bull's entourage leaves by ascending the stairs, all the while, Bull keeps his eye on Mulligan. To best Mulligan at his own materialist game, Bull returns to his table, pulls out coins from his pocket, clinks them in his hands, before selecting one and holding it between both hands, bends it! Bull's guffaw counters Mulligan's sneering contempt. Bull tosses the coin onto the table, then adjusts his coat as he checks for his gat. Before ascending the stairs, Bull mockingly laughs at Mulligan. Once again, Mulligan's crew restrains their homicidal boss.

The rivalry for Feathers plays out in terms of the two mainstays of the criminal underworld—money and violence. Unbeknownst to Bull or Mulligan, a waiter on his knees, hidden by the side of the bar, retrieves the ten spot from the spittoon and cleans it off with his apron. One hundred twenty-five shots comprise this astonishing sequence of nine minutes and fifty-four seconds. Sternberg's camerawork, shadows, and emotional reaction shots provide a new cinematic language, one that expresses unseemly desires, sexuality, and brutality through symbolic images. Outside the Dreamland Café, Rolls Royce and an indignant Feathers wait for Bull, who emerges and dismisses Feather's anger. Bull stares up at large flashing sign covering the upper story of a building and towering over six small-er billboards. It reads: "THE CITY IS YOURS. A.B.C. Investment Co." Bull gestures to Feathers to look up at the sign: "The city is yours, Kid—what'll you have?" Feathers dismisses Bull. Bull looks back to the sign and proudly laughs. Rolls Royce interjects: "Attila, the Hun, at the gates of Rome." A quizzical Bull responds: "Who's Attila? The leader of some wop gang?" Rolls Royce shakes his head and prophesies: "You were born two thousand years too late. You can't get away with your stuff—nowadays." Bull disagrees: "They'll never get me!" Bull pulls out a wad of money and slaps it into Rolls Royce 's hand: "I'm either a missionary or a sucker, but I'm going to put you on your feet." With button-

busting pride, Bull pulls out his vest with his thumbs. To reciprocate, Rolls Royce asks what he can do to help Bull, but Bull dismisses him out of hand: "Help me? Nobody helps me! I help other people!" Bull offers his arm to an accepting Feathers. They stroll away. Cut to a classic noir shot. A long shot of a recently rain-soaked sidewalk before brick buildings lighted from the right to make the wet bricks glisten. Bull and Feathers stroll toward a blackened vanishing point, but Bull, obviously remembering his manners, changes so that he walks on the outside toward the street. Cross-cut to a close-up of a brooding Mulligan, who crushes the flower in his lapel to bits. This sexual symbol now becomes a sign of violence, revenge, and death.

Materialism and money dominate much of film noir and Sternberg incorporates them into two mercantile shop scenes. The first reveals the Mulligan's Flower Shop, his obsession and also front for his criminal finances. The store's window displays a funerary vase with a large card that reads "Mulligan's Special." A hand plucks a flower from the vase. A brooding Mulligan inserts the flower in to his coat's lapel slit. In the backroom, Mulligan pulls out a banner that matches the Rest In Peace sash on the floral crucifix. This banner reads: "Bull Weed." Florist shop girl with her hands on her hips derides Mulligan, who responds viciously: "I'm going to bury that guy while these lilies are still fresh!" FADE TO BLACK.

The inter-title ironically disputes Mulligan's claim: "But Buck should have used wax flowers, for long after his lilies had faded—" The window of a jewelry store displays three necklaces and a large bracelet, along with watches and strings of pearls, which Feathers admires. Bull barks at Feathers: "You don't want that junk. It's too vulgar!" Feathers, with a slight pout and still looking at the jewelry, gives a big sigh. Across Bull's face creeps a knowing smile. Bull escorts Feathers to a Yellow Cab and they depart. Sternberg also ironizes Bull's intention, as the scene shifts to the cab arriving before a tenement. The typical denizens of the lower-class appear as a tableau—a head-scarfed woman leaning out a first-story window, a man in a "wife-beater" reading the newspaper on the top step, a beshawled women with two young boys left of the lower step, a stand of fruits and vegetables right of the lower steps, and debris fills in the street gutter. As Bull and Feathers stand before the tenement steps, Feathers recognizes the place: "Why, it's the old hideaway! Why did you bring me here?" Before

Below, Bull in the hide-out. Right, top and bottom, *He Walked by Night*. Opposite page, foreground bars imprison the entire criminal crew in *The Killing*.

they enter, Bull catches a young boy stealing an apple from the street stand: "Don't you know it's wrong to steal?" Bull gives the boy a swift kick; Feathers laughs at the scene, and Bull admires the apple before biting into it. Bull's sham morality characterizes the ethics of noir, one set of guidelines for society, another code for the criminal class. Bull and Feathers ascend to the doorway, but before entering, Bull gives the man reading the newspaper a kick to move aside for Feathers. Again, Sternberg visually presages violence and retribution that arise out of male rivalry, which will be evident in the hideout scenes.

The hideout scenes establish the narrative elements that lead to *Underworld*'s violent conclusion, prompted by sexual revenge and jealousy. Bull and Feathers make their way to the apartment via a hallway in chiaroscuro shifts from spaces of light to deep shadows. Inside the sequestered apartment, Rolls Royce, now smartly attired, sits reading and smoking. He rises to open the door, after hearing the coded knocking. The window shadow across the door marks out a series of interconnected boxes that suggest a spider's web. A typical noir visual motif of impending entrapment that foreshadows (literally) the film's conclusion, where Bull will fight it out with the cops from this secret hideout. These stylistic patterns often reflects the inner turmoil, paranoia, and sense of hopelessness in noir protagonists, as evidenced by Richard Basehart's cellbar-like shadows when police corner him in his bungalow in *He Walked By Night* (1948), the venetian blinds that cast imprisoning horizontal shadows on Sterling Hayden's bed in *The Killing* (1956), among numerous examples.

In the sequestered apartment behind a cabinet filled with books that operate as a hidden door lies a steel door, itself leading to a small anteroom with another steel door that serves as an escape route: "A perfect getaway—through our warehouse to the next block. And nitro couldn't blow those doors!" After showing an underwhelmed Feathers these secrets, Bull departs for "important business," but before he exits Rolls Royce puts a flower in Bull's coat lapel: "The police all know 'Mulligan's Special.' Plant the little flower where it will do the most good." Of course, the flower will frame Buck Mulligan. After Bull leaves, the second triangle begins to form with Rolls Royce and Feathers as sensitive lovers countering the egotistical Bull. The elegance of their names stand in opposition to the rutting, single-minded Bull and Buck of the triangle of violence. Initially, Feathers ignores Rolls Royce and grabs a book to read, but Rolls Royce turns it right side up in a gesture of mock contempt.

The jewelry store robbery consists of twelve quick shots lasting only forty-four seconds, and yet remains a marvel of condensed cinematic action and visual narrative. The first shot shows the interior of jewelry store with the clerk approaching and opening a glass cabinet filled with clocks, silver bowls, urns, and salt and pepper shakers. As he reaches for a four-pedestal clock on the top shelf, a gun explodes and smoke fills the frame. Cut to the clock face with a bullet hole. The frightened clerk wheels around with his hands in the air. Cut to the window display as a hand grabs the bracelet and the necklaces. A lapel flower drops to the floor, next to a pair of lions' claw legs. Cut to sidewalk with people running, shot from the waist down. Against a jewelry store's wall a legless beggar holds his hat. An unknown man, shot from the waist down, stops before the beggar. Cut to the man's hands bending a coin, which he then tosses. Cut to the beggar's hat on the sidewalk as the coin flies into it. Cut to the beggar's incredulous face. Inside the jewelry store with the clerk viewed outside the store window, he points frantically off to the left. Two men run up to him. He points to the left as a crowd forms around them. Inside the store a detective strolls up to the counter. He notices something on the floor and bends down. Cut to his hand as it picks up the flower from the floor.

Because the police find the flower, they haul in Buck Mulligan from his flower store, which serves as an oppositional space to the jewelry store. Imagery of flowers and jewelry carry sexual connotations, but in this case, both end up as ironic symbols for the impotence of Bull and Buck. After a detective withdraws an envelope from his coat containing a small flower, a fuming Mulligan protests, "Somebody framed me!" Snidely, the detective retorts with a partial grin: "Framed you? Since when are you a picture, Buck?" Before being taken away by the cops, Buck adjusts the "Rest In Peace" sash across the floral crucifix and smiles, knowing full well who has set him up. Meanwhile, another potential set-up occurs in the sequestered hideout with Rolls Royce and Feathers. Sternberg develops their attraction in this second lengthy episode that moves from their inability to ignore one another as they read and their playful laughter to their physical contact and sexual chemistry.

When Rolls Royce asks Feathers about her signature attire, she unabashedly opens her coat and reveals her neckline with the coquettishly inviting phrase: "I wear feathers all over." At a moment when they almost kiss, Rolls Royce pulls back and merely kisses her hand, reminding Feathers: ""Bull Weed's our best friend, isn't he?" Acknowledging her near emotional and sexual betrayal, Feathers shakes her head ever so slightly: "This is the first time in a long while that I've felt ashamed." The sound of Bull's return hastens them back to the separate spots in the room. Bull arrives, gives Feathers her jewels, to which she jumps into his lap. Swelled with pride that the flower frame worked, Bull asks Rolls Royce if he is coming to the Ball that evening. Cut to iris-frame of Rolls shaking his head before a picture of an ancient Roman ruin. The "Attila" remark earlier now has emotional significance. Bull brooks no refusal and orders Rolls Royce to attend: "Beside, I'm going to make Feathers queen of the ball." Bull and Feathers leave and Sternberg cuts to a long shot of Rolls Royce alone, who sits on the sofa, then picks up the ticket to the ball along with a feather. Underworld love triangles occur with some frequency in film noir, such as in *Gilda* (1946) with Rita Hayworth, Glenn Ford, and George

Macready or the imagined affair between Glenn Ford and Gloria Grahame by the psychotic Lee Marvin in *The Big Heat* (1953).

The Mobsters' Ball remains the lengthiest scene in *Underworld*. It serves as an examination of the inner social world of gangsters, an obverse reflection of high society. "Check your gats!" commands a bouncer near the coat room. Bull sells tickets to promote Feathers as Queen of the Ball, the results of which change periodically on a tally board. Rolls Royce and Feathers dance, but a jealous Bull throws Rolls Royce out, which causes both rivals to drink heavily. Feathers surreptitiously approaches Rolls Royce at the crowded bar to dissuade him from drinking, to which he responds: "You're Bull Weed's girl—aren't you?" She hides her face in her hands and with a sense of defeat Feathers returns to Bull. Sternberg captures the decadence and immorality of the underworld: "Elsewhere the night deepened into silence and rest. But here the brutal din of cheap music—booze—hate—lust—made a devil's carnival." He then provides extremely fast-paced montage, thirty shots of the faces of drunken men and women as unsightly masks reflected in a distorted mirror. With Bull passed out, Buck Mulligan has a surrogate invite Feathers to a back office for her award as Queen of the Ball. The sexual subterfuge results in Feathers trapped with Buck as he begins his violent assault. Buck's moll rouses the drunken Bull, who stumbles his way from streamers and confetti to the back office, whose door he kicks in after hearing Feathers scream. Buck flees out the window pursued by Bull, who seems more intent on revenge than comforting Feathers. That job Rolls Royce fulfills when he arrives, holds Feathers, who buries her face in his chest.

Bull tracks Buck back to the flower store and plugs him five times. Fade to a courtroom with the Judge standing and delivering his verdict: "Before sentencing you, I declare to you and your kind that no man, or band of men, can defeat the Law." The Judge's shadow looms over Feathers and Rolls Royce, who are seated together, while Bull seems to ignore the Judge's words as his eyes dart in their direction: "All your life you have dealt with the Law as an enemy. And now, by a final deed of violence, you have compelled it to end your career." Then, the Judge sentences Bull to be hanged by the neck until dead, to which Bull offers only a smirk."

The cell scenes of Bull's incarceration utilize foreground bars and shots through bars to signal impending doom. The Warden pronounces the sunrise hanging, asks Bull for any last request, which he claims would be a steak from the Dreamland Café. The remainder of the film works out the plan for Bull's escape from the County Jail, filmed in its imagined, successful entirety with Schüfftan effects of looming buildings as the hearse arrives filled with Bull's gang. In reality, the gang fails completely. Still, Bull makes his own escape, at two o'clock no less, and returns to the sequestered apartment. There, Bull frantically paces back and forth awaiting the gang, but only Feathers shows up. She has waited for him on a back road, but returned to the hideout, unwittingly bringing the police with her. In a rage, Bull nearly strangles her, because the prison guard and the newspapers perpetuated the falsehood that Feathers is now Roll Royce's paramour. Bull would have killed her, but the cops open fire as Bull barricades the room. Police evacuate tenements. Police tommy guns destroy windows and the brick wall of the apartment. Rolls Royce, learning of Bull being trapped returns with the keys to the steel doors, all the while the siege continues. The only clear shot that Bull gets off is to wound Rolls Royce, who ironically tries to save him.

Rolls Royce makes it through the steel doors, Feathers rushes to her injured lover, and Bull recognizes true loyalty and forgives the couple. In the end, Bull grants them his blessing and admits his jealous error. He gives himself up and Sternberg frames the final moments in a chiaroscuro lit stairwell, with the shadows of the police captain, Bull, and an unseen police officer's shotgun barrel dominating the background. Bull explains to his captors: "There was something I had to find out—and that hour was worth more to me than my whole life." Again, the underworld code prevails over the social code.

In September, 1927, Billboard announced that the success of *Underworld* had led to a long-term starring role contract with Paramount for George Bancroft, the next venture also to be directed by Sternberg.[11] *Underworld* cost around $275,000 to make and Sternberg's salary was relatively low at "$250 a week for directing it."[12] A review of *Underworld* in *The Film Spectator* proclaimed that Sternberg took "a dramatization of the first page of a penny dreadful" and infused what could have been "only another lurid movie" with the touch and feel of an artist, one with a noir sensibility:

> But Von Sternberg is not conventional. The soul of the poet still shines in his work, but it is hard and harsh and stark, and it hurries along at a breath-taking rate that makes you sit still and breathe hard; that makes you love George Bancroft while you are hoping that he will be hanged. . . .He subjugates everything to the story and achieves the greatest art of all—the art that conceals art.[13]

"Pictures and People," in *Motion Pictures News* delivered high praise for *Underworld* proving that "fine pictures are being made—and what is more, pulling in crowds all by themselves," as well as leaving the "'arty' critics high and dry," as *Underworld* "the great art that has made the motion picture great."[14] Laurence Reid further praised the film for its "uncompromising" portrayal of the "graphic lay-out of crime" in a manner that "celluloid matter" can present "life in the raw."[15] When *Underworld* opened at the Paramount Metropolitan, *The Los Angeles Times* kept a hard-boiled edge to its praise: "If the baby has to go barefooted this winter, if the roof leaks like a sieve, and even if the lizzie needs gasoline, dig down into the jeans and go see *Underworld*."[16] *Photoplay*, using the vernacular of the day, claimed *Underworld* to be as compelling as "the bark of a machine gun."[17] *Billboard* understood the artistry of *Underworld*'s multi-dimensional filmmaking, including reference to camera work: "Many things combine to make *Underworld* an absorbing, spellbinding picture. The acting, titles, photography, camera angles, story and action are a few of them."[18]

An announcement in *The Film Daily* revealed "in enormous public favor" a new genre—"underworld stories."[19] Paramount held sway during the late summer of 1927 with three films dominating the marketplace, *Underworld, Wings*, and *The Way of All Flesh*. *The Film Daily* revealed that Paramount had changed its "weekly policy," so that *Underworld* could have an indefinite run at the Rivoli Theatre.[20] Paramount suspended its pattern of weekly changes for motion pictures at theaters for *Underworld*, as editor Maurice Kann explained this new business model, because this melodrama "rings true," has "punch" and "suspense," and "It hits," "so it stays right on the big street."[21] In its review of *Underworld, The Film Daily* extolled Paramount for anticipating film audience's unconscious desire for violence:

> Chicago in its worst days couldn't be any more thrilling than *Underworld* Paramount's latest contribution to the crowd that demands action of the blood and thunder order. The story is indeed gripping providing the spectator's sensibilities will not be offended by scenes showing gang warfare in wholly realistic vision—shot of one bandit pounding lead into a rival leader, a machine gun set-to, a riotous ball and other pertinent bits of life amongst the gangsters. With its very flagrant expose of up-to-date crimes (which may not be altogether smart) *Underworld* certainly offers seven and a half reels of stirring action.[22]

In its first week at the Paramount Theatre in New York, *Underworld* earned $81,782, the second highest first-week box office, just behind Paramount's Pola Negri vehicle, *Hotel Imperial* (1927), which netted $81,802 in its first week.[23] At the Rivoli Theatre, during its first week, *Underworld* set a new record of $41,000.[24] A major factor for Underworld's success was the creating of a noir ambience by having a "midnight show stunt" showing Tuesday through Friday nights, "after the last deluxe performance had closed," thereby giving *Underworld* a new market.[25] Paramount, in a bold move, trimmed down the usual fare that comes with a new film and just had *Underworld* only on this midnight bill, "shown with music, but without the other long features of the program and stage presentation."[26] The result of this new genre's success could be traced to Paramount's stock closing "at 104 3/4, a gain of over two points during the week and 15 points above the low point a few weeks back."[27] For this economic boon, the Paramount Theatre would award von Sternberg its Medal of Honor "stamped in solid gold" and present him with a $10,000 check.[28]

Its success continued nation-wide, as evidenced by its endorsement by the Tampa Police Chief, who found the film essential for its portrayal of "the eternal battle of law versus crime."[29] Even a mock-report had Jesse James's ghost exiting a screening of *Underworld* looking "very pale," but claiming that "he would have liked to have that guy Bancroft in his gang."[30] In Rock Island, Illinois, the sheriff displayed in the lobby of the local theatre the items associated with the underworld—"tears bombs, brass knuckles, lead pipes, dope, and other miscellaneous weapons."[31] A Pueblo, Colorado sporting goods store displayed copy from *Underworld* along with "an array of firearms" used in the film, with a warning from the police "that illegal use of these firearms brought long jail sentences."[32] An insurance rep tried to cash in on *Underworld*'s success by running an advertisement that read: "Protect yourself from prowlers from the 'Underworld.'"[33]

The popularity of *Underworld* and this new genre's appeal in general sparked interest among other studios to join this "new vogue in productions in Hollywood."[34] Fox decided to adapt the play "Romance of the Underworld" with its new star Mary Astor. Tiffany-Stahl Productions assigned William Christy Cabanne to produce "an underworld story," Famous Players-Lasky showed *The City Gone Wild* with Louise Brooks, Warner Brothers came out with *Brass Knuckles* and the Myrna Loy underworld melodrama, *The Girl From Chicago,* and Lumas Film Corporation announced its "Great Underworld Love Drama," *San Francisco Nights*.[35] In its columns on "The Studio," *Exhibitors Herald* recognized this emerging genre that produced a cinematic "crime wave" began with *Underworld* and in 1928 was followed by: *Square Crooks* by Fox, *Crooks Can't Win* for Film Booking Office Picture Corporation (FBO), *The Devil's Skipper* for Tiffany-Stahl, *Fallen Angels* for Universal, *Hell's Angels* for Caddo-United Artists, *Honor Bound* for Fox Films, *The Four Devils* also for Fox Films, and C.B. DeMille's *The Godless Girl* for Pathé.[36] William Ince's *Chicago After Midnight* (1928) for FBO Pictures Corporation received a two-page advertisement spread that proclaimed it "Greatest Underworld Thrill Show Ever Filmed," which would appeal to exhibitors because crime melodramas were the "cry of the hour . . . the demand of the public!"[37] Such demand there was for crime films that T. O. Service in "Service Talks" saw the trend to big city underworld cinema as "the greatest untouched picture material since Rome did a nosedive."[38] Just as the 1910s and 1920s had produced their own cycles of paleo-noirs, that cycle would soon become repeated in gangster and criminal films of the proto-noir period.

Roland West's *Alibi* even more that Sternberg's *Underworld* paved the way for proto-noirs. The opening sequence of *Alibi* indicates the original play's title, *Nightstick*, and several noir conventions with sight and sound. The prison guard's hand twirls a nightstick before the silhouette of the guard, a rhythmic short tap accompanies each twirl. A hand reaches for a fire bell cord that peals with each tug, again with the shadow upon the wall. A medium low-shot, from the waist down, has marching convicts moving in a diagonal line from background right to foreground left and their unified steps provide a new rhythm. A long shot of a uniformed guard facing the camera, lit from the right to

Alibi.

create his silhouette upon the wall, taps his nightstick to the cadence of the prisoners' march. A long shot of the cell corridor places a guard in foreground right along a diagonal two-tiered wall; on the left, a diagonal row of cells and cell doors correspond to the right side wall; both walls run to form a framed rectangle with another guard as the vanishing point; and, a diegetic sound of nightstick taps and feet marching continues. The cell doors open, convicts emerge, and the diagonal procession repeats itself, as though sight, sound, and time remain perpetually trapped without interference.

The foreground guard points to one convict with his nightstick, who responds by leaving the line of marching convicts, approaching the guard who indicates with his thumb for him to move out, which he does out of frame foreground right. The sound bridge of tapping and marching continues as the convict enters a large room with a diagonal long desk, one guard, and a cabinet of four vertical rows of drawers. The only illumination comes from a high, barred window, whose lines create noir shadows of entrapment upon the desk, and cabinet. The guard removes two packets and hands them to the prisoner. A file reads "No. 1065" before transforming by superimposition into his name "Chick Williams." Chick (Chester Morris), now dressed in suit and tie, shakes the guard's hand and departs, while his fate can be discerned by the intense shadows of bars falling upon him. Worth noting, silhouette openings figure in several film noirs, such as the credit sequence for *Double Indemnity* (1944), the brutal beating in silhouettes in the opening moments of *Crossfire* (1947), Jane Greer's sexually sadistic pleasure at watching, then killing Steve Brodie during his fist fight with Robert Mitchum in *Out of the Past* (1947), and the alley thug stomping in *Underworld U.S.A.* (1961).

Roland West experiments with sound throughout *Alibi*, as evidenced by five nightclub girlie dance numbers punctuating the action at almost every ten to fifteen minutes. Connecting underworld milieu with dancehall and lounge performances became a standard in film noir. So many film noirs contain scenes in lounges, restaurants, and clubs with female talent as the entertainment. Toots (Irma Harrison), the main lead in these risqué chorus lines of skimpy outfits and long legs at Bachman's cabaret, flirts with Danny McGann (Regis Toomey), a police detective posing as a high-life, fun-loving dipsomaniac within the criminal gang. Unwittingly, Toots barges in as Danny has the drop on the gang before they can kill him, and her distraction affords Chick Williams the opportunity to plug the informer.

Throughout most of *Alibi,* Toots' presence has been the object of the camera's gaze; in fact, for one chorus line scene, West shot it through a contorted iris-eye so that only feminine waists to toes occupied the frame. Toots, like the later feminine singers in film noir, thematically represents the object of male sexual aggression and violence; in this case, not Toots directly, but rather her open sexuality reflects and simultaneously deflects Joan Manning's (Eleanor Griffith) sexual and moral position as daughter of police Sgt. Manning (Purnell Pratt) and new wife of ex-convict Chick Williams. Toots, then, represents what Robert Miklitsch so artfully analyzes in *Siren City* as "one of the fundamental questions of film noir: Is she or isn't she? In other words, is she a 'good girl' or a 'a bad

girl'?"[39] For Miklitsch, chanteuses of big lounge numbers in film noir often provide feminine discourse as well as thematic content, as he demonstrates for Rita Hayworth in *Gilda* (1946), Lauren Bacall in *The Big Sleep* (1946), Ann Blythe in *Mildred Pierce* (1946), Lizabeth Scott in *Dead Reckoning* (1947), and Ida Lupino in *Road House* (1948), among others.

At the center of *Alibi*'s plot stands or falls Joan Manning's loyalty to truth, since she provides the concert hall tickets to The New York Follies for Chick's alibi and she, as a narrative double to Toots, leads to her husband's death. Joan Manning exemplifies the feminine conundrum of film noir that so often denotes moral ambiguity.

Along with sound innovations, West explored nuances with lighting and camera work that would find their way in the film noir repertoire. Four major scenes demonstrate West's experimental work: the fur coat warehouse heist, the re-enactment of the time sequence for the heist, the interrogation of one of the heist gang, and the death of Chick Williams. The heist occurs during the intermission of the New York Follies precisely at ten o'clock, in a one minute and thirty-three second sequence of twenty shots. The scene outside the concert hall fades to black, then to a close-up of beat policeman's pocket watch reading ten o'clock. He observes a cab fly by him and around a corner in a urban street scene of what would become typical film noir technique, with intensely lit sections sporadically off-set by deep shadows on pavement and walls. The policeman pursues, sees the driver now acting as the look-out, confronts him, and then holds the others thieves at gunpoint. He taps his nightstick on the sidewalk, which resounds to other officers, including detective Sergeant Glennon (Pat O'Malley). From out of the cab appears a hand holding a revolver, which fires four shots into the policeman's back. Two of the gang run away, while the driver hops back into the cab and speeds off.

The re-enactment of the heist's time schedule and distance from the National Theatre introduced the noir convention of filming the cityscape through a moving vehicle at night. The one minute forty-five second sequence begins with a fade from the chorus line of only legs dancing to a cut-in of the detective's pocket watch, which reads five until ten o'clock, and then fade to the detective and sergeant entering the cab and leaving the National Theatre, all the while the sound bridge of the chorus number, "Then I'll Know Why," plays. Fade to POV from windshield of the cab looking over the hood with the headlights illuminating a major urban street ahead as a bright circle of light. The cab moves at considerable speed with city lights glaring from marquees and signs along either side of the street as the vanishing point converges into blackness. The only sound is the metallic, rhythmic sound of the cab's engine. Fade to the cab making a severe left turn onto a dark side street and heading into a tunnel, while a trolley car passes by. Fade to an almost black street with sporadic lights along the sidewalk as a couple darts quickly across the street in front of the on-coming cab, which then takes a sharp right onto a completely blackened street. Fade to the studio shots of the cab rounding the corner of the fur warehouse then to a match-on-action of that turn in front of the warehouse, where the detective hops out of the cab and checks his watch. Cut-in of the pocket watch now reading ten o'clock and back to the detective hopping into the cab as it takes off.

Fade to black, then the bright front of the National Theatre as the cab pulls up with the detective hopping out. A shot of the pocket watch which reads five after ten. Cut to the detective announcing his destination to the cabbie, "Detective Bureau," as he climbs in. Final cut of the sequence is the cab in front of the Theatre pulling away. Fade to black. This in-the-automobile shooting would become highlights of both proto- and standard film noir, such as the exciting sequence in *The Secret 6* (1931) and, of course, incredible from back seat shooting sequence for the bank robbery in *Gun Crazy* (1950), a decade before Jean-Luc Godard's *À bout de souffle*.

The nine minute forty-four second interrogation scene of Soft Malone (Elmer Ballard), the cab driver in the fur heist, begins with the shadow of extended fingers of a hand upon a wall; a hand

Opposite, *Alibi*: Buck Bachman (Harry Stubbs, right) confronts Daisy Thomas (Mae Busch) and Danny McGann (Regis Toomey).

enters the frame and presses down on its shadow, then a fade to a single man with an eye mask, and then another fade to rows of men with eye masks who observe the systematic line-up and finger-printing on an intensely lit stage before them. As Detective Sergeant enters his office with Sgt. Manning, West frames the very theatrical space through four iron bars in the foreground. The motif of foreshadowing cage-like lines of entrapment bode ill for Soft Malone, as they will for so many future film noir criminals. The third-degree and coercion studio stage has one hanging light in the center of the room, which provides intense illumination on Glennon's desk area. When a detective tosses Malone into Glennon's office, the cabbie immediately complains about brutality, not waving extradition from New Jersey, and demands a "mouth piece." When Glennon shows Malone the gun, the cabbie claims that the police planted "in me pocket." When Glennon indicates for the detective to stand outside the door, where his silhouette appears on the frosted glass of the door. When Glennon informs Malone that he saw him in the cab driving away from the scene, Soft produces a ticket for the same Friday the 13th (of course!) performance at the National Theatre that Chick Williams used for his alibi.

Glennon threatens Malone with the story of the disappearance of Gimpy Jackson after he killed a cop, but Soft protests "I wouldn't croak nobody! Honest, I wouldn't, not even a cop." Glennon pushes Malone further by informing him, "That's tough, being you've been elected to take the rap for murder!" When Malone dismisses Glennon with "Don't make me laugh," the two police sergeants confab at the back of the office, all the while Malone nervously eyeing the clock, trying to eavesdrop on them, and being spooked to paranoia by the detective's face outside the door appearing in the silhouette. Edward Dmytryk would use a similar type of anxiety-producing moment in *Murder, My Sweet* (1944), when Moose Malloy's (Mike Mazurki) image appears above Philip Marlowe's (Dick Powell) on Marlowe's office window.

Sgt. Manning opens the window shade, then opens the window, as Glennon wipes off the gun, to remove fingerprints. Glennon puts on gloves, forces Malone to hold the gun, then takes it and loads it as Manning circles around the cabbie. They threaten him with staging a self-defense shooting, which entails Malone trying to escape through the open window after having grabbed the gun, fired at Manning, missed, and dies from the return fire of Manning. Manning puts a pistol at Malone's head as Glennon repeatedly asks who murdered O'Brien (De Witt Jennings), the beat cop at the fur heist. In his panic, Malone experiences a paranoid, kaleidoscopic rotation of Glennon's and Manning's faces until he spits out the murderer's name—Chick Williams. The POV hallucination technique would achieve a number of variants in film noir, most of them associated with acts of violence, such as Philip Marlowe's forced narcotic dream sequence in *Murder, My Sweet*, Jeff Lebowski's Busby Berkeley-esque, mickey-induced fantasy in *The Big Lebowski* (1998), as well as entire films as hallucinatory or productions of mental aberrations, among them *The Woman in the Window* (1944) and *Memento* (2000). The third-degree interrogation scene ends as it began with West shooting through the four bars in the foreground as Malone babbles on about the murder of O'Brien.

Chick Williams' death remains one of the most spectacular moments in early sound films. The Art Deco patterns on the doors' fragmented lines visually suggests the confusion of Williams' escape, a departure from the usual horizontal and vertical bars of entrapment. Here, the displacement of lines indicate incompleteness as they also appear to be a cascade of a falling linear figure. *Alibi*'s ending begins with a simple stage trick. While the cops congratulate themselves on capturing the murderer Williams, he switches off the lights, improbably hurls a floor vase at a pistol-firing detective, smashes a small vase over the head of uniformed policemen, and, even more improbably, ducks behind a leather wingback chair. To deflect away from his position, Williams hurls a leather ottoman through the apartment window, which the detectives misconstrue as his escape route and commence unload their pistols out the broken panes. All the while, Williams crawls to and then flees out the door. His wife, now on the side of the law, screams out, "The door!" and the chase is on. Here, West makes an ingenious and strategic move. The chase lasts six seconds and has only four shots, the most spectacular being Williams's attempt to leap from the ledge of one building to the ledge of the next building. West shoots this moment from a high angle so that the chasm of lighted apartment windows descends into darkness. Of course, Williams initially makes the jump for a split second before his tragic fall. Falls to deaths in film noirs serve as poetic justice for malefactors, such as Agnes Moorehead's marvelously unexpected fall out a window in *Dark Passage*, and the descent by John Garfield in *Force of Evil* (1948), the explosive falls at the end of *White Heat* (1949) for James Cagney or for Harry Belafonte and Robert Ryan in *Odds Against Tomorrow* (1959).

Alibi: Daisy with Chick Williams (Chester Morris. left) and Sgt. Manning (Purnell Pratt). Below, Daisy and Chick.

For its New York run, this "underworld feature," the first talkie for United Artists, will have a "$2 run" on Broadway, after being "enthusiastically received at a special morning review at Grauman's Chinese Theater."[40] According to *The Billboard*, the film's title would be changed from *Nightstick*, the original title of the stage production, to *Alibi*, because the studio concluded that customers "in the hinterland" were "unversed in big-town ways" and would not know what a nightstick was.[41] *The Film Weekly* mentioned *Alibi*'s historical significance as "the first film yet shown to make a serious attempt at a 'talkie' form, and for that reason, if for no other, is definitely a milestone in film history."[42] In March, United Artists, in a two-page advertisement for its four features, Douglas Fairbank's *The Iron Mask*, D. W. Griffith's *Lady of the Pavements*, Mary Pickford's *Coquette*, and Roland West's *Alibi*, claimed *Alibi* was "hailed by 1500 at a recent preview in Hollywood."[43] In April, United Artists' Advertisement campaign for *Alibi*, "the greatest $2.00 top picture" in New York, cited critics for several New York papers, among them, Irene Thirer of *The Daily News*, whose endorsement related the audience's experience:

> A crackerjack thriller. *Alibi* is so tense, so full of gripping drama it makes one grasp his theatre seat and absolutely shiver with excitement. You're going to go strong for it.[44]

To increase public interest in *Alibi*, United Artists set up a forty-seven station "hook up through the Columbia network" so that *Alibi* could be broadcast on Sunday night, April 21, with Chester Morris and Eleanor Griffith, as well as director Roland West, playing radio parts.[45] Of course, radio served as a perfect advertisement medium for the new sound pictures from United Artists.

In May, *Variety* featured an advertisement to exhibitors that proclaimed that *Alibi*, the "All Talking-Musical Melodramatic Sensation," would prove to be "one of the greatest box-office bets of a year of many good pictures."[46] A *Billboard* review of *Alibi* praised Chester Morris' screen presence and added, in a hard-boiled bit of sarcasm to sum up the plot of the film: "The story of *Alibi* concerns the break-down of the alibi of Chick Williams which had been carefully prepared, but the police find has one hidden little hole in it. The detective (Pal O'Malley) is in love with the cop's daughter (Miss Griffith), who spurns him for the crook, but the ending is a happy one, with the girl's crook husband plunging to his death in attempting a sensational escape."[47]

In April, *Variety*'s review of *Alibi* describes the plot with the quick urban diction associated with hard-boiled fiction:

> *Alibi* starts out to give the cops the losing end of an expository tract on brutality. It winds up by hinting that the gendarmes have to be tough. Morris impersonates a clever young rodent with the instincts of a Chinese brigand. Quick to shoot when his adversary's back is turned, he is a sniveling, groveling, contemptible coward when cornered himself. Without stressing the moral, picture is dedicated to the proposition that the man with a gun is a dirty name to start with—and was born that way.[48]

Of course, this "moral" resonates with most proto-noirs, film noirs, and neo-noirs.

In many respects, this chapter makes an appeal to noir scholars and critics for a paleoarchaeology of film noir. This appeal calls for theoretical reconsiderations of international silent film contributions to film noir, as well as for film theorists to re-examine transnational silent film in terms of its aesthetic, stylistic, film linguistic, thematic, and narrative lineage to film noir. Because the vast number of silent films remains lost to scholars, this appeal welcomes some speculation about thematic content, aesthetic values, narrative structures, and cinematic language that might only be obtained through partial restorations, through studio, actor, and director archives, and through film and even fan magazine archives that might open up a window to the archaeological strata in cinema history that not only produced film noir, but also continues to keep that noir tradition alive.

No stylistic, narrative, and thematic genre exists in film history with the expansive reach of film noir. Even the Western, that foundational of fundamental American genres, does not have the archaeological sustained literary, visual, and cinematic coherence of the noir tradition. This essay hopes to open up film noir to numerous discussions, analyses, and debates among film scholars, critics, historians, literary critics, and popular culture mavens, as well as to open this paleo-to-neo-noir timeline to greater scrutiny, debate, and expansion among global art forms.

Notes

1. "The Gangsters of New York," *Reel Life* (March 7, 1914): 6.
2. Advertisement in *The Motion Picture World* (June 10, 1916): 1802.
3. "From the Deep," *The Moving Picture World* (November 4, 1916): 692.
4. "The Better Instinct," *The Moving Picture World* (October 28, 1916): 568.
5. "The Perils of Our Girl Reporters," *The Moving Picture World* (December 16, 1916):1588.
6. "Ignorance," *The Moving Picture World* (December 2, 1916): 1351.
7. "Pidgin Island," *The Moving Picture World* (November 18, 1916): 1022.
8. "Pictures To Be Eliminated Entirely," *The Motion Picture World* (June 10, 1916): 1921.
9. Henry B. Fuller, *The Cliff-Dwellers—A Novel* (New York: Harper & Brothers, 1893): 1-2.
10. Ben Hecht, *Underworld—an original story of Chicago* in *3 Silent Classics by Josef von Sternberg*, Criterion Collection 2010: 45-46.
11. "Long Contract for Bancroft," *The Billboard* (September 3, 1929): 34.
12. " 'Underworld' Prize Film," *Variety* (Wednesday, January 11, 1928): 11.
13. "Von Sternberg Scores with 'Underworld,'" *The Film Spectator* (July 23, 1927): 9.
14. "Pictures and People," *Motion Picture News* (September 9, 1927): 763.
15. Laurence Reid, "Underworld. Graphic Melodrama. Raw but Real." *Motion Picture News* (September 9, 1927): 784.
16. " 'Underworld'—Paramount Metropolitan, L.A," in "Newspaper Opinions on New Pictures," (September 19, 1927): 863.

17. "The Stage Shadow—A Review of New Pictures," "Underworld—Paramount," *Photoplay Magazine* XXXII (September, 1927): 52.

18. "Paramount Film: 'Underworld,'" *The Billboard* (September 3, 1927): 35.

19. "More facts and signs of the times," *The Film Daily* (Wednesday, July 7, 1927): 4.

20. " 'Underworld' at the Rivoli For an Indefinite Run," *The Film Daily* (Thursday, August 25, 1927): 4. See also "The Broadway Parade," *The Film Daily* (Monday, August 29, 1927): 2.

21. Maurice Kann, "An Unusual Procedure," *The Film Daily* (Friday, August 26, 1927): 1.

22. "'Underworld.' Paramount. Length: 7453 ft. REAL BLOOD AND THUNDER MELODRAMA. VIVID PICTUR-IZATION OF CRIMES THAT THRILLS EVEN IF COLD-BLOODED." *The Film Daily* (Sunday, August 28, 1927): 6.

23. " 'UNDERWORLD' EARNS $81,782 IN ONE WEEK," *The Film Daily* (Monday, August 29, 1927): 1.

24. "'Sorel and Sons' Gross $35,928," *The Film Daily* (Tuesday, November 22, 1927): 6.

25. " 'Underworld' Grosses $81,782 in One Week," *The Film Daily* (Monday, August 29, 1927): 4.

26. "Paramount Showings at Midnight Permanent," *Motion Picture News* (September 9, 1927): 773.

27. "Steadiness in Loew's is Feature of Week," *The Film Daily* (Thursday, September 8, 1927): 9.

28. "Sternberg Wins Director's Prize; Badger Second, Stiller Third," *Exhibitors Herald and Motion Picture World* (January 14, 1928): 12.

29. "Exploit-O-Gram—Daily Tips Which Mean Dollars For Showmen," *The Film Daily* (Sunday, October 2, 1927): 10.

30. Phil M. Daily, "And That's That," *The Film Daily* (Monday, October 24, 1927): 1.

31. " 'Underworld' (Paramount)," *The Film Daily* (Monday, December 5, 1927): 8.

32. "Exploit-O-Gram," *The Film Daily* (Wednesday, December 14, 1927): 12.

33. "Exploit-O-Gram," *The Film Daily* (Sunday, October 30, 1927): 1.

34. "Underworld Is Newest Vogue. Here They Come in Row Paramount Leads," *Variety* (Wednesday, June 15, 1927): 5.

35. "Cabanne Making Underworld Film," *The Film Daily* (Monday, November 28, 1927): 4; Lumas Film Corporation ad from *The Film Daily* (Wednesday, December 21, 1927): 6.

36. "The Studio," "Crime Films in Vogue," *Exhibitors Herald and Moving Picture World* (January 29, 1928): 45.

37. "Chicago After Midnight," *Exhibitors Herald and Moving Picture World* (February 4, 1928): 6-7.

38. "Chicago After Midnight," *Exhibitors Herald and Moving Picture World* (February 18, 1928): 48.

39. Robert Miklitsch, *Siren City: Sound and Source Music in Classic American Noir* (New Brunswick, NJ: Rutgers University Press, 2011): 221.

40. " 'Alibi' at $2," *The Billboard* (March 23, 1929): 26.

41. "'Nightstick' Now 'Alibi,'" *The Billboard* (February 16, 1929): 21.

42. "A Film Man's Diary," *The Film Weekly* (March 25, 1929): 11.

43. "Can it be possible," *Variety* (Wednesday, March 13, 1929): 22.

44. "Oh! Boy! What a jolt this guy handed Broadway Monday Night April—8th," *Variety* (Wednesday, April 10, 1929): 21.

45. " 'Alibi'" Over Radio," *Variety* (Wednesday, April 17, 1929): 4.

46. "The World's Greatest—Alibi," *Variety* (Wednesday, May 22, 1929): 33.

47. "'Alibi' (UNITED ARTISTS) At 44th St. Theater," *The Billboard* (April 20, 1929): 22.

48. "ALIBI (Dialog)," in "Film Reviews," *Variety* (Wednesday, April 10, 1929): 23.

Film noir, American painting and photography: a question of influence?

Tom Ryall

> The archetypal noir shot is probably the extreme high-angle long shot, an oppressive and fatalistic angle that looks down on its helpless victim to make it look like a rat in a maze. (Place and Peterson)[1]

Edward Hopper's etching *Night Shadows* (1921) is just the kind of image identified by Place and Peterson as central to the film noir, anticipating its presence as a key defining motif in the postwar Hollywood crime film some twenty years before the first films noir began to appear.[2] Indeed, one critic has described the etching as looking "like a storyboard for a high-angle shot in a Fritz Lang movie."[3] In 1945 Arthur Fellig (Weegee) published *Naked City*, a book of photographs of New York drawn from his work as a photojournalist for the tabloid press. The book's title was acquired by producer Mark Hellinger and used for his 1947 film noir, *The Naked City* (Jules Dassin, 1948); Hellinger also hired Weegee "as a consultant to the film," and gave him "a small part as a news photographer."[4] As Ellen Handy has suggested, Weegee's collection of images of crime scenes, of dead bodies on the streets of New York, "recalls the look of films noir, which share with Weegee's work an emphasis on crime, drama, and dark urban passions."[5] Weegee, a "night prowler,"[6] obtained his candid photographs of urban disorder—crime scenes, fires, automobile accidents—working through the night, utilizing a police radio, "monitoring emergency calls like a hunter waiting for his prey."[7] In the early years of the 20th century, before Hopper's etching and Weegee's *Naked City* corpus, many of the artists usually referred to as the "Ashcan school" began their careers as newspaper illustrators providing drawings of urban life for the developing tabloid press. Their methods as well as their sensational subject matter prefigure Weegee in particular; as Rebecca Zurier has noted, "(i)n pursuit of stories, news artists·learned to follow fire engines, prowl city streets, and sketch in morgues and courtrooms."[8] The semiotic parallels, the affinities of mood and tone between Hopper and noir images, the prowling observations of the Ashcan artists and Weegee, together with other examples from illustration, painting and photography, have been noted in scattered comments by many writers on film noir and by art and photographic historians. They suggest other contexts to accompany German Expressionism, French Poetic Realism, and hard-boiled fiction, the sources usually identified as the primary influences on the cycle.[9] However, such examples do not merely supplement the familiar influences; they indicate a relationship between the film noir and a range of indigenous American cultural practices in the face of a critical literature which, according to Sumiko Higashi, "remains highly Eurocentric and apart from hard-boiled fiction, pays scarce attention to the American origins of noir, specifically 19th-century realism and its construct, the city as a social matrix."[10]

Higashi's work broadens the base of source material for the film noir but adds to the problem, noted by many critics, of the amorphousness of the term, its anarchic heterogeneity, its elasticity, perhaps best summarized in Paul Kerr's "highly amusing, bric-à-brac list"[11] of supposed influences on the cycle extending from German émigrés, Hemingway, and Orson Welles to fears about bureaucracy and the nuclear bomb. It is an inventory offered in the spirit of critical scepticism.[12] However, the remote contexts of other art forms, other artistic practices both contemporary and historical, may

Opposite, John French Sloan, *Wet Night in the Bowery* (1911). Next page: Edward Hopper: *Night Shadows* (1921).

at least merit a little probing. Is the Hopper example misleadingly suggestive, just a matter of coincidence? Can the iconographic affinities between the various mediums be explained in general terms? Robert Warshow's famous characterization of the Hollywood gangster film as appealing "to that side of us which refuses to believe in the 'normal' possibilities of happiness and achievement,"[13] effectively a counter-cultural strand to the positives of American life, is one possible umbrella under which the film noir, Hopper's images, and Weegee's photographs may be considered. Are there specific currents of American culture such as the one nominated by Warshow to which the different cultural practices of film, art and photography contribute and accordingly share a pool of thematic and iconographic elements?

The method of soldering cultural practices together, through the use of overarching notions of social temper and ideological current, is familiar in the critical literature of film noir which frequently deploys what Richard Maltby has termed "a Zeitgeist theory of film as cultural history."[14]

Film noir, American painting and photography:
a question of influence?

103

Recurrent motifs and themes have been interpreted as metaphorical renditions of the underlying social and psychological conditions of the time. Crudely speaking, the pessimistic contours of the film noir, its doomed characters, its fatal narrative trajectories, are seen as emblems of the bleak postwar mood of America facing postwar readjustment, the Cold War, and the nuclear bomb. However, as Maltby and others have suggested, this approach is too prone to unverifiable generalization and highly selective in its attention to a small part of Hollywood's output during the period. It may well be that *Double Indemnity* (Billy Wilder, 1944) and *The Big Sleep* (Howard Hawks, 1946), pinpointed key elements of the American psyche in the mid-1940s but what elements were being pinpointed by other titles of the time, by Abbot and Costello comedies, by Fred Astaire and Judy Garland musicals? As Mike Chopra-Gant has argued:

> It is not so much the case of the mood of early postwar America having been either entirely gloomy or totally optimistic: in reality it was a complicated and often contradictory mixture of both.[15]

The pessimism of the film noir co-existed with the optimism of *Meet Me in St Louis* (Vincente Minnelli, 1944) and *Easter Parade* (Charles Walters, 1948), articulating a negativity to set against the cheerful view of the world embodied in the musicals and comedies of the time. Film noir was not alone, not an isolated expression of contradiction, as Edward Dimendberg has suggested:

> Cultural historians increasingly have recognized the contradictory character of the 1940s and 1950s, one in which extraordinary American prosperity and supremacy on the international stage coexisted with domestic cultural responses ranging from euphoric celebration to anxiety and fear. From Abstract Expressionism to beat culture to film noir, postwar culture in the United States possessed an often sombre underside that contrasts markedly with the allegedly optimistic public face of the period.[16]

1940s crime films were a major constituent of this "sombre underside." As Paul Schrader has argued, "(n)ever before had films dared to take such a harsh uncompromising look at American life,"[17] while cultural historian, Warren Susman, has suggested that the "most important contribution of a major subgenre of detective and gangster movies in the forties, film noir·served to reduce the optimistic American vision to dust."[18] Other strands of American visual culture, in particular painting and photography, both pre-dating and contemporary with the film noir, can be seen to share the film noir's "counter-cultural" perspectives, which contribute to what Robert Warshow defined as the " 'no' to that great American 'yes' which is stamped so big over our official culture and yet has so little to do with the way we really feel about our lives."[19]

Evidence for the familiar influences on film noir—American and German films, hard-boiled fiction—is marshalled in various ways: the evolving traditions of American genre cinema in which the gangster film of the 1930s transmutes into the film noir of the 1940s, the contribution of directors and cinematographers from the German cinema (Lang, Siodmak) to the noir canon especially in terms of style, and the practice of adapting hard-boiled novels for the screen together with the involvement of writers such as Hammett and Chandler in their production. These factors provide a plausible dossier of support for the notion that the film noir emerges from various traditions in American and European cinema and from a powerful current in popular literature. Less proximate cultural phenomena—art, photography—may be more difficult to present as influences tout-court. Yet, some critics have been quite specific arguing, for example, that painters such as Edward Hopper, Reginald Marsh, and John Sloan made a "seminal contribution·to the visual underpinnings of film noir: its intensely luminous detail, jagged perspectives, vertiginous heights, hallucinatory geometry, and bold compositional methods."[20] The "contribution." one presumes, is as an "influence," a complex notion embodying both conscious and unconscious relationships between artists, and between cultural phenomena. Distinguishing the concept from related terms such as "pastiche" and "imitation," Richard Dyer defines "influence" as "a demonstrable process rather than just semiotic similarities or connections

Tommy Udo (Richard Widmark) confronts Nick Bianco (Victor Mature) at a local eatery in *Kiss of Death* (1947). Opposite: bars and restaurants are frequently depicted in the work of John French Sloan: *McSorley's Back Room* and *Renganeschi's Saturday Night* (1912).

Above, another painting of 1912 McSorley's by Sloan. Clockwise from top right, encounters in bars and clubs from the classic period: glistening surfaces, patrons, even cigarette girls do not distract the interacting characters in *Dark Corner* (1946), *Phantom Lady* (1944), and *Railroaded* (1947).

Film noir, American painting and photography:
a question of influence?

107

between works of art of which the parties involved may or may not have been conscious."[21] The problem here is defining "demonstrable processes"—what could constitute a demonstration of influence? "Semiotic similarities" are a starting point for such a relationship but what else is required for "influence" to be established? Much of the literature which attempts to correlate film noir with painting and photography, with Hopper and Weegee, suggests a broader, more general influence, dependent on similarities in iconographic material, especially related to the city and twentieth century urban life, traceable across film and the visual arts.

American Art I: The Ashcan School

It is the Ashcan painters' focus on depicting urban life, New York in particular, that has prompted noir critics to cite their work as prefiguring the film cycle. For example, Larry Ford although acknowledging the influence of German cinema, suggests that the film noir's "urban images were also derived from American Realist artists such as George Bellows, Reginald Marsh, and Edward Hopper. City scenes were presented as strangely stark and aloof."[22] Foster Hirsch provides a more extensive visual lineage for the ways in which the film noir depicts the American city:

> The image of the city as a place of terror and seduction, as a modern wasteland, an environment indifferent to people, a carnival edging towards disorder, has striking parallels in the work of artists of the twenties, thirties and forties. Anticipations and echoes of the noir city appear in the work of John Sloan, George Bellows, Franz Kline, Reginald Marsh, Edward Hopper, Martin Lewis. American artists who chose city scenes as their subject devised a style that blended American realism with Expressionism.[23]

This is a diverse list of artists: Sloan was a key member of the "Ashcan school" described as "twentieth-century America's first school of modern artists";[24] Bellows belongs to a second generation of Ashcan painters; Hopper is linked to the Ashcan school through his studies with Henri and the urban subject matter of his work; Kline is more closely associated with Abstract Expressionism in the 1950s though his early work did include figurative urban paintings; Marsh and Lewis are usually linked to the American Scene painters of the 1930s. Most of them, however, do have some relationship to the "Ashcan school," and have used the city as an important though not exclusive source of subject matter, and most operate some version of "realism" in their aesthetics.

The term, "Ashcan school," refers to a distinctive strand of American art, the origins of which lay in the work of a small group of artists including Sloan, led and taught by Robert Henri; though originally from Philadelphia, the group eventually settled in New York. Other artists joined the original members and in 1908 the group mounted an exhibition—Eight American Painters—at the Macbeth Gallery in New York which was intended as a protest against the conservative art establishment and as a presentation of the new "realist" approach to painting adopted by the group. Though their work was quite varied and included nudes, portraiture, and landscapes, the "Ashcan" designation alluded to the quotidian sometimes sordid nature of their subjects: tenement life, trains and tramcars, bridges, street scenes, back alleys, night clubs, restaurants, shops, music halls and theaters, amusement parks, movie theatres, and boxing matches. As Erika Doss has noted:

> Critics called them the 'Apostles of Ugliness' and 'the revolutionary black gang,' and later dubbed some of them 'ashcan artists' in reference to their 'pictures of ash cans' (garbage cans) and other gritty details of modern urban life.[25]

The Ashcan painters, who had established themselves in New York by 1904, depicted the city, especially its popular and public dimensions, in all its aspects but in styles which distinguished their work from earlier American genre painting. In particular, the considered nature of academic painting gave way to an approach "better suited to their vision of the offhand encounters and dynamism of a modern city."[26] Paintings characterized by a "hasty, painterly execution" reflected the background of Sloan

Compare Sloan's *Wet Night in the Bowery* on page 100 with *Sixth Avenue Elevated at Third Street* (below) and *Phantom Lady:* left, Carol "Kansas" Richman (Ella Raines) approaches the El Train and, opposite, she discovers that the bartender (Andrew Tombes) has followed her onto the platform

[See also page 110]

Left, Kansas alone on the El platform. Center quasi-Expressionist, quasi Ashcan prop painting by John Bender for Scarlet Street (1945). Bottom, elevated platform above the train tracks in *Mystery Street* (1950).

and others whose work as newspaper illustrators influenced their work as painters. As Rebecca Zurier has written, "Sloan and the other Ashcan artists sought to convey a sense of movement and spontaneity through the abbreviated, sketchlike handling associated with news illustration."[27] Their work aimed at capturing the developing modern city in all its diversity—new crowded ways of living, new buildings, new forms of transit, new forms of entertainment, the new fast developing consumer culture.

The busy and crowded street and tenement life of the city is reflected in a number of works such as Henri's *Street Scene with Snow* (1902), Sloan's *Wet Night on the Bowery* (1911), Shinn's *Tenements at Hester Street* (1900), Luks' *Hester Street* (1905) and *On the Steps* (1910), and George Bellows' *New York* (1911) and *Cliff Dwellers* (1913). In addition, Sloan's work included a number of studies depicting intimate moments of life including *Turning Out the Light* (1905), *Roofs Summer Night* (1905), *Three A. M.* (1909), and the somewhat voyeuristic *Night Windows* (1910). The technological environment of modern city life—skyscrapers, stations, trains, buses, bridges—is depicted in Shinn's *Sixth Avenue Elevated after Midnight* (1899), Sloan's *Six O' Clock, Winter* (1912) and *Sixth Avenue and Thirtieth Street, New York City* (1907), Glackens' *The Green Car* (1910), and Ernest Lawson's *Queensborough Bridge* (1909) and *Old Grand Central* (1910). The perils of city life are also reflected in Shinn's *Fire on Twenty-fourth Street, New York City* (1907), and *Night Life—Accident* (1908). The developing world of consumer culture and institutionalized leisure is depicted in various ways. *Window Shopping* (1903), *Sixth Avenue Shoppers* (n.d.), Glackens' *The*

Shoppers (1907-8), *Skating in New York* (1910) and *Crowd at the Seashore* (c.1910), Sloan's *Sunday South Beach Bathers* (1907) and *Afternoon in Union Square* (1912). Cinemas and vaudeville theatres feature in Sloan's *Movies, Five Cents* (1907), Shinn's *The Orchestra Pit, Old Procter's Fifth Avenue Theater* (1906-7) and *Revue* (1908), and bars and restaurants in Sloan's *Chinese Restaurant* (1909) and *McSorley's Bar* (1912). Sports especially boxing appear in a number of works including Bellows' *Club Night* (1907), Both *Members of the Club* (1909) and *A Stag at Sharkey's* (1917), and Glackens' *The Boxing Match* (1906); other sports featured in Bellows' paintings such as *Polo at Lakewood* (1910), *Golf Course—California* (1917), and *Tennis at Newport* (1920), and in Glackens' *Skaters, Central Park* (1912). As Robert Snyder has argued:

> These artists sought themes that mirrored their time and place: the creation of an urban ethnic culture in immigrant neighborhoods where a dozen languages were spoken, the glaring contrasts between the wealth of upper Fifth Avenue and the poverty of Cherry Street on the Lower East Side, the glitter of show business, the bustle of city streets, the construction of new public spaces, the encroachment of commerce into everyday life, and the ferment over the proper roles of men and women.[28]

The Ashcan artists' work adds up to a kaleidoscopic picture of New York during the first decades of the twentieth century, a period of rapid urbanization, of mass immigration from Europe, of the industrialization of the cityscape, of skyscrapers, the elevated railway, motor cars and trams; a period of rapid transformation captured in the illustration work and paintings of Henri, Sloan, Glackens and others.

American Art II: Reginald Marsh and Edward Hopper

Much of the meaning and significance in the urban imagery of Henri, Sloan and Bellows is continued in the work of two contrasting artists, Reginald Marsh and Edward Hopper, both of whom had studied with the members of the Ashcan group. While the Ashcan artists can be seen as a general backdrop within which an iconography, a realism, emerges in American visual art, Marsh and Hopper have been specifically cited by critics as producing bodies of work which can be related more directly to the film noir. Their work can be seen as a development from the Ashcan ethos, one which took the image of the city into a darker register though in markedly different ways. Marsh's work has been neatly characterized by Kathleen Spies:

> Deemed "America's Hogarth" by contemporary critics, Marsh is best known for his depictions of Coney Island amusement parks, crowded New York Streets, and gaudy, run-down burlesque houses. He focused on what he viewed as uniquely American and modern about the city: spectacle, crowds, consumer culture, and popular, democratic forms of entertainment in loud, boisterous places with relaxed attitudes toward moral propriety.[29]

This focus has been picked up by film critics with Marsh's paintings of the Bowery and Coney Island producing a garish version of New York simmering with tension. Foster Hirsch writes:

> Ablaze with a nervous energy, a quicksilver intensity, Marsh's city, like the noir city, is a place of sexual promise and release. It glitters with temptation. In Marsh, as in noir, the visually striking city is a potent, galvanizing force, as beautiful as it is corrupt, as majestic as it is also putrid.[30]

And, more specifically, Edward Dimendberg draws attention to the credits of an early film noir, *Street of Chance* (Jack Hively, 1942), "in which drawings of street signs, an apartment building, and a corner luncheonette evoke the New York etchings of Reginald Marsh."[31] Like many of the Ashcan painters, Marsh began his career as an illustrator in the 1920s but he is usually linked to the Social Realist artists of the 1930s whose work, in Erika Doss's words, "captured urban America at its rawest, eschewing aesthetic idealism and New Deal cultural uplift for art that documented Americans living in severe economic and social duress."[32] Marsh's subjects were those of the Ashcan School – the streets of New

York in the prints *The Bowery* (1928*)*, *East Tenth Street Jungle* (1934) and *Union Square* (1934), movie and burlesque theaters in paintings such as *Twenty Cent Movie* (1936) and *They Pay to See* (1934), the elevated railway in *Why Not Use the El?* (1930), and beach scenes as in *Coney Island* (1936). His treatment though differed and his depiction of New York life, especially in the beach and funfair paintings, stressed a physicality, present in a muted version in Sloan's etchings, but blown into something much more extreme in Marsh. Peter Conrad has suggested that "Marsh changes from a realist to a mythologist, for whom New York is a romping bacchanal, a feast of blowsy, corpulent, promiscuous gods."[33] Foster Hirsch amplifies and develops this as follows:

> Marsh's characteristic treatment of the city, in his numerous Coney Island and Bowery scenes, is as a place of terrific energy. In his packed street scenes, muscular, sensual characters jostle each other in the spirit of Mardi Gras. But beneath the holiday pleasure, there is always the suggestion that the bursting scene is about to erupt into violence— the swelling crowds of pleasure-seekers are a potentially destructive force.[34]

The subversive undercurrents of Marsh's city are replicated in the film noir and, as Hirsch suggests, the "city as a cradle of crime and a cauldron of negative energy is the inevitable setting for film noir."[35] Warshow's "dangerous and sad city of the imagination"[36] is to be found in places other than in the gangster films that he was writing about.

Edward Hopper studied with the Ashcan painter Robert Henri who directed his students to the importance of everyday life as significant subject matter, one of the familiar tenets of realist art; his students, however, developed this realism in different directions:

> Henri believed that beauty could be found in ordinary life, even in daily news, if seen by an extraordinary artist. This attitude differed slightly from that of a later generation of Henri's students whose work achieved disturbing expressionistic power through its exploration of dark emotions. In images by Bellows, Davis and Edward Hopper, attraction and repulsion exist in uneasy balance.[37]

In contrast to Marsh's work and despite their common Ashcan heritage, Hopper's work is more muted and bleak than the garish, energetic images of his contemporary. Barbara Rose suggests that Marsh's paintings "represent responses to the bewildering vulgarity of the carnival of American life and the orgiastic fantasy of the American dream" while "Hopper's lonely filling stations reflect its barrenness and lack of fulfilment."[38] Marsh captures an important and exuberant dimension of the American sensibility; Hopper, probably the most cited of all American painters in relation to the film noir, provides a pessimistic more downbeat alternative. Deborah Lyons has characterized his work as follows:

> Hopper's characters exist in a strangely quasi-narrative stasis. They conduct silent commerce, are bewildered travelers, or are embroiled in dysfunctional relationships in which an oddly cold sexual tension simmers under the surface.[39]

It is a comment which, for example, could also be used to describe *Double Indemnity, Out of the Past* (Jacques Tourneur, 1947), and *The Postman Always Rings Twice* (Tay Garnett, 1946), films replete with "barrenness and lack of fulfilment," films which share the tense alienation and the lonely ethos of the Hopper oeuvre. Alain de Botton has suggested that Hopper's characteristic choice of subject matter includes "threshold spaces, buildings that lie outside homes and offices, places of transit where we are aware of a particular kind of alienated poetry,"[40] and, like Lyons' comment, the description could also apply to the noir cycle with its frequent use of "threshold spaces." For Vivian Sobchack, such places as "the cocktail lounge, the nightclub, the bar, the hotel room, the boardinghouse, the diner, the dance hall, the roadside café, the bus and train station, and the wayside motel"[41] are central to the film noir. As she suggests:

> These are the recurrent and determinate premises of film noir and they emerge from common places in wartime and post-war American culture that, transported to the screen, gain hyperbolized presence and overdetermined meaning.[42]

The "hyperbolized presence and overdetermined meaning" of such venues, generates for the viewer, in the words of Borde and Chaumeton, the founding chroniclers of the cycle, "a shared feeling of anguish or insecurity, which is the identifying sign of film noir at this time."[43] For many writers it is this thematic feature—anguish, alienation, a bleak world-view—which defines the cycle:

> It is the underlying mood of pessimism which undercuts any attempted happy endings and prevents the films from being the typical Hollywood escapist fare many were originally intended to be. More than lighting or photography, it is this sensibility which makes the black film black for us.[44]

The film noir's "mood of pessimism." Hopper's "doomed yearning of lonely figures in cold offices and desolate hotel rooms"[45] are of a piece, at least at a general level.

In more concrete terms, Hopper's relationship to the film noir has been explored in relation to mise-en-scène and style, to specific urban motifs, and to specific films. Abraham Polonsky, the director of *Force of Evil* (1947), cites Hopper as a consciously sought "influence." Polonsky's instructions to George Barnes, the cinematographer on the film, were quite specific in terms of seeking a "Hopper effect" for the visual aesthetics of the film:

Film noir, American painting and photography: a question of influence?

115

I tried to tell George what I was looking for, but I couldn't quite describe that to a cameraman, because I didn't know what to say. I went out and got a book of reproductions of Hopper's paintings–Third Avenue, cafeterias, all that back-lighting, and those empty streets. Even when people are there, you don't see them; somehow the environments dominate the people.[46]

Force of Evil opens with an extreme high angle shot looking down on Wall Street (at right), an image reminiscent of Hopper paintings such as *American Village* (1912, see below) and *The City* (1927), though unlike the paintings there are numerous human figures in the film image. Later in the film the shots of Joe Morse (John Garfield) walking down a deserted Wall Street are taken first from a high angle then from an extreme low angle; both perspectives reinforce the notion that "environments dominate people." The finale when Joe finds his brother's body on the bank of the East River was shot at New York's George Washington Bridge (see bottom right); it exploits the striking structure placing the human figure in an overpowering and monumental environment. To take another film example, Foster Hirsch comments that the mise-en-scène of *Scarlet Street* (Fritz Lang, 1945) evokes Hopper's paintings:

> In *Scarlet Street*, there is no sense of life outside the frame; all exterior scenes are stripped of any sense of city density and rhythm. The film's unpeopled streets, the elongated shadows, the angular buildings that guard empty space like grim sentinels, recall the eerie nighttime cityscapes in the paintings of Edward Hopper.[47]

Hirsch refers specifically to the "strange and rigorously choreographed" opening street scene with its difference "in rhythm from the location shots in Neo-Realist films, where the movement of a real city is presented in all its randomness."[48] It is this quality of "orchestration" in the urban images which "recalls" Hopper though many critics would probably suggest that the rigour and angularity of the mise-en-scène is also a feature of Lang's style. In a similar vein, Peter Conrad suggests that Hopper's cityscapes have an abstract quality:

Force of Evil: pan down:"This is Wall Street." Bottom, the ending

"Hopper looks at the city and sees only a pattern of planes and startling angles."[49] While many of his paintings incorporate the human figure, the most chilling and abstract of his city images do not. *Approaching a City* (1946), one of his bleakest paintings and one without any human figures, exemplifies Hopper's abstract style and has been described as embodying the tone of the noir cycle:

> It suggests how impersonal edifices, a familiar New York locale, and the train (invisible apart from its spatial traces) congeal in the representation of an uncertain postwar moment that centers upon a void. The emptiness of the tunnel elicits the fear and promise of entering the urban realm pervasive in the film noir cycle.[50]

The painting most often cited as an instance of "Hopper noir" with a close kinship to the film cycle is *Nighthawks* (1942), a work described by Gail Levin as "essentially dramatic, capturing the sinister aspect of a disquieting urban night."[51] Art historian Erika Doss suggests that the painting, which depicts an American diner at night, "mirrors Hopper's cognizance of 1930's film themes and subject matter, especially the gangster theme, and it parallels or anticipates the stylistic development of film noir in the early 1940's."[52] The argument is based partly on the iconographic elements of the work especially the diner itself, but also on the sombre mood evoked by the lighting effect. A further link to the cycle is suggested by Gail Levin who draws attention to Hopper's admiration for Ernest Hemingway's short story "The Killers" which begins in a diner. "There is something in the setting and mood of this story that evokes *Nighthawks*," she argues; the story, of course, was the basis for one of the best noirs of the 1940s, *The Killers* (Robert Siodmak, 1946).[53]

Inside *Nighthawks*: the title figures and counterman at Henry's Diner in *The Killers*.

Hopper spent a short period early in his career making posters for silent films and was a frequent cinemagoer throughout his life. Whatever influence his work had on film-makers or on the film noir was reciprocated by the influence of the cinema on his own work. At an obvious level, the cinema building provided subject matter for his work although it is also worth noting that this was a popular source of material for many of Hopper's contemporaries including Sloan and Marsh. Hopper depicts figures in cinema auditoriums as in the etching *The Balcony* (1928), in paintings such as *The Sheridan Theatre* (1928), and in the better known *New York Movie* (1939) which focuses upon a pensive usherette.

However, in terms of Hopper and film noir, it is the aesthetic and formal relationships between his work and the film medium that are important. Gail Levin has suggested that his paintings were "often influenced by cinematic devices such as cropping and unusual angles of vision"[54] while Erika Doss argues that Hopper's frequent movie-going meant that he "was well aware of the cinematic devices of framing and editing."[55] In terms of specific works, Levin suggests of a 1949 painting, that "(t)he setting of *Conference at Night*, with its strong theatrical light, was probably inspired by the movies, particularly the urban melodramas now known as film noir."[56] An earlier work, *Night Windows* (1928), which depicts "a woman in her slip, glimpsed from behind, in an illuminated interior observed through windows from the dark," suggests another dimension of Hopper's work—voyeurism—which invites comparison between his work and cinema. As Levin observes:

> The subject is unaware of being watched, making the viewer into a voyeur, as so often in Hopper's own development of similar themes in his series of transitional etchings. The curtain blowing at the open window seems cinematic, as does the intimacy of the view. In fact, Hopper's voyeurism would find an outlet in his lifelong affair with the cinema.[57]

It is a voyeurism that can be traced back to the Ashcan painter, John Sloan, and his 1910 etching with the same title. In the context of cinema, the director most closely associated with the theme is, of course, Alfred Hitchcock. Hitchcock's films, though not central to the film noir, are sometimes cited as adjacent to the cycle. It has been suggested by Sheri Biesen that Hitchcock's 1930s thrillers "were notable preludes to film noir" and that films such as "*Shadow of a Doubt, Spellbound,* and *Notorious* venture closely to the noir series."[58] *Night Windows*—both the Sloan (next page) and Hopper ver-

Below, women's portraits with blank stares: left to right, *Bohemienne* by Charles Sprague Pearce (1909); *Katherine "Kitty" Marsh Self-Portrait* by John Bender (1945); and *Madeline Davis* by George Bellows (1914).

sions—do seem like "preludes" to Hitchcock's *Rear Window* (1954, see bottom of page) which was based on a story by Cornell Woolrich, "the writer whose sensibility is most deeply noir."[59] Hitchcock also "credited the idea for the house in his film *Psycho* to looking at *House by the Railroad*," a Hopper painting from 1925.[60] Hopper's links with the cinema spread in a number of directions and, in particular, suggest a "noir" artistic sensibility. As Gail Levin has suggested, the film noir "with its potent dramatic scenes and generally pessimistic outlook on life, appealed to Hopper."[61]

Film noir, American painting and photography:
a question of influence?

119

Photography

New York was the focus for the Ashcan painters, and for Marsh and Hopper and though the city was the setting for many films noir, some of the most famous titles were set in other locales such as Los

Angeles (*Double Indemnity, Criss Cross* [Siodmak, 1949]) and San Francisco (*The Maltese Falcon* [John Huston, 1941]). Yet another city, Washington, D. C., was the setting for a series of wartime photographs by Esther Bubley for the Office of War Information related to the film noir and specifically to the images of women the cycle presents. During 1943, Bubley photographed "single working women living in rooming houses or picking up men at bars, (and) a series of women working at their government and industry jobs."[62] As

Below, arcade booth in *The Dark Corner* where the ticket girl strikes a Weegee-esque pose. Far left, an image by Weegee; near left, Ruth Roman is a slightly more glamourous Hollywood taxi dancer in *Tomorrow is Another Day* (where dance tickets are only ten cents).

Left, "Western Union Gummer Kathleen McCarthy" by Esther Bubley (1943).

Above, Lucille Ball as Secretary Katheleen Stewart in *The Dark Corner*.

with Hopper there is a convergent iconography, an affinity between the rooming houses, diners, and bars in the photographs and their equivalents in films such as *The Killers* and *Phantom Lady* (Robert Siodmak, 1944). However, Paula Rabinowitz has argued that the main feature of Bubley's work which links it to the film noir is related to a key icon of the cycle—the femme fatale:

> Bubley's work among these young women in Washington D. C., incarnated the iconography so central to the film noir's sense of dislocation: the lonely aggressive female who can adroitly use a series of mundane objects—telephones, cigarette lighters, radios—with deadly results and who inhabits and works in a world full of others like her.[63]

These government sponsored documentary photographs of ordinary women provided templates for the femme fatale characters played in the film noir by Barbara Stanwyk, Jane Greer, Ava Gardner, Joan Bennett and a host of lesser stars.

However, it is Weegee's New York photographs that are most frequently discussed in relation to the cycle. New York has been well documented by photographers from the late nineteenth century socially committed work of Jacob Riis, the fine art photography of Alfred Stieglitz, and Walker Evans' photographs of apartment blocks, to the near-abstract images of skyscrapers in the work of Georgia O'Keefe. It is Weegee's particular rendition of the city though which most resonates with the cycle. Gordon Theisen, linking Weegee with Hopper, has drawn attention to the similarity "between the feel of film noir and that of two nonfilm artists who excelled at atmosphere, one being the 1940s crime scene photographer, Arthur 'Weegee' Fellig, the other being Hopper."[64] In a more detailed observation of the stylistic qualities of the photographer's work, Ellen Handy suggests:

> Weegee's work is defined by searing chiaroscuro. His preference for working at night, the glaring light of the city streets, and the particularly inky darkness of New York nights all contribute to the intense tonal contrast in his work.[65]

The links to film noir—"searing chiaroscuro, inky darkness, tonal contrast"—reside in the expressive strategies of the photographer as well as in the focus on urban life. Indeed, Alan Bergala implicitly suggests a stylistic affinity between Weegee's photographs and the films of key noir directors such as Siodmak and Lang:

> There is a disturbing intersection between the very frequent expressionistic chiaroscuro and filmic settings of his images and the Central European-derived aesthetic which he shares with the émigrés of cinema who in large part fashioned the aesthetic of the forties films noirs.[66]

As noted previously, Weegee did have some concrete links with the cinema. Apart from his involvement with *The Naked City*, he played bit-part roles in *The Set-Up* (Robert Wise, 1949) and *M* (Joseph Losey, 1951), and also had played the violin as accompaniment to silent pictures.[67] However, the connections are not substantial though it has been suggested that his influence on *The Naked City* can be extended to its imagery. In Edward Dimendberg's words, "at least a few of its shots – those of children opening up fire hydrants and a cleaning woman in a deserted bank – might well have been inspired by his photographs."[68] The images of children in particular do recall Weegee's photographs, *Summer*, the *Lower East Side* (c. 1937) and *Police End Kids' Street Shower—Under Orders* (1944), both of which were included in the *Naked City* book.[69] The collection is a kaleidoscopic picture of New York, its districts such as the Bowery and Harlem, Coney Island, a series of blazing buildings entitled "Fires." and audiences in various cultural and sporting venues including a Frank Sinatra concert and the Metropolitan Opera House. Its most notorious images, however, are in the chapters devoted to death—"Murders" and "Sudden Death"—which, together with a chapter on arrested people on their way to police stations ("Pie Wagon"), push Weegee's image of the city towards the film noir. As Linda Brookover suggests:

> A case of parallel art movements, Weegee's photography and film noir were the expressions of an era when the American dream began to crumble and crime stories in the news helped initiate a cycle of film violence that has yet to end.[70]

The subject of murder and death was a particular preoccupation for Weegee and his first solo exhibition in 1941, organized by the influential cooperative the Photo League, was entitled "Weegee: Murder is my Business." The murder photographs, both those in *Naked City* and others, are varied. Some such as *Murder in Hell's Kitchen* (c.1940), *Shot and Killed on East Side Street* (1942), and *This was a friendly game of Bocci* (c.1939), feature the classic blood-stained corpse lying on the ground— familiar from the gangster film of the 1930s as well as the noir pictures of the 1940s. But, as Orvell has pointed out, Weegee's treatment of the subject "encompasses not only the act of murder itself— with the victim shown, usually lying face down on the sidewalk in a pool of blood—but the spectator's perspective as well."[71] Especially striking is *Their First Murder* (1941) which captures the immediate responses of mainly young people to a killing in Brooklyn. In Orvell's words, the photograph "shows us a grieving woman in the center of a moving crowd, jostling for a better look at the corpse; their faces, many of them children, reveal, by turns, triumphant glee, fierce anger, and demonic ferocity."[72]

Another, *Balcony Seats at a Murder* (1939), is a full shot of a tenement building with the residents leaning out of their windows looking at a corpse in the doorway below. The collection also includes a photograph, *Weegee at a Murder* (1942), in which the photographer appears Hitchcock-like in "his own work." Weegee's perspectives on New York were distinctively nocturnal and voyeuristic, preying upon the seamy underside of an affluent urban center:

> The city as pictured by Weegee was a place of disorder and upheaval—violence, accidents, fires, gang wars, social deviance, privation and isolation, conditions that were not the result of temporary economic problems or that were remediable by acts of benevolence; rather, disorder seemed to spring from the natural and human world, is was part of the human condition, which for Weegee seems to oscillate between lonely isolation and the fleeting comforts of a quick embrace.[73]

Again, as with Hopper, general characterizations of their work could also be comments on the film noir; the lives of many noir characters are marked by "lonely isolation and the fleeting comforts of a quick embrace."

Conclusion

A number of the cited comments on the links between the film noir and the visual arts are based upon similarities, upon resemblances, often left as simple observations as in Brookover's "case of parallel art movements," Handy's suggestion that Weegee's work "recalls the look of films noir," Hirsch's "echoes of the noir city in the work of John Sloan...Reginald Marsh, Edward Hopper." and Erika Doss's comment on Hopper that "many of his paintings demonstrate an extraordinary kinship both formally and in terms of subject matter, with the popular films he watched." Some writers move towards a causal relationship, a sense of "influence," as in Ford's "urban images were also derived from American Realist artists," and Bergala on Weegee referring to *The Naked City* with its "street shots that are directly inspired by photographs of his." Although most of these references are parenthetical and assertive, and not developed in significant detail, they do move the discussion of the film noir into a specifically American cultural context. Traditional accounts, of course, usually make reference to Hollywood genres of the 1930s and to American hardboiled crime literature. However, writers such as

Vernet and Higashi broaden the lineage somewhat to include further material for a substantial indigenous cultural and artistic line of descent. As Higashi has suggested, the "Ashcan painters and DeMille's early features are indeed intertextually related works that are expressions of American pictorial realism and a source of noir stylistics."[74] It is an ancestry which predates the more familiar European antecedents of the film noir providing a tradition of urban representation in the Ashcan painters' attention to the commonplace and public details of urban living—"realism" in a classic sense of the term—together with a visual and stylistic repertoire drawn from Cecil B. DeMille's melodramas from the 1910s made a few years before the more frequently cited German Expressionist films of the 1920s.[75]

Supplemented by the work of artists such as Sloan, Marsh and Hopper, and photographers such as Bubley and Weegee, the thread of a richer indigenous background for the film noir is adumbrated if not defined in detail, forming a counterbalance to the Eurocentric analyses criticized by Higashi. An

Left top, *Traveling Carnival, Sante Fe* by John French Sloan (1924), Left, *Ride the Pink Horse*: Gagin (Robert Montgomery, star and director) approaches the Tio Vivo carousel from Taos, New Mexico.

Film noir, American painting and photography:
a question of influence?

123

additional dimension is provided by cultural commentators and historians identifying a somewhat bleak sensibility which underlies certain aspects of American culture. The focus of much of the art discussed and, indeed, the film noir itself, is on the seamy underside of urban life, on Warshow's "dangerous and sad city of the imagination which is the modern world"[76] and runs counter to the generally optimistic cast of the Hollywood film. The search for "influence" from the visual arts may have some local authority with film directors such as Polonsky and Hitchcock citing Hopper in relation to aspects of their work; a more credible set of relationships, however, lies in the pessimistic cultural strand and its somewhat negative depiction of urban life. This, together with the voyeuristic elements to be found in the work of John Sloan, Edward Hopper and Weegee, and reflected especially in the work of Hitchcock, indicates the shared world of fear and anxiety, paranoia and prurience, threaded through painting, photography, literature, and cinema, and given a very distinctive focus in the film noir.

Notes

1. Janey Place and Lowell Peterson, "Some visual motifs of Film Noir," in Alain Silver and James Ursini (eds), *Film Noir Reader* (New York: Limelight Editions, 1996), p. 68.

2. All of the images (paintings, photographs) mentioned can be found on various websites including Mark Harden's Artchive (www.artchive.com/) and Artcyclopedia (www.artcyclopedia.com/).

3. Philip French, "From Nighthawks to the shadows of film noir," *Observer*, 25.4.04, Review Section, p. 7.

4. Miles Barth, "Weegee's World," in Barth (ed.), *Weegee's World* (Boston: Little, Brown and Company, 1977) p. 30.

5. Ellen Handy, "Picturing New York, the naked city: Weegee and urban photography," in Barth (ed.), *Weegee's World*, p. 157.

6. Miles Orvell, *After the Machine: Visual Arts and the Erasing of Cultural Boundaries* (Jackson: University of Mississippi Press, 1995), p. 71.

7. Ibid. p. 72.

8. Rebecca Zurier, *Picturing the City: Urban Vision and the Ashcan School,* (California: University of California Press, 2006), p. 24.

9. The term "cycle" is used for ease of reference and is not intended as a contribution to the vexed debate about the correct terminology to use in categorizing the film noir.

10. Sumiko Higashi, "The American origins of film noir. Realism in urban art and *The Naked City*." in Jon Lewis and Eric Smoodin (eds), *Looking Past the Screen. Case Studies in American Film History and Method* (Durham & London: Duke University Press, 2007), p. 354.

11. Marc Vernet, "Film Noir on the edge of doom." in Joan Copjec (ed.) *Shades of Noir* (London: Verso, 1993), p. 2).

12. Paul Kerr, "Out of what past? Notes on the film noir." in Kerr (ed.) *The Hollywood Film Industry* (London: Routledge & Kegan Paul/British Film Institute, 1986), pp. 221-23.

13. Robert Warshow, *The Immediate Experience* (New York: Atheneum, 1970), p. 136.

14. Richard Maltby, "The politics of the maladjusted text." in Ian Cameron (ed.), *The Movie Book of Film Noir* (London: Studio Vista, 1992), p. 41.

15. Mike Chopra-Gant, *Hollywood Genres and Postwar America* (London: I. B. Tauris, 2006), p. 4.

16. Edward Dimendberg, *Film Noir and the Spaces of Modernity* (Cambridge, Mass.: Harvard University Press, 2004), p. 8.

17. Paul Schrader, "Notes on film noir." in Silver and Ursini (eds), *Film Noir Reader*, p. 53.

18. Warren Susman, "Did success spoil the United States? Dual representations in postwar America." in Lary May (ed.), *Recasting America* (Chicago: University of Chicago Press, 1989), p. 29.

19. Warshow, *The Immediate Experience*, p. 136.

20 Nicholas Christopher, *Somewhere in the Night. Film Noir and the American City* (Emeryville, CA: Shoemaker Hoard, 2006), p. 15.

21. Richard Dyer, *Pastiche* (London: Routledge, 2007). p. 49 fn. 21.
22. Larry Ford, "Sunshine and shadow: lighting and color in the depiction of cities on film." in Stuart C. Aitken and Leo E. Zonn (eds), Place, *Power, Situation, and Spectacle: a Geography of Film* (Maryland: Rowman & Littlefield, 1994), p. 123.
23. Foster Hirsch, *The Dark Side of the Screen: Film Noir.* (New York: Da Capo Press, 1981), pp. 82-3.
24. Erika Doss, *Twentieth-Century American Art* (Oxford: Oxford University Press, 2002), p. 33.
25. Doss, *Twentieth-Century American Art* p. 35.
26. Zurier, *Picturing the City*, p. 26.
27. Ibid.
28. Robert W. Snyder, "City in transition." in Zurier et al (eds), *Metropolitan Live: The Ashcan Artists and their New York* (New York: National Museum of American Art in association with W. W. Norton & Company), p. 29.
29. Kathleen Spies, " 'Girls and gags': sexual display and humor in Reginald Marsh's burlesque images." *American Art*, 18: 2 (2004), p. 34.
30. Hirsch, *The Dark Side of the Screen*, p. 83.
31. Dimendberg, *Film Noir and the Spaces of Modernity*, p. 122.
32. Doss, *Twentieth-Century American Art*, p. 102.
33. Peter Conrad, *The Art of the City. Views and Versions of New York* (New York: Oxford University Press, 1984), p. 98.
34. Hirsch, *The Dark Side of the Screen*, p. 83.
35. Ibid.
36. Warshow, *The Immediate Experience*, p. 131.
37. Rebecca Zurier, "The making of six New York artists." in Zurier et al (eds), *Metropolitan Lives*, pp. 63-4.
38. Barbara Rose, *American Art Since 1900*. A Critical History (London: Thames and Hudson, 1967), p. 214.
39. Deborah Lyons and Adam D. Weinberg, *Edward Hopper and the American Imagination* (New York: Whitney Museum of American Art in association with W. W. Norton & Company, 1995), p. XII.
40. Alain de Botton, "The Pleasures of Sadness," *Tate Etc.* Issue 1/Summer 2004. (www.tate.org.uk/tateetc/issue1/article1.htm).
41. Vivian Sobchack, "Lounge time. Postwar crises and the chronotope of film noir." in Nick Browne (ed.), *Refiguring American Film Genres: History and Theory* (Berkeley, Los Angeles: University of California Press, 1998), p. 130.
42. Ibid.
43. Raymond Borde and Etienne Chaumeton, *A Panorama of American Film Noir 1941-1953* (San Francisco: City Lights Books, 2002), p. 13.
44. Robert G. Porfirio, "No way out: existential motifs in the film noir." in Silver and Ursini (eds), *Film Noir Reader*, p. 80.
45. Rose, American Art Since 1900, p. 124.
46. Eric Sherman and Martin Rubin (eds), *The Director's Event; interviews with five American film-makers* (New York: Atheneum, 1970), p. 20.

Right, *Girl on Stage,* Everett Shinn (1906).

Film noir, American painting and photography:
a question of influence?

125

47. Hirsch, *The Dark Side of the Screen*, p. 78.

48. Ibid.

49. Conrad, *The Art of the City*, p. 102.

50. Dimendberg, *Film Noir and the Spaces of Modernity*, p. 17.

51. Gail Levin, "Edward Hopper's 'Nighthawks' ." *Arts Magazine*, May 1981, p. 160.

52. Erika Doss, "Edward Hopper, Nighthawks and film noir." *Postscript: Essays in Film and the Humanities*, 2:2, Winter, 1983, p. 21.

53. Levin, "Edward Hopper's 'Nighthawks' ." p. 156.

54. Ibid.

55. Doss, "Edward Hopper, Nighthawks and film noir." p. 16.

56. Gail Levin, *Edward Hopper. An Intimate Biography* (Berkeley, Los Angeles: University of California Press, 1998), p. 408.

57. Ibid., p. 218.

58. Sheri Chinen Biesen, *Blackout. World War II and the Origins of Film Noir* (Baltimore: The Johns Hopkins University Press, 2005), p. 36.

59. Hirsch, *The Dark Side of the Screen*, p. 43.

60. Levin, *Edward Hopper*, p. 536.

61. Ibid., p. 408.

62. Paula Rabinowitz, *Black & White & Noir: America's Pulp Modernism* (New York: Columbia University Press, 2002), p. 38.

63. Ibid., p. 39.

64. Gordon Theisen, *Staying Up Much Too Late: Edward Hopper's Nighthawks and the Dark Side of the American Psyche* (New York: Thomas Dunne Books, St Martin's Press, 2006), p. 190.

65. Ellen Handy, "Picturing New York, the naked city: Weegee and urban photography." in Barth (ed.), *Weegee's World*, p. 149.

66. Alan Bergala, "Weegee and film noir." in Barth (ed.), *Weegee's World,* p. 77.

67. Orvell, *After the Machine,* p. 88.

68. Dimendberg, *Film Noir and the Spaces of Modernity*, p. 56.

69. Weegee, *Naked City* (New York: Da Capo Press, 2002, reprint of the original 1945 edition), pp. 110-11.

70. Linda Brookover, "Blanc et Noir: Crime as Art." in Alain Silver & James Ursini eds *Film Noir Reader 2* (New York: Limelight Editions, 1999), p. 215.

71. Orvell, *After the Machine*, p. 85.

72. Ibid., p. 86.

73. Ibid., p. 78.

74. Higashi, "The American origins of film noir." p. 354.

75. Vernet, "Film Noir on the edge of doom." pp. 9-10.

76. Warshow, *The Immediate Experience*, p. 131.

Opposite page center right, Robert Henri (left), Everett Shinn (center) and John French Sloan, part of "The Eight" in Paris in 1896.

Right, Arthur (Ascher) Fellig aka "Weegee the Famous."

This Day and Age: Louis Garrett (Charles Bickford) guns down dry-cleaner Herman (Harry Green) with the remark: "From now on we'll do the cleaning and you'll do the dying."

Proto-noir—DeMille Style

Alain Silver and James Ursini

With those two oft-blamed events of 1929—the coming of sound to movies and the Wall Street crash—the playful and sometimes naïve decadence of the previous decade's motion pictures met a sudden and unexpected death. But in keeping with the mythical nature of Hollywood, a new phenomenon was born out of the ashes of blue chip certificates and cellulose nitrate, a phenomenon that can best be described as dark, in both theme and visual style, populist films (*The Public Enemy*, *I Am a Fugitive from a Chain Gang*, *Wild Boys of the Road*, *Gabriel over the White House*, etc.) which foreshadowed the socially conscious and progressive strains in many of the films of the noir classic period.

Even legendary producer-director Cecil B. DeMille, the master of 1920s Jazz-age decadent and visual extravagance (*Male and Female* [1919], *Manslaughter* [1922], *The Ten Commandments* [1923], *The Godless Girl* [1929], etc.), saw the writing on the walls of his "temple" at Paramount studios. So he began to shift, at least temporarily, to narratives that considered the problems of filmgoers ravaged by the Great Depression but also desperate for a little distraction, DeMille's forté. DeMille grafted his decadence onto selected films from 1929 to 1933, films that act as proto-noirs with their emphasis on violence, sexuality cocooned inside a quasi-populist world view.

In these films made before 1934—the year when the Production Code Office, under pressure from the Catholic Legion of Decency, decided to strictly enforce their puritanical morality rules and thereby bring about a freeze on artistic freedom—DeMille revealed, in spades, the dual side of his

Below, *Madam Satan*: Trixie (Lillian Roth, left), Jimmy Wade (Roland Young), and Angela Brooks (Kay Johnson) in a pose—a man and woman in bed—specifically forbidden by the production code.

artistic personality. On the one hand, he was a moralist who led his blissfully "perverse" characters into hellish catastrophes and ambiguous futures. At the same time, the attention to detail in visual style and the lush attractiveness he lent to the portrayals of these "perverse" and socially unsanctioned acts made clear where his interest lay. He was, in other words, a traditional moralist with a taste for vice. As the raucous, liberated 1920s faded into the desperate 1930s, DeMille followed suit, tailoring his films to the times, often metaphorically, most particularly in four movies: *Dynamite* (1929), *Madam Satan* (1930), *The Sign of the Cross* (1932), and *This Day and Age* (1933).

Femme fatales, a powerful archetype in film noir, were a particular favorite of DeMille. In both *Dynamite* and *Madam Satan* (both co-written by one of DeMille's most influential collaborators, Jeanie Macpherson) men are something to be bargained for and occasionally to be fought over. Kay Johnson, portraying the wife Angela in the wacky *Madam Satan*, answers Lillian Roth's (portraying the femme fatale Trixie, who has seduced Angela's husband) taunts about being an "ice cube" by claiming that when she gets going (and she is about to) an engine company will be needed to put her out. Consequently, the real climax of the movie is not the "hand of god" destruction of the dirigible in which the depraved and idle rich, involved in a near orgy of outlandish pleasures, fall to their uncertain fate (much like the apocryphal stories of investors falling out of windows after the Great Crash). Rather the real climax is the earlier sexual showdown choreographed like a Western-movie gunfight that features Angela in her black silk Madam Satan outfit by designer Adrian and the concupiscent

Below, proto-femme fatale Kay Johnson exotically garbed as the title figure in *Madam Satan.* Opposite Claudette Colbert gazes out like a confident dominatrix as Empress Poppaea in *The Sign of the Cross.*

Trixie in feathers and glitter, a sequence in which the two women sing and slink towards each other while displaying their considerable physical "weapons." The husband is ultimately punished for being a "buffoon" by his fall from the disabled dirigible while Angela and Trixie escape unharmed. In fact to Trixie's delight she glides in a parachute through the skylight of Turkish bath filled with shocked half-naked men.

DeMille's women, like the lions which appear in so many of his films, are ever ready to bare tooth and claw and are really part of the same deterministic "jungle" law that underlies much of classic noir. Consequently, the brave gestures and noble sacrifices are reserved for the male characters, usually in attempts to save the women they idolize. They are forerunners of the many outwardly strong "chumps" in film noir, doomed by their interactions with femme fatales and typified by Jeff Bailey in *Out of the Past* and the Swede in *The Killers*. A case in point is the climax of *Dynamite*. In the film a spoiled heiress Cynthia (Kay Johnson again) must marry by a certain date or lose her inheri-

Below, *Dynamite*: like many proletarian noir protagonists in the future, incarcerated and condemned Hagon Derk (Charles Bickford) still manages to get embroiled with a scheming con-woman Cynthia Crothers (Kay Johnson). Opposite, social irony in a DeMille set piece: spoiled and wealthy Roger Towne (Conrad Nagel) sacrifices himself to save Derk and Cynthia after a mine accident.

tance. She is however having an affair with Roger, an effete married man. He can only get a divorce if he pays off his avaricious wife. So Cynthia makes a deal with a working class convict on death row to marry her in return for money for his sister. In a twist, Derk, the convict, is unexpectedly exonerated and so pursues his "wife." The film plays upon the clash of classes, extremely relevant for working-class audiences, as well as the conventions of a ménage à trois romance. The wedding scene in the prison—staged to the sound of hammers beating nails into Derk's gallows—demonstrates the social consciousness of the movie as DeMille evokes the injustice of a system which is about to send an innocent man to his death. In the final scene the trio is trapped in a mine shaft. But this time it is not Derk who must sacrifice himself for a woman. It is the playboy Roger who in order to save the woman he adores hits a bundle of TNT with a sledge hammer, a sacrifice that reduces his own body to rubble but creates an escape for Cynthia as well as his rival.

Contrary to the parade of hysterical, helpless women in a Hollywood DeMille helped create, DeMille often suggests that the "weaker sex" compensates for any physical disadvantage to men by the use of their wiles. Once they set out to take/re-take possession of a man or money or power, as does Kay Johnson's character in both films, rivals are treated more like cattle rustlers or claim jumpers than simple competitors. Although the perils for men in DeMille's films, as they would be in film noir, can be fatal, the temptations of his 1930's femme fatales are almost impossible to resist. Even the barrel-chested, lead-fisted, curly-haired ex-con of *Dynamite* is not impervious to them. For once he has broken down the door of Cynthia's "boudoir" and gotten an ample look at her charms, there is no doubt that this prudish coal miner, too, will succumb. The husband in *Madam Satan* is lucky to get off with only a broken arm and multiple lacerations.

Above, a clunky sign of the times in *The Sign of the Cross*: the 1944 prologue: clueless airman "Hoboken" (Tom Tully) gets a history less from Chaplain Lloyd (Stanley Ridges) before they rain down heavy-handed irony along with bombs on Italy.

Opposite, *This Day and Age*: the vigilante high schoolers capture and torture the smart-aleck gangster Louis Garrett.

Stylistically, DeMille frequently reveals a very modern taste for sadism and violence as do many later noirs such as *Brute Force* or *T-Men*. In *The Sign of the Cross*, his allegory about the class and ideological warfare beginning to appear in both Europe and the United States—a correlation DeMille underscores in the wartime re-release of the film in 1944 by adding a prologue from the view point of American bombers flying over Mussolini's dying "Second Roman Empire." In the core narrative DeMille pits innocent Christians and a sympathetic rugged Prefect Marcus against a corrupt ruling class overseen by a dissolute bisexual couple, Poppaea and Nero. The movie is a cornucopia of perverse pleasures. Poppaea. (Claudette Colbert) bathes in the milk of asses, her breasts bobbing tantalizingly near the surface, as she seduces both men and women. Charles Laughton in heavy make-up camps it up as Nero, playing his lyre as Rome burns. The lesbian Ancaria attempts to seduce the virginal Christian Mercia with a "Naked Moon" dance. Crocodiles munch on Christians while a gorilla molests a naked female Christian tied to a post. An Amazon horde skewers its pygmy opponents with scimitars. This battle between Christianity and Paganism for all practical purposes ends in an artistic stand-off.

This Day and Age fits neatly into the gangster film genre, a seminal influence in the development of film noir. DeMille again draws on his seemingly unlimited images of sadism and perversity for this tale of a group of middle-American teenagers on a vendetta against a gang of criminals who have corrupted their small town. When the local Jewish tailor is murdered (the references to the beginnings of Jewish persecution in Germany are obvious) and one of their friends is jailed on trumped up charges, the teens go after the real culprit, the gunsel Garrett (played by Charles Bickford, who also limned the role of Derk in *Dynamite).* Disillusioned with legal methods which are hopelessly compromised by the collusion of bribed officials with the gang bosses, the teens become vigilantes. The formerly clean-cut teen leader Steve convinces his sexy girlfriend Gay (Judith Allen) to become the femme fatale of the piece by distracting the crime boss with her charms, while they go after Garrett. As Gay flirts with the boss, who has no qualms about sex with a teenage girl ("I like my olives green"), Garrett is kidnapped, tied by ropes over a pit filled with rats and interrogated. In a sadistic scene worthy of the most violent in noir (such as the murder in the laundry room in *Brute Force* or the steam bath killing in *T-Men*), Garrett cracks and confesses. The teens have won but the price they paid, the film implies, was great. They can never regain their small-town-America innocence.

After the Production Code crackdown in 1934, DeMille retreated into the world of big budget epics, historical and biblical, culminating in 1956 with his bland remake of his own decadent 1923 epic *The Ten Commandments*. None of these films ever reached the heights or the depths of his Pre-Code proto-noirs.

An unusual proto-femme fatale:
Katharine Hepburn in *Mary of Scotland* (1936).

Proto-noir Pictorialism in the 1930s Films of John Ford

Alain Silver

In the abundant critical writing about the films of director John Ford, very few have associated his body of work with the noir movement in any way, and most instances have been merely to ask "Is *The Searchers* a noir Western"? That question is not considered here.

Hitchcock, DeMille, Florey, Lang, von Sternberg, Zinnemann and the other directors whose features are mentioned in this volume—including Hawks, LeRoy, and Wellman for the early entries in the Gangster cycle and such diverse filmmakers as Karl Freund and Edgar G. Ulmer working the 1930s horror genre—none have more than a passing relationship to Ford and his world view. Auteurism aside, Ford's work is rife with the prototypical examples of the visual style and character types that would bind together noir films of the classic period. Those examples coupled with Ford's already long-established pre-eminence as a pictorialist would influence the visual methods of directors and the figurative readings of viewers from beginning to end of the film noir movement. As Orson Welles famously observed: "...John Ford was my teacher. My own style has nothing to do with his, but *Stagecoach* was my movie text book. I ran it over forty times" [in Peter Cowie, *The Cinema of Orson Welles*, New York: A.S. Barnes, 1965, page 27]. That is the phenomenon that underlies this visual survey.

Hard side light models the face and underscores the apprehension of Tom Joad (Henry Fonda) in *The Grapes of Wrath* (1940).

The Informer (1935): a desperate Gypo Nolan (Victor McLaglen) stands with outstretched arms in a crucified pose that externalizes his self-image. Insets, clockwise from top right: Ford uses high-lights and reflections when Nolan (face in glass) stands with Madonna/whore Katie Madden (Margot Grahame) in front the travel poster that promises escape to America for £10 pounds that neither of them has; Nolan with the wanted poster that assures twice what he needs if he informs; Madden in a proto-femme fatale pose; dramatic rim light and Nolan's shadowy figure on the foggy street outside the travel bureau.

138.

Another dramatization of "the troubles" in Ireland in *The Plough and the Stars* (1936): low light casts dark shadows behind the troubled figures of Jack Clitheroe (Preston Foster) and his wife Nora (Barbara Stanwyck) leaning towards each other and away from Padraic Pearse (Arthur Shields, opposite page). Opposite top: an even more conspicuous Madonna, a prayerful Nora with head shawl and cross around her neck. Opposite bottom, character modeling with side light of a worried Nora and her reflection generates another emotional doppelgänger.

Right, a pose common to gangster and hapless noir heroes, the manacled and unjustly accussed Dr. Samuel Mudd (Warner Baxter) is *The Prisoner of Shark Island* (1936). Left, light models the face to create a mask of shadow as John Wilkes Booth (Francis McDonald) declaims, "Sic semper tyrannis." Below, hard side light stylizes the escape attempt of Mudd. At bottom, his wife and doctor create a pieta pose with Mudd.

Opposite, Claire Trevor as an even more explicit proto-femme fatale, the prostitute Dallas in *Stagecoach* (1939). Above, more side light to underscore emotion, Driscoll (Thomas Mitchell, left) and Olsen (John Wayne) keep a vigil with the dying Yank (Ward Bond) in *The Long Voyage Home*. Below, Ringo (John Wayne) watches Dallas walk away down a shadowy corridor in *Stagecoach*.

Ominous low light illuminates the faces of characters with an emotional burden: Tom Joad (Henry Fonda) and Jim Casy (John Carradine) in *The Grapes of Wrath* (1940). Inset, a synecdoche often used in film noir: slender shadows represent the unseen human figures.

A method often used in film noir, source light in *The Grapes of Wrath* beams reflect off the river bed and nate the desperate faces of Joad a father (Russell Simpson). Below, th lamp on the table in the confined the tent through dark shadows be figures. Opposite, rim light cuts ac forehead of Joad's scarred face an foreground scaffold to suggest his ment.

Universal Horror and Film Noir—*The Mummy* and *The Black Cat*

James Ursini

> Do you have to open graves to find girls to fall in love with?
>
> Helen in *The Mummy*

Universal's horror series of the 1930s has often been cited as a source of film noir, particularly in its visual style. Under the influence of German expressionism, émigré filmmakers like Karl Freund (cinematographer on Fritz Lang's *Metropolis*—1927), Edgar G. Ulmer (who worked with German expressionist director F.W. Murnau), and James Whale (who created *Frankenstein* [1931] and *Bride of Frankenstein* [1935]) planted the extravagances of expressionism in the more "realistic" soil of the Hollywood look. Stretching from *Dracula* in 1931 (which Freund photographed), through *Frankenstein* and *Bride of Frankenstein*, *The Mummy* (Freund) in 1932 and *The Black Cat* (Ulmer) in 1934, the first leg of the Universal horror series combined chiaroscuro lighting with alienated anti-heroes and obsessive love, essential elements of the classic period of film noir.

This article focuses on two movies: *The Black Cat* and *The Mummy*, both of which are more securely rooted in graphic and narrative "realism" within the preternatual conventions of the horror film than others in the series, a realism which permeates the film noir cycle. While the *Frankenstein* and *Dracula* films are more "fantastic" in setting and characterization, both Ulmer and Freund

Below, the brides in *Dracula*, where cinematographer Karl Freund applies expressionistic lighting to Gothic sets. Opposite, Helen (Zita Johar) transformed into a proto-femme fatale in Freund's *The Mummy*.

(according to studio publicity releases of the time—found in the Margaret Herrick Library at the Academy of Motion Picture Arts and Sciences) attempted to create a "believable" milieu for their horrific stories. Ulmer who had studied architecture based the main setting of his film (the art deco mansion) on the designs of the Bauhaus school of modernist architecture and the California houses of Frank Lloyd Wright. Freund for his part was intent on recreating the settings of ancient Egypt, the Cairo Museum, and the English mansions of the wealthy with an attention to detail within the confines of the studio back lots.

The Mummy

Universal's classic *The Mummy* (1932) plays off two sources. The first is the success of Universal's *Dracula.* Its cinematographer Karl Freund, acted as director on *The Mummy*; two of the actors, David Manners and Edward Van Sloan, played virtually the same parts; and *Dracula* co-writer John Balderston worked on its script. The second is the worldwide fascination with everything Egyptian following the discovery of Tutkankhamun's tomb by Howard Carter in 1922. Even by the 1930s Egyptian motifs continued to influence fashion and design, particularly art deco.

The story itself revolves around the character of Helen Grosvenor (Zita Johann) who is the reincarnation of the dead Egyptian princess Anckesen-Amon. She is the object of not one obsession but two. In her former life during the eighteenth dynasty (which we see in a flashback, shot entirely as a silent movie with no dialogue) she died young and was buried in the Valley of the Kings. Her lover,

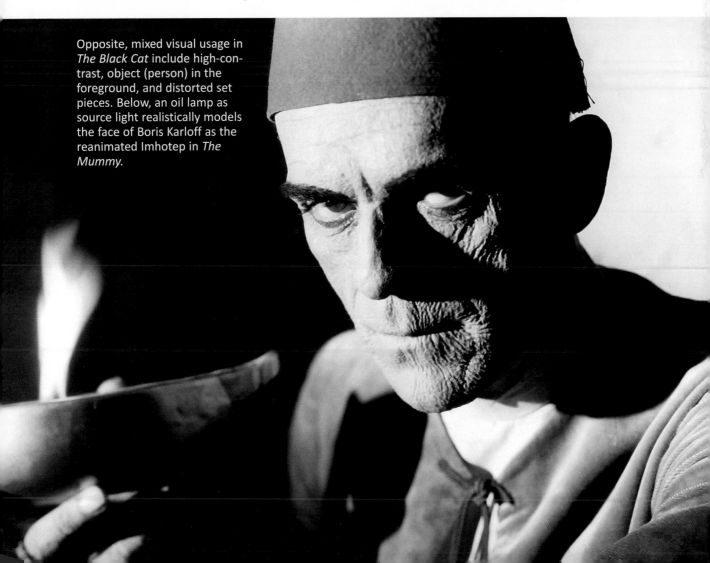

Opposite, mixed visual usage in *The Black Cat* include high-contrast, object (person) in the foreground, and distorted set pieces. Below, an oil lamp as source light realistically models the face of Boris Karloff as the reanimated Imhotep in *The Mummy.*

The Mummy: reflections from a mirror cut across the faces of both Imhotep and Helen, who gazes at herself transformed into a princess of ancient Egypt.

Above, realistic detail in an ancient setting as Imhotep is led to his emtombment in *The Mummy*.
Opposite, *The Black Cat*: Werdegast (Béla Lugosi) flays the murderous cultist Poelzig (Boris Karloff).

however, Imhotep (Boris Karloff), could not bear her death and tried to bring her back from the dead using the forbidden scrolls of Thoth. Caught in the act, he is sentenced to be buried alive, wrapped in the bandages of a mummy. More than three thousand five hundred years later, in 1921 he is accidentally returned to life by a too enthusiastic archaeologist who unwittingly reads the Thoth scrolls out loud (after the mummy comes to life and leaves, he laughs madly, "He went for a little walk."). Imhotep is clearly the anti-hero/protagonist of the piece. His obsession defies the space-time continuum and even any normal sense of morality. He is "extraordinary" in the Nietzschean sense, a "superman" who rises above his existential angst through force of will.

Ten years later a desiccated looking Imhotep returns to aid another expedition to uncover the tomb of his beloved princess. When her remains are removed to the Cairo museum, he spends his nights there on his knees, reading the scrolls of Thoth in order to effect her revivification. During one of his vigils the camera pans from the image of the princess to that of Helen, staring distractedly out at the pyramids, and in that way clues the audience in on the connection between the dead princess and Helen.

Helen as portrayed by Johann is an exotic, imperious woman who spends much of the film lying on couches with men before her on their knees, further reinforcing her connection to the original princess. Her attitude as well as her fatal lure mark her as a femme fatale in the tradition of nineteenth century fin-de-siècle literature and art.

Frank (David Manners), one of the archaeologists, falls in love with Helen almost immediately, innately sensing her connection to the mummy of the princess he had helped unearth. When he relates to Helen how he fell in love with the dead princess after fondling her clothes, her toiletries (Helen: "How could you do that?") and seeing her face on the coffin, Helen teases him by asking, "Do you have to open graves to find girls to fall in love with?" His attempts at lovemaking are interrupted shortly by Imhotep himself who has felt Helen's presence across the city. Imhotep stares at her forlornly and asks, "Have we not met before?" And soon he too becomes enamored, for a second time in his case.

The pain and torture associated with obsessive love (a key film noir theme in classics like *Double Indemnity*, *The Postman Always Rings Twice*, *Gilda*, etc.) becomes a major theme as the film progresses. After Imhotep shows Helen her past in a pool of water (the flashback), he tells her, "No man ever suffered as I for you." And she agrees. But Frank also suffers. He sleeps outside her door like a devout dog, is attacked by Imhotep telekinetically, and agonizes over her mysterious attraction to Imhotep. At one point he tells Helen, "It's been such torture. I love you so."

The theme of gender power (another film noir staple) also weaves its way through this film. All the men in the movie try to protect, coerce, and cajole Helen into doing their will: her psychiatrist Muller (Van Sloan), Frank, Imhotep, her medical doctors. She tells them, "I can't be shut up all the time," after they confine her to bed. She reprimands her doctor angrily with the words, "I'm not a child." But still they treat her like one.

It is a tribute to the filmmakers and to a more progressive attitude towards women in evidence in the 1930s and 1940s that Helen is allowed to become an active participant in her own destiny. As Imhotep dresses her in royal garments and prepares to kill her in order to revive her as the dead princess, she appeals to Isis, the supreme goddess, for a return of her powers. And it is she, not Frank or Dr. Muller who are both incapacitated by Imhotep's spell, who finally destroys the mummy, returning his brittle body to the earth.

The Black Cat

Ulmer's one and only A-film in his long career was *The Black Cat* (1934), made for Universal and starring the studio's top horror stars Boris Karloff and Béla Lugosi. Drawing on all his training under Murnau in Germany, Ulmer constructed an expressionistic tour de force redolent with Wagnerian liebestod.

Vitus Werdegast (Lugosi) meets a newly married couple—Peter and Joan (David Manners and Julie Bishop aka Jacqueline Wells) on a train heading for a honeymoon site in Hungary. After softly caressing the hair of the sleeping Joan, he explains his actions to the suspicious husband. He lost his wife, as beautiful as Joan (he tells them), during the war. He is, in fact, returning to the mansion of an associate—Poelzig (Karloff), an architect who has built his art deco masterpiece atop the remains of a fort in which ten thousand men died. And so Werdegast immediately establishes his credentials as a noir conflicted protagonist, tortured by loss and seeking revenge, as we later find out.

After an accident on the rain-damaged road, Werdegast and his two companions seek refuge in this "palace of death." Poelzig, who had stolen the wife of Werdegast and then mummified her after her death, is now married to Poelzig's stepdaughter Karen (Lucille Lund), unbeknownst to Werdegast.

Poelzig's first appearance is calculatingly disturbing. In silhouette he rises from the bed he shares with Karen and goes to greet his guests. Like the décor around him, Poelzig is angular and imposing with his thin but muscular stature, sculpted face, and geometric hairdo. Unperturbed by the presence of Werdegast who has returned, Poelzig senses, to seek revenge for the loss of his wife and the betrayal of the Austrian army by Poelzig during the war, Poelzig welcomes his guest, looking lustfully at Joan as she embraces her husband. Filled with lust, Poelzig grasps the torso of the art deco statuette of a naked female.

Poelzig not only incarnates death and depravity (two themes which criss cross noir films like *Scarlet Street* and *Kiss Me Deadly*) but he also epitomizes perversity in his desire for beautiful women whom he sees as decorative objects (in fact, he keeps several of his former lovers, including Werdegast's wife as mentioned earlier, embalmed and hanging in glass boxes in one of his underground caverns). While Werdegast bides for time, playing chess with Poelzig for the fate of the young couple (a game Werdegast loses), Poelzig arranges for Joan to become his new bride. He then kills Karen for disobeying his will and embalms her as well. He even shows Werdegast her body and admits to sleeping with the man's daughter.

In another underground chamber of the abandoned fort (lit in classic chiaroscuro style), Poelzig makes arrangements for the ritual. He kidnaps Joan and chains her to an asymmetrical cross. But before the ceremony can begin, Werdegast and his servant interrupt the proceedings and free the woman. As the couple escapes, Werdegast chains Poelzig to the same cross and begins flaying him alive, Poelzig's screams echoing through the fortress. The dying servant, under orders from Werdegast, ignites the dynamite charges underneath the fortress and, as the young couple escapes, the architectural dream above shatters into pieces as Poelzig and Werdegast join the ten thousand dead below them.

Opposite, Werdegast gets the drop on Poelzig, in front of the display of the dead body of his daughter Karen (Lucille Lund) in *The Black Cat*.

Film Noir Graphics: Origins

Alain Silver and James Ursini

When post-War audiences went to see a "film noir," they certainly did not refer to the movie by that term. Nonetheless they knew what kind of movie they were going to see. They might have called it a thriller, mystery, action movie, or even psychological melodrama. Whatever the sobriquet, advertising displays that boldly announced titles that were "coming soon" with expressive icons and menacing catch phrases evoked the noir cycle's dark and deadly vision and told them exactly what to expect. As Arthur Lyons suggested in *Death on the Cheap,* in some ways "film noir did not originate as a genre but as a faddish way of packaging the crime flm." From the earliest days of cinema sensational graphics often promised a movie ride to a world where danger lives.

In every era of Hollywood including the classic period of film noir, guys with chiseled chins and dames with curves were easy enough to cast for minimum salaries. From 1940 to 1960 film noir was a staple product from the major studios to poverty row. Consequently A-list actors might sometimes share a marquee with faded idols from past decades or up-and-comers, who never made it past the first-rung on the ladder to stardom. Republic, Monogram, PRC and still lower-grade releasing companies could all manage to come up with a few extra dollars and buy some decent poster art. It might not be a level playing field in most respects, but as with certain black-listed writers, directors, and even actors, the work of some talented graphic artists could be had for a price.

Unlike some stylized posters for German Expressionist cinema, most precursors of noir graphics used faces and their expressions to suggest fear or anger, love or hate. Even a hand overlaid with an "M" for Fritz Lang's proto-noir (opposite) keys on a human element (compare the hands on pages 166 and 168). Just as the style and content of classic period film noir were influenced by such varied

Below, the worried looks in the 1931 gangster sagas *The Public Enemy* and *City Streets* subconsciously color the more romantic pose in Fritz Lang's bleak 1937 pre-noir *You Only Live Once.*

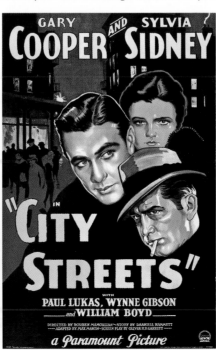

WESTERN, DETECTIVE & ADVENTURE STORIES

★BLACK MASK★

THE

MALTESE

FALCON

By

DASHIELL

HAMMETT

SEPT. 1929·20

IN CANADA 25¢

Opposite, 1929 pulp cover.

Right, graphic for the 1931 film version of *The Maltese Falcon*.

Below, the dust jacket of the first edition of the novel.

Evolution of the femme fatale: below Bebe Daniels in the 1931 version and Bette Davis (bottom and right) as the same character in the 1936 *Satan Met a Lady*.

antecedents as hard-boiled fiction and gangster movies of the early 1930s, film noir graphics adapted elements from proto-noir sources. When Dashiell Hammett's novel was serialized in "Black Mask" Magazine, it was sold by using the sensational and violent art seen two pages back. The hardcover Knopf adopted a more restrained approach, one befitting "serious" literature, for its dust jacket. As seen on the previous page, the first adaptation in 1931 lifted the elements of the Falcon and the stylized hand from that cover.

As the lobby card for the 1931 adaptation suggests, the top-billed Bebe Daniels—sex kittenish star of such silent movies as *The Campus Flirt, She's a Sheik,* and *What A Night!*—does not portray Miss Wonderly as much of a femme fatale. Five years later, the pose struck by Bette Davis as Valerie Purvis (Wonderly) in *Satan Met A Lady* is more seductive and more menacing. In case there was any doubt about her potentially lethal character, on the insert card, she's the one holding the gun. Whether from book or movie, nothing in these graphics contains the explicit violence embodied in the 1929 pulp cover where Hammett's prose first appeared.

The cover from late 1935 at left garishly combines the detective with a gun and a languid siren in a thin crepe dress.

Below a 1941 pulp cover goes even futher: the man is neither a smooth-shaven nor smoothly handsome but considerably more hard-bitten. The woman also has quite an edge, plus a wound on her arm not to mention an oversized revolver.

The next adaptation of *The Maltese Falcon* is generally

accepted as the first major release of a film noir during the classic period. It also defines the elements of many film noir graphics to follow over the next two decades. The key figure is now male and the top-billed Bogart combines elements of the men on all three pulp covers. He has the fedora and the automatic, of course, and the clear-eyed expression is not placid but subtly focused. Mary Astor as the latest Wonderly—here named Brigid O'Shaughnessy—is noir's first femme fatale. Like the "Black Mask" tart she also wears a crepe dress and leans back but not into a man's shoulder. More importantly she looks staight ahead, charming, beckoning, and. as the viewer will discover, scheming.

In the early 1930s Warner Bros. was the key studio for the gangster genre. While not entirely embracing the pulp approach, the one-sheet on the next page for the Warners adaptation of *Little Caesar* moves from the stylized violence of the book jacket—again from Knopf, which overlayed a

literary patina onto the grisly content of the novel—into an explicit association of sex and guns. The couple (Douglas Fairbanks, Jr. and Olga Stassoff) who stare longingly into each other's eyes and the thuggish Edward G. Robinson in a hat with a gat are equally prominent. It's a small step from there to the poster art for the 1941 *Maltese Falcon*.

Mervyn Leroy, who directed *Little Caesar* for Warners, also produced *Johnny Eager* for MGM. Although released the year after the Bogart/Astor *Maltese Falcon* the poster on the opposite page is a slight throwback. The smaller figures with guns blazing recall the dust jacket for *Little Caesar*. Although the black-and-white version of Robert Taylor as the title figure in the lower left certainly has a noir tinge, the key element is the couple, which romantized the sexual double entendre in the "TNT."

As the noir movement modified the elements from various antecedents to define its own set of graphic connotations and key iconic indicators, there was a reciprocal effect. With its slick-haired ethnic Rico pointing his piece at some unseen antagonist, the noir influence is quite visible in the 1945 cover for the Avon paperback of *Little Caesar* at right. On the next page, the caricaturish art found on the original one sheet of *Scarface* somewhat mitigates the violence.

The art rendering of the title figure is somewhat recognizable as actor Paul Muni; but actual co-star Ann Dvorak hardly seems the inspiration for the shocked female figure. Compare that to the poster below used for the 1947 reissue at the peak of the classic period.

There are obvious and esoteric links between film noir graphics and their antecedents. Some are strikingly similar such as the claw-like hands depicted on the pulp cover and a poster for Hitchcock's *Shadow of a Doubt*, at left. There are also the more subtle effects like the diagonal slash of red graphics and the shadowed face common to the title lobby card from the silent *Underworld* (1927) and twenty years later in the six sheet for the proto-typical noir *The Dark Corner* (1946).

The Verlocs (Oscar Homolka and Sylvia Sidney) are a desperately unhappy couple in *Sabotage*.

Hitchcock Before Noir: Hitchcock's Gaumont British Thrillers as Film Noir Prototypes

Richard L. Edwards

> French writers after the war might have recognized the equally significant contributions of other European nations to the evolution of the crime or espionage film. For example, they could have alluded to Alfred Hitchcock's British thrillers of the 1930s and—had they known it—to Carol Reed's *Night Train to Munich* (1940). These were the films with which American reviewers compared the 1941 version of *The Maltese Falcon*; in fact, when Billy Wilder completed *Double Indemn*ity, he told the Los Angeles Times that he intended to 'out-Hitchcock Hitchcock.'
>
> James Naremore, *More Than Night: Film Noir in Its Contexts*

1. The Distinctive Qualities of Hitchcock's Prewar Thrillers (1934-1938)

Between 1934 and 1938, Alfred Hitchcock made six films as a director in the British film industry: *The Man Who Knew Too Much* (1934), *The 39 Steps* (1935)*, Secret Agent* (1936)*, Sabotage* (1936), *Young and Innocent* (1937), and *The Lady Vanishes* (1938). Often referred to as the "thriller sextet," Hitchcock made these films at Gaumont British Picture Corporation—after beginning his career during the silent film era and in the early sound era at two other British film studios, Gainsborough and British International Pictures (B.I.P.). The films of the sextet established Hitchcock's international reputation as the "Master of Suspense" and the box office success and positive reception of these films in particular helped Hitchcock to cross to the other side of the Atlantic and enter into the Hollywood studio system through a contract with David O. Selznick in 1939. Collectively, the films of the thriller sextet shared narrative constructions, formal experiments, and generic conventions built around tales of spies and saboteurs. As a kind of mini-cycle in Hitchcock's *oeuvre*, the films he made at Gaumont British helped him to hone his own particular and successful brand of dark and moody suspense thriller in the first two decades of his long and prolific career.

These six films have been analyzed by scholars in terms of their importance on Hitchcock's career arc—especially as a transitional and transformational moment between Hitchcock's silent films like *The Lodger* (1927), his experimental early sound films like *Blackmail* (1929) and his fine first batch of Hollywood studio films, including *Rebecca* (1940), *Suspicion* (1941), and *Saboteur* (1942). However, the Gaumont British films are less well known in terms of their impact on the development of film noir in 1940s Hollywood. I will address reasons that might account for the absence of these films in the film noir literature, while also demonstrating, through specific examples, how these thrillers operate as significant film noir prototypes in their own right. Moreover, I will advance the idea that Hitchcock's thriller sextet put down evolutionary and experimental roots that fed into the soon-to-be flourishing family tree of film noir.

Following along this line of inquiry, I propose three major reasons as to why this phase of Hitchcock's film career might not have been previously considered as a significant prototype for film noir. This assessment comes about due to Hitchcock's position as a British film director in the 1930s, the transgeneric nature of Hitchcock's overall influence on modern crime thrillers, and the distinctive and indelible qualities and characteristics of his personal authorial signature and style as a noted film *auteur*.

First, Hitchcock, in general terms, tends to be considered a less significant influence on the direct development of film noir because he does not quite fit the mold of the iconic Hollywood film noir director. Partly this is a result of working in the British film industry of the 1920s and 1930s, and partly due to Hitchcock's independent status as a star director/producer for multiple studios under unique picture deals on both sides of the Atlantic. As Foster Hirsch notes:

> Since he is neither a German expatriate nor an idiosyncratic American, Alfred Hitchcock, the most renowned directors of thrillers, does not belong to any group predominately associated with noir. Hitchcock, in fact, is seldom labeled as a noir director—certainly he is not linked with the genre to the same degree as Fritz Lang or Robert Siodmak or early Jules Dassin. And yet, as he continued working in that narrow vein of the thriller that he has made distinctly his own, Hitchcock is pre-eminently a noir stylist: *Shadow of a Doubt, Rope, Spellbound, The Paradine Case, Strangers on a Train, I Confess, Rear Window, The Wrong Man, Vertigo*, and *Psycho*, are richly, demonstrably noir. (*The Dark Side of the Screen*, 139)

It should be noted that Hirsch makes a distinction between Hitchcock as a noir director and a noir stylist in an almost philological sense, where presumably, in this kind of formulation, Hitchcock should be considered as his own stylistic off-shoot in the tangled written annals of film noir. Furthermore, while he mentions Hitchcock's more famous American films noir, Hirsch's list does not cite or reference the six noir-inflected thrillers of his 1930s Gaumont British period.

Additionally, Hitchcock's ambivalent status as a source for the early development of American film noir was likely a by-product of early scholarship on film noir. For example, in their early, influen-

Noir lighting in *The Secret Agent* wiyh Peter Lorre as The General and John Gielgud as Brodie/Richard Ashenden.

tial study of film noir, first published in the 1950s, *A Panorama of American Film Noir, 1941-1953,* Borde and Chaumeton argue that the British film industry as a whole was a "feeble" influence on American film noir, though they do give a small nod in Hitchcock's direction as a possible exception to that "rule:"

> ...in the best of cases the influence of Europe seems to be *feeble*...In England, there'd hardly be anything worth retaining, from our angle, apart from Hitchcock's oeuvre, with its mysterious and fascinating atmosphere (*The 39 Steps, Sabotage*) and its unforgettable villains (*Jamaica Inn*). (22-23) [Italics mine]

Borde and Chaumeton's framing of Hitchcock as a less significant influence on film noir is not unusual in early noir writings. Nino Frank, who coined the term "film noir" in his seminal article, "A New Kind of Police Drama: the Criminal Adventure," identifies Hitchcock's *Suspicion* (1941) as part of the realm of "criminal psychology" but Frank mentions it parenthetically while privileging other early 1940s films as "particularly masterful" in the film noir vein such as John Huston's *The Maltese Falcon,* Otto Preminger's *Laura,* or Billy Wilder's *Double Indemnity.*

In general, the dark thrillers and spy melodramas made by the British film industry in the 1930s, including those of Hitchcock, do not get much scholarly attention in noir studies or histories, especially in light of other films produced in key national cinemas of the 1930s such as Germany and France. German Expressionism and French Poetic Realism are referenced more commonly as sources

Young and Innocent: Old Will (Edward Rigby) looks on as Derrick (Robert TIsdale) and Erica (Nova Pilbeam) hold on to Guy (George Curzon).

of film noir. Therefore, in this version of noir's cinematic origins, Hitchcock's films at Gaumont British are not considered as influential or generative as films like Fritz Lang's German Expressionist *M* or Marcel Carne's French Poetic Realist *Le Jour Se Leve*.

Second, even when Hitchcock's films and his influence are acknowledged by noir scholars, his overall positioning or status within the history of film noir is often called into question or marginalized, as can be seen in this entry from the *Historical Dictionary of Film Noir* (2010). Andrew Spicer opens his remarks on Alfred Hitchcock as follows:

> Born in Leytonstone, northeast London, Hitchcock had a major career on both sides of the Atlantic, and his contribution to American and British film noir was immense. Hitchcock was involved in every aspect of filmmaking—scripting, art direction, cinematography, music, and editing—and his films constitute a body of work with its own personal 'signatures' both visual and thematic. Therefore, many of his crime and spy thrillers...exist on the fringes of film noir. (135)

Spicer's entry on Hitchcock offers yet another issue that is typically raised when discussing Alfred Hitchcock and his films in relation to the body of film noir. Hitchcock made "immense" contributions to films noir in general, while many of his own crime and spy thriller films exist mainly on the fringes of the movement or fall out of the noir canon completely. While Spicer does acknowledge Hitchcock's "immense" contribution to film noir, that overarching claim lacks a certain sense of specificity. It can be argued that the kind of influence that Spicer is referencing could be applied to any crime film made in the Hollywood system in the twentieth century, whether films noir or not. Furthermore, there is an implication that if we consider Hitchcock's films in terms of their own particular themes, stylistic techniques, or story constructions, such determinations will place Hitchcock's films on the outer fringes or the periphery of the classic film noir cycle, if they are to be considered at all.

Third, beyond questions of the influence of British film industry in 1930s and the general

Faces and figures modeled with high-contrast lighting in *Sabotage*, centered around Ted Spencer (John Loder).

nature of Hitchcock's impact on other films and filmmakers, it also can be argued that there might be intrinsic or unique qualities found within the films of Hitchcock's thriller sextet that make them poor candidates to be film noir prototypes of any kind. In other words, while they might appear in their visual design, narrative structures, or tonal qualities to have certain affinities to the films noir of the 1940s, Hitchcock's authorial signature and his own brand of thematic preoccupations undercut or challenge their perception as a meaningful influence on other films noir.

Scholar James Naremore makes this kind of assessment in his essay, "Hitchcock at the Margins of Noir." Naremore argues that "intrinsic qualities of subject matter, tone and style...make [Hitchcock's] films appear slightly alien to the *noir* universe – especially when we think of *noir* as a phenomenon produced by Hollywood in the 1940s and 1950s." (266) Naremore enumerates four major qualities he observes in Hitchcock's Hollywood films after 1940, namely the director's Britishness, Hitchcock's preference for classical suspense, his celebration of romantic unions, and a specific nostalgia for a pre-modern world. While Naremore concludes his essay by stating that Hitchcock "seems marginal [to film noir] only in a somewhat parochial context," such a caution runs up against the larger points of the essay that seem to place Hitchcock outside mainstream renditions of film noir history.

To investigate if Hitchcock's films have intrinsic qualities not compatible with other films noir, Naremore lays out a particular line of inquiry: "If we define *noir* in terms of a post-World War II Hollywood, we can use the concept as a kind of foil, bringing certain distinctive qualities of Hitchcock's 'world' into bold relief." (266) Naremore focuses on the "bold relief" of Hitchcock's films against an expansive definition of film noir in order to more clearly discover or determine distinctive qualities that do not quite fit with even the broadest definitions of film noir. Yet what if we use that same methodology and apply it to Hitchcock's Gaumont British thriller sextet? What if we flip the line of inquiry and look instead for how Hitchcock's British thrillers contribute to the evolution of film noir? In other words, what if instead of looking for reasons to exclude Hitchcock from film noir studies, we seek evidence in the 1930s British films themselves to justify their inclusion into discussions of significant noir prototypes?

As might be expected, we will have to be cautious with such an approach. Writing (or re-writing) the imposing figure of Hitchcock either into or out of the film noir story seems fraught with risks and challenges. When Hitchcock as a major stylist is conspicuously written out of the noir story as one of its chief practitioners, his films will appear more closely aligned with a set of personal preoccupations that elevate him as an elite *auteur* but leave his contributions to film noir as a marginal outcome. On the other hand, if we re-write Hitchcock the director back into the film noir story, we do so at the risk that he might be a special case in film noir studies. In this case, his inclusion would unnecessarily broaden the definition of film noir to mean any stylish or modern crime film of the twentieth century—thus rendering the film noir category virtually meaningless. It is worth noting that most of the time when scholars or fans are performing these categorical exercises, the films that are under discussion are the ones Hitchcock made after 1940, such as *Shadow of a Doubt*, *Notorious*, or *Strangers on a Train*—the films he made during the heyday of film noir in Hollywood.

While Hitchcock's 1940s and 1950s contributions to film noir have been a subject of sustained scholarly inquiry in many books and articles, his 1930s spy and espionage thrillers from Gaumont British have not typically been viewed as a major influence on the film noir style. In this essay, I will examine three of Hitchcock's pre-World War II thrillers of the 1930s: *The Man Who Knew Too Much*, *The 39 Steps*, and *Sabotage* to see how they influenced the future directions of film noir. It might seem strange to learn that these British noir prototypes are centered around tales of espionage and not hard-boiled pulp and detective fiction as in the early American films noir. Instead of Raymond Chandler and Dashiell Hammett, the sextet relied on novelists like Robert Buchan (*The 39 Steps*) and Joseph Conrad (*Sabotage*). But in Britain, the popular spy novels and stories occupied a similar cultural niche to pulp fiction in the U.S., and in a similar vein, spy stories were one of the ways that Edwardian Britain shared cultural anxieties about imperial decline and painful cultural shifts occurring before, during and after World War I.

Hitchcock as a filmmaker constantly pursued, developed, and refined techniques, styles, performances, and stories that pushed the bounds of crime and spy melodramas into new and unsettling dimensions. While Hitchcock was experimenting, he was also achieving good box office results during his years at Gaumont British in ways that would not have gone unnoticed in Hollywood circles and among the financiers. Hitchcock was a key stylist and cinematic innovator who became a model (and sometimes a rival) for film noir directors in the Hollywood studio system. Through his Gaumont British thrillers of the mid to late 1930s, Hitchcock showcased for other filmmakers, studios, and audiences how his film noir prototypes developed a trenchant visual design anchored in silent film aesthetics, innovated and experimented in pursuit of new and exciting ways to relate spy/detective stories, and playfully incorporated mordant humor and black comedy amidst a steady dose of shock, suspense, and horror. In this sense, Hitchcock and his Gaumont British films made an "immense" contribution to the Hollywood film industry by providing a kind of mass market blueprint for how to broaden the commercial appeal for downbeat crime films and how to whet the audience's appetite for the ever-growing slate of noir films in the 1940s.

2. Sly, Silent, and Stylized: Hitchcock as Silent Filmmaker in His Noir Prototypes

To understand some of Hitchcock's stylistic innovations that contributed to the development of film noir is necessary to revisit the earliest parts of Hitchcock's experiences in the British film industry. Hitchcock began his career in the silent film business and many scholars such as Sidney Gottlieb and others believe that Hitchcock remained a silent filmmaker at heart for his entire career. The Gaumont British thriller sextet shows many elements of visual innovation that were first learned by Hitchcock during his early years working on silent films.

In 1921 a young Alfred Hitchcock got his first job in the movie business when he was hired by Famous Players-Lasky (FPL) to create title cards for upcoming silent film productions. As Peter Ackroyd notes, FPL was probably a fortuitous first job for Hitchcock. Even though FPL was located in Islington, London and "was in essence an American studio with a largely American staff." (2016) Hitchcock learned many lessons about filmmaking before he ever set foot behind a camera, often with an American perspective and with a focus on words and scripts. Ackroyd describes Hitchcock's experiences at FPL as follows:

> From the beginning [Hitchcock] learned how to cooperate with the studio's scenarists, essentially scriptwriters, who were usually American women; [Hitchcock] once said he was steeped in the cinematic learning of "the middle-aged American women" who worked in Poole Street. It was under their guidance that he also learned to write scripts. He learned also that it was possible to change the tone or meaning of a film by inserting very different title cards than the ones intended; in this manner a poor film might be saved. (*Alfred Hitchcock: A Brief Life*, 2016)

The use of words and text on screen was a practice Hitchcock first used extensively in his silent film projects and he continued to use the technique very effectively in the thriller sextet. He would use a handwritten note to relate a clue or a secret code for the characters, or use a theater ticket or a travel brochure to give a sense of place. These textual close-ups advance the plot and bring the

Right and opposite top, four examples of textual notes and handwritten clues in *The Man Who Knew Too Much.*

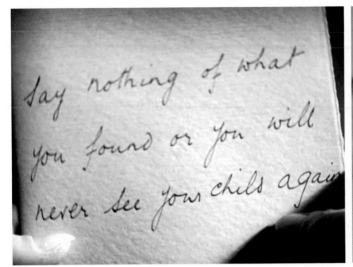

audience up to speed without the use of dialogue or excessive narration. Hitchcock's uses could be very sly as in the dramatic of a secret note in *The Man Who Knew Too Much* (1934) that was hidden in the handle of a hairbrush. Similar techniques would be popular in films noir in the 1940s and 1950s.

Beyond his early experiences with intertitles, Alfred Hitchcock began his directing career by going to Germany in 1925 to direct his first silent film, *The Pleasure Garden* (1925). As part of his visit to Germany, the young Hitchcock visited UFA, Germany's premier film studio, and was exposed to German Expressionist techniques through the work of F.W. Murnau and Fritz Lang. He proceeded to make many silent films, including what was likely his strongest pre-noir prototype of the silent film era in *The Lodger* (1927).

As a silent filmmaker at heart, German Expressionist techniques remained a part of Hitchcock's visual repertoire for his entire career. Given Hitchcock's use of German Expressionism in his films, it is strange that he is not considered more central to the development of film noir. Hitchcock was one of the first filmmakers outside of Germany to deploy the lighting and set design strategies associated with Germany Expressionism, but inflected through the sense and sensibility of a different national context. While Hitchcock was capable of shots that would not be out of place in the bleakest German films of that era, his version of expressionism was less an homage and more of an interpretation—many film noir directors and directors of photography followed similar uses close to Hitchcock, and were probably inspired by Hitchcock's work. And Hitchcock, following Murnau, was willing to use German Expressionist techniques in some unlikely and non-urban settings as in the night-time and fog-bound backdrop (at right) as police detectives search for Richard Hannay across the Scottish moors in *The 39 Steps* (1935).

Earlier examples of Expressionistic/pre-noir lighting in *The Lodger* (Ivor Novello as the title figure below) and *Blackmail* (inset).

3. Expressive, Experimental, and Entertaining: Hitchcock's Experimentation in His Noir Prototypes

Early in his career, under the tutelage of independent producer Michael Balcon, Hitchcock was encouraged to experiment in his film techniques and he remained experimental through his entire career. From the beginning of his film career, Hitchcock displayed an interest in inventive uses of set design, lighting, editing (especially in the spirit of Soviet montage), and sound design. A Hitchcock film like *Blackmail* (1929), which precedes the Gaumont thriller sextet by a few years, demonstrated Hitchcock's commitment to expressive sound design. He would use sound design in elaborate ways that advanced the story in *The Man Who Knew Too Much* (1934) with an assassination plot timed to synchronize with a musical performance at the Royal Albert Hall. Or he would show his interest in unconventional camera angles and camera movements during a hypnotism

Below, Nurse Agnes (Cicely Oakes) during an act of hynoptism in *The Man Who Knew Too Much*.

scene in the same film during a scene at The Tabernacle of the Sun. Frequently, in his experimentation, Hitchcock would look for visual analogues to simulate different kinds of perceptual states.

In *Sabotage* (1936), Hitchcock's experimentation is on full display. In ways that are reminiscent later of Orson Welles' *The Lady from Shanghai*, Hitchcock expands the settings for these kinds of films in ways that will resonate in later films noir. There is a scene in an aquarium that is reminiscent of the aquarium scene from *The Lady from Shanghai*, and both the Welles and Hitchcock films have major scenes take place in a movie theater. But Hitchcock got there first.

Left, celebrated, pre-noir use of public space as a location: the British Museum chase in *Blackmail*. Below, meeting at the aquarium (left) and scene behind the screen (right) in *Sabotage*.

The Man Who Knew Too Much: Smoke from the cigarette of Abbott (Peter Lorre) gets in the eyes of the desperate father Bob Lawrence (Leslie Banks).

An experimental sequence for Hitchcock in *Sabotage* that draws a lot of attention as a noir precursor is the explosion of a bomb on a bus. The sequence utilizes Hitchcock's skill in creating suspense and a feeling of dread through skillful editing and montage aesthetics. Hitchcock has always claimed that he made a "mistake" with the bomb going off and killing a little boy. As he explains to Francois Truffaut: "I made a serious mistake in having the little boy carry the bomb...[He] was involved in a situation that got him too much sympathy from the audience, so that when the bomb exploded and he was killed, the public was resentful." This comment reveals one of the reasons why Hitchcock tends to get excluded from discussions of film noir. *Sabotage* is one of his bleakest films, and when Hitchcock creates a sequence that makes implicit sense within the bounds of the narrative, Hitchcock feels he misread the audience and he regrets how he assembled the story beats. It was a lesson for Hitchcock that he never forgot, and it can be argued that in later films Hitchcock tempered such sequences if he felt that they might not sit well with an American middle-class audience. Other film noir directors would push their films to make the audience feel uneasy, but Hitchcock, after *Sabotage*, seldom would approach his films with as random a moment of fatal doom as we have in this film with the little boy on the bus. This sequence is bleak and merciless in a way that will become more common in the 1940s with film noir.

4. Dark, Downbeat, and Droll: Hitchcock's Mordant Humor in His Noir Prototypes

In *The Man Who Knew Too Much* (1934), Peter Lorre—his first film outside of Germany after the world-wide success of Lang's *M* and his first English-speaking role—delivers an almost comedic performance at times in the role of the principal villain of Abbott. The light playful touch of his performance here is in a sharp contrast to Lorre's grim portrayal of a child murderer in Lang's *M*. In Hitchcock's film, there is a droll delivery in the lines of dialogue given to Peter Lorre's character. For example, when Abbott is relaying a threat on their daughter's life to her parents, he says: "Tell her they may soon be leaving us. Leaving us for a long, long journey. How is it that Shakespeare says? 'From which no traveler returns.' Great poet." Lorre delivers the line with a smile on his face, while looking away in the middle distance of the room and with a mischievous playfulness. While the lines are intended to be a veiled threat (and we clearly see the look of fear on the faces of the parents in the background), these words come out with a touch of deadpan humor that adds a layer of complexity that problematizes our sympathies for Abbott in this story. Abbott's bemused demeanor, his sly expressions, his black hair with its distracting white streak, and his natural brio make him more charming than the average villain. Film noir stylists in the 1940s and 1950s will frequently use a similar tactic with humor or wit to complicate the audience's reading of tough guys, bad guys, and villains in many a noir picture.

In the thriller sextet, Hitchcock continued his use of mordant humor and black comedy that can be traced back to his earliest silent films. In the *New York Times* review of *The 39 Steps*, Andre Sennwald wrote back in 1935 that Hitchcock was "[a] master of shock and suspense, of cold horror and *slyly incongruous wit*, he uses his camera the way a painter uses his brush, stylizing his story and giving it values which the scenarists could hardly have suspected." [Italics added] Hitchcock's droll sense of humor is characterized as "slyly incongruous wit" which fits the

Right, Abbott (Peter Lorre) threatening Bob and Jill Lawrence (Leslie Banks and Edna Best) with disarming humor and a smile in *The Man Who Knew Too Much.*

narrative of the film as the film is a fast chase through various parts of the British isles. Even though the films of the thriller sextet can be very downbeat and darker in tone than typical melodramas, Hitchcock leavens each of the stories with a suitable amount of humor and wit.

Richard Hannay (Robert Donat) must prevent his reluctant travelling companion Pamela Shaneakwa (Madeleine Carroll) from revealing their position in *The 39 Steps*.

A film like *The 39 Steps* operates along the lines of screwball comedy, with its double chase structure also involving a running meta-commentary on the perils and pitfalls of marriage (with a provocative image of handcuffs as part of that commentary). There are literal points in *The 39 Steps* that move even more aggressively than *The Man Who Knew Too Much* (1934) into the realm of comedy. In the opening scenes with Mr. Memory, members of the audience yell out humorous questions to add an element of rambunctiousness to the entire proceedings. When Hannay (Robert Donat) begins his life on the run, there is a very humorous exchange with a milkman who asks him if he is married to which Hannay replies: "I am. But don't rub it in." There is an exchange on a train where Hitchcock blends elements of sexual innuendo with humor during a discussion of women's lingerie. Hitchcock is also particularly enamored of using humor as a self-reflexive device as when he has a character say: "These sex dramas don't appeal to me."

In large and small ways, Hitchcock's noir prototypes likely have more humor than the typical 1940s film noir. It is not that other films noir do not have mordant humor or black comedy, but it is an especially constitutive feature of Hitchcock's body of work. Given Hitchcock's box office success, perhaps part of his successful formula for these kinds of dark melodramas was to lighten up the story at key times. It is possible that this lesson did not completely transfer to other noir filmmakers who incorporated fewer moments of droll or mordant comedy than is found in a typical Hitchcock film.

5. After Gaumont: The Further Evolution of Hitchcock's Noir Prototypes in the Hollywood System

After the thriller sextet at Gaumont British, Hitchcock would make one more film in England (1939's *Jamaica Inn* with Charles Laughton) before coming to Hollywood to work for David O. Selznick. If we look more closely at the various films and production crews that Hitchcock uses in the early 1940s in the Hollywood system, it is possible to see more ways in which Hitchcock influenced the evolution of noir. Hitchcock's influence on the film industry and film noir itself was not always directly communicated through the films he made and the images that appeared on the silver screen. Some of Hitchcock's influence would have been shared during his script conferences, in pre-production meetings, on studio sound stages, and in the editing booth. Creative personnel and crew members who worked with Hitchcock on his American films would have picked up some of the lessons learned by Hitchcock during the making of the thriller sextet and then later films. Conversely, Hitchcock would receive new insights and new techniques from talented Hollywood production crews that had experience in gothic romance, horror films, social problem films, and gangster films—which when brought together and further stylized was a primary creative engine behind the rise of film noir.

In this regard, RKO has a special place in noir history as a Hollywood studio that was instrumental in making some of the first films noir of the 1940s including:

> *Stranger on the Third Floor* (Boris Ingster, 1940)
> *Citizen Kane* (Orson Welles, 1941)
> *Suspicion* (Alfred Hitchcock, 1941)
> *Journey into Fear* (Orson Welles, 1943)
> *Woman in the Window* (Fritz Lang, 1944)

In such a list of early films noir, it is difficult not to notice that directorial talents like Hitchcock, Welles, and Lang are not only working at RKO, but they are making films that are connected to the film noir tradition. In this sense, a studio like RKO will have "below the line" talent that will not only make major contributions to film noir, but the "below the line" talent will work with more than one director. For example, Alfred Hitchcock makes *Notorious* for RKO in 1946. Most noir scholars consider *Notorious* to be a classic film noir. Hitchcock makes *Notorious* while on loan from David O. Selznick, and as such, Hitchcock has to assemble his own crew on the RKO lot to make *Notorious*. He works with art directors Carroll Clark and Albert D'Agostino. These art directors would help influence the noir look of *Notorious*. Albert D'Agostino's first film at RKO was *Stranger on the Third Floor* (1940), which is an

The final installment in the "thriller sextet," *The Lady Vanishes*, has the same sort of dark comedy as its antecedents. Above Gilbert Redman (Michael Redgrave) has finally helped Iris Henderson (Margaret Lockwood) find the vanished lady Miss Froy (Dame Witty), who is an unlikely British spy. When Iris first approached Gilbert to ask if he has seen her, he asks for detail: "What was she wearing? Scotch tweeds wasn't it?" "Oatmeal tweeds." "I knew it had something to do with porridge. "

example of the German Expressionist style in Hollywood. An interest in German Expressionism, that predates Hitchcock's arrival at the studio, permeated many films at RKO: "when Albert D'Agostino replaced Polglase as supervising art director, RKO and Clark turned to a more expressionist style of production design that perfectly answered to the moody, claustrophobic interiors and dark and rain-swept urban landscapes of film noir…" (*The Wrong House: The Architecture of Alfred Hitchcock*, 315-316). I bring up this point to address that talents like Clark and D'Agostino worked with Welles, Hitchcock, and Lang, thus there is overlap at RKO below the line on many key films noir. It is no accident that D'Agostino also worked on what might be the quintessential film noir, *Out of the Past* (1947). Increasingly in the 1940s, film noir would become a kind of house style for RKO and Hitchcock's own brand of stylized thriller, first developed during his British filmmaking period, would find resonance at a studio like RKO.

Furthermore, in his noir films, Hitchcock could assemble camera personnel, editors, lighting crews, or production designers to enhance his ideas on his suspense thrillers at Hollywood studios (most typically at Universal or RKO) as many technical employees of the studios had experience in Gothic horror pictures, gangster films, and other kinds of expressionist-inflected films, or even, after World War II, certain kinds of documentary realism. It is within this particular milieu, where technical personnel worked on movies produced by many different kinds of directors, that Hitchcock would make further contributions and add his own brand of expressionism and realism into the working memories and experiences of professional crews at RKO and Universal. His cinematographer from *Notorious*, Ted Tetzlaff, would go onto make his own film noir picture, 1949's *The Window*, showing how these lines of influence might be happening on the front lines of the studio sound stages and not always readily apparent in the finished films themselves. In a related vein, Welles' *Citizen Kane* has always seemed very influenced by Hitchcock's *Rebecca*, down to the cameramen themselves. Hitchcock's director of photography on *Rebecca* was George Barnes, and Welles' director of photography was Gregg Toland. Perhaps unexpectedly, this creates a kind of connection between the work of Welles and Hitchcock as Gregg Toland had tutored under George Barnes at Samuel Goldwyn.

What if Hitchcock's "intrinsic qualities of subject matter, tone and style" were not considered as a determining factor of whether or not his noir prototyping work at Gaumont British and then at various Hollywood studios place his films inside or outside of the noir tradition? Instead what if the possibility of exhibiting such a profoundly personal signature (or the ability to exhibit the mark of an *auteur* inside the studio system) was what was noticed by other Hollywood talent, especially directors and other front-line artists? What if Hitchcock gave audiences and filmmakers not only a series of well-made British films, but a larger creative challenge: what would it take to pursue a similar cinematic approach as Hitchcock, or to even out-Hitchcock Hitchcock? In other words, what if it was that Hitchcock showed other directors how to approach filmmaking with a new vim and vigor, daring other directors to push their creativity and experimentation inside the Hollywood studio system—with each new creator adding their own deft touches and personal signatures? What if it was Hitchcock's mode of production that was *the* decisive factor to the development of film noir in the Hollywood film industry of the 1940s and 1950s? The lessons learned from Hitchcock's approach to filmmaking at Gaumont British might be part of the foundations of film noir in ways that can be widely acknowledged (as in Spicer's mention of "immense contribution") but harder to perceive. This kind of directorial influence might be hard to trace retroactively because it always operated behind the scenes, below the line, and outside the bounds of normal textual analysis in film studies. But what would it mean if Hitchcock's most significant contribution to noir prototypes is that he inspired subsequent creators to take their own personal and particular visual approaches, in a spirit of experimentation, with their own blend of melodrama and comedy, infused with the spirit of the age and responsive to their own lived experiences of a psychologically scarred and existentially vertiginous world? If that was Hitchcock's contribution to the development of film noir, then that creative legacy can be traced back to the pre-noir journey he embarked upon during his time at Gaumont British and the making of the thriller sextet.

Works Cited:

Ackroyd, Peter. *Hitchcock: A Brief Life*. (Doubleday, 2015).

Borde, Raymond and Etienne Chaumeton. *A Panorama of American Film Noir, 1941-1953*. (City Lights Books, 2002).

Hirsch, Foster. *The Dark Side of the Screen: Film Noir*. (Da Capo Press, 1983).

Naremore, James, "Hitchcock at the Margins of Noir," in *Alfred Hitchcock's Centenary Essays*, eds. Richard Allen and S. Ishii Gonzales. (BFI Publishing, 1999).

Naremore, James. *More Than Night: Film Noir in Its Contexts*. (University of California Press, 2008).

Spicer, Andrew. *Historical Dictionary of Film Noir*. (Scarecrow Press, 2010).

Truffaut, Francois. *Hitchcock/Truffaut*. (Simon and Schuster, 1966).

The Face Behind the Mask: Peter Lorre as Janos Szabo.

Noir Revealed: Robert Florey and *The Face Behind the Mask*

James V. D'Arc and Todd Erickson

Variety was unsure how to identify director Robert Florey's *The Face Behind the Mask* in its December, 1940 review just prior to the film's January 1941 theatrical release. It is a mordant tale, as scripted by Allen Vincent and Paul Jarrico, from Thomas Edward O'Connell's play, about Janos Szabo, a hopeful European immigrant, who exudes naiveté and unbounded enthusiasm on his arrival in 1940 Manhattan to begin a new life, but whose face becomes so horribly disfigured in a hotel fire that it subsequently prevents his obtaining much-needed employment. In despair, he is saved from suicide by Dinky, a likeable bum and petty thief who informs Janos of the miracle of plastic surgery. Together—reluctantly on Szabo's part—they embark on a life of crime with a gang that Dinky belongs to in order to pay for Szabo's costly operations. Well into his gangster lifestyle, Szabo and a blind woman accidently meet and soon fall in love with plans to marry but, by film's end, both end up dead.

Florey's direction of this grisly narrative was judged by *Variety's* staff reviewer as "not so much likely to scare audiences as make them a little sick." After his exposure to this trim 69-minute Columbia B picture, the reviewer was struck by a paradox: the acting, story, and production "are all of a fairly high order." Nevertheless, he concluded, "it's all too unpleasant." Even today, this film is little known, having never appeared on home video and only sporadically broadcast on cable television. Yet, its verbal as well as visual articulation of fear, fate, desperation, alienation, duplicity and despair appears well before this now all too familiar shaken-and-stirred cocktail of film noir elements became iconic. That *The Face Behind the Mask* was directed by a man with European origins in birth as well as visual sensibility should not be surprising, but what is noteworthy is its arrival in the American cinema with such flair before more celebrated noir titles made their appearance. From a director who came close to making one of the most iconic horror films and ended up directing one of the better ones, *The Face Behind the Mask* was rated by Florey's biographer as "perhaps even his greatest film."[1]

The Macabre Influence

The Paris-born director was 39 years old when he began work on *The Face Behind the Mask* for Harry Cohn's Poverty Row studio. By that time, Florey had already plied his directing talents in stints with Warner Bros., M-G-M, Universal and Paramount (twice), including a handful of European projects sandwiched in between his return to the United States in 1931. Florey's first two projects at Universal were *Frankenstein* (1931) and *Murders in the Rue Morgue* (1932) and they serve as important reference points regarding his fondness for the macabre. Richard Schayer, head of Universal's story department, was intrigued by Florey's involvement with The Théâtre du Grand-Guignol de Paris, a small theater in Paris known as the "Theater of Horrors" for its graphic and violent melodramas, and approached him about ideas for a new horror film to star Bela Lugosi. They agreed that the "Frankenstein" story was the best option. In developing *Frankenstein,* Florey produced an extraordinarily detailed script that contained over 600 shots with camera angles, special effects even lens specifications. He even came up with the idea for the electrodes on the monster's neck. According to cameraman Paul Ivano, the 20-minute test reel that Florey produced had directors on the lot salivating to make the film themselves. However, the studio's shiny penny British import, James Whale, claimed the coveted assignment and had at his disposal all of Florey's preparatory work.[2]

As a consolation, Carl Laemmle, Jr., *Frankenstein*'s producer gave Florey *Murders in the Rue Morgue* (1932), starring Bela Lugosi, as Dr. Mirakle, the malevolent carnival barker who strives to crossbreed humans with apes. The film's imaginative camerawork and expressionist sets of Paris, its perpetual setting at night and the brooding atmosphere (in spite of the nagging comic relief by Bert Roach) attested to the influence of *The Cabinet of Dr. Caligari* (1920) on Florey's work, as well as having worked as an assistant to Louis Feuillade in southern France early in his career.

The Face Behind the Mask was Florey's first film for Columbia as he worked his way *down* the Hollywood ladder rather than up. However, as we will note, Florey did not hold back on his creativity; rather, he infused this little melodrama with elements that signaled a transition from both the horror film that was perfected in the United States from the mid-1920s through the 1930s, as well as the American gangster film during roughly this same period.

The Horror Film Influence

The American horror film had, by 1941, flourished with the influx of European filmmakers escaping both a worsened economic climate and the rise of Hitler and his targeting of Jews. Curt and Robert Siodmak, Billy Wilder, Fritz Lang, Fred Zinnemann, Rudolph Maté, Curtis Bernhardt, and other directors, writers, cameramen, and set designers brought to American film a European visual look that was palpable, stemming from German Expressionism and a cultural pessimism from the economic devastation and a deterioration of morale following World War I. The poorly managed and economically teetering Universal Pictures found temporary profitability in cornering the horror market with its modestly-budgeted, but highly successful series of horror films that began with *Dracula* and *Frankenstein* (both 1931) and continued with *The Mummy* (1932), *The Invisible Man* (1933), *The Werewolf of London* (1935) and their many derivatives. These forays into the macabre mushroomed during the pre-Code era, but just a few years later, after the enforcement of the Production Code, they were heavily circumscribed and faced severe censorship in Great Britain. Despite increased scrutiny from the Hays Office, *The Bride of Frankenstein* (1935), *The Invisible Ray* (1936), *Son of Frankenstein* (1939), *The Wolf Man* (1941) and numerous sequels continued to provide reliable profitability to the San Fernando Valley-based studio even as the Laemmles lost control of their organization.

In *The Face Behind the Mask,* Florey flirts with standard horror conventions limned out by films made by Universal and others, from Poverty Row to the Big Five. This perhaps explains the consternation experienced in print by *Variety's* reviewer presuming that this was intended as a horror film, but then, in another sense, was not. It was something more sickening than scary. If despair and tragedy, told in the graphic terms that Florey chose to show it in this modestly-budgeted film can be otherwise described as "sick," his Janos Szabo character was more immediately horrifying as a human being who had *become* a monster by choices made to conceal this "other" Janos behind a very real mask.

Audiences of the 1930s who were familiar with monsters—whether created, as in *Frankenstein,* from sundry body parts or, as in *The Werewolf of London,* from a transformation arising from a curse—as threatening, hideous-looking beings, were treated by Florey to a new type of "monster," borne out of Szabos' own moral choice. He was identified from the film's early moments as honest and highly skilled (watchmaker, aircraft technician, pilot), who found stealing repugnant. His choice of a life of crime with

Right, an exaggerated, Expressionistic look from Lorre as Janos Szabo. Opposite page: Lugosi to Karloff in *The Raven:* "Maybe if a man looks ugly, he does ugly things."

Dinky, and then becoming a member and eventual leader of a gang, while stemming from a forgivable, if still wrong-headed, motive to change his appearance, prefigures his tragic end. In fact, his disturbing facial appearance not only was highly offensive to others, but the film seemed to confirm that it was a significant influence on Szabos' own perceptions of himself, as he reveals to the blind woman, Helen, shortly before they become engaged ("I was an outcast, so I did things I should not have done."). The motivation to accumulate money so he can repair his face leads Janos to crimes from which he can never turn back and spells tragedy for both himself and the woman he was to marry. This would become a staple noir sensibility, not frequented in the mainstream horror genre at the time. However, the notion that ugliness in physical form makes ugliness in motivation was explicitly explored in one of Universal's better horror films of the 1930s, Louis Friedlander's *The Raven* (1935), starring the "twin titans of horror," as studio publicity billed its stars, Boris Karloff and Bela Lugosi.

In *The Raven,* Friedlander (better known as Lew Landers after this film) seized on an intriguing aspect of horror that saw a talented but unscrupulous physician, Dr. Richard Vollin (Bela Lugosi), using the plea of escaped convict Edward Bateman (Boris Karloff) to change his facial appearance though plastic surgery to avoid recognition and his capture by police. Bateman remarks to Vollin on his own unattractiveness as a possible factor that contributed to his life of crime: "Maybe if a man looks ugly, he does ugly things." To which Vollin, in astonishment, replies, "You are saying something profound." Vollin performs the surgery, but when Bateman sees himself in the mirror following the surgery he does not see the face of a normal man looking back at him, but one with a pronounced, drooping eye and mouth. Bateman rages at Vollin for doing such a horrible thing to him and unleashes a guttural roar that is reminiscent of Karloff's performance as the Frankenstein monster four years earlier. "Your monstrous ugliness breeds monstrous hate!" declares an obviously pleased Vollin. "Good! I can use your hate." Vollin promises Bateman that he will alter his disfigured face to a normal one, but only when he consents to murdering his houseguest, Judge Thatcher, the father of the woman he loves, who forbids the mad doctor's marriage to his daughter. However, that is as far as Friedlander and screenwriter David Boehm take this point. Florey takes this horror-based notion, develops it, and, indeed, makes it the "profound" centerpiece of Szabo's fatalism that leads to his death and almost everyone in his sphere. A device used in horror film—entrapment and blackmail—becomes, in Florey's vision, a skillfully saturated atmosphere of doom.

Above, foreshadowing the gangster's milieu.

The Gangster Film Influence

The other standard element in *The Face Behind the Mask* that drives the narrative, and was certainly common during the time that Florey's little film was made, was gangsterism. Hollywood's—and America's—uneasy fascination with both the attraction and revulsion to a cocky, successful hoodlum began in the crime-ridden era of Prohibition during the 1920s and continued through the 1930s. With *Underworld* (Paramount, 1927), *Little Caesar* (Warners, 1930), and *Scarface* (Caddo/UA, 1932), Josef von Sternberg, Mervyn Le Roy and Howard Hawks respectively established the archetypal gangster protagonist who rises from the mean streets of an economically oppressive metropolis as a small-time hood and, fueled with an uncontrollable ambition, strives to topple the mob boss. His motivation is typically the accoutrements of success: money, women (though rarely romantic attachments, recognizing them only as an important accessory), and status. Even in pre-Code years, von Sternberg's "Bull Weed," Le Roy's "Caesar Enrico Bandello" and Hawks' "Tony Camonte" lived out their unbridled aggrandizement of material wealth to their tragic ends. Acquisitiveness in these three films as well as others like *The Public Enemy, G-Men, Angels with Dirty Faces,* and *The Roaring Twenties* was confirmed as one of the pillars of the American dream, notwithstanding gangsters accumulated their wealth through violence, force, and theft. After being riddled by police machine gun fire at the film's climax, Little Caesar (Edward G. Robinson in his star-making vehicle), registers genuine surprise to actually reaching the limit of his criminal success as he gasps, "Is this the end of Rico?" The message of these films and dozens of others from the major studios during the 1930s became clear: the gangster was the flip side of the American dream, a nightmare vision of the Horatio Alger myth of starting at the bottom and working one's way up to success.

In *The Face Behind the Mask,* Janos Szabo's orientation to American criminal conduct began within minutes of his arrival in New York City. After seeking the assistance of a sympathetic plain-clothes detective, Lt. O'Hara (Don Beddoe), thinking that he had been robbed of his money, Szabo excitedly tells the lawman that he had been "gangstered," only to discover shortly thereafter through

Below, hopeful in a new country: a new friend, a new job, a new place to live.

the detective's questioning that he had not been robbed at all, but had forgotten that he had hidden his meager fortune in his clothing. In rushing to such a conclusion, might Szabo have been conditioned by what he had read in the newspapers in his native Hungary, or had seen in American gangster movies? Certainly, lawless conduct on the scale practiced by mobs or crime syndicates was not limited to the United States, but it was definitely enshrined to the extent it was both celebrated and scorned in American gangster films screening worldwide.

Above, Janos' inferno.

Following the hotel fire that drove him from his lodging, a dejected, hopeless Szabo, whose hideous face repels nearly all who meet him, wanders onto a lonely dockside pier late at night, presumably to throw himself into the waters of the East River. He is asked by an elderly man of means to light a cigarette, but at the sight of Szabo's disfigured visage, registers shock, drops his wallet, and abruptly scurries away. It is at that moment the down-on-his-luck dock urchin Dinky (George E. Stone) comes out of the shadows to retrieve the man's wallet. Dinky comes across as a small time grifter who robs only to make ends meet following a string of bad breaks that brought him to his hand-to-mouth existence ("I tried to go straight six or seven times, but something always went wrong—something happened."). Of greater importance to the story, Dinky is not repulsed by Janos' appearance and the two find much-needed companionship with Janos attending to the tubercular-like coughing Dinky and, in turn, Dinky's success in lifting Janos' downcast spirit, by telling his new friend that he can "buy a new face" through the artistry of plastic surgery. Dinky even dubs Janos with a new name ("Johnny"), and tells him it will take a sizable bankroll to accomplish the transformation: "You can buy anything with money."

After spending a night in a junkyard, the two use the limited funds from the stolen wallet to stay in a succession of flop houses. Dinky is contacted by a former gang confederate who wants him to make a heist. However, he is too ill to follow through on the job and, out of sympathy for his valued friend, but against his principled instincts, ("You can't do wrong and find happiness in life"), Janos volunteers to do the job himself.

Following the successful robbery, the two gang members locate Dinky and Janos in a hotel to get their cut of the take, only to learn that it was Janos and not Dinky who pulled the heist. Janos is immediately inducted into the gang, whose nominal head, Jeff Jeffries (James Seay), is soon to be released from a prison stretch. With money from a string of robberies, Janos consults a plastic surgeon's assistant who creates a mask based on Szabo's passport photograph to conceal his disfigurement. As he makes clear to Dinky, the *only* reason that he continued his uncharacteristic life of crime was to get a new face and to become respectable by gaining employment in a decent job. ("I had only

Below, a contrast in reactions from the hospital (left) to Dinky (right).

one goal – to get money and to get it fast."). So successful was the gang under Janos' guidance in plotting and executing a series of heists, that he becomes its leader and thwarts an attempt by the newly-released Jeffries to regain his former position with the mob.

During a visit to the plastic surgeon, Janos is told that his face has become irreparably damaged from the hotel fire. He would only have the mask to hide behind for the rest of his life. Preoccupied with the bad news as he exits the doctor's office, Janos bumps into Helen (Evelyn Keyes), causing her to spill a box of costume jewelry onto the sidewalk. After angrily reproving her to "watch where you are going," he quickly realizes that Helen is completely blind. His native compassion that was evident in his first meeting with Dinky returns and he volunteers to accompany Helen to her apartment. There, he finds himself attracted to the uncomplicated, pretty, upbeat woman who, he is told, has been blind from childhood, and makes a modest living stringing beads into necklaces for local stores. She invokes memories of Janos's Hungarian fiancé, Maria, whom he planned to bring to America and marry until his accident compelled him to end their engagement. Janos becomes protective of Helen and commits to getting enough money to pay for an operation to restore her sight.

Above, gang boss Jeffries says to Janos/Johnny: "You're just as false as that face and you know it."
Below, three images as Janos finds refuge from the city and hope for a new life.

Following his confession to Helen of his disfigurement from the hotel fire, his meeting with Dinky and subsequent gangster activities, Janos announces to the mob his intention to retire and return the gang leadership to Jeffries, who, with the others, have come to rely on Janos' brilliance and success as their boss. Jeffries is suspicious that Janos' motive for exiting the gang is not purely personal, and his concerns appear to be justified when, rifling through Janos' desk, he discovers Lt. O'Hara's business card with an ambiguous note on the back ("Please call me when OK") that O'Hara had left with a nurse at the hospital after the fire. He wrongly surmises that Janos' clean break from his partners in crime was

to rat them out to the police and, owing to his apparent cozy relationship with O'Hara, escape the consequences of his ill-gotten fortune. In retaliation, Jeffries and his gang track down Janos at the new country home he has purchased for Helen and himself and plant a bomb in their car that will detonate when the dashboard radio is turned on. The mob had tortured Janos' location out of Dinky, whom they thought had been fatally shot and dumped beside the road before arriving at Szabo's country residence.

Seriously wounded, but not dead, Dinky manages to limp to a gas station where he contacts Janos by telephone to warn him of the car bomb. However, Janos arrives too late to warn Helen who is already in the car, and following the explosion she dies in his arms. After getting Dinky medical treatment and learning of Jeffries' plans, Janos promises his loyal friend that he will be taken care of, as he departs to intercept the gang before they escape to Mexico.

Above, Florey's mise-en-scène and extreme camera angles punctuate Janos' decision to quit the life of crime. Below, no escape, paradise becomes prison.

An airplane and a pilot are hired only to discover on landing in the desert, well short of their escape destination, that the pilot is Janos! He knows that none of them can fly a plane, that they are out of fuel and miles away from civilization. Janos welcomes the quick death their bullets would provide, but they can't risk killing him, despite his taunting, "Go ahead, it won't hurt as much as being alive, surrounded by my treacherous friends. Then I won't have to wait as long as you."

One by one, each admits the futility of escape. An insert montage shows the grains of sand diminishing in an hour glass as it dissolves to a shot of a search plane carrying the owner of the missing airplane and Lt. O'Hara. After discovering that every member of the gang had expired not far from the aircraft, Lt. O'Hara eventually comes to find Janos' dead body strapped to the strut of the plane's landing gear where Jeffries and the others had restrained him. A note on Janos' body, addressed to O'Hara, reveals both his plan to eliminate Jeffries and the mob, and a $5 bill to repay the gift the kindly detective had left with a hospital nurse to give to the "hopeful" little man during his recovery.

Unlike the perverse hoodlums lionized and then taught a socially-appropriate lesson in dozens of successful gangster films during the era in which *The Face Behind the Mask* was made, Janos' singular motivation for his life of crime is associated with respectability (to make his face

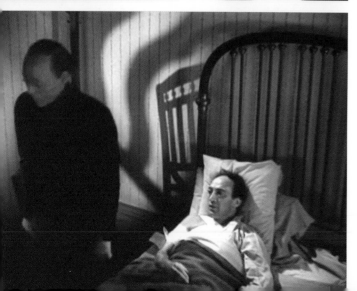

normal in order to gain honest employment and, later, to marry Helen), and not status, power, or unbridled greed. Florey takes an otherwise routine gangster plot and uses it to dramatize the conflicts of an essentially good man gone wrong who, out of necessity during the working out of these conflicts, must conceal himself from others. It is Janos' inherent goodness, therefore, that results in the death of his criminal associates as well as, in practical terms, his own suicide. The tragedy of Szabos' belated awareness of how far he had gone in his illicit activities and recognizing where they *must* lead—doomed self-sacrifice—is the essence of what would later become a foundational concept embodied in film noir.

The Lorre Influence

The suitability of Peter Lorre's casting by fellow European Florey in *The Face Behind the Mask* should be noted before concluding our analysis of this film. Like the character of Janos Szabo, Lorre (1904-1964) was born in Hungary and became an itinerant actor in Europe before his breakthrough role as the child molester in Fritz Lang's *M* (Ufa, 1931). Escaping Hitler's rise to power, he came to America where he proved that he could be an effective protagonist on both sides of the law, as crime boss Abbott in Alfred Hitchcock's *The Man Who Knew Too Much* (Gaumont-British, 1934) and as the obsessed Dr. Gogol in *Mad Love* (M-G-M, 1935); then, successfully interpreting the role of the Japanese insurance investigator, Mr. Moto, in the popular series of eight films made by 20th Century-Fox, from 1937 to 1939. He subsequently became a morally compromised companion to the equally shady Sydney Greenstreet in a number of mysteries made by Warner Bros. in the 1940s. No doubt Florey knew of Lorre's disturbing performance in the title role of a minor RKO programmer, *The Stranger on the Third Floor*, directed by Boris Ingster and released in August, 1940, just before production began that fall on *The Face Behind the Mask*. The hallucinatory dream sequences in Ingster's film, coupled with Nicholas Musuraca's dazzling chiaroscuro cinematography, has often been identified as a *bona fide* precursor of film noir.

The Florey Influence

It is clear to us that *The Face Behind the Mask* should be recognized as an essential precursor that anticipated the film noir movement. Robert Florey, in this important transitional film, utilized familiar conventions that had for more than a decade been pre-sold to audiences of both horror films and gangster dramas, and he infused the narrative with an arc of optimism that ended in doom. Throughout the plot elements in between, fate (trapped in a hotel fire, meeting Helen), deception (the mask, both physical and psychological), the contrast of the corruption of the City and the tranquil innocence of the Country (the hotel fire and mob activities in the city, Janos and Helen's home in rural New York), and doom (too deep into adverse behavior to escape its consequences)—just to name a few—are expressed in such a manner as to presage motion pictures that would enshrine these qualities. Revealed now in hindsight *The Face Behind the Mask* is one of those significant "little" films that marked a quick dissolve to the breed of films that would reflect America's changing culture, and the acceptance of noir as popular—albeit unsettling—entertainment.

Opposite three images, The stylistics of Expressionism: distorted shapes and exaggerated shadows. At right, Janos tells the gang of their doom and accepts his fate with the dismissive comment: "Your little brains are turning round and round in circles looking for a way out."

Notes

1. Taves, Brian. *Robert Florey, The French Expressionist.* (Oklahoma: Bear Manor Media, 2014), p. 231.
2. Taves, pp. 124-127.

Crime and Punishment—the Mother of All Noir

James Ursini

> Pain and suffering are always inevitable for a large intelligence and a deep heart. The really great men must, I think, have great sadness on earth.
>
> Fyodor Dostoevsky
> *Crime and Punishment*

Fyodor Dostoevsky published his landmark novel *Crime and Punishment* in 1866. Drawing on his own existential angst as a young intellectual and his experience of redemption in a Siberian prison camp (he was sent there for revolutionary "activity"), the work is considered one of the most influential novels in world literature. For the purposes of this article, I will concentrate on its profound effect on film noir by examining the archetypes, motifs, and themes of the novel and how those elements are exemplified through five adaptations of the novel itself: three protonoirs, one classic noir, and one neo-noir.

Film Noir Archetypes

The anti-hero: the protagonist of Dostoevsky's novel is the student Raskolnikov. He struggles with poverty, illness, and delusions of grandeur. He is alienated from his family and his few friends. He is haunted by a repressed compassion for "les miserables" around him coupled with a sense that he is superior to them all. Writing articles about what the German philosopher Nietzsche would later call the "ubermensch" (superman), Raskolnikov begins to believe that he is one these "extraordinary" individuals who are exempt from bourgeois rules of right and wrong. Acting on his beliefs, he murders an avaricious pawnbroker (along with her innocent sister). Racked by guilt and fear of detection, he searches for answers to his existential dilemma and finds it in the arms of a saintly prostitute.

Opposite, Peter Lorre as Raskolnikov with his painting of Napoleon. Clockwise from left, a gallery of existential angst: Vincent Kartheiser; Burt Lancaster (in *The Killers*); Gregori Chmara; George Hamilton; Tom Neal (in *Detour*); and Pierre Blanchar.

Proto-femme fatale Marian Marsh as
Sonya in 1935. Opposite, new genera-
tions: Mary Murphy (right) as Sally in
Crime and Punishment USA and
Monica Keena as Roseanne in *Crime +
Punishment in Suburbia.*

The sly detective: Raskolnikov finds his match in the person of the police inspector Porfiry Petrovich. Porfiry keeps his suspects off guard by pretending to be friendly and to lack true understanding. He however suspects Raskolnikov as soon as he faints at the police station. He never has enough hard evidence but knows that Raskolnikov's guilty conscience will bring him to confession. He is the forerunner of so many noir detectives from Hammett's Spade, through Chandler's Marlowe, to TV's Columbo.

The good bad girl: Sonya is a teenage prostitute, the sole support of her parents and siblings. Sacrificing herself for them, she still maintains a sense of integrity and a deep spirituality which appeals to the conflicted Raskolnikov. She is the main impetus behind Raskolnikov's surrender (falling down in the middle of the city and confessing as he kisses the ground as Sonya had demanded). She follows him to Siberia. Sonya is a version of the much misunderstood femme fatale who populates such noir films as *Gilda* and *The Postman Always Rings Twice*.

Film Noir Motifs

The urban jungle: St. Petersburg in the 19th century is an analog for the modern "naked cities" of film noir. It is bustling, noisy, teeming with desperation as well as ravaged by pockets of poverty. Raskolnikov's world is one of cramped, dingy apartments, bars frequented by alcoholics like Sonya's father, streets filled prostitutes and customers, and bridges from which young women jump.

Claustrophobia and darkness: the novel features a plethora of night scenes as Raskolnikov wanders the streets, lost in his tormenting and often contradictory thoughts (which although in third person point of view are an analog for the first person narrations of many film noirs). He darts in and

out of alleys as he escapes from the scene of his crime. He encounters figures in the darkness who seem to accuse him of "murder."

Film Noir Themes

Existentialism: even though *Crime and Punishment* predates the naming of "existentialism," it is considered one the best exemplifications of this philosophy. The first half of the novel revolves around Raskolnikov's stream of consciousness as he tries to give meaning to his depressing, poverty-ridden existence. He finds solace in the concept of the "extraordinary man" and his mission to exert his will and thereby change the world around him (e.g.,murdering the pawnbroker to end his poverty as well as rid the world of an "insect," as he calls her).

Redemption: Sonya incarnates the theme of redemption. She is a source of wonder to Raskolnikov because she combines a child-like innocence with a sensuality which causes Raskolnikov to fall to his knees before her and kiss her feet even as he berates her for selling herself. Noir protagonists are often seeking redemption and finding it at times in the arms of a female savior, if only temporarily, as Jeff Bailey does in *Out of the Past*.

Violence and Crime: the murder of the pawnbroker and her sister is particularly graphic and bloody as is the "dream" Raskolnikov relates in which a horse is beaten to death in the streets. The potential for violence lurks around every corner whether it is the accident in the street that kills Sonya's father, suicides including that of the pedophile Svidrigailov, or random beatings. It is an explosive milieu like those environments which permeate most film noirs.

"Perverse" Sexuality and Obsession: The character of Svidrigailov who becomes a major figure in the last quarter of the novel acts as a dark doppelganger for Raskolnikov—a reflection of what he might have become without Sonya. Svidrigailov is a pedophile who is responsible for the suicide of a servant girl he has molested and is obsessed with Raskolnikov's sister, an obsession developed when she was a teenager. He tries to blackmail her into returning to him. When she refuses and tries to shoot him, he falls into depression and commits suicide. Film noir often restricted by the production code of its time has traveled the road of non-conformist sexuality and obsession with films like *The Killers, Criss Cross, The Lodger,* and *The Locket.*

Unlike Al Roberts in *Detour* or the Swede in *The Killers,* Jeff Bailey (Robert Mitchum) does find a redemptive woman (Virginia Huston) in *Out of the Past* but not even that can save him.

The Films: *Raskolnikow* (1923)

Writer-director Robert Wiene, who was responsible for one of the most important films in the German Expressionist film movement—*The Cabinet of Dr. Caligari* (1920), put together a largely Russian cast and adapted *Crime and Punishment* under the title *Raskolnikow* (1923). The film follows the story's outline fairly closely but through an expressionist lens. Much like *Caligari,* Wiene creates a distorted nightmarish world filled with canted angles, low ceilings, slanted walls (see frame at right), and chiaroscuro lighting—all of which became a major influence on film noir.

The expressionist mode is particularly apt for this story as it allows the director, who does not have the option of dialogue or narration other than in periodic title cards, to externalize the mind of Dostoevsky's tormented anti-hero. Wiene opens on Raskolnikov's cramped garret. The ceiling seems to force him to sit hunched over, the slashes of light through the off-center window cuts into his environment. In the first tight close-up of his face, the audience sees a visage marked by lines of worry (see frame below), eyes enlarged, almost bulging, features distorted by angst. Even when Raskolnikov exits his tenement apartment building, he is still not free of his environment as the buildings seem almost ready to topple onto him.

Wiene further enhances this externalization of Raskolnikov's anxiety in several dream sequences original to the film. A random bystander comes out of the darkness to accuse Raskolnikov of murdering the pawnbroker and her sister (from the book) but in Wiene's adaptation the accuser appears to him as a guide in his dream, leading him back to the scene of his murder where he attempts to repeat the murder of the insect-like pawnbroker. But in his guilt-ridden dream she is invulnerable, her face superimposed multiple times on the space before him as he attempts to strike her down with his axe.

The good/bad girl of the piece, Sonya, is the weakest element in this adaptation. The actor playing her is far too mature to effectively capture her combination of innocence and sensuality. In addition the detective-inspector who hounds Raskolnikov is played in the film with far less self-dep-

recating humor and more menace. As he sits in front of his spider web-style windows (painted on as are so many of the windows, giving the sets an even more two-dimensional and claustrophobic mood), the detective seems far more interested in simply harassing Raskolnikov than trapping the guilt-ridden suspect.

Opposite, top: Marian Marsh makes Sonya a true ingenue, who captures the affection of Peter Lorre as a manic depressive Raskolnikov. Bottom, Raskolnikov fairly cringes in the presence of Edward Arnold as the portly Porfiry.

Crime and Punishment (1935)

The illustrious director Josef von Sternberg found himself on hard times after losing the object of his obsession in life and in film—Marlene Dietrich. Having helped to develop her decadent, glamorous femme fatale persona on screen in films like *The Blue Angel* (1930), *Morocco* (1930), and *Blonde Venus* (1932), the two separated artistically and personally after the quasi-autobiographical *The Devil Is a Woman* (1935). While Dietrich went on to a lengthy career, the temperamental von Sternberg stumbled from project to project and studio to studio, often taking on projects that he did not initiate. *Crime and Punishment* was such a project.

Shot at the minor major studio Columbia Pictures, von Sternberg reportedly had little say in either the script or the casting of the film. But as the director would show over and over in noir films like *The Shanghai Gesture* (1941) and *Macao* (1952), von Sternberg still attempted to elevate the project by his masterly use of visual style.

Crime and Punishment opens on a sort of prologue (not in the novel) which shows Raskolnikov graduating from the university. A pompous president lectures the students about their promising future and the importance of ideals. The film intercuts between the president's radiant face and a group of graduates standing in front of a gray blank wall, their faces and figures covered by dark shadows. In this manner von Sternberg contrasts the platitudes of the speaker with a visualization of the fears and misgivings of the group of graduates. Presently the president calls up Raskolnikov and extends his praise to him personally. The prologue continues as Raskolnikov shakes off his depression and roughhouses gleefully with his best friend, his sister, and mother. In all this Raskolnikov's mood is far more jovial than Dostoevsky's protagonist.

This ironic, almost comic tone on the part of von Sternberg's Raskolnikov extends even beyond the prologue. Peter Lorre as Raskolnikov does not neglect the deep depressions of the bipolar protagonist but pushes the limits of his more manic moments by treating the audience to buffoonish imitations of his hero Napoleon, whose picture hangs above his bed, including his hand-in-coat poses and hair-do, as well as his merciless mocking and physical stunts, such as a slapstick hat routine, when dealing with his sister's pretentious fiancé.

As one would expect from such a female-centered director as von Sternberg, the director's Sonya comes closer to Dostoevsky's original than Wiene's version of the teenage prostitute. The director has costumed and coiffed the actor (Marian Marsh) to resemble Dietrich. He also treats her to luminous close-ups which emphasize her innocence (her child-like voice helps in conveying this) but also suggest an alluring sensuality which edges her into the femme fatale category. At the same time, this Sonya has a redemptive quality. "I forgot that there was still some kindness in the world," she remarks early on to Raskolnikov, "Thank you." His counter observation—"I forgot there was still some beauty in it"—reflects the fact that his initial attraction to her is physical; but it is Sonya's faith that later holds him back from the brink of complete existential despair. In a scene where she proffers a Bible and recalls the raising of Lazarus, Sonya will not descend into the self-pity Raskolnikov embraces with his comment "What have you or I to hope for out of life?" Her defiant reply is "Don't take away my faith. I need it!"

Von Sternberg also effectively portrays the angst-filled cat-and-mouse play between Raskolnikov and Inspector Porfiry (Edward Arnold). Unlike Wiene's inspector, Arnold's Porfiry plays up the self-deprecating façade the inspector-detective uses to put Raskolnikov off balance. When Raskolnikov finally confesses in the inspector's office, Porfiry accepts him graciously as the Imperial Orthodox cross on Porfiry's desk casts a shadow on the figure of the redeemed Raskolnikov.

Crime et Châtiment (1935)

Pierre Chenal's adaptation, released in France the same year as von Sternberg's film, is part of the French Poetic Realist movement of the 1930s (*Le jour se leve, La bete humaine*, etc.), a movement which greatly influenced American film noir. In fact, Chenal made yet another landmark film in the poetic realist mode, *Le dernier tournant* (1939), an unauthorized adaptation of James M. Cain's noir novel *The Postman Always Rings Twice*.

Chenal effectively conveys the dark mood of the novel with shadowy interiors and exteriors like the films before it. The film also boasts two powerful performances in Harry Baur's Inspector Porphyre and Pierre Blanchar's Raskolnikov. Their battle of wits and nerves dominates the film, leaving little room for the relationship between Raskolnikov and Sonya, his savior.

Crime and Punishment U.S.A. (1959)

A unique adaptation of the novel from the classic period of film noir. Updated to the present day (1959) writer Walter Newman (*Ace in the Hole, The Man with the Golden Arm*, etc.), co-directors (and brothers) Denis and Terry Sanders (known for documentary work), and cinematographer Floyd Crosby (who worked with the great expressionist director F.W. Murnau on *Tabu* in 1931 and with Roger Corman on his series of Edgar Allan Poe adaptations in the 1960s) collaborated on a low-budget but highly literate noir adaptation of Dostoevsky's novel.

The film opens, in the tradition of many noir films, in media res. Sirens sound on the track and a police radio dispatch reverberates as the camera tracks away from an apartment building and a group of police to center on the figure of Robert Cole (George Hamilton) walking away in a daze, and then falling to the ground in a swoon. Considering the period and the setting—Venice-Santa Monica, a center of beat culture in the 1950s—the film then introduces its effectively appropriate jazz score.

Crime et châtiment: Pierre Blanchar as Raskolnikov and Madeleine Ozeray as Sonia.

Left, Toni Merrill as Mrs. Cole and the newspaper and bottom George Hamilton as Bob Cole with Mary Murphy in a thread-bare local diner. Such images epitomize the docu-noir style of directors Denis and Terry Sanders and cinematographer Crosby that resembles the contemporary features of Samuel Fuller.

A helicopter shot introduces the audience to Southern California as it flies by the Santa Monica pier and the boardwalk strip extending from Santa Monica to Venice. As in the rest of the film Crosby's photography is crisp, filled with noirish shadows even in the midst of fabled California sunshine.

The sequence ends on an interior of Bob's cramped studio apartment where our anti-hero hides himself from the world he is alienated from. Hamilton plays the Raskolnikov character with an arrogance much closer to Dostoevksy's original, to the belief that "an 'extraordinary' man has the right...to decide in his own conscience to overstep... certain obstacles." In that sense he is as close to the characters inspired by the actions of Leopold and Loeb that were dramatized in *Rope* (1948) and *Compulsion* (1959) as the cinematic predecessors in this survey. He rudely rejects the help of his friend and a doctor. He keeps his sister and mother at a distance. When he encounters the Sonya analog in the movie, the prostitute Sally—played with a world-weary cynicism and sensuality by Mary Murphy, who in John Payne's *Hell's Island* (1955) incarnated one of the noir's most powerful femme fatales— Bob, although attracted to her, mocks her spiritual readings (Kahlil Gibran, popular during that period among New Age adherents) and throws her poetry at her, demanding that she read it. Sally holds her own, accusing him of "getting his kicks" from abuse, a criticism which hits home.

Chastened by Sally, the morose Bob returns to his wanderings at night: at the pier framed by the flashing lights of the pier roller coaster, "sleepwalking" into alleys, sitting in all-night diners, nervously tapping a beat on his coffee cup, and playing the cat-and-mouse game with the detective character (played with great subtlety by veteran actor Frank Silvera, pictured above questioning Cole).

Crime + Punishment in Suburbia (2000)

Like many neo-noirs of the new millennium, this film grafts the conventions of film noir onto a distinctly post-modern sensibility, that is, a heightened sense of irony, multiple perspectives, and pop culture references. The filmmakers have fractured the points of view in the novel through several methods. First of all, they have created two major noir protagonists, the teenagers Vincent and Roseanne, both of whom incarnate characteristics of Raskolnikov and Sonya, although by the time of the murder, it is clear that Roseanne has fully taken on the role of Raskolnikov and Vincent the role of Sonya, in a very post-modern bit of gender-reversal.

Vincent (Vincent Kartheiser) begins as the first-person narrator of the piece. He is a "goth boy" outsider obsessed with a beautiful, sexually alluring cheerleader—Roseanne Skolnick (Monica

Crime + Punishment in Suburbia: after leaving prison, Roseanne Skolnick (Monica Keena) rides off "into the sunset" with Vincent (Vincent Kartheiser). Opposite, Roseanne with boyfriend Jimmy (James DeBello).

Keena). He stalks her, taking photos of her from a distance as she frustrates boys with her revealing outfits and taunts her "jock" boyfriend with promises of sexual privileges. While Vincent tattoos nihilist sayings like "por nada" ("for nothing") on his body, Roseanne lives her "mean girl" life at the local suburban high school. But as Vincent learns, Roseanne's life at home is not quite as "bright and sunny" as it is at school.

Like Sonya Roseanne has an abusive, alcoholic father figure and an angry, disillusioned mother. As her parents fight, Roseanne retreats into her books and expresses her anger by stabbing her stuffed animals. The situation worsens when her mother begins an affair with a younger man. In a drunken fit, Roseanne's stepfather rapes her. After this heinous act, Roseanne's world spins out of control. In role reversal, she shifts into a Raskolnikov mind-set, which leaves the love-struck Vincent to assume the redemptive posture of Sonya.

Roseanne enlists her dense boyfriend to help her murder her stepfather, which is seen in graphic detail (like the book and unlike the other movies in this survey). Before and after the murder, the filmmakers intercut images of a nearby forest fire and the orgiastic high school homecoming ceremony to enhance the dark violent mood. After the murder, Roseanne sinks further and further into depression, especially when her mother is arrested as a suspect in the murder. (The first-person narration here also begins to gradually shift to Roseanne's point of view.) Ultimately, she turns to Vincent who gives her spiritual advice and offers himself as a victim to her, his arms stretched out like Christ on the cross.

Eventually, Roseanne confesses and is put in prison. Again, unlike the other films in this survey, the film follows the Raskolnikov character all the way to her redemption. Seen in slow motion, wandering like a zombie in her orange jumpsuit, Roseanne becomes mute, wondering why Vincent no longer visits her. But like Dostoevsky's Sonya, he does return, this time wearing a t-shirt with an image of Christ.

The final shots of the movie are of a squeaky clean Roseanne leaving prison, smiling as she sees Vincent gallantly waiting for her on his motorcycle. As they speed off down the road, Roseanne tightens her grip on her savior.

Expressionistic low-light and horizontal shadows in a posed shot of Jane Bryan as Peggy and George Raft as Cliff Taylor, an ex-con trying to avoid recidivism in *Invisible Stripes*.

The Gangster in Film Noir

Alain Silver

This article revisits the central idea in the most recent version of "The Gangster <u>and</u> Film Noir" in *Film Noir Light and Shadow:* that the style and substance of the gangster film in the late 1920s and early 1930s are essential parts of the cinematic line leading to the noir cycle. In the process of transforming several genres of fiction into a movement such as film noir, icons and characters mutate. Instead of tommy-guns blazing out of car windows, discrete gats are concealed under double-breasted suits. Molls wearing diamonds and furs to the speakeasy are succeeded by femme fatales crooning love songs in smoky nightclubs. But the male protagonists of the pre-noir gangster film and many of those in the noir movement have the same character core: men driven to success and capable of extortion, larceny or even murder to achieve it. If one defines gangsters simply as criminals allied with others of like mind and intention—as opposed to the more complex structure of a Mafia-style group—then a movement as rife with criminal enterprise as film noir must also be full of gangsters. In noir, however, many if not most of the gangs are ad hoc: small, one-project entities put together with a mind to the requirements of the enterprise at hand. Films such as *The Killers* (1946), *The Asphalt Jungle* (1950) or *The Killing* (1956) are typical. Writers, producers, directors, cinematographers, and actors who began their association with criminal narratives in the gangster genre continued to work in that vein as they brought the gangster archtetype into classic-period film noir.

The ad-hoc gang in *The Asphalt Jungle*: from left, Sam Jaffe as Doc Riedenschneider, Sterling Hayden as Dix Handley, Anthony Caruso as Louis Ciavelli, and James Whitmore as Gus Minissi.

Classic period portrayals derived from gangster prototypes include Alan Ladd as Raven (above) in *This Gun for Hire* and Barry Sullivan as the scarred Shubunka in *The Gangster* (above center).

The gangster archetype that originated in the United States with the titled-character performances of Paul Muni as Scarface (opposite, top right) and Edward G. Robinson as Little Caesar (bottom left) spread across both oceans to be channeled by Japan's Joki Oka (with Kinuyo Tanaka, opposite top left) in *Dragnet Girl* (1933) and Britain's Esmond Knight (below right) in *Crime Unlimited* (1935) and John Mills (bottom left with René Ray) in *The Green Cockatoo* (1937). It continued postwar with Richard Attenborough as Pinkie (below, with Carol Marsh) in the 1947 adaptation of Graham Greene's *Brighton Rock*.

The influence of the gangster film on the noir style is arguably more comprehensive that any other antecedent genre of movement. Noir is rife with faces and places taken from the characters and decor of the antedecent genre. The explicit gangster figures, are mostly antagonists to the alienated detectives or federal agents in pictures that range from *The Glass Key* (1942), *The Big Sleep* (1946), and *T-Men* (1948) to *The Big Heat* (1953), *The Big Combo,* and even *Kiss Me Deadly* (both 1955), by which time such low-rent goons Sugar Smallhouse and Charlie Max, incarnated by Jack Lambert and Jack Elam, become postwar semi-parodies in name and action of syndicate hard guys. Often the gangster himself, from small time gambler to hit-man to syndicate mouthpiece, is the principal of the noir narrative: *This Gun for Hire* (1942), *Nobody Lives Forever* (1946), *The Gangster* (1947), *Force of Evil* (1948), *White Heat* (1949), *Kiss Tomorrow Goodbye* (1950), *Night and the City* (1950). The supporting peformances of Kirk Douglas as the smooth, well-groomed small timer in both *Out of the Past* (1947 and *I Walk Alone* (1949) derive directly from the often misguided sartorial preoccupations of Rico Bandello in *Little Caesar* (1931) and Tony Camonte in *Scarface* (1932) that quickly evolved into Clark Gable as the dapper "Blackie" Gallagher in 1934's *Manhattan Melodrama.*

Opposite, top left, Rico poses proudly in his new three-piece suit in *Little Caesar.* Bottom right, Clark Gable as Blackie Gallagher, who often sports a tuxedo in *Manhattan Melodrama.* Bottom left, even while pulling a job with Burt Lancaster's Frank Madison, Douglas' Noll Turner in *I Walk Alone* channels Whit. Top right, even in a tight spot, Noll is poised and never rumpled.
Below, Kirk Douglas (left) as gangster Whit Sterling poses with smiling confidence next to Robert Mitchum as P.I. Jeff Bailey whose usual garb is a rumpled overcoat.

Whereas the dapper but tough George Raft, with Muni in *Scarface* (above right) and Humphrey Bogart in *Invisible Strips* (opposite page) continued to be cast in the same roles crossing over into film noir, Bogart's more accessible figure evolved from gunsels, most notably as Duke Mantee (right) in *The Petrified Forest*, to the old-school criminal with a code of honor "Mad Dog" Roy Earle (opposite page inset with Ida Lupino) in *High Sierra* and finally the chivalrous Philip Marlowe in *The Big Sleep* (above).

The juvenile gangsters in *The Public Enemy* (opposite, bottom left) meet in a proletarian location, the local speakeasy. Noir gangsters in similarly proletarian include the title figures in *The Killers* (below) in a diner and Shubunka (opposite top left) holding court in a soda fountain.

In both the gangster genre and film noir, criminal protagonists often end up behind bars. Ironically James Cagney's in *Each Dawn I Die* (opposite top) was a journalist framed by corrupt officials (George Raft's character "Hood" Stacey was not that innocent). A decade later Cagney was again in prison as one of film noir's ultimate sociopaths, Cody Jarrett in *White Heat* (above). While none of Riedenschneider's gang end up in prison, the pose of Dix Handley (opposite, bottom) next to the bars of the bank vault effectively foreshadows the fact that their caper will doom them all.

Some French Films of the Occupation: The Silence of the Noir

Tony Williams

As Ginette Vincendeau once stated in her article on the French antecedents of film noir in *The Book of Film Noir*, "Noir is also a French word"[1] and much has been written on the fusion of German Expressionism and French Poetic Realism in terms of this international visual style.[2] Yet the key era for the development of this French version was the period of the German Occupation of France when the country was divided into the Nazi controlled area and the puppet Vichy Government of Marshal Petain. Due to French shame at national humiliation this era has received relatively little critical examination in contrast to the glory days of the twenties and thirties and the post-war era noted for the triumphs of the French New Wave and beyond. However, French film noir continued in the Occupation era as it did before and after but its most notable characteristic along with other generic works was the complete absence of any reference to the German Occupation. It was not until the appearance of Jean-Pierre Melville's first feature film *Le Silence de La Mer* (1949) that such references occurred with its former French Resistance director uncovering the lid on what had been deliberately suppressed up to that point.

Adapted from a well-known Resistance novel but filmed on a low-budget that intuitively facilitated Henri Decae's use of film noir lighting, a style the director would be long associated with, *Le Silence de La Mer* opens with a pre-credit sequence in which all the stylistic components of film noir

The main set of *La Silence de la Mer* lit by Henri Decae: the uncle (Jean Marie Robain) and the niece (Nicole Stéphane) in

appeared. Commencing with a high angle shot in night-for-night cinematography, a solitary Frenchman walks near a bench before he deposits a suitcase and walks away. Another man enters from the shadows to open the suitcase. Both anticipate those later members of Melville's *L'Armeé des Ombres* (1969). As the second man opens the suitcase he uncovers a manuscript hidden amidst the clothes and Resistance bulletins. It is the book which the adaptation narrates. Credits follow and the action begins.

This act of excavation is one of the central themes of Melville's first feature. The director unveils an item that epitomizes a particular "return of the repressed" of French Occupation Cinema, namely a taboo historical event that stimulates the noir style of a "certain tendency of French Occupation Noir Cinema."[3] If American noir literature evokes the negative side of the American Dream during certain eras, then its French cinematic counterpart also unveils the dark side of its own national cinema, especially concerning a time whose significance is still hotly contested today particularly in regard to the heroic myth of The Resistance which Marcel Ophüls's *The Sorrow and the Pity* (1971) later exposed.

Although I may be mistaken, I can find no evidence of any French film made during the period of the Occupation that acknowledges either German Occupation or the presence of German troops in the street. Any references occur in an oblique and throwaway manner as in Maurice Tourneur's Inspector Maigret film *Cécile est Morte* (1944) where one character remarks on having Royal Rabbit for dinner in a plush hotel the previous evening, an obvious reference to contemporary French food shortages. The rest of the film exists in an ahistorical "No Man's Land," French cinema's attempt to disavow the grim nature of the actual period. Any references to the Fall of France appear oblique and up to the viewer to discern as in *Les Inconnus dans la Maison* (1942) when one of the young French delinquents appears in court wearing military uniform following his enlistment. Due to evasiveness, the film could have been made any time prior to May 1940 after which the French Army faded into

insignificance. *Le Silence de La Mer* contains exact historical references at a time it is safe to do so. Set in 1941 with credit caption, the film deals with the code of silence a Frenchman and his niece use against a German officer billeted on them. However, many aspects of the noir visual style appear. On his first appearance (at left), von Ebrennac (Howard Vernon) is filmed with traditional German expressionist lighting making him a relative of Murnau's Nosferatu. His image also evokes the realm of fantasy that several Occupation noirs chose to escape within as certain examples such as *La Nuit Fantastique* (1942) and *La Main du Diable* (1943) show. Yet the outsider is no vampire eager to devour the flesh and blood of his French hosts but someone versed in world culture, especially French, hoping for a cultural (and implicit physical) marriage between the best traditions of both nations. He is a naïve idealist but also one who has closed his eyes to the circumstances surrounding his arrival in the same

way that the French uncle and niece deny his presence by refusing to either speak to him or recognize that he is there. The Uncle asks his niece "Perhaps it's inhumane to refuse to speak to him?" However, the niece remains silent. Despite the officer's difference from the stereotypical German, she remains resolute in her wish to deny his very presence. The Uncle's question is ironic since it also questions the strategy of French Occupation film in their denial of the historical situation whether in noir or elsewhere.

One day von Ebrennac announces that he is to visit Paris. Successive scenes show him as a tourist visiting well known sites before he is reunited with his former student room mate who persuaded him in vain to join the Nazi Party in Munich.[4] Significantly before this scene, one shot contrasts with previous scenes as it anticipates the beginning of the flashback narrated by von Ebrennac to his reluctant hosts, one now fully informed by what he has learned in Paris. It shows the presence of German soldiers in the streets of Paris almost as if von Ebrennac's idealistic vision will soon confront the grim reality of his presence there. In the next sequence his friend informs him of the Final Solution as the camera slowly tracks in to a close-up of Hitler's image. Von Ebrennac later learns of the German plan to eliminate all traces of French culture and gradually erode the status of a nation he admires. As he arrives back at the railway station, he now looks at a noticeboard he had ignored prior to his journey. It lists hostages shot for the murder of a German soldier. When he enters a shop to acquire a box of matches his gaze is alerted to a sign on the right forbidding access to Jews.[5] On his return von Ebrennac announces his intention of returning to combat having elicited the only spoken words from Uncle and Niece. He speaks to invite him inside after he has knocked on the door while she expresses "Adieu."

Apart from its merits as Melville's first film, *Le Silence de La Mer* has other distinctive characteristics, the most notable being its unveiling of the repressive veil French film noir utilized to disguise the effect of national humiliation. Instead of encountering the German presence directly on the streets of France, the occupied French film industry chose instead to substitute its own form of oblique style to veil the imposed German presence creating an ominous world also characterized by sublimated mise-en-scène in several productions. Selected examples form the basis of this presentation that will reveal the full development of French film noir from its well-known Poetic Realist antecedents such as *Pépé Le Moko* (1937), *Quai des Brumes* (1938), and *Le Jour se Lève* (1939). During the period of the Occupation French Cinema was as diverse as its pre-war and post-war periods but it was within this era that French film noir matured in the same way as its American counterpart at the same time. Certain films did contain brief flourishes of noir as *Cécile est Morte* and the Hollywood influenced romantic triangle *La Ferme aux Loups* (1943) reveal. Starring young Paul Meurisse and Francois Perier as newspaper reporters eagerly pursuing Martine Carol, the film features a dark night noir sequence set in

Pépé le Moko: Jean Gabin and Mireille Balin.

an "old dark house" obviously influenced by James Whale's celebrated 1932 film but otherwise it follows the conventions of the American newspaper/detective film both in style and content.

Clouzot or The Ambiguities

Later celebrated for several varied but distinctively post-war noir films such as *Quai des Orfèvres* (1947), *Manon* (1949), *Le Salaire de la peur* (1953), *Les Diaboliques* (1955), *Les Espions* (1958), and *La Vérité* (1960), Henri-Georges Clouzot (1907-1977) has many claims to be regarded as a key figure of French film noir both as writer and director. While the noir work of Christian-Jaque remained confined to the Occupation period, Clouzot's work continued well into the post-war era suggesting his special temperamental affinity with this visual style that, despite its later variations, exhibited continuity rather than disjuncture from its genesis in the Occupation period. Like many directors, he made several films with the same actor working as screenwriter on the Pierre Fresnay film *Le Duel* (1941), *Le Dernier des six* (1941), before directing him in *L'Assassin habite au 21* (1942) and the celebrated *Le Corbeau* (1943) that became the quintessential film of French Occupation noir. Clouzot had also scripted *Le Duel, Le Dernier des six,* and later co-wrote *L'Assassin habite au 21* and *Le Corbeau*. His emphasis on the dark side of human nature was not just due to his experiences under German Occupation but also four year hospitalization due to TB in the 1930s. As he later stated, "I owe it all to the sanitorium. It was my school. While resident there I saw how human beings worked."[6] Clouzot's life was later marked by tragedy in one way or another including the sudden death of his wife Véra from a heart attack and the difficulties encountered in finding projects that matched his earlier achievements. But there can be no doubt that the Occupation period set the stamp on his tendency for dark, nihilistic projects as well as a tendency towards black humor. *Le Corbeau* managed to upset both Vichy and the Resistance, the latter attempting to blacklist him in the post-war era and delaying the continuing exhibition of his adaptation of the Georges Simeon novel into *Les Inconnus dans la Maison* (1942).

Directed by Henri Decoin later well known for his post-war noir *Razzia sur la Chnouf* (1955) featuring Jean Gabin and Lino Ventura who had previously appeared in Jacques Becker's *Touchez pas au Grisbi* (1954), the film was derived from a novel written in 1940 completed well before the defeat of France. Celebrated as the creator of Inspector Maigret, Simenon was also a highly prolific writer of dark fiction many of which not only depicted a Gallic version of noir literature but also a bleak description of internal and external lower depths forms of existence that paralleled the bleak thirties world of Graham Greene's fiction associated with the term "Greeneland."[7] Banned for a time after the Liberation because its screenplay was "with its strong undertones of anti-Semitism was held to constitute anti-French propaganda"[8] not present in the original novel, *Les Inconnus* is a much more ambivalent film than this description suggests. Its visual style certainly parallels well-known film noir motifs with dark images, tormented characters, and claustrophobic entrapment especially in the confined interior of the old Loursat house with its attic revealing the presence of a dead body and the later courtroom scenes. With one presence of mobile overhead camera shots craning over spectators in a courtroom, the defender, and accused, the motion ends with a tracking shot into the presiding judge overseeing a situation of what

Below, the opening sequence from *Les Inconnus de la Maison.*

It's raining on the city,
and in the middle of this deluge

André Reybaz Andre as Emile and a robed Raimu as attorney Hector Loursat in *Les Inconnus de la Maison.*

appears to be a conclusive case against the defender. The novel appeared in 1940 before the French defeat as seen in the enlistment of one of its young juvenile delinquents into the Army. The film opens with images of a small French town at night, a voice-over describing the rainy landscape with the evocative line, "But today, the icy rain dampens our spirits" equally applicable to both the atmosphere of a crime novel as well as a country under occupied rule symbolically depicted by a stormy climactic atmosphere.

As in *Psycho*, the camera moves into the interior of an old house revealing its occupants: shrewish housekeeper, an alcoholic former lawyer father who has remained inside for the past twenty years ever since his wife left him, and his young daughter Nicole who suffers from parental neglect. This is Simenon's version of a "Bleak House" as well as Clouzot's symbolic representation of an occupied nation denying the existence of the outside world. The noir cinematography through most of the film presents an evocative stylistic counterpart to the narrative of a film whose main character is oblivious to the presence of "strangers in the house."[9] A discovered corpse will stimulate its drunken owner out of his lethargy towards achieving justice for a victimized young working class Frenchman. Awakening to his neglected daughter's involvement with a gang of mostly affluent juvenile delinquents who have turned to petty crime due to parental neglect, suffocating mother love, or lack of healthy physical opportunities as opposed to the cinema and dubious bistros and brothels, Hector Loursat delivers a very un-Simenon condemnation of irresponsible parents in court before identifying the guilty party.

Portrayed by Raimu (1883-1946) acclaimed by Orson Welles as the greatest actor who ever lived and internationally known for his role as César in the Marcel Pagnol trilogy (1931, 1932, 1936), Hector Loursat is one of Simenon's most positive characters. He is someone who has fallen into lethargy but awakes at the end to recover his former energies to ensure justice is done. No explicit reference is ever made to the historical circumstances of the film's production but certain lines such as "No, at times like this, it's every man for himself" and "The law is pretty hard these days. In Nevers they executed a 19-year-old" relate equally to pre-war and Occupation conditions. Delivering one of

Yeah, he fell on Manu's fist.
Poor old Edmond.

his great speeches during the final courtroom scene, Raimu's Loursat appears like a sleeping tiger roused into action to disclose the real murderer young Justin Luska. It is significant that his first name is changed from that of the original novel "Ephraim" having obvious Jewish connotations that would support the charge of anti-Semitism made against Clouzot's screenplay. However, although the young French-Algerian actor Marcel Monloudji (at left) playing Luska has a vague "Le Juif" resemblance, no explicit reference to his origins ever appears in the film as it does in Book Three, chapter 2 of the original French novel where Justin Luska is described as "son of a tradesman...because of his red hair, his name, his real first name, Ephraim, the Eastern origin of his father, was the object of ridicule of his schoolmates."[10] Luska's cinematic father has no identifiable Jewish traits as suggested in the book.

Although Loursat's critiques of parents, the cinema world of "heroes of the week" and the revealing "legs of starlets"[11] as opposed to the more alternative physical sports activities of stadiums and swimming pools rather than 132 bars and 4 brothels may resemble a Vichy family values speech, it is also a very familiar one from many historical periods. This detailed condemnation of bourgeois parental failure does not appear in the novel but belongs to Clouzot's screenplay foreshadowing his attack on Vichy village values in *Le Corbeau*. At best, the film is ambivalent, deliberately choosing not to address the outside world but implying the existence of certain external negative forces that determine events, something Clouzot will perfect later in *Le Corbeau*. The final scene is affirmative. Loursat reunites with his estranged daughter, her lover saved from execution and his mother whose working class sacrificial character strongly contrasts with the affluent, indulgent bourgeois families seen earlier in the film who represent the same type of decadent images also embodied within those aristocrats in Jean Renoir's pre-war *La Règle du Jeu* (1939) who collaborate in their own form of denial at the end of the film. The film is ambivalent. It may be seen as an affirmation of Vichy family values or as an allegory of French resilience like Jean Grémillon's *Le Ciel est à vous* (1944), another Occupation film that lends itself to dual readings. Yet the noir overtones of *Les Inconnus dans la Maison* suggest much darker reverberations concerning the existence of an oppressive world outside whose existence cannot be recognized openly. As with the victorious matron female aviator of Grémillon's film, a specific non-political type of French resistance appears – in this case a Frenchman awakened from alcoholic stupor ready to take an active part in the world outside, a world he has hitherto denied until it affects his own family relationships.

Directed by Georges Lacombe, *Le Dernier des Six* is more notable for its screenplay by Clouzot and noir visual style flourishes than for any distinguished form of direction. Adapted from the 1931 source novel by Belgian writer Stanislas-André Steeman (1908-1970) well-known for his "romans policiers," the film is the first one to feature one of his well-known detective heroes Inspector Wenceslas Vorobeitchik, aka Monsieur Wens. Portrayed by Pierre Fresnay, the master sleuth is called upon to investigate the mysterious deaths of several men who swore an oath years ago that the survivor would inherit all the money one of them won at gambling. The film begins with five men waiting for their associate in a darkened room whose interior matches the gloomy world outside. Whether shot in noir style for economic reasons or not, the opening scene depicts a claustrophobic darkness within where agency is limited. Apart from some scattered daylight scenes and a brightly lit nightclub, the whole film is dominated by the noir style that overwhelms its" roman policier" framework of the master detective eventually solving the crime. Also featuring Clouzot's then mistress Suzy Delair as Wens's mistress Mila Malou, the couple often operate according to the conventions of a screwball comedy team (something the next film will develop) suggesting not just a muted self-awareness of the fact that other repressed elements condition the narrative in addition to its detective framework at a time when Hollywood films were banned but also an inherent form of self-reflexivity intermittently appearing throughout the narrative visually suggesting that things are not what they seem. The teaming of Fresnay and Delair suggests Clouzot's awareness not just of American screwball comedy conventions but also a Gallic version of Nick and Nora Charles from Dashiell Hammett's last novel *The Thin Man* (1934). Until the German Occupation prevented screenings of American films at least three of the cel-

ebrated series starring William Powell and Myrna Loy—*The Thin Man* (1934), *After the Thin Man* (1936) and *Another Thin Man* (1939)—were probably shown in France.[12] Self-reflexivity not only appears in certain lines such as "You're so silly. You should have written pulp novels" and "That sounds like something from a movie" but also artificially cinematic trick effects seen during Lolita's sharpshooting cabaret act and an overheard objective shot straining at the formula of cinematic verisimilitude showing

Above right, Pierre Fresnay as Inspector Wenceslas Wens.

Right, a darkly lit interior from *Le Dernier des Six.*

French showgirls performing in a Busby Berkeley manner. Compared to Clouzot's later work *Le Dernier des six* is limited in conception but the underlying noir elements and the theme of French betrayal would not fail to resonate with the bleak mood of Occupation audiences who would not experience the type of escapist "mindless entertainment" they expected.

Clouzot's first film as director and co-scenarist *L'Assassin habite au 21* is much more cinematically and thematically fertile than its predecessor. Shot in the French noir style and co-scripted with the author from his 1939 novel, with whom Clouzot would finally work on *Quai des Orfèvres* adapted from *Légitime Défense* (1942), this film again features Fresnay and Delair in an even more excessive screwball comedic partnership placing them much more firmly in the dark world of the Occupation. The main premise involves the activities of a serial killer murdering several Frenchmen in the dark streets and leaving his calling card as signature to his deed. The opening scenes represent a mastery of visual suspense. The film begins with a close-up of a door opening and camera tracking out to end with the dialogue "It wasn't opened by me. It opened by itself." Following scenes show a clochard who has won a lottery seen through the subjective point of view of the murderer before he claims his victim with a swordstick. Anticipating the opening shot of Michael Powell's *Peeping Tom* (1960) and John Carpenter's *Halloween* (1978), the scene evokes elements of the horror film rather than

a detective story. Lasting some seventy-five seconds, it is almost as if the viewer is temporarily placed within the realm of the fantastic, viewing the stalking through eyes evoking vampire imagery foreshadowing the introduction of von Ebrennac in *Le Silence de la Mer*. The mysterious killer is later compared to a "vampire from Düsseldorf." The identity of the killer remains a mystery until the end when both Wens and Mila independently discover that there is not one killer but three, all believing themselves to be artists in crime, their Nietzschean form

L'Assassin habite au 21: top left, an Expressionistic staging by director Clouzot. Left and below, an early example of a series of stalking shots from the killer's POV.

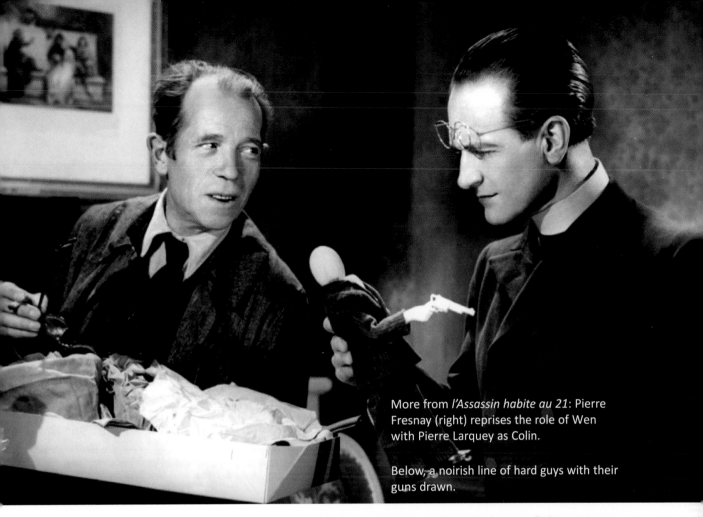

More from *l'Assassin habite au 21*: Pierre Fresnay (right) reprises the role of Wen with Pierre Larquey as Colin.

Below, a noirish line of hard guys with their guns drawn.

of rivalry going back to school day experiences. One of the murderers clearly regards his victims as "untermensch" when he remarks "I did kill one of those *grubs* in a building yard" (italics mine). As we have seen, the first victim in the film is a tramp, a disposable element in any society, Vichy or otherwise.

L'Assassin habite au 21: left, more noir style from Clouzot a "money" scene with shadowy imagery. Below left, gun in one hand, Insp. Wens lights up after solving the crime.

Noir cinematography is on prominent display in this film with one shot showing the shadow of the accused Linz in the police station anticipating a later one of the deranged professor in *Le Corbeau* (1943). Although the three killers revelation may derive from Steeman's novel, the visual context of the film hints that they are allegorical representations of the Axis powers. This is not beyond the bounds of possibility since Clouzot reveals his hand in a brief, but very daring manoeuver at the end of the film that lasts a second or so clearly designed to escape the eye of the censor. All three master criminals have their hands in the air at the end when they are surrounded by the police. However, in the final shot, Wens stands opposite the real ringleader of the three, getting him to lower his right hand while his left clearly remains in the air as if giving the traditional Nazi salute! Intentional or not, this certainly suggests that Clouzot aimed at a subversive depiction of the Occupation, one that he will refine in his next film that managed to offend both the Nazis and their Vichy allies as well as the French Resistance who considered it unpatriotic and attempted to blacklist Clouzot permanently after the Liberation.[13]

Again starring Pierre Fresnay, *Le Corbeau* is the archetypal French film noir of the Occupation whose strategic use of ambiguity and allusive allegory paints accurately the mood of the time. As Truffaut later wrote, "the film seemed to me to be a fairly accurate picture of what I had seen around me during the war and the post-war period – collaboration, denunciation, the black market, hustling."[14]. It is based on a real incident that occurred between 1917 and 1922 when a sexually repressed former civil servant disseminated over a thousand anonymous letters that provoked several suicides in the southern town of Tulle. Expertly employing film noir techniques, style is now unified to content without any need for allusive self-reflexivity nor briefly glimpsed hesitant ambiguous allegorical references. *Le Corbeau* perceptively paints the picture of a divided society whose inhabitants are at each other's throats as a result of deep tensions that poison pen letters evoke rather than create. Merging several different cinematic styles such as classical Hollywood prestigious studio cinematography with noir shadow imagery seen in *L'Assassin*, Clouzot depicts a divided French village that is less unified than Vichy propaganda suggested. The mysterious informant tears apart the hypocritical façade of a community already divided. Criticized by German and Vichy authorities as well as the French Resistance for undermining the supposed unity of the French nation, *Le Corbeau* utilizes its own stylistic weapons to reveal the dark side of the Occupied society.

Le Corbeau: Pierre Fresnay as Dr. Germain and Ginette Leclerc as Denise.

Le Corbeau: Denise strikes a classic femme fatale pose (compare Joan Bennett on page 22). Opposite top, two guilty men confront each other. Center and bottom, intercut tight close-ups.

Starring Pierre Fresnay, the Gallic noir icon of this era as American actors such as Humphrey Bogart and Robert Mitchum were of theirs, this film stands supreme among its group not just as the French Occupation film prematurely interrogating the post-Liberation myths that sought to conceal a dark era in national history but also one foreshadowing post-war cynical noir explorations of its director who would later film *Les Diaboliques* from the two novelists Hitchcock would later adapt *Vertigo* (1958) from.[15] Fresnay's Dr. Germain is a very un-Vichy type of hero performing abortions to save the life of village women rather than sacrificing them at the altar of Vichy ideological production designed to ensure continuity of a (hopefully) male species. Women are never idealized according to the values of Nazi and Vichy propaganda as seen in Laura Vorzet's (Micheline Francey) unpatriarchal revelation to Germain towards the end of the film as well as the morally ambivalent figure of its femme fatale Denise (Ginette Leclerc) who is a forthright woman "who knows too much" in speaking honestly about the village's moral malaise. Denise's physical deformity as well as her later attempt at inducing an abortion, place her well outside the pale of acceptable Aryan-Vichy values. Yet she is one of the most sympathetic characters in the film despite her gold-digger attitude. Her behavior forms a stark contrast to those accusing villagers and police who arrest an innocent suspect (Helena Manson who portrayed Emile's mother in *Les Inconnus* and another mother in *L'Assassin*) in a manner evoking the actions of the Gestapo in one of the most celebrated sequences in the film. In *Le Corbeau*, the nature of guilt is ambiguous and diffuse as revealed in that striking scene between Germain and the guilty party Dr. Vorzet (Pierre Larquey) who asks the former whether he trusts his own reflection as an overhead light swings back and forth casting each character in light and then darkness. Near them both is a globe evoking that earlier one seen in *L'Assassin* that, here, has more definite meanings in terms of "Today, France. Tomorrow the World."

As Bertrand Tavernier, director of one of the rare films dealing with the Occupation Film industry *Laissez-passer* (2002) points out in his interview featured in The Criterion DVD edition, *Le Corbeau* is an extremely sophisticated film that reductive readings by both Vichy conservatives and Resistance forces failed to comprehend. Everyone is guilty in one way or another and the ambiguous ending following the death of Dr. Vorzet suggests no easy resolution. Yet, some residue of hope does exist. As Germain states earlier, "This kind of crisis has a purpose. Like a convalescence you come out stronger, It's horrible to admit but evil is necessary." Also, as Denise states, "We can't sacrifice the future to the present." It is possible to survive as the unexpected union of Germain and Ginette reveals, especially after a supposedly stereotypical femme fatale condemns the film's nominal hero. "You may be right, doctor. But I feel sorry for you. You are what is saddest and strangest...a bourgeois." As Clouzot's earlier screenplay for *Les Inconnus* revealed, it is this class that another flawed figure, a drunken lawyer, condemns for creating the circumstances surrounding murder. Here Denise's speech evokes a familiar discourse emanating from one of the more radical groups forming a very diverse French Resistance. At this period of time, Clouzot can only hint at the fact that the village of St. Robin is certainly no idyllic "little fatherland" for the rural ideology of Pétain's New Moral Order. Those who still criticize the director should remember that this was the film that got him fired from the German controlled French film company Continental Films.

The French Occupation Noirs of Christian-Jaque and Jacques Becker

Like Clouzot, these two directors would continue their careers after the Liberation but while Christian-Jaque became one of the many targets of the *Cahiers du Cinema* group for his later frivolous films and celebrity marriage to Martine Carol, Becker would receive acclaim for films such as *Touchez pas au Grisbi* and *Le Trou* (1960) that, unlike the work of Christian-Jaque, continued the noir tradition into the post-war era. By contrast Christian-Jaque's brief moment of glory occurred in the Occupation era where circumstances dictated the type of films he would make.

Co-directed with Roger Chapatte, *L'Assassinat du Père Noël* (1941) is set in an enclosed snow-bound French village. Like other Occupation films, it depicts a timeless zone with no reference to recent historical events. Yet, this touching film contains a yearning for French values involving community, Church, and the celebration of Christmas that may be either read as pro-Vichy or as an alternative utopian hope that things will be better in the future. Featuring the ill-fated Harry Baur as a villager who takes on the role of Santa Claus every year, the anti-Semitic actor Robert Le Vigan (referred to often in the works of rabid right-winger Louis Ferdinand Céline depicting the cataclysmic fall of the Third Reich), the narrative focuses upon equally catastrophic events in a small community—the murder of Santa Claus and the return of a prodigal son, the Baron, who may have contracted leprosy during his exile. The visual style of the film contrasts daylight snow scenes (such as the investigators below), comforting and threatening interiors, with a dark world outside expressing that mood of visual uncertainty associated with French noir Occupation films that repress any reference to those forces controlling the destiny of French people. Eventually, following the revelation of the actual murderer (someone who is an integral part of the village) the film moves to a touching resolution where the Baron's Prince Charming finds that his Cinderella has always been within his own domain and the late

arrival of Père Noël on Boxing Day delivers a special gift to a crippled boy – the power to walk again.

As well as depicting the French noir Occupation mood of enclosure and fear, the film also not only employs subjective POV similar to that in *L'Assassin* but also contains one sequence anticipating Hitchcock's 360-degree panning shot in *Vertigo* (1958). During the post-Midnight Mass celebrations while Cinderella (Renée Faure as Catherine, right) waits for her absent Prince Charming, revelers led by Le Vigan circle around her (center and bottom right) with the camera swirling in a 360-degree accelerated pace. Another shot anticipates Hitchcock's using a revolving plinth in *Vertigo*, used to represent Scotty's successful achievement of his dark desires in finally transforming Judy into Madeleine that Brian De Palma will later perfect at the end of *Obsession* (1976) with an actual 360-degree panning shot. Here the heroine becomes surrounded by revelers suggesting her entrapment in a Dance of Death orchestrated by Le Vigan's character. Although LeVigan's infamy became common knowledge after the Liberation leading him to flee into permanent exile, his anti-Semitic, pro-Nazi sympathies were probably well known at the time, making the significance of this scene obvious, whether conscious or not. At the same time, Hitchcock began his Hollywood experiments with film noir, Christian-Jaque was already doing the same thing but significantly anticipating and exceeding the visual techniques of his Hollywood contemporary. The dark era of the Occupation gave particular resonance to such experiments as *Voyage sans Espoir* (1943) reveals.

Karl Marx's remark that human beings never make history under circumstances of their own choosing also applies to Christian-Jaque's 1943 noir since he appears never to have ventured into this territory again in the post-Liberation period. Fusing French poetic realism with recognizable traits of the shadow world of film noir, the film deals with issues of escape from a France set in no explicitly defined historical period but one dominated by the Occupation as its overpowering dark imagery and bleak mood suggests. Containing several distinctive mobile camera movements that would make Hitchcock envious if he ever saw this film, *Voyage sans Espoir* employs some striking mise-en-scène elements of visual confinement and entrapment set

My beautiful love.

Roger Richebé

présente

in a railway compartment, the interior of a ship, a supposedly safe apartment, nightclub, or hideaway adjacent to a stormy wave-ridden jetty. Featuring the accidental meeting of two "French Strangers on a Train," Pierre Gohelle (Paul Bernard) and Alain Genestier (Jean Marais) appear opposites to each other but actually have much in common similar to those later Patricia Highsmith creations. Both seek their own versions of ways of escape to distant lands such as America (an impossibility for 1943). Based on a novel by Pierre McOrlan (who also wrote the source material for Marcel Carné and Jacques Prévert's equally doom-laden Poetic Realist Popular Front drama *Quai des Brumes*), *Voyage sans Espoir* functions as a dark film noir mirror image to both its earlier predecessor as well as Julian Duvivier's *Pépé le Moko* (1937), not only in having its heroine die from a gunshot wound at the end as she bids farewell to her naïve young lover (above left) but also implicitly echoing a different type of disillusionment for its era as the decline of the Popular Front ideals was for those earlier Poetic Realist films that became models both for American and French film noir.[16] It is hard not to see a deliberate reworking of the Poetic Realist tradition into French film noir with its countless canted angles, rain-swept streets, gloomy interiors and an opening that appears to reverse the beginning of Jean Renoir's *La Bête Humaine* (1938) with railway tracks viewed upside down (above right) from the front of a speeding train "as the camera drunkenly rolls upright and titles come flying towards us, slapping flat across the frame likes flies hitting a windshield."[17]

Marie-Ange (Simone Renant) and her naïve would-be victim Alain Ginistier (Jean Marais) in *Voyage sans Espoir*.

Jacques Becker (1906-1960) had worked as an assistant to Jean Renoir during 1932-1939 but unlike his mentor had remained in France. Following his release from a German P.O.W camp after the defeat of France, he began his career directing two Occupation noirs – *Dernier Atout* (1942) and *Goupi Mains Rouges* (1943) continuing his career after the Liberation with *Falbalas* (1945) starring Micheline Presle, who had appeared in *La Nuit Fantastique* (1942) and Christian-Jaque's *Boule de Suif* (1945) whose Franco-Prussian war setting implicitly criticized French bourgeois hypocrisy. The heroine's forced "horizontal collaboration" would gain added relevance in the immediate period of the Liberation and the film makes clear that cowardly French citizens have exerted pressure on this unfortunate woman. The frivolous nature of *Dernier Atout* may be due less from frustration of a former Renoir collaborator forced to direct a commercial film to prove his box-office capability but more to a covert exhibition of the type of ambiguity and ironic play on audience sensibility characterizing several Occupation noirs. Shot in high key lighting until its dark action noirish climax at the end and set in the mythical South American "imaginary country" of Carical, the film initially appears to be little more than a French caper comic pastiche of American formulas. Though certain characters are supposedly American like Rudy Score (Pierre Renoir) and his sister Bella (Mirielle Blain) they are 100% French like the cops who pursue them despite surnames such as Gonzalez (Noel Roquevert) and Montez. Despite the production date characters are able to travel freely from America to any country they choose. Vying with his colleague Montez for the cherished prize of police college valedictorian, heroic young Clarence (Raymond Rouleau) infiltrates himself into Rudy Score's entourage to solve the murder of Chicago gangster Tony Amalo (Gaston Modot). With exterior scenes shot on location in Vichy Mediterranean France, bizarre cops pursue American gangsters by car and motorcycles in an exciting noirish night-for-night chase ending in a shootout in a tunnel and the demise of the Big Boss himself thanks to a strategically aimed flashlight wielded by Clarence to allow his colleagues to demonstrate the marksmanship prowess seen in the film's opening scenes. Becker certainly never took his first film seriously nor did he expect audiences to, deliberately blending incongruous elements with interiors in the Hotel Babylonia and exteriors in Vichy's Deep South stronghold that makes the area less one promoting Pétain's conservative values but resembling more a bizarre, crime-ridden, banana republic.

Night-for-night chase with motorcycles and ambush in the back roads of "Caracal" in *Dernier Atout.*

Above, two members of the Goupi Clan, brothers Eugène (Georges Rollin) and Léopold (Fernand Ledoux) aka Goupi Red Hands.

If special pleading is needed to regard *Dernier Atout* as a hybrid satire strategically employing noir elements in its action finale, Becker's second film expertly engages in ambiguity, cinematic hybridity, and paradox to challenge contemporary censorship codes. Set in a border region between the German Occupied Zone and Vichy France, the film indirectly challenges the virtues of the country and its peasantry espoused by Pétain's regime. Adapted from a 1937 crime novel by Pierre Véry who also wrote the source material for Christian-Jaque's 1938 noir *Les Disparus de Saint-Agil* starring Erich von Stroheim, *Goupi Mains Rouges* is a French film noir demolition of countryside values (similar to Jacques Tourneur's later criticism of rural life in his 1947 *Out of the Past*) in a manner evoking both Stella Gibbons' *Cold Comfort Farm* (1932) that parodied the rural idyllic world created by Mary Webb as well as Emile Zola's caustic *La Terre*. Becker's Goupis are no paragons of rural virtue but a family dominated by economic greed. Following the death of sharp tongued Goupi Tissane whom one critic compares to a Nazi,[18] the family close ranks especially against their city slicker relative who arrives in darkness in a scene resembling the opening of *A Canterbury Tale* (1944). Finally, the appropriately surnamed, deranged Goupi Tonkin (appropriately played by Robert Le Vigan) dies a sacrificial victim on the altar of family guilt and French colonial exploitation based on economic greed. Although the film moves to a supposedly happy ending with black sheep Goupi Mains Rouges (Fernand Ledoux) restored to the family table by patriarch Goupi Les Sous, all espousing Vichy conservative values, the film actually ends with a suggestive mobile shot symbolizing the continuing influence of economic greed that has characterized this rural family throughout the entire film.

Two Occupation Noirs by Maurice Tourneur

Following a distinguished career in American silent cinema, Maurice Tourneur (father of Jacques) had returned to France in 1926 following a dispute with MGM over the production of *Mysterious Island* (1929). Tourneur had already revealed his attraction to fantasy themes with films such as *The Blue Bird* (1919) so, in some ways, it is not surprising that he directed a remarkable horror-noir such as *La Main du Diable* that forms an interesting parallel to his son's Van Lewton produced RKO films *Cat People* (1942), *I Walked with a Zombie* (1943), and *The Leopard Man* (1943). If fantasy appears an unusual genre for this time, we must remember that Occupation Cinema allowed the release of *La Nuit Fantastique* (1942) by French avant-garde director Marcel L'Herbier, Carné's *Les Visiteurs du Soir* (1943), and Jean Delannoy's Jean Cocteau-inspired *L'Eternel Retour* (1943). Despite Nazi and Vichy imposed censorship restrictions, French Occupation cinema permitted a surprising degree of latitude for the time also allowing for certain degrees of ambiguity both in production and reception.[19] Produced by Continental Films overseen by a sympathetic German administrator Alfred Greven that also released *Le Corbeau*, the film may be viewed as another deliberately ambiguous representation of the Occupation with its noir style and doom-ridden hero Roland Brissot (Pierre Fresnay) embodying a contemporary version of the similarly trapped Jean Gabin figure of *Le Jour se Lève* (1939). This time the protagonist is an unsuccessful artist seduced into a Faustian bargain of success at the cost of eternal damnation. Beginning in an isolated mountain inn and leading to an extended flashback, the victim narrates his doom-laden narrative to a group of guests until he finally returns an accursed talisman to its rightful owner, a medieval monk whose hand the Devil acquired after death. Like *Le*

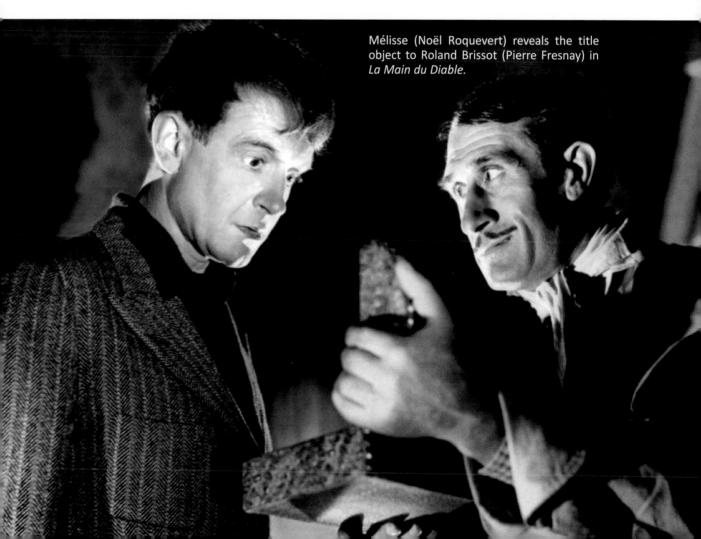

Mélisse (Noël Roquevert) reveals the title object to Roland Brissot (Pierre Fresnay) in *La Main du Diable*.

Corbeau, the film ambiguously plays with two possible meanings: condemnation of an anti-Vichy decadent lifestyle leading to the sinner's just deserts as is the case with the victimizer in Clouzot's film or as a dark allegory of Occupation oppression. Released a few months after *Les Visiteurs du Soir* with Jules Berry's villainous persona well-known from Renoir's *Le Crime du M. Lange* (1935) and Carne's *Le Jour se Lève* playing the Devil, Tourneur's Lucifer, played by Pierre Palau, resembles more Hannah's Arendt's Adolf Eichmann influenced conception of "the banality of evil." As James Travers notes, "With his complete lack of human feeling and his ability to perform mathematical calculations at lightning speed, he is the very epitome of the Vichy bureaucrat, cold, efficient, and ruthless – a stealer of men's souls if ever there was one."[20]

Filmed in a less expressionistic noirish style, Tourneur's *Le Val d'Enfer* (1943) is an equally bleak depiction of Life under Occupation as *Le Corbeau* and *Le Main du Diable*. On the surface, it appears as propaganda for Vichy family values with its resolution of a family restored after the convenient death of femme fatale city girl Marthe (Ginette Leclerc) and the reunion between repressive father Noël Bienvenu (Gabriel Gabrio) and his estranged prodigal son Bastien (Andre Reybaz) who returns home suitably chastised following a jail term. Like the delinquent youngster who enlists in *Les Inconnus*, institutional discipline has redeemed him. As father and son walk side by side in the final shot, the villagers approvingly note the period of imprisonment "that made him a man." Another notes, "like the army." However, despite propaganda resonances, the film operates on a more ambivalent note like many French Occupation noirs. Despite Leclerc's stereotypical depiction as femme fatale, like her counterpart in *Le Corbeau*, her character is more than one-dimensional. Tourneur suggests that she has also been let down by her own father in the same way that Noël refuses to help his errant son in the opening scene. It appears that she has been forced into a life of prostitution and initially appears happy to start a new life by marrying Noël despite the difference in age between them. Asked by a dying friend to take care of his daughter, Noël offers to marry her revealing the truth of that old axiom, "There's no fool like an old fool." With full knowledge of his new wife's past life as a prostitute Noël becomes putty in her hands even agreeing to put his parents into an old people's home in one of the most poignant scenes in the film. The screenplay suggests that Marthe becomes a femme fatale less by conscious design but more to circumstances overwhelming her through no fault of her own. She is finally killed by a convenient accident in a quarry explosion indirectly facilitated by one of Noël's workmen. Vichy family values rule once more but their success is not too remote from similar family operations in *Goupi Mains Rouges*. Both films suggest the dark presence of devious patriarchal manipulations.

Ginette Leclerc as Marthe in *Val d'Enfer*. Opposite, screaming at the deadly explosion.

Tourneur blends several cinematic styles in this film. Like Fritz Lang's *Human Desire* (1954) it opens and closes with naturalistic images of a world of work showing a Haute-Provence quarry intimating a realm of Zola-like determinism well-suited to Vichy propaganda praising the virtues of family against those represented by city girl Marthe. Yet several interior and night scenes exhibit familiar noir cinematography suggesting the questionable foundations of Vichy family values. It suggests a particular "heart of darkness" surrounding the family in this film that deliberately counterpoints its ideological associations. For all her faults, Marthe acts more as an unconscious catalyst for deep rooted insecurities and tensions already embedded within the Bienvenu family that needs a conveniently complicit voyeuristic accomplice to return it once more to unity. In *Val d'Enfer* Tourneur reveals dark, homicidal implications behind Petain's rallying cry of "Work. Family. Country." The film employs a particular operation of ambiguity characteristic of Occupation noir, making possible several readings ranging from a pro-Vichy slant to an indirect attack on those who collaborated with the enemy. Noël "collaborates" with his femme fatale "stranger in the house" complying with her every wish before the more than convenient action of one of his workers in eliminating an external threat in much the same manner as a Van Helsing operating within a traditional horror film. The film does make clear that the patriarch invited a dangerous femme fatale into his house, denying her well-known background very similar to the way many French citizens collaborated with the enemy by denying what they really represented.

French Film Noir of the Occupation or the Historical Ambiguities

Writing in the immediate aftermath of the Liberation, André Bazin commented that the Occupation period contained inspiration for several great films, ones capable of "suggesting new dreams for us."[21] He also regarded it as a mistake to oppose realism to escapism and that "Escapist cinema does not exclude the use of the contemporary scene."[22] All the above French film noirs did represent various "ways of escape" from the grim realities of the Occupation with very little reference to the reality of that historical period. However, the use of this particular noir style suggested contemporary hesitation and unease as to the fact that things were not what they seemed and that dark factors lurked in the background. Noir operated as it always did to suggest a conscious suppression and repression of the grim realities of everyday existence. This was the era when Poetic Realism merged with German expressionism to create a distinctive French variant of the Noir and it is doubtful whether this would have ever happened were it not for the German Occupation. If Evelyn Ehrlich defines French Occupation Cinema as one of paradox then its noir components represent a mechanism of stylistic ambiguity necessary for an era that chose not to reveal disturbing historical features in its entertainments in an industry in which it was impossible to distinguish the output of the German controlled Continental Studios that produced *Le Corbeau* and *Le Main du Diable* from any other French Company at a time when only two overtly propaganda films were made.[23] Like its UFA counterpart, French Cinema chose entertainment over propaganda as Dr. Goebbels' well-known reservations over the effectiveness of explicit propaganda films such as *S.A. Mann Brand* (1933) and *Hans Westmar* (1933) revealed. French Occupation Noir was characterized paradoxically by a silence concerning content and by the paradoxical employment of a significant choice of visual expression suggesting the presence of dark historical forces whose implications could not be consciously named.

French Occupation noirs deserve more study especially concerning visual techniques anticipating many later Hollywood examples involving style and camera mobility. One such example involves a striking 360-degree tracking shot that lasts over two minutes in a hotel basement kitchen in the non-noir Inspector Maigret film policier *Les Caves du Majestic* (1944). French Occupation noirs comprise a cinema of silent ambiguity, produced not freely but under extreme conditions of restraint. They may lend themselves to further examination according to that concept of ambiguity formulated by G. Cabrera Infante that results in a certain creation of meaning through a controlled expenditure of visual style.[24] Rather than being an aberrant interlude in the history of French Cinema these films represent a process of development whereby French Poetic Realism fused with its German expressionist heritage to develop a national cinematic style that would progress further in the post-war era. Their heritage is unmistakable.

Later Developments

Melville's *L'Armée des Ombres* forms an epilogue not just to French Resistance history but also to the French Occupation legacy of film noir where poetic realism of the 1930s finally fused into a Gallic version of film noir. Marcel Carné and Jacques Prévert's final collaboration *Les Portes de la Nuit* (1946) is an appropriately atmospheric noir dealing with the issue of collusion with the occupying forces that could not be explicitly addressed during the 1940-1944 period. Starring Yves Montand and Serge Reggiani (who would play a similar betrayer role in Clouzot's 1949 noir *Manon*) the film is now able to unite

Above, Melville revisits Germans at the Arch of Triumph.
Right, Ebrennac visits in *La Silence de la Mer.*

its historically influenced style with a particular content that had to be expressed ambiguously a few years before. Now there is no need for ambiguity or fantasy since the later film can now develop its noir heritage in a much more realistic manner. Unlike *Le Silence de la Mer* where von Ebrennac gradually discerns the German military presence half-way through the film, in *L'Armée des Ombres* Melville films the triumphal march of the Wehrmacht past the Arc de Triomphe to confront the audience by marching into the frame in the very opening shot of the film. This documentary representation brings the repressed German presence masked by Occupation styles of noir and the fantastic directly in front of the camera. The rest of the film reproduces the post-war visual style of Melville's gangster movies with color added from *Le Samouraï* (1966) onwards. This later film represents his significant use of neo-noir cinematography continuing the trajectory of earlier films such as *Le Doulos* (1963) and *Le Deuxième Souffle* (1966) in the same way Roman Polanski's *Chinatown* (1974) and Robert Aldrich's *Hustle* (1975) added new visual inflections to the classical American black and white noir style. Where noir really succeeds is in its alliance of style and historical context, the latter aspect important whether expressly or indirectly. *L'Armée des Ombres* employs noir imagery to represent visually the insecurity and everyday internal fear experienced by all those who chose to resist the Occupation whether directly or indirectly rather than submitting passively. Due to French Occupation film constraints the trauma of that era could not be represented directly but rather indirectly as opposed to Melville's later film where form and content complement each other in stylistic and contextual unity. French film noirs of the Occupation could not express the fears of their historical moment directly unlike those American noirs such as *Crossfire* (1947), *Body and Soul* (1947), and *Force of Evil* (1949) before the forces of reaction expelled their content, leaving indirect traces via visual style allowing for a deliberate strategy of ambiguous reading. If the political associations of post-war American film noir leave open the door for repressed sublimated meanings so, too, do several French film noirs of the Occupation era. Although the charge of collaboration can be easily leveled against those French directors who chose to work in the industry at this particular time so also can a similar allegation be made against those American cinematic talents who survived blacklist surveillance and chose, nevertheless, to work and subtly protest at what was going on in their country, a situation over which they had no agency to oppose or react against via explicit protest. In both cases such allegations are manifestly unfair.

Various talents working on several French film noirs of this period realized that no explicit protest was possible under much more dangerous circumstances than those affecting blacklist Hollywood cinema but they actively chose to articulate visually the dangerous circumstances surrounding both their country and the industry within which they worked. They attempted making their form of sublimated message no matter how compromised it was at the time and chose the noir style to do so.

It took many decades for French society to recognize the fact that the Occupation was a much darker episode in its history, eschewing any simple binary oppositions between the majority of people being on the side of the Resistance against collaborators such as Laval and Pétain who had made their Faustian pact with the Satanic "Boche." Despite the initial effect of *The Sorrow and the Pity* on French audiences, it took some time for it to resonate on French society. The hostile reception against Louis Malle's *Lacombe Lucien* (1974) was one of the reasons for his relocation to America. As late as 1995 Claude Lelouch's 1995 version of *Les Miserables* set in the Occupation period starring Jean-Paul Belmondo as a twentieth-century Jean Valjean was withdrawn from one international film festival despite its un-Hugo "happy ending." While French cinema made tentative efforts to come to terms with the 1954 defeat in Dien Bien Phu in the 1990s releases of Jean-Jacques Annaud's heavily nostalgic *L'Amant* (1991); Regis Wargnier's *Indochine* (1992) starring Catherine Deneuve as a French colonial Marianne mother-figure; and Indo-China war veteran Pierre Schoendoerffer's *Dien Bien Phu* (1991), it was not until much later that a dark chapter in French history could be explicitly treated with the release of Robert Guediguan's *Army of Crime* (2009). It contrasted the courage of a mixed group of Armenians and Jews with the willingness of most French people to accept or assist the Germans in contrast to the myth of the Resistance celebrated earlier in Rene Clément's *La Bataille du Rail* (1945). The French television series *Un Village Francais* (2009-2016) was able to use a different visual style than Occupation noir to address openly what could not be depicted in earlier representations of the era, whether noir or not.[25] The dark era of Occupied France could not be explicitly addressed in any of the films made then but it was the contemporary French version of the noir style that attempted to express the fear, hesitancy, and uncertainty within this particular era. Restraint often calls into play the role of subversion and many of the best examples of these films especially those of Clouzot engage in such practices. This is an era deserving further attention not just for noir but also other Occupation cinematic adaptations of Georges Simenon novels that indirectly expressed the contemporary mood in their own specific ways.

    [I wish to thank Rob Cochran for his generous help in supplying material for this article as well as Greg Wendt for screener assistance.]

Notes

1. Ginette Vincendeau. "Noir is also a French Word: The French Antecedents of Film Noir." *The Book of Film Noir*. Ed. Ian Cameron. New York: Continuum Publishing Company, 39-48.
2. See especially the special edition of *Iris* 21, "European Precursors of Film Noir." Spring 1996.
3. My ironic play on Truffaut's celebrated article is, of course, intentional. See Francois Truffaut, "A Certain Tendency of the French Cinema." *Movies and Methods*. Ed. Bill Nichols. Berkeley: University of California Press, 1976, 234-237.
4. See Rui Nogueira, *Melville on Melville*. London: Secker & Warburg, 1971,29-30 According to Brett Bowles details of this Paris visit are absent from the novel. Images showing the German presence on the streets derive from selections from the official state newsreel Deutsche Wochenschau with several re-enacted scenes. Also, the solitary shots of von Ebrennac as tourist evoke Hitler's 1940 visit in a car through empty streets. See Bowles, "Documentary Realism and Collective Memory in Post-War France, 1945-1955." *Historical Journal of Film, Radio, and Television* 27.2 (2007): 202. This not only suggests the cultured German's unwitting involvement with Nazi goals but also a common type of denial that also appears in French Occupation cinema.
5. Ginette Vincendeau, *Jean-Pierre Melville: An American in Paris*, London: British Film Institute, 2006, 56-57, who notes that this is another detail not in the book.
6. Quoted from Fiona Watson, "Henri-Georges Clouzot. Great Directors," http://www.sensesofcinema.com/2005/great-directors/clouzot/ (accessed March 2, 2017).
7. During 1960-1963, BBC TV ran the popular series Maigret featuring Rupert Davies, a choice that pleased Simenon. Michael Gambon reprised the role for ITV in 1992. The BBC TV series also inspired a 1966 series of thirteen hour long non-Maigret crime stories *Thirteen Against Fate,* many of which were noirish by nature. As well as Jean Valjean of Victor Hugo's *Les Miserables*, Maigret has long represented a rite of passage for many French actors such as Pierre Renoir, Albert Préjean, Jean Gabin, and Bruno Cremer.
8. Fenton Bresler, *The Mystery of Georges Simenon*. New York: Beaufort Books, Inc. 1983, 127.
9. This English translation of the French title of Simenon's novel also echoes the title of the later 1966 English version starring James Mason, *Stranger in the House*. Another French version was made starring Jean-Paul Belmondo in 1992.
10. I owe this reference to Francis M. Nevins who consulted an English translation of the novel in his 2/24/17 email. He covers film and novel in his monthly column "First You Read, Then You Write." www.mysteryfile.com/blog/?p=46301 (accessed March 20, 2017). The 1961-published French version of the book also refers to the first name Ephraim. So does the 2006 *New York Review of Books* English translation, *The Strangers in the House* translated by Geoffrey Sainsbury with revisions by David

Watson and others which contains several references to Luska's Jewish origins despite the claim by P.D. James in her introduction that Justin Luska's "Jewishness is hardly mentioned" while "emphasized" in the film. (ix). However, in this recent translation, Simenon mentions "a Jew like Luska" (70) whose "real first name was `EphraIm'." (150) According to certain French sources, the film was later re-synchronized after the War changing "Ephraim" to Amedée but since Raimu had died in 1946, he is the only person in the film to call the character by his real first name in the novel. "*Les Inconnus dans la mason* de Henri Decoin: quand Decoin et Clouzot adaptent Simenon ou 'une petite ville francaise sous l'occupation'." www.newsstrum.wordress. com/2016/6/10. See also David Cairns. "Henri Decoin – *Les Inconnus dans la maison* aka *Strangers in the House* (1942)." www.worldscinema.org/2016/11 (accessed March 20, 2016). This issue deserves an entire article but it seems to be the case that Clouzot probably down-played the Jewish angle yet had to use the name "Ephraim" since the source novel was widely known and any deliberate change would arouse suspicions against him. Significantly, although Vichy eliminat-ed the double bill system of exhibition, it seems to have made an exception in the distribution of *Inconnus* by putting it on a double bill with one of the only two anti-Semitic films produced at the time – *Forces Occultes* (1943). See Roy Armes, *French Cinema* . London: Secker & Warburg, 1985, 110, 119.

11. When we first see Nicole's cousin Edmond with his mother, he has just returned from the cinema and faints like a demure female when he hears about the murder!

12. As Vincendeau notes (58) all the key elements of French film noir that Hollywood had already borrowed from were well in place by 1939 as seen in *Le Dernier Tournant* (1939) directed by Pierre Chenal. Furthermore, Anglo-American crime fiction had appeared in French translations since 1927 with Hammett's *Red Harvest* and *The Glass Key* already available in 1932. (57)

13. See Watson.

14. Francois Truffaut, *The Films in My Life*. London: Allen Lane, 1980, 3.

15. For Clouzot's influence on Hitchcock see Patrick McGilligan, *Alfred Hitchcock: A Life in Darkness*. New York: Regan Books, 2003, 494, 542.

16. See Vincendeau, "Noir is also a French Word" and ""Deep focus: How the French birthed film noir." *Sight & Sound*. BFI. http://www.bfi.org.uk/news-opinion/sight-sound-magazine/features (accessed March 24, 2017.) For the distinctive nature of French Poetic Realism see Dudley Andrew, *Mists of Regret: Culture and Sensibility in French Film,* Princeton, Jew Jersey: Princeton University Press, 1995.

17. David Cairns, "The Forgotten: Aglow and Askew." https://mubi.com/notebook/posts/the-forgotten-aglow-and-askew. (Accessed March 10, 1917)

18. See James Travers,"Goupi mains rouges/It Happened at the Inn/Jacques Becker/1943." http://www.filmsdefrance.com/review/goupi-mains -rouges-1943.html; Tony Williams, "Goupi mains rouges." http://www.sensesofcinema.com/2014/cteq/goupi-mains-rouges. (Accessed March 25, 2017).

19. See Armes, , 121, 123. The standard work on this period in English is still *Evelyn Ehrlich, Cinema of Paradox: French Filmmaking under the German Occupation*. New York: Columbia University Press, 1985. Although André Bazin mentions several noir titles in his study of this period, he never uses the term "film noir" nor does he categorize any film accordingly. See André Bazin*, French Cinema of the Occupation and Resistance: The Birth of a Critical Esthetic*. Tr. Stanley Hochman. New York: Frederick Ungar Publishing Co., 1981.

20. http://www.filmsdefrance.com/review/la-main-du-diable-1943.html (accessed March 15, 2017).

21. André Bazin, *French Cinema of the Occupation and Resistance*, 99.

22. Op. cit.

23. Armes, 109, 110.

24. See Kenneth E. Hall, *Guillermo Cabrera Infante and the Cinema*. Newark, Delaware: Juan de la Cuestra-Hispanic Monographs, 1989, 16-17, 87.

25. Season Two contains an indirect reference to *Le Corbeau* where a poison pen letter informing on French schoolteacher Lucienne uses the same format as that in the earlier film.

A posed shot of Dan Duryea and June Vincent in the adaptation of Cornell Woolrich's *Black Angel.*

That Sinking Feeling: Cornell Woolrich and the Uncanny Noir Mood

Marlisa Santos

The world of film noir criticism loves to play the "noir/not noir" game. We amuse ourselves, and perhaps our students, by hunting the elusive element that makes a film a bona fide noir. When all is said and done, it is not the lighting nor the cinematography nor the plot nor the characterizations that define noir—it is the feeling that the viewer gets when entering that world. And no writer evokes that peculiar mixture of despair and dread more distinctly than Cornell Woolrich. Woolrich was the most adapted author of the classic noir period, with a lucky 13 of his short stories and novels turned into films noir. Chandler, Cain, and Hammett hold their rightful place as noir source creators but, as Woolrich biographer Francis M. Nevins quips, Woolrich's universe is so twisted and dark that "[t]he world of Hammett is a Victorian drawing room by comparison."[1] It is precisely Woolrich's unpredictability, bent for the uncanny, and lack of adherence to what would be considered conventional realism that set him apart from other noir progenitors and set him firmly as one of the greatest architects of film noir.

Considered a literary prodigy from his early days at Columbia in the 1920's, Woolrich moved from Jazz Age fiction to mystery and suspense sometime in the early 1930's, selling such an extraordinary number of tales to pulp magazines such as *Detective Tales, Argosy, Black Mask*, and *Detective Fiction Weekly* that he had to begin to use pseudonyms (William Irish, George Hopley) to further saturate the market with his particular brand of darkness. As Nevins points out, even his earliest straight suspense stories held a twinge of the twisted shades of ordinary life, as seen in 1934's "Death Sits in the Dentist's Chair," which tells the story of a sadistic dentist who preys upon the most desperate, down-and-out victims of the Depression. Though Woolrich himself was comfortably well-off, from both family money and his prolific writing sales, his stories vividly reflect the economic trials of the Depression, and most importantly, how these trials wove themselves into the fabric of human experiences and their accompanying existential anxieties. As film noir developed, themes of post-WWII angst, including gender role shifts and global fears of communism and nuclear annihilation, became significant markers of the cycle. But it is in the Depression-era crises that the roots of noir can be found. The depth of these crises is emphasized by Philip Hanson, who argues, "[i]ntensifying the collapse of prosperity was the sense that the reputations of society's pillars had been illusory; intensifying the dissolution of respected reputations was a fear that fundamental American values had themselves been an illusion," adding that Charles Schwab himself claimed in 1932, "'I'm afraid, every man is afraid. I don't know, we don't know, whether the values we have are going to be real next month or not.'"[2] The fundamental security that has been shaken by economic collapse seeps into the deepest corners of the American psyche and cannot be righted. The world of which Woolrich conceives reflects this core uncertainty from which equilibrium could not be recovered and is, in fact, only further reinforced with the aforementioned forces of the social and political upheavals of the 1940s and 1950s.

It is precisely one of the greatest criticisms of Woolrich's work—his wildly improbable plot turns and almost obsessive attention to detail—that creates the noir quality that would influence so many filmmakers. According to Nevins, "these are not gaffes but functional elements that enable him to integrate contradiction and existential absurdity into his dark fabric...[l]ong before Theater of the Absurd, Woolrich knew that an incomprehensible universe is best reflected in an incomprehensible story."[3] Woolrich forces the reader—and by extension, the viewer—to confront the cracks in what we believe to be the stability of reality, and will not entertain such stability in his world. As Tom Quin, the wrongly accused protagonist in *I Wouldn't Be in Your Shoes* (1948), muses, "I remember the trial as if through a fog...it was all unreal. Funny how the realest things in your life always seem that way." In Woolrich, the real is unreal, and the unreal is real. You are an innocent man...until you are not. You know who you are...until you do not. In this way, Woolrich manufactures a singular uncanny dread—not to be confused with fear—that permeates his fiction.

Dread can be distinguished from fear in its breadth and its object—whereas fear is localized and specific, dread is global and general. In its inability to be pinned down, it is a crushing form of human anxiety, without form or cause or potential relief. Robert Porfirio identified the noir atmosphere as "one in which the familiar is fraught with danger and the existential tonalities of 'fear' and 'trembling' are not out of place, even less that sense of 'dread' which is taken to mean a pervasive fear of something hauntingly indeterminate."[4] The way that Woolrich's dread manifests itself—and indeed defines noir—bears resemblance to Freud's examination of the uncanny. In his explorations of

the concept, Freud considers various etymological and philosophical definitions of the term, the German *unheimlich,* meaning "unfamiliar," or more literally, "un-home-like." He focuses on Schelling's particular interpretation of the uncanny, which is "everything that ought to have remained secret and hidden and has instead come to light."[5] That peculiar unsettling feeling, then, derives not just from something being unknown or unfamiliar, but a quality of being familiar and not familiar at the same time—something that is simultaneously partially known and unknown, and moreover, that should have stayed where it belonged in the dark. Naturally, Freud's interest in this idea focuses on the disturbing prospect of the unconscious. But it could be argued that the idea could be applied to the collective American unconscious simmering during the post-Depression to pre-Cold War era that we associate with classic film noir. The permeating dread that seeped into everyday life was broadly colored by anxieties that, though fueled by economic and social uncertainties, were often difficult to define and terrifying in their scope—related to fundamental questions of stability and consistency in social, political, and even ontological realms. It certainly appears that Woolrich was tapping into this uncanny quality of everyday life, and the recurrent themes and motifs that are seen in his fiction, notably amnesia and the wrongfully accused, point to larger issues of instability of identity that become central to films noir as the cycle develops.

Nevins aptly characterizes Woolrich's universe as "a trap, an incomprehensible place where beams happen to fall, and at the same time are predestined to fall, and at the same time are toppled over by malevolent powers."[6] The most unnerving quality of Woolrichean fiction is its refusal to maintain consistency within its own world, and this is the feature that makes it appear uncanny, at once both strange and familiar, ruled by fate and chance at the same time. Noirs from the classic period based on Woolrich's fiction spanned from 1942-1956. Many source novels were filmed seemingly as quickly as he could write them—for instance, *Street of Chance* (1942, Jack Hively) was based on 1941's *The Black Curtain*, and *Phantom Lady* (1944, Robert Siodmak) was based on the 1942 novel of the same name. But many of these novels were based on earlier short stories published in the aforementioned crime rags in the 1930's—for instance, *Black Angel* (1946, Roy William Neill) was based on the 1944's *Black Angel*, which found its roots in a 1935 story entitled "Murder in Wax," published by *Dime* magazine. Therefore, while it may seem that there was a certain simultaneity in Woolrich's influence on film noir, his particular brand of noir narrative had long been read in the popular community in the 1930's, and though it was grounded in Depression-era desperation, blossomed as World War II anxieties mounted, both during and after. Even so, since films noir based on Woolrich were produced until 1956, the focus for this essay's purpose should more rightly be the earliest noirs, as those likely had the most formative influence on later films.

The first of these was *Street of Chance*, an arguable prototype for what would become the ubiquitous noir amnesia film. The film's "dangerous random accidents," according to Sheri Chinen Biesen, parallel the unnerving effect of the Japanese attack on Pearl Harbor, having "lethal consequences and a labyrinth of chaos spiraling out of control. The film's convoluted, elaborate, and unlikely psychological crime plot was just the stuff noir was made of."[7] Indeed the opening of both the film and *The Black Curtain* thrust the viewer and reader abruptly into the protagonist's amnesia predicament, wherein a falling piece of debris has knocked him—and his memory—out cold. The opening shot of *Street of Chance* displays the agent of this debris: "Empire House Wrecking Company: We Move Anything." It is a fitting motif for the ensuing trials of Frank Thompson/Danny Nearing, the dual identity of the character played by Burgess Meredith. Frank/Danny has no real home and his existence is a constant moving target. It is the particular details that Woolrich supplies in the novel, duplicated

Opposite, *Street of Chance:* amnesiac Frank Thompson (Burgess Meredith) with Ruth Dillon (Claire Trevor) is repeatedly stymied as he tries "to unravel the mystery of his own self."

in the film, that place his experience squarely in the realm of the uncanny. After regaining consciousness from the opening blow on the head, he examines his personal effects, some of the most personal items one could carry, his cigarette case and hat, only to find not only general unfamiliarity, but also a set of initials that point to no name he associates with himself. Yet, these items are physically on his person, so they must be his. A boy who tries to help him after the accident, queries, "Don't you know your own hat, mister?" This disconnect creates the initial disorientation that frames the rest of his pursuits and also provides a blueprint for creating the singular noir uneasiness.

Through a series of revelations, Frank Thompson learns that he has been "missing" from his previous life for three years, living as someone named Danny Nearing, and moreover, this Nearing is wanted for murder. The process by which he learns this and eventually clears himself, is another narrative device that would become commonplace in noir: the "wrong man" who must become a detective to unravel the mystery of his own self. The condition of amnesia injects a ready-made identity crisis that makes such investigation necessary, wherein the protagonist discovers any number of unwanted details about himself or the self he thought he was and knew. Thompson's wife, Virginia (Louise Platt), in an effort to help him through the experiences says, "Hold on to the things you're sure of." However, these sureties are few to none—ultimately, the only one to which Thompson clings is a sen-

Below, another Woolrich character deficient in "street smarts," Vince Grayson (DeForest Kelley) buttonholes Cliff Herlihy (Paul Kelly) in *Fear in the Night*.

timent that comes directly from Woolrich's text: "The me that's inside wouldn't let me kill anyone." Though Thompson continually feels as though he is "dead" or "in a bad dream," his only anchor is the overriding—and illogical—idea that whoever "he" is at the core could not have committed the crime. And generally in Woolrich, this sentiment proves to be correct. One might suppose, then, that Woolrich believes in the existence of a stable identity, grounded in a core morality. But this answer too proves unsatisfying; regardless of how many Woolrichean novels and films resolve this way, one always feels that it is only by chance that they do so. Out of 100 stories that prove this idea true, the 101 would be the one that does not. This sensation is a testament to Woolrich's ability to construct a world so precarious that if there were such thing as immutable human morality, it is a hair's breadth away from collapse at all times.

Thompson's efforts to exonerate himself involve gathering clues from those who might have known him, and these are extremely uncanny experiences. He is pursued by a nefarious-looking character, who seems to want to kill him, but who turns out to be a police detective, Marucci (Sheldon Leonard). In this reversal of worlds, the cops bear striking resemblance to the criminals, especially if you may be a criminal yourself. Thompson is now required to impersonate a self that he does not know, even though others do know that self. He is learning about this other self by impersonating it and drawing out his own characteristics from interactions with others. For instance, when he tries to pawn the cigarette case, he learns that he had already appeared in the pawnshop to sell it several times before. And Nearing's girlfriend, Ruth Dillon (Claire Trevor), tells him he is "no good." Such characterizations are at odds with Thompson's mild-mannered appearance; there is usually nothing hard-boiled about Woolrich's hapless male protagonists, and Burgess Meredith, like DeForest Kelley being cast in 1947's *Fear in the Night*, is an appropriate choice. The lack of street-smarts in these characters reinforce their uncanny experience and distance from their "other" selves. The idea of social construction of identity is also clearly at work, as will be apparent in other early noirs based on Woolrich's work. And the only possible savior for Thompson comes in the form of another marginalized figure, the mute and paralyzed mother of the murdered man, who witnessed the crime, but cannot tell what she saw. A desperate Thompson devises a way to communicate with Grandma Diedrich (Adeline DeWalt Reynolds) through a system of eye blinks and yes/no questions. In *The Black Curtain*, this character is the dead man's mute and paralyzed father who communicates through eye blinks that convey Morse code. In Woolrich's world of gray, Thompson's innocence must be proven through systematic revelations from black and white options and tortured attempts at discovering stable knowledge.

Garrett Fort's screenplay, like those of other future Woolrich adaptations, one-ups the noir quality by making Ruth Dillon the real murderer, rather than the greedy relatives from the novel; she is the most significant casualty of Thompson's venture into an alternative life, since she claims she did it for him, for the money that he told her would allow them to run away together. In another indication of Thompson's questionable core character, it would appear that his influence indirectly caused both Diedrich's murder and her own. And it is not so neat a resolution as it seems, for Thompson to be cleared and resume his previous middle-class life and marriage. The gaping hole in the narrative, of both novel and film, is what caused the original occurrence of amnesia, and the subsequent steps that led him to become Danny Nearing, who was, by all accounts, a two-bit petty criminal and chiseler. Though Thompson tries to push this disturbing question aside, the fact remains that Frank and Danny are the same person, even though one has no conscious memory of the other. As Mark Osteen argues, Thompson "reinhabits his old self only through the ministrations of Nearing, who is then sacrificed for his trouble...[e]ven at the conclusion Frank Thompson remains a partial person, as disabled in his own way as Grandma Diedrich—and far less honest."[8] Thompson's parallels with Grandma Diedrich are multiple and rich—not only do they share a barrier in communicating knowledge, their access to this knowledge is mediated. Grandma sees Ruth kill her son as a reflection in a mirror, and Thompson can only learn about his other self, whom he must try to exonerate, through the descriptions of others. In the end, Thompson is more fixed in the uncanny unknown than even Grandma, since he fills in only enough to free Nearing, not to explain himself. And Woolrich forces us to accept this lack of resolution. Like the film's final shot of Detective Marucci pensively smoking a cigarette on the street after Ruth's demise, Woolrich leaves the players in the kind of suspended uncertainty that will become standard operating procedure in film noir.

The next earliest Woolrich noir adaptation, *Phantom Lady* (1944, Robert Siodmak) establishes another noir convention, that of the wrong man and the female savior-detective, through uncanny means. The experience of *Phantom Lady's* Scott Henderson (Alan Curtis) is the classic "thought crime" of noir: the hostility of a bitter argument with his wife, which begins the evening and leads him to the company of a mysterious unknown woman, becomes physically realized when he returns home to find her dead and police accusing him of the murder. As Foster Hirsch argues, the entrapment of these characters "may spring from guilty thoughts more than guilty deeds, and from an unconscious masochism."[9] The idea that one can be condemned by a guilty thought certainly appeared in the first arguable film noir, *Stranger on the Third Floor* (1940, Boris Ingster), and appeared in many Woolrich stories during the 1930's, including the aforementioned "Murder in Wax." It could be argued that Woolrich's own tortured psyche, including his repressed homosexuality, might account for the predicaments of such characters, who may not be guilty, but perhaps feel guilty. In *Phantom Lady*, for instance, it not only looks bad for Henderson because of the crime scene's circumstantial evidence; it also is bad, as witness after witness claim never to have seen the "phantom lady" he claims he was with and who can be his only alibi. These machinations are similar to those in Woolrich's later *The Black Path of Fear*, wherein the protagonist, Bill Scott, is accused of murdering his girlfriend, and shown witnesses and pieces of evidence that directly contradict his own experience. In *Phantom Lady*, according to Thomas C. Renzi, "the question is not whether he can find her but whether she existed at all. The story becomes an existential exercise in that we suddenly must wonder whether the event, told from Henderson's viewpoint, was an imagined reality. Even if he did not deliberately formulate it, he might have resorted to a defense mechanism by which his guilty conscience enabled to him to deny the murder he really did commit."[10] It may seem as though portraying this ordeal on film might make it less subjective, since the viewer can actually see the mystery woman. However, the situation is still conveyed as decidedly questionable because of exactly that kind of supposition regarding eyewitness testimony, the supreme confidence in perception as epistemological certainty. How could so many witnesses be mistaken or lying? Viewers may feel less sure that Henderson created the woman than readers of the novel, but they are no closer to explaining what is happening to him. Henderson himself acknowledges the existential crisis this situation creates, commenting. "If I did that, I'd never be sure of anything again in my life."

As in many Woolrich stories, when logic fails, blind faith must take over, because it is the only resort left. Henderson's girlfriend, Carol "Kansas" Richman (Ella Raines), sets out to prove his innocence because she refuses, in her love and loyalty, to believe that he could have committed murder. As one of many Woolrich avenging angels, she sheds her staid appearance to become first barfly, and then, hep kitten in her dogged pursuit of the real killer. Night after night she appears in the bar that Henderson and the mystery woman appeared, staring mercilessly at the bartender (Andrew Tombes) who did not acknowledge that the mystery woman existed. The bartender's guilt slowly emerges, projected onto her Fury-like gaze, and here again is exposed the idea of the uncanny, the disquieting feeling of the familiar in the unfamiliar—he does not know this woman, but he knows quite well his own guilt, the thing that should be left buried, but has instead surfaced. Her disturbing presence drives him nearly to murder her and then to his own accidental death in trying to escape from her. She also indi-rectly causes the death of jazz drummer Cliff (Elisha Cook, Jr.), who tells her he got "500 smackaroos for looking at a dame and sayin' I didn't…no matter who asks, say no, and keep on sayin' no." The real killer, Henderson's "friend" and ex-lover to his wife, Jack Marlow (Franchot Tone), strangles him when he suspects that Cliff has revealed his deception. The forays of Kansas into these various underworlds in order to unearth the truth reveal the precariousness of what we assume to be an objective reality. Innocence and guilt are in no way stable conditions, and the pursuits of the law to make them so prove to be faulty when money or whim drive the expression of "truth." This ever-shifting quality of noir narrative shows, according to J.P. Telotte, "how much the stories we tell—individually and cul-turally—always seem to depend on an elusive, phantom fundament, and to argue for their truth largely through an ability to disguise absence, assumption, or common prejudice with narration's own rhetorical presence, especially its sense of certainly and objectivity, or by relying on a pattern of mutu-al consent."[11] This "mutual consent" is key to Woolrichean instability and the Kafka-esque uncanny situations in which his protagonists find themselves. All trust, in oneself and in one's fellow humani-ty, becomes compromised when a collective—and perhaps false—agreement of truth rules over an individual's conviction.

Further iterations of both the avenging angel and amnesia "wrong man" stories are seen in the next two Woolrich film adaptations, two of three released in 1946: *Black Angel* and *Deadline at Dawn* (Harold Clurman). *Black Angel's* protagonist is not the wrongly accused man, but rather his wife, and one significant difference between the novel and film is the nature of her knowledge-seeking

"Night after night, she appears in the bar": Ella Raines as the dogged Carol "Kansas" Richman in *Phantom Lady*.

journey—whereas the novel focuses in great detail on the multiple shady personalities that she encounters to find the mysterious "M" who she believes actually committed the murder, the film simplifies these possibilities and throws more attention on the figure of Marty Blair (Dan Duryea), the ex-husband of the murdered woman, who is helping the wife, Catherine (June Vincent) exonerate her husband. Blair is an alcoholic who suffered from "Korsakoff's psychosis," a.k.a. alcohol amnesia, and so does not remember that it was actually he who killed Mavis Marlowe (Constance Dowling). This detail is only revealed at the end of the film, and so ironically, the detective work that he and Catherine do is all in vain, and do not even lead to this discovery. As in *Phantom Lady*, when Marlow is discovered only at the point that "Kansas" finds herself in peril at his hand and the investigation has simply seemed to have run out of suspects, Blair realizes himself that he is the murderer after there are no other options.

It is significant that these dead ends and in-the-dark stumbling begin with an important assumption, again on faith, of Catherine regarding her husband's innocence. Whereas in Woolrich's novel, Alberta knows her husband could not have committed the crime because he calls Mavis' apartment at the exact time that Alberta, in her wronged wife anger, has sought out Mavis and discovered her body, in the film, Catherine simply takes her husband's word that he is innocent. Therefore, an immediate absence of knowledge grounds the entire action and indeed the moral core of the narrative. The uncanny experience of seeking this elusive knowledge is ironically the purview of Blair and Catherine, not Kirk Bennett (John Phillips), who in both novel and film, is more or less a non-character, as he awaits the outcome of his disastrous circumstances. Similar to *Phantom Lady*, when a spec-

Marty Blair (Dan Duryea) and Catherine Bennett (June Vincent) search for leads to solve the murder of his ex-wife in *Black Angel*.

tator coughs over the verdict being read, Bennett's judgment is delivered indirectly; the news is transmitted via reporters and newspaper headlines. As in the novel, the prison sends Catherine his belongings, "as if he were already dead." He is quite separated from his own identity and fate, as Catherine takes on this responsibility as his surrogate. Blair becomes an unlikely ally, as he is the initial suspect for Catherine, but his alibi is strong enough for her to rule him out: his friend Joe (Wallace Ford) swears that he brought him home to his room, the door of which is curiously equipped with a slide bolt on the outside, for his own protection when he drinks himself into a dangerous state. Locked in as such, Joe says, he could not have committed the crime. Blair himself is also thereby convinced of his own innocence, and "Heartbreak," as he is called, after a hit song that he wrote for Mavis to sing, begins to feel that in the course of his helping Catherine, he may finally find a new beginning and real love.

However, similar to Alberta's influence leading to the destruction of each of her suspects in the novel, it is Cathy's romantic rejection of Marty that sends him into the bender that ultimately reveals his guilt. Each stop in the drinking montage that occurs peels away further layers of Marty's buried memory, culminating in a feverish dream as he is strapped to a bed in the psych ward. Marty spotted a woman in one of these bars wearing the heart-shaped brooch that he had given Mavis, and which he and Cathy had been searching for all along, as the only definitive clue to the killer's identity. At her claim that he gave her the brooch, he angrily starts arguing and fighting; once in the hospital, a dream sequence filled with mirage-like dissolves reveals that he was actually the killer of Mavis. One of the most surreal and sinister aspects is the revelation that the hotel caretaker unbolted his door that night, saying "Heartbreak? I'll let you out for a quarter." As out of *Pandora's Box*, all of Marty's love-fueled despair and rage is released and finds murderous ends. And like Cassandra, even when he tries to tell police that he is actually the murderer, no one believes him. Even when Marty's deepest secret has become unburied, the uncanny result is heightened by his voice not being heard and believed. It is not insignificant that the Woolrichean wrong man murders are often strangulation—the wife of *Phantom Lady's* Scott Henderson is strangled with a necktie and Mavis is strangled with her own scarf—signifying the silencing of voice, the suffocation of knowledge.

While Marty Blair's uncanny amnesia is so buried that it is not even known to himself, and Frank Thompson is dimly conscious of a whole life lived and unremembered over the course of a year, *Deadline at Dawn's* Alex Winkler (Bill Williams) knows who he is, but also knows that he cannot remember a few hours the previous night—and that these few hours will mean life or death for him. A chance meeting with shady and now-dead blackmailer Edna Bartelli (Lola Lane) has left him hungover and doubting his own actions, leading him to enlist the help of taxi dancer June Goffe (Susan Hayward) to retrace his steps and determine whether he indeed committed the murder. Donald Phelps characterizes Woolrich's "low-income heroes and heroines: white-collar scramblers, dancehall hostesses, watch repairers—as determined amateurs; committed, however fearfully and fumblingly,

Philosopical cabbie Gus (Paul Lukas) helps June Goffe (Susan Hayward) and Alex Winkler (Bill Williams) in *Deadline at Dawn.*

to salvaging their negligible, yet threatened worlds"[12] This description is particularly apt for *Deadline at Dawn*; nearly every character we meet is damaged in some way, yet desperately trying to preserve his or her own piece of the world. The opening shot of the film sets the tone for these struggles: an upside-down close-up of Edna's closed-eyed face with a fly lighting twice upon it. As she opens her eyes to a pounding knock at the door, we see she is merely drunk, not dead (at this point); however, the suggestion of living death is reinforced throughout the entire film, giving the tenor of the action a peculiar uneasy quality. Aside from June and Gus (Paul Lukas), a kindly philosophical cabbie, other ancillary characters complete this picture, any of whom might also be murder suspects, including Edna's violent brother Val (Joseph Calleia), Sleepy Parsons (Marvin Miller), Edna's ex-husband, a morose blind piano player, and Helen Robinson (Osa Massen), a working-class housewife with a limp and an unfaithful husband. Alex, unless or until he can determine Edna's actual killer, is a less-than-living man himself, his sailor's leave likely to become a death sentence. Most of the action in the film in fact centers on how many hours Edna's death might be kept a secret from the police, while time is bought to solve the crime, her dead body treated like an object of little consequence or care. Ultimately, and ironically, even though these characters are loners in the urban jungle, their lives are intertwined from the beginning of the narrative, as signified by a close-up of Sleepy's white lapel carnation swirl-dissolving into the top of Alex's sailor hat as he is awakening at the newsstand. And as will become clear, such interconnection can spell salvation or destruction.

Against the backdrop of all this corruption, Alex's naiveté and childlike outlook on life is particularly striking and almost out of place. He is continually surprised at his own situation, referring to his alcoholic blackout and his general ineptitude, as a chronic mental failing on his part, repeating "non compos mentis" and tapping his head when these shortcomings arise. He is surprisingly stoic, even at the prospect of that he could be the murderer and that this could mean his own destruction.

Opposite, June the taxi dancer wistfully contemplates her evolving relationship with serviceman Alex. Above, a dramatic staging: June can only watch as the violent Val Bartelli (Joseph Calleia) threatens Lester Brady (Jerome Cowan) partially obscured by set pieces and shadow in *Deadline at Dawn*.

He says, "I was dead once, drowned in a river," but was revived after two hours and feels "nothing more can happen to me." It is as though once touched so strongly by death, the threats of the living world no longer frighten him. His boyish countenance and seemingly wide-eyed view of the world continually surprise June; she keeps calling him a "baby" and through her own jaded perspective, feels the need to help him and take care of him. She is another amateur female detective character, one who gradually learns that her bitter perceptions can in fact produce insights that could save a man's life. When Alex brings her to Edna's apartment, she examines lipstick, perfume, and a cigarette dismissively, until it dawns on her that she might actually be able to discover something important, such as the shade of lipstick not being one that Edna would wear because of her coloring, and later, the idea that she might use the scent of the spilled perfume on herself to test Sleepy Parson's reaction to it. Characters such as June, Catherine Bennett, and "Kansas" Richman pave the way for the noir "good-bad" girl—not femme fatale or sterile homebuilder, but savvy helpmate. Moreover, they contribute in general to the catalogue of noir detectives outside the law that begins with Woolrich's lost souls who must dig to uncover themselves. Phelps argues that there is nary a professional detective in Woolrich's fiction, adding that "[t]he idea of an authoritarian protector of natural order…seems to be remote from Woolrich's skewed romanticism."[13] This lack of order protection is the foundation of the uncanny experiences of Woolrich's characters as they must navigate all-too-real bizarre experiences.

Much of the detecting experience arises from an imaginative exercise, as June asks Alex, "You've just done it—where do you go, what do you do?" Alex himself might have indeed done it, but he erases that haunting possibility for the moment to completely imagine what another person might do, and his first instinct—to buy some juice for his dry throat—leads them to Helen, who we discover later is the reason for the murder, committed on her behalf by her father, the sympathetic Gus. Gus is a fascinating counterpoint to the world-weary June; he has lived with heartache and disappointment too, but seems to have found peace with his life and the world's injustices. "Where's the logic to it?" June says. "Golly, the misery that walks around in this pretty quiet night..." He responds, "The logic is that there is no logic. The horror and terror comes from being alive. Die and there's no trouble." Gus says the only antidote to the situation is love, and ironically his murder of Edna is for love of his daughter and wanting to preserve her marriage, into which Edna had inserted herself as mistress and blackmailer. As Alex has been trying to find clues to regain his memory of that portion of the night (which he never does), Gus has been on his own uncanny journey, trying to disguise his own very familiar guilt at the same time that he preserves Alex's innocence. And so, his confession is a final act of love, for the future of Alex and June and the hope that they might escape the un-home-like atmosphere of the cruel city. The discovery of the real murderer, moreover, has nothing to do with objective police process and everything to do with Gus' own sense of morality and humanity. When police are interrogating Alex, his initial claims that he is innocent are transformed, by the admonition of the "good cop" to "be sincere," to the admission that it was possible he did commit the murder; this is "good enough" for them to arrest him for the crime. For the final time in the film, June's woeful musing, "I hear the whistle blowing" signifies the depth of chance at work here. The mere admission of possibility creates a yawning abyss of probability. Gus' repeated interjections that "statistics tell us" various certainties on which we can rely ends with his confession, and also his admission that "statistics tell us...nothing."

Deadline at Dawn deviates significantly from Woolrich's novel in most ways aside from the chance meeting of two young people who see in each other a chance to escape the vagaries of urban life. Even the amnesia is not part of the original story, prompting Renzi to comment that "Odets' version of Woolrich's novel is less an adaptation of *Deadline at Dawn* than it is an offshoot of *Nightmare* and *The Black Curtain*."[14] But it is this kind of transformation that shows film noir's gradual absorption of the Woolrich aesthetic to the point that it became an undeniable part of its fabric. Film adaptations often became what Woolrich would have or might have done, in addition to what he actually did do in his fiction. A particularly striking example of this phenomenon is *The Chase*, the final Woolrich film released in 1946, adapted from *The Black Path of Fear* (1944). The novel is an extremely bleak portrait of how Bill Scott, as a consequence of his affair with his boss' wife, endures the accusation of her murder, a terrifying flight from police and dealing with the opium underworld of Cuba to prove his innocence. This journey culminates with his own murder of his previous boss, who ordered his wife killed and Scott framed. Director Arthur Ripley and screenwriter Philip Yordan retain much of the core plot, but narratively transform it into a tale of mental instability and amnesiac dream disturbance. Honesty as a rare commodity is highlighted in both versions, however, as Scott (Robert Cummings) meets Eddie Roman (Steve Cochran), his future boss, because he is returning Roman's wallet. An added detail in the film is that Scott is a veteran, a further sign of wartime influence over noir and the layering of the cultural fallout it produced. When Roman sardonically asks his henchman Gino (Peter Lorre) to go buy Scott a medal for his honesty, Scott replies, "I've got a medal." When Scott meets Roman, his pockets are empty, borrowing money from the wallet to have a single meal before returning it. After being hired as Roman's chauffeur, his stomach may be fuller, but he is less free. Roman is a ruthless gangster, cruel and controlling, who has even installed overriding brake and accelerator pedals in the back seat of the car, so that he can control –or test—the driver. It is not difficult to understand why his wife, Lorna (Michele Morgan), is eager to escape him, via Scott's sympathetic attention. Cuba is not a far enough destination, however, because she is knifed to death in a crowded bar, and Scott is accused of the murder. Similar to Henderson's predicament in *Phantom Lady*, Scott has the uncanny experience of hearing witnesses tell the police things that his own experience tells him are untrue. The most damning of these is his purchase of a knife that appears to be the murder weapon. Scott insists he bought the "hear no evil" knife of a "three wise monkeys" set, whereas the shop's owner insists that it was the "see no evil" knife, which was embedded in Lorna's body. This discrepancy also signifies the breakdown of sensory experience in the pursuit of truth. Thus begins Scott's journey away from the law, and seeming objective reality, in his escape to prove his innocence.

Where film adaptation drastically deviates from the novel is the fact that the largest portion of the plot, that of Scott's terrifying adventures in Cuba, are in the movie appropriated to a dream that he has, a result of ongoing war trauma, "anxiety neurosis," for which he was apparently being treated at the naval hospital. Cornered by Gino, Scott appears to die from gunshots, but then a cut to Scott's room in Roman's house shows him awakening, taking pills, and calling the naval psychiatrist, telling him, "It's happened again." Not only was the whole ordeal a fantastic dream, Scott does not remember any of it except for its end and there being a Cuban connection—and does not even

Below, haunted veteran Chuck Scott (Robert Cummings, center) is ushered in an exotic room to meet the sinister henchman Gino (Peter Lorre) by Joe the Butler (James Westerfield) in *The Chase*.

Above, Lorna Roman (Michele Morgan) is killed while in the arms of her husband's driver Chuck Scott by a souvenir knife that he had purchased in *The Chase*.

remember how he ended up at Roman's house in the first place. As he speaks to the doctor, he keeps looking at the clock, feeling as though there is something he was supposed to do. Scott's dream experience and subsequent disorientation, though it does not occur in Woolrich's novel, is exactly of the sort Woolrich might have constructed: the sensation that life is simply an exercise of running out of time, a surreal feeling that you are always forgetting something, that part of your life is unlived and should have been—or that something you have lived is better left forgotten. As it turns out, Scott remembers enough to find Lorna and make the ship in time for their escape to Cuba. Roman is in pursuit, but because of his own hubris, he accelerates his car from the back seat enough to collide with a train, in contrast to the near miss that occurs in the early part of the film. According to Osteen, "Chuck's dream, unlike those of most noir vets, is not a memory of war but the forecast of a future that he ultimately avoids. Yet he does little to alter his destiny and instead saved by a deus ex machina..."[15] The viewer may feel as though the future is less bleak without the shadow of Roman darkening the path of Scott and Lorna, but there is a significant unsettling and uncanny quality to the resolution—if Scott's identity is this unstable, what other dangers might the future hold?

In contrast to that of his other contemporaries, Frank Krutnik argues, Woolrich's style is "avowedly Expressionistic, apparently influenced by the capacity of film to generate expressive effects rather than its ability to record reality."[16] Woolrich's early forays into films adapted from his works could very well have colored his eventual ability to set a scene with such visual arrest that Gary Indiana, of the *Village Voice*, commented that "one reason Woolrich's books were so readily bought by Hollywood must have been that nobody had to bother with a shooting script."[17] Following the aforementioned five film adaptations, over the next ten years, film noir would hold other rich interpretations of Woolrich's work, including *Fall Guy* (1947, Reginald Le Borg), *The Guilty* (1947, John Reinhardt), *I Wouldn't Be in Your Sh*oes (1948, William Nigh), *Night Has a Thousand Eyes* (1948. John Farrow), *The Window* (1949, Ted Tetzlaff), and *No Man of Her Own* (1950, Mitchell Liesen). The story "Nightmare" even inspired two noirs by Maxwell Shane, *Fear in the Night* (1947) and *Nightmare* (1956). These earliest noir examples, though, show how Woolrich's vision left an indelible imprint on the development of existentialist film, applying Depression-era desperation and questioning of economic and political systems onto post-World War II apocalyptic anxieties. The result is a unique kind of dread that blurs the lines between objective reality and dreamlike sensibility, ultimately arguing that there is no line at all. Woolrich's uncanny tales of living dead characters suffering amnesia and false accusations reinforce what would become noir commonplaces—at turns the unluckiest is also the luckiest, and that the act of selfhood is one of creativity and also faith.

Notes

1. Francis M. Nevins, Jr., *Cornell Woolrich: First You Dream, Then You Die* (New York: The Mysterious Press, 1988), 117.

2. Philip Hanson, "The Arc of National Confidence and the Birth of Film Noir, 1929-1941," *Journal of American Studies* 42.3 (Dec. 2008), 392.

3. Nevins, 121.

4. Robert Porfirio, "No Way Out: Existential Motifs in the Film Noir," in *Film Noir Reader*, Ed. Alain Silver and James Ursini (New York: Limelight Editions, 1996), 92.

5. Sigmund Freud, "The Uncanny," in *The Standard Edition of the Complete Psychological Works of Sigmund Freud,* Trans. James Strachey. 17. (London: Hogarth, 1957), 224.

6. Nevins, 116.

7. Sheri Chinen Biesen, *Blackout: World War II and the Origins of Film Noir* (Baltimore: Johns Hopkins University Press, 2005), 89.

8. Mark Osteen, *Nightmare Alley: Film Noir and the American Dream* (Baltimore: Johns Hopkins University Press, 2013), 50.

9. Foster Hirsch, *The Dark Side of the Screen: Film Noir* (Boston: Da Capo Press, 1981), 178-79.

10. Thomas C. Renzi, *Cornell Woolrich: From Pulp Noir to Film Noir* (Jefferson, NC: McFarland, 2006), 202-203.

11. J.P. Telotte, "Siodmak's Phantom Women and Noir Narrative," *Film Criticism* 11.3 (Spring 1987), 4.

12. Donald Phelps, "Cinema Gris: Woolrich/Neill's Black Angel," *Film Comment* 36:1 (Jan/Feb 2000), 64.

13. Phelps, 64.

14. Renzi, 236.

15. Osteen, 32-33.

16. Frank Krutnik, *In a Lonely Street: Film Noir, Genre, Masculinity* (New York: Routledge, 1991), 41.

17. Gary Indiana, "Man in the Shadows," VLS 74 (May 1989), 26.

Women and Film Noir: Pulp Fiction and the Woman's Picture

Julie Grossman

Many discussions of film noir are dominated by the categories of the hard-boiled detective and the femme fatale. While these character patterns tend to govern our thinking about the genre, classification of films *as* noir itself poses problems because of the term's cultural pervasiveness. This essay reconsiders the categories conventionally associated with film noir, not only because these labels tend to overshadow discussion of narrative, but also because focusing on such stock characters excludes consideration of other generic associations that can shed light on some of the most intriguing films from the classic period. The most compelling film-noir movies, finally, are blends of male and female stories that don't reinforce patriarchy; they feature both good and bad kinds of agency (rather than being mere primers in moralistic thinking). Lastly, film-noir movies cross genres to include what we conventionally refer to as melodrama, as is certainly the case in all three versions of *Mildred Pierce* (the novel, film, and HBO miniseries).[1]

Far from providing a pat repetition of familiar character patterns and narrative clichés, the best film-noir movies, like much of the fiction that these films adapt, have had an important role in depicting gender distress in modern culture. This essay explores the conversations that take place between classic noir films about love, violence, and gender and the female-authored fiction that served as their sources.[2] Looking at 1940s novels written by women that were brought to the screen as "film noirs" underscores the problems inherent in limiting discussion of film noir to the "classic" character patterns—specifically, the "femme fatale" and the "hard-boiled" male protagonist.[3]

Linking noir with its female-authored source material will, I hope, help to reorient (and reorder) gender associations with film noir so that male experience is not its exclusive focus. Rather, such linkage renders the shared concerns of film noir and melodrama (and its often-discussed sub-genre, the "woman's picture") more evident and interprets the relationship between gender and genre more as a dialogue, less as an opportunity to rank texts in terms of an evaluation-laden hierarchy.[4] Seeing women as the literal source of film noir will, I hope, advance a discussion of the centrality of women *in* noir, but my hope is also that in connecting several film noirs to their female-authored sources, this analysis will promote broader ways of thinking about adaptation spearheaded by Linda Hutcheon, Thomas Leitch, Robert Stam, and other post-fidelity adaptation theorists. The dialogical, performative, nonhierarchical models for adaptation articulated by these critics offer more fruitful and creative ways of talking about film and literature than are available in the context of dyadic or heavily evaluative models that borrow the language of origins and fidelity.[5] A relational model of reading film and literature can recognize how different media, as well as cultural contexts, transpose form and content. More important, this approach also focuses on the meanings that emerge when we think of texts as being discrete, while still being in some sense connected: texts in dialogue *with,* rather than in opposition *to,* one another. Looking at classic film noir in proximity to feminist sources is one example of how relational models of adaptation can enrich our understanding of culture, society, and textual production.

In what follows, I look first at Dorothy Hughes's novel *In a Lonely Place* (1947) and Nicholas Ray's film *In a Lonely Place* (1950); second, at Vicki Baum's novel *Mortgage on Life* (1946) and Ray's film *A Woman's Secret* (1949); and, finally, at Vera Caspary's novel *Laura* (1942) in relation to Otto Preminger's film *Laura* (1944). These works, all made within an eight-year period, exemplify the non-schematic presence of gender issues in noir and the continuities between the treatment of gender in the genre and the exploration of gender in the source novels. While the feminist force of film noir generally comes from a variety of factors that can include writing, acting, and mise-en-scène, the fascination with gender in these particular films derives in large part from the female-authored source material.

Feminist film critique has begun to dissociate film noir from the masculinist perspective that dominated earlier discussions of the genre. Critical work by feminist scholars such as E. Ann Kaplan, Elizabeth Cowie, Helen Hanson, Philippa Gates, Jans Wager, and others has shown the centrality of women to film noir.[6] While popular associations with film noir still seem strongly connected to conventional gender stereotypes (the tough though often righteous male protagonist; the evil seductress), these works on gender and noir, dating from the first publication in 1978 of Kaplan's *Women in Film Noir,* have significantly changed scholarly views of the genre. Whether these critics focus on female protagonists, the subversive nature of the femme fatale, or a feminist critique of the male position in the genre, the revised focus on women in noir has rendered the assumption of noir as an *exclusively* male sphere obsolete.

Alongside this feminist upsurge in noir studies has been an increasing concomitant interest in revising strict genre definitions, with some critics suggesting that there are important continuities among the genres of noir, melodrama, and its subset, the woman's picture, that challenge conventional gender/genre associations. For example, Elizabeth Cowie has observed that film noir addresses the psychic worlds of women and rehearses an idea of melodrama that has been rooted in the genre from its beginning in 1940s classical cinema. While critics have recognized that certain noir films may be called "crime melodrama," that a number of noir films are also "gothic melodramas," and that some noir

films take on a female perspective, ostensibly constituting them as "women's pictures,"[7] these observations haven't had a huge impact on the fixity of film noir as a category, perhaps because the term has become such a cultural touchstone. However, the many films talked about in relation to film noir offer stories and stylistic approaches to narrative that run the gamut across conventional genre boundaries, and, as Cowie has noted, such hybridization was in fact part of the early history of film noir, when studios tried to merge genres in order to tap into as wide an audience as possible: "[W]hat has come to be called *film noir,* whilst it does not constitute a genre itself, does name a particular set of elements that were used to produce `the different' and the new in a film; hence the term *film noir* names a set of possibilities for making existing genres `different.' With this view of genre and of *film noir,* it is no longer possible to speak of `the' *film noir,* as so many writers seek to do."[8] Cowie's reminder that film noir as a category grew to some extent out of a commercial interest in overlapping genres spurs a reconsideration of the relationships among noir and other classic film genres.

Opposite, *A Woman's Secret*: a demurely dressed Susan Caldwell (Gloria Grahame) under the male gaze of Luke Jordan (Melvyn Douglas), although her standing position facing-the-camera accords some visual dominace.

Above, a more balanced pose between the title character in *Laura* (Gene Tierney) and her would-be Pygmalian Waldo Lydecker (Clifton Webb). Although Lydecker looks down at Laura's brightly-lit face, his shadowed profile counters his visual dominance.

Reevaluation of standard genre associations will hopefully continue to loosen the grip of noir enthusiasts on "fatal" character patterns. Helen Hanson has, for example, explored the subjectivity of women in the female gothic and film noir in *Hollywood Heroines,* and Thomas Schatz has discussed the "family resemblance" between the female gothic and the hard-boiled detective film,[9] coining the phrase "femmes noires" to refer to postwar thrillers in which women are central: "The female viewpoint, meanwhile, was privileged in films like *The Strange Love of Martha Ivers* and *Temptation*...thus effectively melding the woman's picture with the *noir* thriller."[10] Attempts to nuance an understanding of film noir are, however, often thwarted by the figure of the femme fatale, who dominates discussions of gender and noir, certainly in popular consciousness but also in critical studies. Jon Lewis, for instance, subscribes to the feminist reading of the "fatal women" in noir as a reflection of postwar anxiety about female independence but asserts that the "castrating woman" is at the heart of film noir: "At the center of many noir films is a devouring woman, a femme fatale."[11] As I've argued elsewhere, the presence of an unambiguous evil woman in the genre is wildly overstated.[12] In fact, the most interesting noir films construct a sliding scale of narrative types—from malevolent seductress, to intrepid and victimized female characters, to ambitious yet helpless females—in suggestive and intriguing ways.

Lizabeth Scott as Mona Stevens with Dick Powell as insurance investigator John Forbes in *Pitfall.*

Close examination of film-noir movies reveals a systematic representation of female characters who cannot express their desire or attain satisfaction within conventional social roles. Examples of such characters who are given subjectivity in film noir while still often being tagged as simply femme fatales abound. Lizabeth Scott's Mona Stevens in *Pitfall* (1948) directly criticizes Dick Powell's John Forbes: "You're a little man with a briefcase" (see opposite page); her insight casts her as the controlling voice of the narrative. Gloria Grahame's Vicki Buckley in *Human Desire* (1954) is also a tragic figure mislabeled as a "femme fatale."[13] Like Mona, Vicki conveys feminist insight in her comments about women's experience: "Most women are unhappy. They just pretend they aren't." Barbara Stanwyck's Mae Doyle in *Clash by Night* (1952) also draws viewer sympathy. She's hard-boiled herself, which may lead viewers to categorize her as a femme fatale, but her story is one of privation, like the situation of many women in film noir; Mae had, on her own report, "big dreams, small results." Debby Marsh in *The Big Heat* (1953) parodies thug Vince Stone's (Lee Marvin) pandering to his boss Lagana in her imitation of Stone's "circus jumping" at Lagana's bidding. Debby's wry commentary establishes her as a sympathetic voice of critique. So, too, in *Notorious* (1946), Alicia Huberman (Ingrid Bergman) perceives and articulates Devlin's (Cary Grant) limitations as a lover. Alicia repeatedly calls attention to his lack of trust in her ("What a little pal you are"; "Not a word of faith. Just down the drain with Alicia").

These characters, like many others, critique male privilege and men's obsessiveness, lack of trust in women, and will to power. The well-known characters whose noir films are named after them—Laura, Mildred Pierce, and Gilda—are certainly not malevolent. Many other female characters (such as Norma Desmond in *Sunset Boulevard* [1950] and Cora Smith in *The Postman Always Rings Twice* [1946]) may behave criminally, but their stories, as in a good Victorian novel, contextualize their behavior in ways that make these characters sympathetic. And yet, our long-standing assumption in discussions of film noir is that such women have no subjectivity. In his interesting discussion of Dorothy Hughes's subversive representation of gender in *In a Lonely Place*, Stanley Orr claims, for example, that the film "stands out as one of the few films noir that permits a female figure to transgress the boundaries of the angel/femme fatale binary in favor of the lonely centrality of authenticating alienation."[14] Orr is certainly right that *In a Lonely Place* doesn't portray women in schematic ways. He's wrong, however, to assume that the character construction in the movie is rare. The portraits that emerge from so many noir films are of men and women brutalized by class and gender roles. Looking at the female-authored sources of several classic film-noir movies helps us to see one way in which the genre shows persistent gender disharmony in American culture.

In her essay "Why Film Noir? Hollywood, Adaptation, and Women's Writing in the 1940s and 1950s," Esther Sonnet takes Richard T. Jameson to task for what she sees as his recuperation of Otto Preminger's *Daisy Kenyon* (1947) by virtue of its noir affiliation. In other words, the film was formerly labeled as a "woman's picture" but should, for Jameson, be instead newly appreciated for its status as a "kissing cousin to film noir." Having "rescued" the film based on its now-recognizable noir elements, Jameson demonstrates for Sonnet the genre's hierarchical privileging of *"masculine affiliation."*[15] Sonnet's claim "that categorization as a film noir will secure for the film some critical value that it might not otherwise deserve" is based on her concern that the feminist source material in Elizabeth Janeway's novel will be obscured. To make her point that *Daisy Kenyon* does not fall easily into the category of film noir represented by *Double Indemnity* (1944), *The Postman Always Rings Twice*, *Gilda* (1946), and *The Big Heat*, Sonnet unfortunately contends that all of these films are "predicated on the function of the femme fatale"—an assumption, certainly for *Gilda* and *The Big Heat* and arguably for *The Postman Always Rings Twice*, that is deeply problematic, as I have claimed elsewhere.[16] Sonnet's questioning of the genre assumptions we bring to our viewing of adaptations is important, especially as it foregrounds the centrality of the female voice and social critique that underlies the source material for classic Hollywood films. However, the assumption that noir is "predicated on the function of the femme fatale" is based on a conventional view of noir derived from a troubling focus on only a few mainstream films, such as *Double Indemnity*. This critical stance fails to take into account the strength of many independent-minded women in noir and their struggle for empowerment, which is sometimes intriguingly connected to the women involved in either the source material or its adaptation.

Although Nicholas Ray's *In a Lonely Place* contains neither a femme fatale nor a hard-boiled detective, it was recently called "one of the finest of all films noir."[17] It is also an example of a film whose noirness derives from a woman's work. As many have noted, *In a Lonely Place* departs significantly from its source novel of the same name. Dorothy Hughes portrays Dix Steele as a hack novelist; in Ray's film, Dix (Humphrey Bogart) is a besieged yet "authentic" artist/writer who must ward off the efforts of the Hollywood machinery to turn his "art" into slavish Hollywood "popcorn" scripts. The trajectory of the narrative is altered, too, since in the novel Dix is in fact the serial murderer the characters in the film only suspect him to be.

While both novel and film address gender psychosis, the tone of the works is also different. Ray's *In a Lonely Place* adds romantic melodrama to Hughes's crime story. In the film, while Laurel

A fearful Laurel Gray (Gloria Grahame) rides with Dixon Steele (Humphrey Bogart) in *In a Lonely Place*. Opposite, happier times just a little earlier.

(Gloria Grahame) grows increasingly fearful of Dix, the lovers' heightened emotion grounds the film. Their exceptional yet ill-fated romance is captured in the lines Dix writes for a script he's been working on: "I was born when you kissed me. I died when you left me. I lived a few weeks while you loved me." These lines are repeated by Dix and Laurel throughout the film, establishing them as the subject of the narrative and exemplifying Jonathan Rosenbaum's description of a "passionately symmetrical relationship" in *In a Lonely Place* and Ray's other films. In contrast, Dorothy Hughes focuses in her novel on Dix's pathology as she charts his actual serial killing. Though Dix's status as a serial killer seems a crucial plot distinction in both novel and film, the presence of the male serial murderer is this story's feminist McGuffin,[18] the seeming central question of the story that is finally irrelevant to the real interest of these works, which is, in the case of the novel, the inevitable violence of conventional gender roles, and in the case of both the novel and the film, the nearness of trauma to everyday American experience. The film's tragedy is that though Dix is cleared of suspicion for the murder at the end of the story, his temper and quickness to violence have so upended his relationship with Laurel that it doesn't matter that he isn't the murderer.

While Dana Polan's reference to *In a Lonely Place* as a "woman's film"[19] depends on its exploration of a female (gothic) perspective on male violence, the film's interest in gender trauma can be directly linked to Dorothy Hughes's exploration of deviant masculinity. Polan contrasts the film's assumption of a female perspective with the novel's point of view: "Significantly, in light of the serious recognition that the film of *In a Lonely Place* gives to a woman's point of view, Hughes does not seem a writer much concerned to give women power in a narrative."[20] While the novel limits perspective to the psychotic point of view of Dix, however, Polan's comparison doesn't acknowledge the extent to which the film's interest in gender and masculinity is derived from the novel's analysis of postwar gender roles. In other words, the film's treatment of masculinity as a form of psychosis adapts the novel's investigation of psychosocial gender disorder. Thus, the distinction Polan draws between Ray's characteristic representation of social milieu and Hughes's psychological portrait of Dix's madness underestimates the extent to which Dix's psychology in the film as well as the novel is a symptom of the impossibility of "normal" human interaction in modern postwar social space.

It is Dix's masculinity that is felt to be under siege in the novel, and Hughes makes a point of delineating the great loss of power associated with men coming home from the war. This is a familiar noir scenario, one nowhere better portrayed than in the first twenty minutes of *The Blue Dahlia*.[21] It is interesting, however, that the most explicit articulations of this motif—violent vets (think Robert Ryan as Montgomery in *Crossfire* [1947]) unable to adapt to "normal" life after the war—can be found in a novel in which the narrator says of the main character, "The war years were the first happy years he'd ever known.... You were the Mister"; "The world was yours."[22] There is a radical feminist assumption at work here: for someone who has been constructed psychologically as a killer by the pressures of masculine role-playing, war would be strangely satisfying. A "normal" world where one

can't kill people would be the harder environment to be in. This alignment of murder and masculinity is the source of Lisa Maria Hogeland's evaluation of the novel. For Hogeland, the book seems to be a consummate portrait of a dangerous misogynist, but "the vet ruse . . . works two ways: on the one hand, it creates suspicion of Dix in relation to the images circulating in the postwar period of veterans as liable to `snap,' while on the other, it connects him to a very large number of `average,' `normal,' American men who have been capable of killing."[23]

The portrait in film noir of postwar America as a place where repressed violence threatens to seep out in unlikely places is familiar to us from many noir films, including *Out of the Past* (1947), *On Dangerous Ground* (1952), *The Hitch-Hiker* (1953), and *The Night of the Hunter* (1955). The fine line that divides the murderers from the romantic heroes is where noir resides.[24] Both the novel and the film version of *In a Lonely Place* locate this observation about the proximity of psychosis to "normal" behavior in masculinity.

However, not only gender but also class consciousness feeds psychosis in the novel *In a Lonely Place.* Hughes makes a point of Dix's contempt for work and his anger at the vulgar Uncle Fergus, who withholds money from Dix because of his failure to work:

Dix knew damn well he'd go through hell at the university. He did. He suffered. God how he suffered, that first year. He'd have quit, he'd have flunked out quick but the alternative was far worse: being packed off like a piece of cattle to a farm Uncle Fergus owned. Either he had to be a gentleman,

The inadvertent revelation by Sylvia (Jeff Donnell, below) angers Dix and draws reactions from policeman husband Brub (Frank Lovejoy) and Laurel.

according to Uncle Fergus' standards, or he could resort to the peasantry. Dix was smart enough to know he couldn't get a job, stand on his own feet. He didn't want to work that hard. He took the first year, working in the hardware store after school, afraid to look anyone in the eye, afraid he'd see the sneers openly, or the pity.[25]

> As this passage suggests, class issues help to explain Dix's violence. Unable to "stand on his own feet," Dix doesn't fit into class-defined categories—"gentleman" or "peasant"—and is helpless to create a place for himself. He is radically alienated from class and gender norms, which fuels his anger and explains his deviance. Hughes's novel reveals noir's submerged feminist sources that powerfully critique the ways in which class and gender make freedom, love, and meaningful agency impossible in the modern world.

While Ray's *In a Lonely Place* focuses more on the impossibility of love and intimacy surviving anxiety about domestic violence, it also adapts the novel's interest in women as victims of male rage. As Polan says, "One can easily read the film as a proto-feminist work that argues that men *per se,* not this or that murderous man, can pose a threat of violence to women."[26] Because women's roles and behavior are directly linked to threatening male behavior and identity, the generic conventions of noir are blurred. Not only is Dix an "homme fatal," but women are neither domestic angels nor femme fatales. Geoff Andrew comments that the film's Laurel is "freed from the conventions of the *femme fatale* to portray a woman at once strong, intelligent, and vulnerable."[27] Similarly, Stanley Orr notes that in the novel, Sylvia Nicolai and Laurel Gray are strong women: Sylvia assumes the role of detective, as she hones in on Dix's secret life as a serial killer, and Laurel "complicates the neat binaries of noir."[28] At the same time, female aggressiveness is not treated as malevolent in these works but instead as feminist rebellion. For example, the script adapts Sylvia's suspicion about Dix via Freudian slips that reveal a suppressed hostility. On the beach with Brub, Laurel, and Dix, Sylvia reveals that Laurel has been to see Detective Lochner (without Dix's knowledge), which sends Dix into a fury (see opposite page). Sylvia immediately repents: "I don't know why I said it. Brub especially asked me not to." Here, Sylvia "acts out" her anxiety about Dix's submerged violence and counters Brub's defense of him as "an exciting guy" by eliciting proof of Dix's dangerous rage. An even more veiled rendering of female agency is Martha the masseuse's warning to Laurel about Dix: "You'll be sorry, Angel" (see below). As Andrew astutely observes, the way the scene is filmed with the use of back lighting, low-angle shots, and extreme close-ups[29] suggests Laurel's repressed fear and desire to escape her relationship with Dix. These instances in the film of female rebellion and "the special solidarity among women"[30] transpose the novel's theme of women under threat who nevertheless assert their agency (Sylvia, for example, appearing as a detective figure).[31]

I have been arguing that the ambiguities in the representation of female experience in film noir are obscured by the heavy weight of the character patterns ("hard-boiled detective," "femme fatale") and generic assumptions that swamp readings of noir narrative. The gendered categories of "film noir" and "women's picture"[32] short-circuit sustained attempts to reorient viewers to a more nuanced reading of gender in film noir. Critical attention, too, has mostly been articulated in categorical terms, not only the femme fatale figure and the hard-boiled detective but also "postwar anxiety" and the "mean streets" of the city.

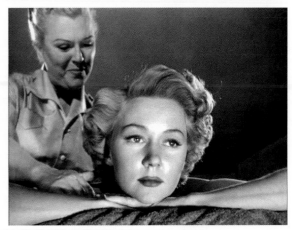

All of these categories have historically been organized around the male figures in these films (post-war trauma for men, the threat that bad sexy women pose to men, interrogation about why modern men in the city are cynical or hard-boiled). Moreover, auteurist attention to directors (in the case of the films discussed here, the prominent directors Preminger and Ray) reinforces critical attention on directors' style and vision as opposed to the films' representation of gender violence drawn from the source material. For example, the romantic light Nicholas Ray shines on Dix Steele—Ray's portrait of an angry artist who imagines that redemptive love can ward off opportunistic Hollywood and a brute social world—taps viewer associations not only with disappointed men in noir but also with Ray's characteristic cynicism and idealism. As Rosenbaum observes, "[E]ven within a vision as fundamentally bleak and futile as Ray's, a clear view of paradise is never entirely out of mind or even definitively out of reach."[33] In connection with *In a Lonely Place,* critical focus on Ray's "naked paw prints"[34] has overshadowed the film's dialogue with Hughes's novel and its portrait of violence specifically linked to gender and culture. This may explain an overidentification with Dix that, as Polan points out, causes some viewers and critics such as Jean Wagner "to believe that Dix deserves more sympathy than the murder victim Mildred."[35] Ray's "deep romanticism," combined with a generic expectation of a hard-boiled protagonist, may eclipse the feminist force of the narrative.

In its exploration of Dix Steele as the "homme fatal," Ray's *In a Lonely Place* modifies noir's conventional gender associations, a refashioning of familiar character types presaged by Hughes's novel. Another Nicholas Ray adaptation of female-authored fiction from the classic Hollywood period similarly explores modern gender trauma and also blurs the generic boundaries that separate the woman's picture from film noir. In 1949, Ray directed *A Woman's Secret,* based on Vicki Baum's 1946 novel *Mortgage on Life.* Critics have noted "noir elements" in *A Woman's Secret*[36] and have also compared the film to "Freudian Gothic melodrama."[37] The mixed tone of *A Woman's Secret* and its cynical treatment of celebrity in contemporary America constitute a hybrid generic model of melodramatic and noir elements difficult to separate. Further, the film pursues an analysis of gender and the objectification of women that is deeply related to its fictional source. Both of these points—the film's complicated generic status and its fascination with gender—are clarified when it is juxtaposed with Baum's novel. Indeed, reading all of the films discussed here in relation with their source novels reveals their generic elasticity and their feminist characteristics.[38]

Deep focus captures the apprehension of Laurel as she listens in on Dix.

In the novel *Mortgage on Life,* the ambitious and intelligent Bess Poker ("Pokey," as she is nicknamed) takes over the life and career of the naïve, "indolent," and beautiful Mary Lynn, renamed "Marylynn." Bess Poker transforms the "disarmingly young and stupid"[39] Marylynn into a Broadway star who leaves men in her trail, while plain-Jane Pokey writhes ambivalently on the sidelines, watching the love of her life, the composer Luke Jordan, chase after Marylynn, writing songs for her that make the two of them famous and successful. Bess's lack of self-esteem is accompanied by "bitterness and hatred," as she negotiates the cynical landscape of "ruthless" men who fall for Marylynn. One of these is A. W. Huysmans, who "had ruined many of his opponents, politically, socially, financially. He had driven some of them into suicide without batting an eyelash."[40] Another suitor is the narcissistic politician Dale Corbett, who is "all ambition" and empty at the core.

There is a fair amount of melodrama in the novel, including some extremely traumatic episodes: the fire at the nightclub that horrifically burns Marylynn (repaired through a grafting of Pokey's skin!); the storm during which Marylynn meets Huysmans; the World War II battle surrounding the foxhole in France, where the soldier Lee Crenshaw protects and saves Marylynn from German fire; and the shooting of Marylynn by Pokey, when the performer insists on leaving her life as a singer to marry Lee Crenshaw and return to middle America. However, there is also a noir commentary: first, on modern social relations that are viewed as utterly objectifying; second, on the nearness of violence to "normal" everyday life in America; and third, on the desperation of men and women in America who resort to such violence because of their narrow prospects for living a fulfilling life. Driving Pokey to "make Marylynn" is her anxiety about her alternative to success as an agent: "scraping, saving, going back to the small life of small people. There were various prospects, and all of them unbearable."[41] Like the women in noir often mislabeled as "femme fatales," Bess is a hard-boiled protagonist who is ambitious yet also frustrated with the limits of her prospects.

Much attention is paid in the novel to Bess's physical plainness, and her physiognomy becomes a metaphor for her overreaching ambition. Bess has "too much of a nose, too much of a mouth, an awful lot of strong, big teeth that must have somehow got out of control at the time there was not enough money for braces."[42] Bess's physical mien reflects her "unnatural" desire to be a player in society, to be empowered beyond the conventional roles available to women in postwar America. It is fascinating to note that Bess's noir act of attempted murder is cast as a "suicide": "I had no life of my own. My life was—Marylynn. And so I shot her." Bess is seen as only "half a woman": Luke says, "Jesus Christ, if I could only make one girl out of the two of you! If you'd have Mary's figure and her sort of voice—or if she'd have your brains and personality—then we would really go places."[43] Luke's fantasy that he can constitute and market the perfect woman reflects the objectifying social gaze and frantic consumerism that characterize living in the modern world. Such attention to the exploited lives of women and the limits of their experience in culture and society is paramount in film noir, as it is in the so-called woman's picture.

A Woman's Secret, the Nicholas Ray film adapted from Baum's novel, begins, as *Mildred Pierce* does, with a flashback sequence and an ambiguous murder. The mystery revolves around whether Marian Washburn (Bess/Pokey in the novel) has killed Susan Caldwell, the film's version of Marylynn (here, Susan's stage name is similarly objectifying, the one-word "Estrellita"). Like *Mildred Pierce, A Woman's Secret* is referred to both as a noir and as a woman's picture. Like many films central to the noir series, it addresses the theme of female ambition and the limited venues for women to express their desires. Ray's *A Woman's Secret* shares with its source material a melo-noir representation of the underbelly of American consumer culture and women's often despairing role as a commodity within that system. If, as Geoff Andrew says, *A Woman's Secret* is "Ray's most anonymous work, and he himself felt no affection for it,"[44] perhaps Cullen Gallagher is right to suggest that "it is precisely because of its position as a studio—rather than a personal—project that *Secret* demands alternative ways of understanding, appreciation, and criticism."[45] I would suggest that a focus on the film's adaptation of Baum's novel rather than an auteurist consideration of its marginal place within the body of Nicholas Ray's work can provide one fruitful "alternative" approach to *A Woman's Secret*.

There is no doubt that Gloria Grahame's portrayal of Susan/Estrellita is the most appealing aspect of the film. Grahame brings her charisma to the part and carries off the best lines of Herman Mankiewicz's script with utter insouciance. Her description of where she comes from, "Azusa" ("it's a made-up name—everything from A to Z"), is a brilliant noir sendup of the emptiness of American culture—again, a vision of America as a void, its inhabitants on a quest for meaning in a denuded cultural landscape. Susan seems to be looked at by others in the film as malevolent, a response out of keeping with the portrayal by Grahame and a misreading then proliferated by Nicholas Ray's biographer, Patrick McGilligan, who writes that Susan "metamorphoses into the torch singer Estrellita, a bewitching monster. Frankenstein never looked so good."[46] Far from a stereotypical femme fatale, Susan/Estrellita comes across to viewers as a sympathetic naïf, meandering through the American wasteland. Figure 3 nicely captures Susan's exploitation by her mentors, Marian and Luke.

A Woman's Secret: Susan Caldwell is menaced by her musical mentors Marian Washburn (Maureen O'Hara) and Luke Jordan (Melvyn Douglas).

McGilligan's misreading of Grahame's character strangely replays the objectification that is already satirized in the narrative. This is evident in the derivation of the name "Estrellita." A popular folk song written by the the Mexican composer Ponce, who died in 1948 (a year before *A Woman's Secret* was released), "Estrellita" means "little star" in Spanish. Susan's objectification in the narrative is thus signaled in her pseudonym, a motif introduced at the very beginning of the film when "Estrellita" sings the song after which she is named.

It is further worth noting that the novel places Mary's "home" as Blythe, California, perhaps a play on the word "blithe," since Mary's life has been anything but carefree. The setting of Blythe is described starkly in the novel as "just a small dump in the desert."[47] Mary/Susan, in the film and novel, is distracted from her rootlessness by the attention of men and the promise of celebrity. The story of both of the women in novel and film repeats a pattern in classic noir of presenting women as trapped, lonely, and either insufficiently armed to protect themselves or extremely ambitious in their attempts to create meaningful lives for themselves. In *Mortgage for Life,* Marylynn has a doll called Emily that (like Mary for Bess) is her other half, a reliable source of comfort and opportunity for emotional expression ("Emily cries at night"[48]). Because she has to be so hard-boiled in her life, Marylynn sublimates her vulnerability in playacting with "Emily." Given the sympathy lent to Mary/Susan in her vulnerability, her dismissive treatment by men, and her objectification by Bess/Marian, the role of the "seductress" is thus complicated in tone. The sympathy for the aggressive yet exploitative Bess/Marian is there too, for she has no self-esteem and is clearly in search of a means for expression of her ambition.

Susan aka Estellita in a happier moment with attorney Brook Matthews (Victor Jory).

Sidebar: British Film Noir and Portraits of Women in the Two *Bedelias*

Vera Caspary's 1945 *Bedelia* and the British film noir adapted from Caspary's novel the following year work in dialogue to portray gender psychosis in the modern period.[1] Caspary's novel is set in Connecticut in 1913, at the moment when Victorian culture was giving way to modernism and New Woman gender politics. The 1946 film adaptation, directed by Lance Comfort, cowritten by Caspary, and starring Margaret Lockwood as Bedelia, is set initially in Monte Carlo, where Bedelia and Charles Carrington (Ian Hunter, portraying an Anglicized version of the novel's Charlie Horst) vacation following their wedding. While Monte Carlo may have appealed to a contemporary postwar audience (the setting projected backward, however, to 1938 before the war), the film then shifts its locale to Charles's home in Yorkshire, England, evoking a Bronte-esque atmosphere of romantic isolation and Victorian domestic constraints. This fascinating pair of postwar portraits of female distress gradually shows the lovely Bedelia to be a psychotic serial killer of husbands.

Margaret Lockwood as the title character in *Bedelia*.

The novel and film both establish a familiar literary setting of Victorian repression. The novel is set in New England, where Charlie Horst's home is haunted by "the ghosts of Puritan ancestors,"[2] and Charlie's dead mother marshals these phantoms through time, as her portrait hangs in Charlie's bedroom. The picture depicts the stalwart matriarch "at seventeen, a righteous girl, her lips tight with disapproval" (30). In stark contrast, Charlie's new wife Bedelia embodies amoral energy run amok. Her crossing of American geography, as she moves from place to place poisoning husbands and trashing the stolid ground of family relations, is thus placed symbolically in opposition to a markedly repressive Puritan view of women.

In the bedroom in which Charlie's mother's portrait radiates her "scorn of weakness," Charlie indulges his desires, glad to have "married a widow" and quietly excited by Bedelia's "careless tresses," which carry "sluttish charm" (26) for him. The contrast between Bedelia and Charlie's mother is drawn distinctly. While the matriarch Harriet Philbrick "never colored her lips and cheeks with rouge," Bedelia's "fervor embarrassed" Charlie (88). Bedelia's presence exposes a Puritan double standard whereby Charlie wishes to maintain the repressive code instilled in him by his mother while unleashing his sexual desire on a woman for whom virginal innocence is no longer a concern. The very beginning of the novel establishes the male fantasy of indulgence and containment, as the fire is stoked and Charlie is pleased with his new mate: "She wore a dark-blue velvet dress whose sheath skirt was slit to show her pretty ankles and high-heeled bronze pumps. The Yule log caught fire. Flames licked the crusty bark. This was a great moment for Charlie" (10). Despite Charlie's "great moment," Bedelia's secret excesses cannot be channeled into acceptable behavior patterns. The "ghosts of Puritan ancestors" are no match for Bedelia, whose "brunette radiance" contrasts with Charlie's "pallid, angular, and restricted" mien. The setting and introduction of the characters as gendered types thus provide an important context for defining Bedelia's psychosis as symbolic, a staged opposition to social norms.

In the film, the theme of trapped women is presented symbolically through repeated scenes of Bedelia being "captured" visually. Recalling Caspary's *Laura*, as well as Otto Preminger's 1944 adaptation of the earlier work, Bedelia is introduced to viewers, first, in a portrait, as Ben Chaney (Barry K. Barnes), the detective pretending to be a painter, describes her in his voiceover as a lethal "femme fatale." Second, she is observed through the window of the French jeweler's shop in Monte Carlo, as Ben and the jeweler watch her. Third, Bedelia is figured as an image when her painting is positioned as the mediating absent "subject" of the conversation between Ben Chaney and Ellen (a possible love interest for Charles). Finally, Bedelia's suicide is captured in a reflection of the mirror. All of these scenes underscore the film's insistence on Bedelia's simultaneous—and paradoxical—power and objectification. The notion of apprehending Bedelia is not only figured in the repeated references to her as a visual object but also thematized in Ben Chaney's repeated taunting of her, as he pretends to be unaware of her past but suggests names and images that subtly convey to Bedelia that he knows her secrets. Ben paints a picture, for example, and signs it "Raoul Burgess," the name of Bedelia's fictional former husband. When Ben suggests to Bedelia and Charles that he has found an "original" "Raoul Burgess" ("Raoul Cochran" in the novel), Bedelia's response repeats the filmic refrain of her wild-eyed desperation, an hysteria that designates her not as an exposed criminal but as Ben Chaney's prey, the object of his predatory detective manipulations.

The repeated images of Bedelia's terror—Bedelia "caught" between Charles and Ben, represented in the camera's slow dolly shots toward Bedelia and the close-ups of her horrified reactions to Ben's subtle accusations—depict a truth that is counter to the plot of her serial killing: Bedelia's hysteria and desperation are expressions of female energy with no outlet and active resistance to masculine power.

Bedelia's object status is also dramatized in her submission to Ben's and Charles's exhortation to "sit" for Chaney's painting sessions (inset at right). In one scene Ben Chaney taunts Bedelia with flirtatious comments about the color of her hair. We later learn in the film that as "Mrs. McKelvey," Bedelia had red hair. As Ben draws her portrait in Monte Carlo, he says, "You ought to have red hair. Nature got her colors mixed when she was making you." Ben's ironic suggestion here that Bedelia is not a "natural" woman echoes his initial voiceover about Bedelia's "curious innocence" that veils a "poisonous flower." "Watching" Bedelia try to evade the false painter's capture invites viewers to imagine a counter-perspective in which Bedelia's actions symbolize a breaking out of the frame, an "acting out" that is, indeed, outside of the social roles women are supposed to assume, including a convention of women "sitting pretty." Ben's comments about Bedelia's red hair thus conflate the "natural" with the conventional, establishing the idea that the story's portrait of a wild murderess, a "femme fatale" of the first order, is a cover for the story's real interest in a female rebellion against gender conventions and domestic settings that entrap women.

Notes

1. This piece is excerpted from a longer version of the essay "The Fervor and Framing of Bedelia: Gender Psychosis in Vera Caspary's Novel and Film Noir," *La Furia Umana* 15 (Winter 2013).

2. Vera Caspary, *Bedelia* (1945; reprint, New York: Feminist Press at the City University of New York, 2005), 27 (subsequent references will appear parenthetically in the text).

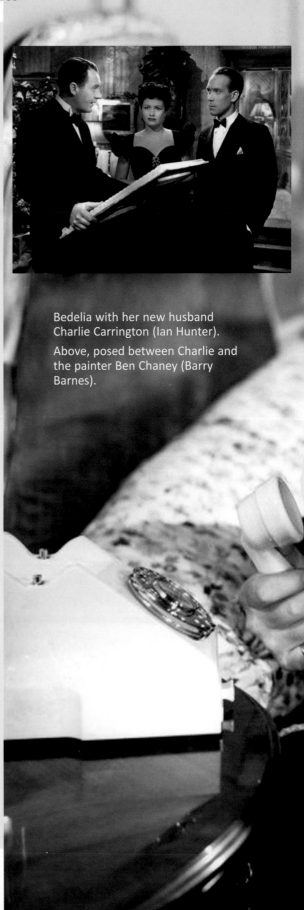

Bedelia with her new husband Charlie Carrington (Ian Hunter).

Above, posed between Charlie and the painter Ben Chaney (Barry Barnes).

Vera Caspary's novel *Laura* also works in tandem with its film adaptation to draw a portrait of a shallow world of possibilities for women. While some critics contrast the film's fetishizing of Laura as an image to the novel's "giving voice" to the independent working-woman Laura, the novel and film seem to me to be in conversation about female independence, about the theme of watching and "detecting" female malfeasance, and about a contemporary social milieu that is generally exploitative and specifically hostile to female ambition. Liahna Babener describes Caspary's novel as a feminist exploration—first, of the difficulties facing independent women in American culture, and second, of the detective's coming to love the "real" Laura as opposed to the image of her with which he has been obsessed. Unlike the novel, the film focuses for Babener primarily on Laura as an image, not as a subject with her own story to tell.

However, I think Babener misses the complexity of Laura's role in the film when she says that Laura is "blameworthy and threatening to masculine composure." Preminger's film is in fact about Laura's *eliciting* of male gender psychosis from the men around her. While Preminger was famously dictatorial and may have been misogynist, and Caspary did object to a number of changes made to the novel in the adaptation,[49] the film's relation to viewers is considerably richer than Babener's blanket dismissal of its gender politics suggests. Babener's claim that "the woman's discourse that propels

the novel is choked off"[50] leaves out the film's analysis (intentional or not) of the overreading of Laura that *is* a major focus of the narrative and mise-en-scène: We are not "with" McPherson when he grills Laura at the police station. We are, on the contrary, with her in her rejection of his "testing" of her. Laura may be "refused a voice-over," in Babener's terms,[51] but her presence in the film defies the conventional idea of the femme fatale. Just as Karen Hollinger suggests that Johnny's perverse narration of Gilda in *Gilda* breaks down and undermines Johnny's authority,[52] here, too, Waldo's voiceover is also symptomatic of sex and gender obsession, the bid for control by an homme fatal who fails to possess Laura. Like the Duke in Robert Browning's "My Last Duchess," as I've noted elsewhere,[53] Waldo must resort to killing her. Tierney's "Laura" does not play as a "reproachable temptress," nor do we read her behavior as simply "coy manipulation."[54] The impulse to read her as such may, in the case of a feminist approach, result from disappointment that the film fails to re-present a source text that functions differently, textually and culturally, an attitude that underlines the problems with using fidelity as a central criterion for evaluating adaptations. Alternatively, the impulse to identify simplistically with McPherson—in the case of some viewers and perhaps Preminger himself—registers a failure to acknowledge the film's deconstruction of sex and gender obsessions. That the film "continues to be revered by viewers" may be less a sign of "how difficult it is to tell women's stories in classical forms"[55] (though Babener's observation here is certainly right) and more an indication of the richness of the film from the standpoint of changing views of the representation of sex and gender in film noir. The film *Laura* is not, in short, simply a masculine bastardization of the novel.

In the novel, Laura strongly resists "positions" held by men that are taken for granted, especially in her striking comments about the smallness of detectives: "I don't like people who make their livings out of spying and poking into people's lives. Detectives aren't heroes to me, they're detestable."[56] An interesting expression of resistance to male intrusions into female experience, the comment is given force by McPherson's ambiguous rifling through Laura's personal things in her apartment. On the one hand, an inflated notion of the detective hero is articulated in Caspary's novel by a "girl detective," who says (rather shockingly) to McPherson, "I shouldn't mind being murdered half so much, Mr. McPherson, if you were the detective seeking clues to my private life."[57] On the other hand, Lydecker's bloated body in the novel and feminized penchant for taking baths in the film contrast with McPherson's brawny detective credentials. Further, and perhaps more to the point, the dubiousness of the classic detective figure is surely distilled in the uncanny moment of mis/recognition when Laura believes an intruder has entered her apartment (see opposite page). In the film, Preminger's mise-en-scène visually symbolizes that McPherson's engagement with Laura has been mediated by powerful fantasy (the framed "image" of Laura). McPherson's narration in the novel goes as follows:

"I spoke with authority. 'You're dead.'"

My wild stare and the strange accusation convinced her that she was facing a dangerous lunatic. She edged toward the door.[58]

The novel's and film's riff on the potentially sinister side—again, the theme of impending violence—of detectives' intrusive power calls into question the practices of the "classic" hard-boiled protagonist, an idea embedded in noir from its source in this case and throughout the noir cycle.

In Preminger's film, there are memorable moments of Laura's independence and determination, even as she faces questionable authority figures—when she says, for example, "I will never do anything that is out of keeping with my own free will." More pointedly, Tierney's Laura asserts her subjectivity when she rejects the light literally cast on her at the police station and calls McPherson to task for his investigation and suspiciousness regarding her.

Opposite, the "dead" Laura (Gene Tierney) returns to find Det. McPherson (Dana Andrews) in her place.

This exchange exemplifies Preminger's "concern with contrasting discourses and gestures,"[59] McPherson sublimating his feelings for Laura in police procedure (pictured opposite). The camera angles and lighting (the scene is "steeped in noir shadows"[60]) cast Laura as a murderess, a role she rebelliously then assumes. "What difference does it make what I say," she says coldly. "You've made up my mind I'm guilty." The scene, like the moment of mis/recognition in Laura's apartment, communicates Preminger's visual theme of disorientation, that sense of "terror and loneliness of the secret emptinesses that surround the fora where dialogue and understanding take place."[61] Such trauma, however, is directly concerned with gender: McPherson's unstable masculinity is insecurely masked by his role as detective, just as Laura's anxiety-provoking femininity is masked by her "mysteriousness."

In Caspary's novel, Lydecker makes a comment about the process of objectifying Laura: "By the necromancy of modern journalism, a gracious young woman had been transformed into a dangerous siren who practiced her wiles in that fascinating neighborhood where Park Avenue meets Bohemia. Her generous way of life had become [in the press] an uninterrupted orgy of drunkenness, lust, and deceit, as titivating [sic] to the masses as it was profitable to the publishers."[62] Lydecker's analysis could be said to predict the making of the femme fatale as an industry. Caspary describes the process by which popular commentary stokes cultural anxieties about what women do to men. "You never know about women,"[63] says McPherson to Lydecker (when the real question in film noir could be, "You never know about men—what do the men do to the women?"). Lydecker's surprising reply, "Don't tell me you're a misogynist," reveals the novel's interest in the process by which interest in women is so easily adapted into sources of male anger and anxiety. In response to Lydecker's reply, "[McPherson] clamped his teeth hard upon his pipestem and glanced at me with an air of urchin defiance." These scenes from Caspary's novel and Preminger's classic film establish a continuity between pulp fiction and film noir in their investigation of thwarted female power and threatened masculinity.

An often-ignored element in Caspary's novel is the portrait of Diane Redfern, whose presence in the film is limited to her role as the one who is mistaken for Laura and thus killed by Lydecker when he finds her at Laura's apartment. Diane's real story is that of down-and-out "Jennie Swobodo," one in a long line of ambitious young women whose dreams turn into brutal realities in noir narrative: "You could tell that Diane had dreamed of Hollywood. Less beautiful girls had become stars, married stars, and owned swimming pools. There were some of those confessional magazines, too, the sort that told stories of girls who had sinned, suffered, and been reclaimed by the love of good men. Poor Jennie Swobodo."[64] McPherson's narrative about Diane Redfern introduces sympathy for an undistinguished female character: "I sat on the edge of the bed and thought about the poor kid's life. Perhaps those photographs represented a real world to the young girl. All day while she worked, she lived in their expensive settings. And at night she came home to this cell." McPherson's insight into Diane Redfern's domestic prison leads to the striking image of a "suicide staircase": "I felt sorry for the kid, being young and expecting something of her beauty and coming home to this suicide staircase."[65] It is worth noting the lineage from Jennie Swobodo to another divided personality, one of whose selves is also called "Diane": *Mulholland Drive*'s tragic Diane Selwyn in David Lynch's 2001 film. The comparison evokes the gendered machinery of modern American industry as it "patterns" women into images that can't be sustained in real psychosocial terms or experience. These submerged stories, I believe, constitute the cynical and desolate tone of film noir as much as the disappointments of the male protagonists, and these stories have been engaged by films conventionally regarded as noir as well as by melodrama and the woman's picture.

Far from being "the male genre" it is still proclaimed to be (despite recent feminist work), film noir is, more broadly, fundamentally about gender and society. The novels that are sources for the

Back at the police station,
McPherson interrogates Laura.

films discussed set the stage for film noir's exploration of troubling gender configurations. Like many melodramas and the so-called woman's pictures now too easily appropriated by Hollywood and by consumers as "chick flicks," film noirs adapt our continual reflection on the failure of conventional social roles to sustain human individuals, forcing a reassessment of the gender assumptions that have transformed over time and those that remain resistant to change. Such reconsideration demands the tight focus required of careful reading as well as broad appreciation for the blended universe of film noir so that the "suicide staircase" of Jennie Swobodo doesn't go unnoticed. My hope is that more sustained emphasis on the submerged stories of women and the sliding scale of concerns shared by melodrama and film noir will more systematically anchor studies of the genre. Further, film adaptations can perhaps more usefully be theorized as being in conversation with their source material rather than in discrete opposition to textual predecessors. The latter approach invokes a model of difference that leads to evaluation and competition between and among texts. The elements of conventionally defined melodrama and noir in each of the works examined here should not only raise questions about the narrow purview of gender and genre labels but also ignite critical discussion about the efficacy of emphasizing textual distinctiveness as opposed to relationships among texts. What, finally, are we talking about when we address the set of texts known as "Laura" or "In a Lonely Place"? Adaptation studies may benefit from a more feminist approach, in which meaning emerges as a by-product of cultural dialogue. A shift in emphasis away from examination of discrete texts and toward investigation of the relations among texts may offer a more productive, culturally relevant, and resonant stream of analyses.

Notes

1. Adaptations of *Mildred Pierce* help to spur considerations of the category of noir and the inflexibility with which so many approach it. Much of the discussion surrounding Todd Haynes's adaptation has centered on its identity as melodrama. However, like James M. Cain's novel and, I would argue, also like the 1945 film with Joan Crawford, the miniseries is largely concerned with the pressures that class and conventional gender roles bring to bear on men and women. Haynes is feminist in a way that Cain is not; through the acting and especially his signature mise-en-scène, the director foregrounds a sympathy for Mildred's desolation that is somewhat different from the more disinterested tone of Cain's novel. Haynes's exploration of the crises that beset individuals in society is much more deeply connected to the cultural work of film noir than has been generally acknowledged.
2. Like Shelley Cobb, I employ the "metaphor of conversation" to talk about adaptation. For Cobb, the language we use to describe the relationship between an adapted text and its source is deeply gendered (thus, hierarchical) and has implications for cultural ideation surrounding gender as well as adaptation studies. See Shelley Cobb, "Adaptation, Fidelity, and Gendered Discourses," *Adaptation* 4.1 (2010): 28-37.
3. See Daniel Hodges's Web site devoted to interrogating clichés about film noir, "The Film Noir File: A Dossier of Challenges to the Film Noir Hardboiled Paradigm," http://www.filmnoirfile.com, accessed October 23, 2012,
4. Examples of such ranking include director Curtis Hanson's "preferential treatment" of the film *In a Lonely Place* in comparison with Dorothy Hughes's novel of the same name. In the DVD commentary for *In a Lonely Place,* Hanson glosses over the extent to which these texts converge and diverge. Another example, one I will return to later in this essay, is Liahna Babener's diatribe against what she sees as the antifeminist rewriting of Vera Caspary's *Laura* in Otto Preminger's film, while, in my view, the novel and film approach the theme of threatened female independence and survival in equally intriguing ways. See Liahna Babener, "De-Feminizing *Laura*: Novel to Film," in *It's a Print! Detective Fiction from Page to Screen,* ed. William Reynolds and Elizabeth A. Trembley (Bowling Green, Ohio: Bowling Green University Popular Press, 1994), 83-102.

5. For some of the most intriguing work in adaptation studies that develops postfidelity models of discourse, see Kamilla Elliot, *Rethinking the Novel/Film Debate* (New York: Cambridge University Press, 2003); Linda Hutcheon, *A Theory of Adaptation* (New York: Routledge, 2006); Thomas M. Leitch, *Film Adaptation and its Discontents: From* Gone with the Wind *to* The Passion of the Christ (Baltimore, Md.: Johns Hopkins University Press, 2007); Brian McFarlane, *Novel to Film: An Introduction to the Theory of Adaptation* (Oxford: Oxford University Press, 1996); R. Barton Palmer and David Boyd, *Hitchcock at the Source: The Auteur as Adaptor* (Albany: State University of New York Press, 2011); Julie Sanders, *Adaptation and Appropriation* (New York: Routledge, 2007); and Robert Stam, *Literature through Film: Realism, Magic, and the Art of Adaptation* (Malden, Mass.: Blackwell, 2004). See, also, my "Literature, Film, and Their Hideous Progeny: Adaptation and ElasTEXTity" (Houndmills, Basingstoke: Palgrave Macmillan, 2015).

6. See, for example, Elizabeth Cowie, *"Film Noir and Women,"* in *Shades of Noir,* ed. Joan Copjec (New York: Verso, 1993); Philippa Gates, *Detecting Women: Gender and the Hollywood Detective Film* (Albany: State University of New York Press, 2011); Julie Grossman, *Rethinking the Femme Fatale in Film Noir: Ready for Her Close-Up* (Basingstoke, U.K.: Palgrave Macmillan, 2012); Helen Hanson, *Hollywood Heroines: Women in Film Noir and the Female Gothic Film* (London: I. B Tauris, 2007); Ann E. Kaplan, *Women in Film Noir* (London: British Film Institute, 1980); and Jans B. Wager, *Dames in the Driver's Seat: Rereading Film Noir* (Austin: University of Texas Press, 2005).

7. Indeed, Pam Cook makes the point that the "the relationship between melodrama and the women's picture has been assumed rather than argued." Pam Cook, "Melodrama and the Woman's Picture," in *Imitation of Life: A Reader on Film and Television Melodrama,* ed. Marcia Landy (Detroit: Wayne State University Press, 1991), 248.

8. Cowie, *"Film Noir and Women,"* 131.

9. Thomas Schatz, *Boom and Bust: American Cinema in the 1940s* (Berkeley: University of California Press, 1999), 236.

10. Ibid., 378.

11. Jon Lewis, *American Film: A History* (New York: W. W. Norton, 2008), 204.

12. Grossman, *Rethinking the Femme Fatale in Film Noir.*

13. See Steve Neale, "`I Can't Tell Anymore Whether You're Lying': *Double Indemnity, Human Desire,* and the Narratology of *Femmes Fatales,"* in *The Femme Fatale: Images, Histories, Contexts,* ed. Helen Hanson and Catherine O'Rawe (Basingstoke, U.K.: Palgrave-Macmillan, 2010), 187-98, in which Neale shows the systematic victimization of Vicki Buckley.

14. Stanley Orr, *Darkly Perfect World: Colonial Adventure, Postmodernism, and American Noir* (Columbus: Ohio State University Press, 2010), 123.

15. Esther Sonnet, "Why Film Noir? Hollywood, Adaptation, and Women's Writing in the 1940s and 1950s," *Adaptation* 4.1 (2011): 1-13 (quotation on 2).

16. Grossman, *Rethinking the Femme Fatale in Film Noir,* 45-48.

17. Anne Hockens, "A Schoolgirl with a Sorceress' Eyes," *Noir City* (Summer 2012): 9-22 (quotation on 13).

18. Dana Polan quotes James W. Palmer's original observation: "In Hitchcockian terms, the murder story is simply this film's MacGuffin." Polan, *In a Lonely Place* (London: British Film Institute, 1993), 13.

19. Ibid., 66.

20. Ibid., 27.

21. In this 1946 film, the World War II vet Johnny Morrison (Alan Ladd) "comes home" to his wife Helen's partying household. An inebriated woman opens the door, and Morrison says, "I'm looking for my wife." The response? "The place is full of wives," then to the partygoers, "Hey, everyone, Helen's got a husband!" Later, Helen: "My husband wants you to leave. He probably wants to beat me up"—a scarcely suppressed expression of postwar disillusionment, a heroism that, for some men, has no outlet in postwar domesticity (this scene suggests) except for domestic violence.

22. Dorothy Hughes, *In a Lonely Place* (1947; reprint, New York: Feminist Press at the City University of New York, 2003), 113-14.

23. Lisa Marie Hogeland, Afterword to *In a Lonely Place,* by Dorothy Hughes (1947; reprint, New York: Feminist Press at the City University of New York, 2003), 225-48 (quotation on 237).
24. I have elsewhere coined the term "Victorinoir" to describe Victorian literary sources for the male and female protagonists in film noir, but here, one can similarly see the continuities in gender representation from a Heathcliff or Rochester, the male romantic figures in classic Victorian novels (respectively, *Wuthering Heights* and *Jane Eyre*). These men, like Dix Steele, or countless other passionate men in noir (played, for example, by Humphrey Bogart or Robert Ryan or Orson Welles), are often living at the border of romance and madness, while women in their midst must navigate their own bid for independence within this context.
25. Hughes, *In a Lonely Place,* 112.
26. Polan, *In a Lonely Place,* 46.
27. Geoff Andrew, *The Films of Nicholas Ray* (London: British Film Institute, 2004), 52.
28. Orr, *Darkly Perfect World,* 121.
29. Andrew, *Films of Nicholas Ray,* 48.
30. Polan, *In a Lonely Place,* 40.
31. In *The Celluloid Closet,* Rob Epstein and Jeffrey Freidman's 1995 documentary based on Vito Russo's book about gay subtext in classic Hollywood film, Susie Bright observes that Martha's evocation of lesbian power and female bonds communicates a theme of female desire for freedom from male dominance.
32. While some critics have interestingly merged the nomenclature—"noir melodrama" or "melo-noir"—my target here is the persistence of an idea of noir that is stubbornly grafted to established character patterns and genre categories.
33. Jonathan Rosenbaum, "Nicholas Ray," *Senses of Cinema* 21 (2002), accessed November 5, 2013, http://sensesofcinema.com/2002/great-directors/raynick/.
34. Rosenbaum, "Nicholas Ray."
35. Polan, *In a Lonely Place,* 37.
36. Hockens, "A Schoolgirl with a Sorceress' Eyes," 11.
37. See Thomas Elsaesser, "Tales of Sound and Fury: Observations on the Family Melodrama," in *Critical Visions in Film Theory,* ed. Timothy Corrigan, Patricia White, and Meta Mazaj (Boston: Bedford/St. Martins, 2011), 496-511 (quotation on 511, n. 7).
38. In a *USA Today* article on his 2013 film *Trance,* Danny Boyle commented on his sense of film noir as "cold": "I wanted to do an updated noir, give it a contemporary spin in terms of emotion. . . . Noir is usually cold. I wanted it to be more emotionally charged. It's the first time I put a woman at the heart of a movie." While Boyle's assumption may be shared by the culture at large, in fact the genre's grounding in issues of gender and society, as well as its close affiliation with melodrama, belies Boyle's reading of film noir as emotionally cool. See Susan Wloszczyna, "Sneak Peek: Boyle Falls into `Trance' with Thriller," *USA Today,* December 27, 2012,
    Accessed http://www.usatoday.com/story/life/movies/2012/12/26/danny-boyle-trance-james-mcavoy-movie/1779189/.
39. Vicki Baum, *Mortgage on Life* (New York: Triangle Books, 1946), 28.
40. Ibid., 155.
41. Ibid., 140.
42. Ibid., 13.
43. Ibid., 37.
44. Andrew, *Films of Nicholas Ray,* 32.
45. Cullen Gallagher, rev. of *A Woman's Secret,* Not Coming to a Theater Near You, August 18, 2008, accessed November 8, 2013, http://notcoming.com/reviews/awomanssecret.
46. Patrick McGilligan, *Nicholas Ray: The Glorious Failure of an American Director* (New York: HarperCollins, 2011), 146.
47. Baum, *Mortgage on Life,* 29.
48. Ibid., 82.

49. These include Caspary's objection to Preminger's vulgar and bombastic insistence that Laura is "a whore" and the change from novel to film in what was to be the murder weapon. See Eugene McNamara, *Laura as Novel, Film, and Myth* (Lewiston, N.Y.: Edwin Mellen Press, 1992), 34. As McNamara observes, Caspary "was furious when she learned that her device of hiding the murder gun in Waldo's walking stick had been changed into a mundane shotgun. To her, the stick was a symbol of Waldo's impotent, frustrated love for Laura, twisted into destructive rage" (9). In his *Otto Preminger: The Man Who Would Be King* (New York: Knopf, 2007), Foster Hirsch comments on the change: "In this case Caspary was right: the phallic symbolism of the gun concealed in the impotent man's walking stick is revelatory, whereas the ending Preminger proposed is merely a narrative device" (97).

50. Babener, "De-Feminizing *Laura*," 88.

51. Ibid., 93.

52. Karen Hollinger, "Film Noir, Voice-over, and the Femme Fatale," in *Film Noir Reader,* ed. Alain Silver and James Ursini (New York: Limelight Editions, 1996), 243-59.

53. Grossman, *Rethinking the Femme Fatale in Film Noir,* 31.

54. Babener, "De-Feminizing *Laura*," 94, 90.

55. Ibid., 100.

56. Vera Caspary, *Laura* (New York: Dell, 1942), 89.

57. Ibid., 44.

58. Ibid., 82.

59. Chris Fujiwara, "Otto Preminger," *Senses of Cinema* 20 (2002), accessed November 8, 2013, http://sensesofcinema.com/2002/great-directors/preminger/.

60. Hirsch, *Otto Preminger,* 112.

61. Fujiwara, "Otto Preminger."

62. Caspary, *Laura,* 35.

63. Ibid., 39.

64. Ibid., 136.

65. Ibid, 135.

Clockwise from right:
A Woman's Secret, *Laura*,
In a Lonely Place, and
Bedelia.

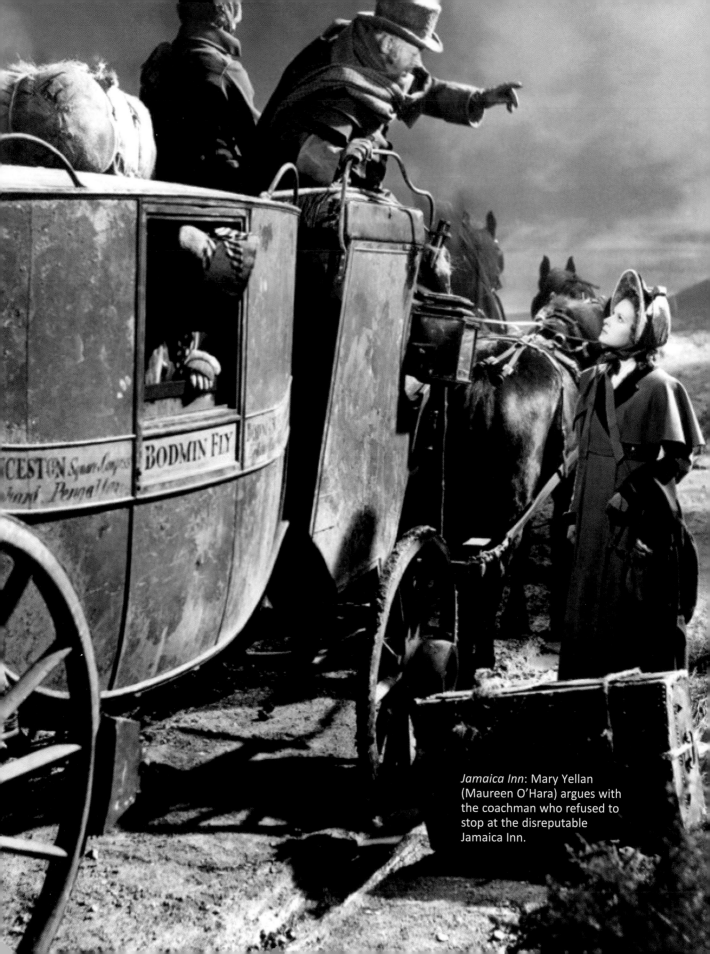

Jamaica Inn: Mary Yellan (Maureen O'Hara) argues with the coachman who refused to stop at the disreputable Jamaica Inn.

"Rawness To Romance": "Gothic" Thrillers as Film Noir Prototypes from Alfred Hitchcock to Orson Welles

Sheri Chinen Biesen

In the 1930s, after the Great War, Prohibition, the Jazz Age, and the onset of the Great Depression, Hollywood censors tried to crack down on unsavory film content and heralded a new era, moving from "rawness to romance." Seeking to avoid depictions of what they called an "orgy of sadism," they proclaimed a sweeping moratorium on violent gangster, crime and horror films. By the end of the decade, however, despite bans on gangsters, horror and grisly "hard-boiled" novels, censors grew alarmed at the increasing number of crime films and a rising array of "crime-horror" pictures. Indeed, the "horrific" criminal nature of these films was not of the typical Al Capone, *Frankenstein* or *Dracula* variety. They were a different sort altogether, churned out like hotcakes by the 1940s. As censors scrambled to deal with the resurgence of deviant hoodlums and cinematic mayhem, the crime trend would eventually proliferate and be termed Hollywood's "Red Meat" "crime and romance" cycle in 1944, soon to be called film noir in 1946.[1]

By 1939, censors recognized a menacing propagation of screen criminality, and added a new picture to their long list of "crime-horror" films: director Alfred Hitchcock and independent producer David O. Selznick's adaptation of Daphne du Maurier's 1938 Gothic novel *Rebecca*. Hitchcock had come to work with Selznick in Hollywood after directing (and producing) an impressive series of crime, espionage, and Gothic thrillers in Great Britain, including a film adaptation of du Maurier's Gothic novel *Jamaica Inn* in 1939. In Hollywood, Hitchcock especially reveled in depicting psychological subjects and insanity onscreen in Gothic films such as *Rebecca* since screen images of insanity were banned in Britain at the time.

Film noir has long been recognized for its psychological depictions, for visually revealing cinematic incarnations of a disturbing "nightmare" underworld on screen. Such nightmarish psychological imagery seen in film noir was also iconic of Gothic novels as in Emily Brontë's *Wuthering Heights*, Charlotte Brontë's *Jane Eyre*, Daphne du Maurier's *Jamaica Inn* and *Rebecca*. Further, filmmakers who were influential to film noir, such as Alfred Hitchcock and Orson Welles, typically thrived on cinematically portraying subjective prisms of psychological anguish on screen in their noir thrillers. Like film noir, Hitchcock called his suspense thrillers "very real" "nightmare" "bad dreams." He observed, "When you dream...Everything seems real... You are glad to wake up, because it's so real. So, you take a dream idea." Evocative of film noir, he explained, "it's a nightmare—and you make it real. The audience [is] looking at a nightmare, and crazy things happen...but it must be real." (Hitchcock) Hitchcock deftly drew on his cinematic experience and extensive background in directing crime, espionage, Gothic thrillers, and noir pictures in envisioning his suspense films.

In fact, Hitchcock insisted his 1959 color Cold War thriller *North by Northwest* (not typically considered noir, but reimagining Hitchcock's 1946 Gothic espionage noir *Notorious* [and Gothic espionage films noir, e.g., *Gilda, The Stranger*]) was actually re-envisioning the conventions of film noir (with its shady iconic "black and white" chiaroscuro shadows) in a new light. The elements of film noir style, so prevalent in crime films of the 1940s and 1950s, eventually became so codified and recognizable in the postwar era that they were later seen as expected, typical, conventional (even ordinary) to filmmakers and anticipated by audiences. "Now," Hitchcock explained, "in every ordinary [noir] film, what is the setting?" Mysterious atonal sounds of jazz (iconic of film noir) are heard. "The setting is night. The corner of a street in the city. The ground, like in every French [noir] film, has cobbles washed with water by rain. He stands under the street light, you know, so we have the atmosphere for terror." This description was certainly evocative of Hollywood's "crime-horror" cycle of which Hitchcock was so influential. "Now, a person looks through a window." [He moves his hand as if opening a window and looks out, leaning into the shadows blackening his face as jazz sounds menacing.] "A black cat runs along the wall. And we wait for the limousine to come and go da-da-da-da-da-da-da-da-da." [He points his hand simulating a staccato machinegun firing across the screen.] "That is the cliché. I say 'No. Cannot do it that way.' It must be done fresh and new. Therefore, I will do the same scene with nothing. No darkness. No lamp. Nothing at all. All sunlight. Everything." Hitchcock explained that he wanted to do something unexpected and "out of the ordinary" in setting a crime film and a murder scene in the middle of nowhere in broad daylight.[2]

Without mentioning the term "film noir," Hitchcock described the typical "urban jungle" atmosphere and setting of a film noir in vivid detail as an example of what audiences would come to expect from an attempted murder scene in a crime film with a dangerous milieu in a distinctively noir nocturnal metropolis. While Hitchcock imagined tormented, framed "wrong man" antihero Cary Grant (star of his 1940s Gothic noir films *Suspicion* and *Notorious*) navigating the obstacles in a "real" waking "nightmare," he wanted to transcend cinematic clichés occurring on shadowy rain slicked city streets in shrouded dark alleys with wet cobblestones and misty fog swirling as steam rises from the

Fred MacMurray lurking as the corrupt cop in *Pushover*.

gutter where street lights reveal the murky silhouette of a mysterious figure in a trench coat and fedora who smokes a cigarette (as at left), when a black limo sedan suddenly screeches out of the darkness firing staccato (machine) gunfire to knock off the noir crime protagonist. And, in shifting the typical setting from an iconic noir urban jungle to an unlikely deadly setting amid a barren landscape of farm fields in the middle of nowhere, Hitchcock not only reimagines film noir, but also deftly evokes noir prototypes, as in the bleak moors and remote rural terrain of his earlier female Gothic thrillers (and Gothic-espionage films), so influential to classic films noir.

These "Gothic" thrillers were important prototypes contributing to the development of film noir. Moreover, "Gothic" thrillers, such as "female Gothic" troubled "dark romance" suspense films, would eventually evolve to incorporate brooding noir style and become heavily influenced by the conventions of film noir itself. Notable "Gothic" preludes to film noir include "female Gothic" thrillers, as in brooding, moody atmospheric "dark romance" films like William Wyler's *Wuthering Heights* (1939), Alfred Hitchcock's *Jamaica Inn*

Another woman in period garb menaced by a "Gothic 'homme fatale'": Anton Walbrook as Paul Mallen and Diana Wynard as his wife Bella in the 1940 *Gaslight.*

(1939), *Rebecca* (1940), and *Suspicion* (1941), Thorold Dickenson's British version of *Gaslight* (1940, as well as George Cukor's 1944 Hollywood remake), and Orson Welles' uncredited contribution behind-the-scenes to the 1943 production of *Jane Eyre* (released in 1944). These female Gothic proto-noir thriller films are fascinating noir prototypes rife with gender distress that offer a more female-centric perspective on noir than typical masculine gangster films or hard-boiled fiction narratives. As influential noir prototypes, it is also interesting how the proto-noir style of these female Gothic thriller films evolve and coalesce by the 1943 production of *Jane Eyre.* In 1946, French critics praised what they termed Hollywood "*film noir*" as "black film" or "dark cinema." These shadowy crime films drew on, and later inspired, the dangerous, mysterious surroundings and lethal gender distress of "*roman noir*" Gothic thriller films adapted in the prewar 1930s through a distinctive World War II 1940s production and reception climate, and continuing into the postwar era, tapping into existential cultural anxieties.

Hitchcock's psychological proto-noir thrillers *Rebecca* and *Suspicion* spurred his Hollywood "female Gothic" film cycle, followed by *Shadow of a Doubt, Spellbound,* and *Notorious*. By the end of the war, *Notorious* combined the female Gothic with elements of an espionage thriller and film noir style. As in hard-boiled "serie noir," the term "film noir" related to "roman noir," or "black novel," which 18th- and 19th-century French critics called the British Gothic novel. Like film noir, gender distress, psychic trauma (or, insanity) and misogynism were essential to Gothic thrillers. The onset of World War II was also a catalyst for a dark breed of film noir pictures as basic Hollywood production materials, sets, and electricity were rationed for the duration amid blackouts in the Los Angeles basin which was considered a theater of war. (Biesen, *Blackout*)

Such Gothic thriller films as *Wuthering Heights*, *Jamaica Inn*, *Rebecca*, *Gaslight*, *Suspicion*, and *Jane Eyre* featured dysfunctional Gothic "dark romance" sexual relationships, troubled domestic love triangles, murder, illicit affairs and marital infidelity, supernatural tendencies, and often included a trapped or deceased female object of desire imprisoned in remote, treacherous surroundings. In fact, these dark variations on crime film narratives drawn from Gothic novels typically centered on tumultuous settings visually projecting the disturbing events and brooding emotions of the characters embroiled in doomed Gothic romances in an unlikely criminal milieu. Action revolved around huge, creepy "toxic" mansions or haunted "great" houses, such as Wuthering Heights, Jamaica Inn, Manderley (in *Rebecca*), and Thornfield (in *Jane Eyre*), which seem to be possessed by a menacing ghostly spirit which troubles disturbed inhabitants who are isolated from human contact and far away from urban centers because of their remote, perilous locations atop steep cliffs precariously looking out over a raging sea on the Cornwall coast. These macabre Gothic manors are also typically surrounded by a harsh, barren landscape pelted by violent storms and howling winds blowing across the moors as in dark Gothic *roman noir* romantic thrillers *Wuthering Heights* and fiery infernos destroying haunted castles like Thornfield in *Jane Eyre* and Gothic mansions like Manderley in *Rebecca*, both possessed by the ghoulish spirit of a woman.

While film noir featured a self-destructive tormented antihero and an alluring lethal femme fatale, Gothic thrillers centered on a more naïve victimized Gothic ingénue embroiled in dark romance with a comparatively worldly mysterious, unpredictable masculine "homme fatale" who preys on her innocence and hides deadly secrets which threaten her well being and possibly lead to her demise, as

Jane returns to Gateshead Hall in *Jane Eyre*.

in Laurence Olivier's troubled "homme fatale" Heathcliff in *Wuthering Heights* and melancholy Maxim in *Rebecca*, Orson Welles' brooding Rochester in *Jane Eyre,* Charles Laughton's sinister bootlegger in *Jamaica Inn*, and Cary Grant's menacing ne'er do well in *Suspicion*. Gothic ingénues such as Joan Fontaine's naïve heroines in *Rebecca, Suspicion,* and *Jane Eyre,* can also be seen as noir prototypes for the innocent "good girl" female "redeemer" who often offsets the femme fatale in film noir.

Disturbing stories set against dangerous landscapes involving toxic relationships centering on murder, psychological insanity with tormented unstable psyches, hysteria, and crimes of passion were hallmarks of "female Gothic" *roman noir* narratives. Hollywood's female Gothic film cycle developed a darker visual style and revolved around "gender difference, sexual identity, and the 'gender distress' that accompanied the social and cultural disruption of the war and postwar eras." Thomas Schatz observes that, like hard-boiled detective narratives, the Gothic centered on an "essentially good though flawed and vulnerable protagonist at odds with a mysterious and menacing sexual other." (Schatz 236; Waldman) In the Gothic, in this harsh remote setting of stormy moors, steep cliffs, violent surf and haunted mansions, an innocent young woman meets, becomes romantically involved with, and marries a suave enigmatic stranger. The Gothic heroine's charming mysterious older lover or husband (such as Laurence Olivier's brooding Heathcliff in *Wuthering Heights* and Maxim in *Rebecca,* and Orson Welles' moody Rochester in *Jane Eyre*), with a dubious past and with secrets to conceal, becomes an alluring but potentially predatorial sexual presence.

Such Gothic *roman noir* thriller films as *Wuthering Heights*, *Jamaica Inn, Jane Eyre, Rebecca* and *Suspicion* concerned anxieties which resonated with women during this period regarding entanglements with misogynistic lovers and husbands, especially as World War II approached. In the postwar era into the Cold War, Gothic gender images eventually transformed into Gothic espionage thriller films of dangerous liaisons with Nazis or Cold War criminals in deadly Gothic surroundings which shifted from the mansion to the home and perilous natural landscapes (e.g., Cornwall coastlines, Gothic mansions in *Wuthering Heights*, *Jamaica Inn, Jane Eyre, Rebecca* and *Suspicion*) as lethal sites of crime, murder and passion. In the wake of the war, these Gothic "homme fatales" would eventually morph into Axis enemies in Gothic espionage hybrid noir films, as in Claude Rains' "Nazi momma's

Orson Welles as the
enigmatic Rochester
with Margaret O'Brien as Adele and Joan
Fontaine as the title heroine in *Jane Eyre*.

boy" Alex (sparing with Cary Grant's repressed spy Devlin) in *Notorious*, Orson Welles' Gestapo war criminal in *The Stranger*, or George Macready's murderous Aryan menace in *Gilda* and *My Name is Julia Ross*.

Hitchcock's 1940s Gothic thrillers frequently centered on women, especially during World War II and just after the conflict. By 1946, Hitchcock acknowledged that he had gained a substantial domestic and Allied "home front" audience of women viewers engaged in his increasingly noir styled female Gothic thriller films. A *New Castle News* article in September 1946 described Hitchcock as "the movie director who gauges trends like Gallup measures opinions" and who "says women set the standards of sex appeal. The male just falls in line." After many years with men overseas serving in the war, insisting, "It's women—women moviegoers who make up 80 percent of the audience—who create the Betty Grables, the Lana Turners and the [Ingrid] Bergmans." Although Hitchcock was acclaimed for directing suspenseful crime films involving murder, many of his wartime 1940s pictures were proto-noir female Gothic thriller films which not only contributed to the development of film noir, but also targeted women who made up a large portion of the domestic (and Allied) home-front viewing markets during the war and were influential in determining screen sexuality and appeal. As a result, filmmakers like Hitchcock and Welles were keen to reach female viewers (as well as masculine noir crime viewers) in these more female centered Gothic noir prototype films during this wartime to early postwar period: "It isn't the male wolf who keeps [Lana] Turner sweating out scene after scene in a sweater. The British-American director swears it's the bobby-soxer, the little gals between 15 and 18 who take their boy friends along just to buy the ticket." As Hitchcock explained, "It's identification, that's what it is. The bobby soxer wants to look like Grable and Turner. The older woman wants to look like Bergman and Colbert. The whole process starts with a mirror. When a woman looks in her mirror she sees what she wants to see. When she looks at a movie screen, she wants to see some of the same—only more so." Hitchcock was described as the "man who has turned out more stars than he can name" and the director who was convinced that "stellar personalities" with "sincerity" and "intelligence" on screen transcended sex appeal. (Hitchcock)

These atmospheric 1940s female Gothic films developed in relation to the chiaroscuro, expressionistic style of films noir. As in film noir, dysfunctional romantic relations in suspenseful female Gothic melodramas embodied a sexual threat to disturbed protagonists. The mature hard-boiled protagonists and deadly seductive femme fatales of film noir were joined by young naïve Gothic ingénues (or redeemers) opposite menacing older masculine antiheroes. The presence of these ingénues created a female Gothic film genre that coincided with a wartime labor market of aging men and younger women in Hollywood as younger men went off to war. (Biesen, *Blackout*) Both film noir and female Gothic thrillers involved toxic "dark love" romances and lethal fatal attraction. The harsh atmospheric milieu in female Gothic thrillers visually reflected their "seeds of romantic estrangement." In this brooding, perilous noir Gothic setting, the homme fatale's "moodiness and unpredictability sometimes signal potential danger to the heroine even before she marries," as in George Cukor's *Gaslight* (1944), where a menacing criminal spouse Charles Boyer preys on a young unsuspecting Ingrid Bergman. Helen Hanson observes the "rapid move from the romance stage of the narrative to one of suspicion and investigation shows the transition in the heroine's perception of her husband." (Hanson, 67) Cukor's 1944 Gothic *Gaslight* was a transatlantic Hollywood adaptation of Thorold Dickinson's fine 1940 British Gothic thriller featuring an extraordinary performance by Gothic homme fatale Anton Walbrook. During and just after World War II, films noir and Gothics also featured scrappy young "Rosie the Riveter" working-women heroines, as in *Phantom Lady* (produced by Hitchcock protégé and *Jamaica Inn, Rebecca, Suspicion* writer Joan Harrison), *Spellbound, Notorious, Gilda, Ministry of Fear,* and *My Name is Julia Ross.*

In his Gothic thrillers, master of suspense Hitchcock drew on his earlier expressionistic experience working at Weimar Germany's UFA studio and collaborated with German producer (of expressionist psychological horror masterpiece *The Cabinet of Dr. Caligari*) Erich Pommer on *Jamaica Inn*. Although as a British Gothic noir prototype, *Jamaica Inn* resembles more of a shady pirate movie and an historical costume period drama than a typical film noir. Hitchcock's *Jamaica Inn* revealed a Gothic thriller evocative of seafaring adventure films with a mysterious remote location on the cliffs of the British Cornwall Coast where murderous gangs of pirates and bootleggers hide in a haunted house called Jamaica Inn. Charles Laughton plays the squire kingpin who runs the deadly black market from his estate sending his band of criminals to lure, attack and destroy ships, knock off their crews, and steal their treasure. Young orphaned Gothic ingénue Maureen O'Hara comes from Ireland and becomes entangled and entrapped in the deadly unsavory surroundings and tries to uncover the culprit. Like O'Hara's young Irish émigré lass in British Gothic *Jamaica Inn*, director Hitchcock moved across the Atlantic to America and directed his first Hollywood film, *Rebecca*. With the war in Europe by the late 1930s and early 1940s, many talented Europe émigré creative artists (including noir stalwarts like Robert Siodmak [who directed Gothic noir hybrid *Phantom Lady*], Fritz Lang, Curt Siodmak, and Jean Renoir) and filmmakers from Great Britain such as Hitchcock and actors Charles Laughton, Laurence Olivier, Judith Anderson, and Irish actress Maureen O'Hara flocked to the American film industry and contributed to Hollywood's burgeoning film noir and Gothic thrillers. Émigrés such as Hitchcock, his colleague and collaborator Joan Harrison, and a young brilliant American Orson Welles (who had spent time working and acting in Ireland and the United Kingdom), would cultivate a vibrant Gothic noir prototype aesthetic in 1940s Hollywood.

Rebecca: in Monte Carlo "Maxim" de Winter (Laurence Olivier) meets the unnamed young companion (Joan Fontaine) to Mrs. Von Hopper (Florance Bates).

Evoking the turbulent Gothic terrain of *Jane Eyre, Jamaica Inn,* and *Wuthering Heights*, Hitchcock's adaptation of du Maurier's *Rebecca* opens with a shadowy wooded nightscape outside Manderley mansion where Joan Fontaine's Gothic ingénue recalls in voice-over narration a psychological dream evocative of the noir nightmare Hitchcock described in his thrillers: "Last night I dreamt I went to Manderley again. It seemed to me I stood by the iron gate leading to the drive and for a while I could not enter, for the way was barred to me. Then, like all dreamers, I was possessed of a sudden with supernatural powers and passed like a spirit through the barrier before me." Inspired by the brooding iconography of Gothic thrillers such as *Jane Eyre*, in Hitchcock's *Rebecca*, the ghost of Rebecca haunts Manderley and seems to possess its inhabitants, such as Mrs. Danvers (Judith Anderson), enthralled in memories of her lesbian affair with the deceased Mrs. DeWinter embodied in the spirit of the "touched" great-house.

As film noir emerged in the 1940s, World War II transformed the Hollywood motion picture industry as America mobilized for the war and studios shifted from a pre-war to wartime climate affecting studio production conditions, creative personnel, censorship and the types of films produced. Film noir capitalized on these unique wartime production conditions such as war-related blackouts in the Los Angeles basin; restrictions on location shooting, rationing of film, lighting, electricity, set materials; and use of recycled sets shrouded in shadow, fog, rain, cigarette smoke, mirrors and shrewd camera angles so distinctive of noir's cinematic milieu. (Biesen, *Blackout*) New advances in technology also enabled noir filmmaking innovations with lightweight cameras and better, deep focus lenses (and "faster," light sensitive film stock), which enhanced noir's distinctive shadowy chiaroscuro

Rebecca: the new Mrs. de Winter with the disapproving Mrs. Danvers (Judith Anderson).

look and aesthetic visual style with high contrast, "low-key" lighting and cinematography, as evident in the 1944 noir styled shadowy Gothic noir prototype *Jane Eyre*.

The changing wartime Hollywood production and reception climate affected motion picture viewers exposed to grislier film portrayals and stronger women that resonated with tougher film noir and Gothic thrillers. While earlier noir prototypes *Rebecca, Suspicion,* and *Shadow of a Doubt* are not as dark and shadowy in visual style as film noir, Gothic preludes like the wartime production of *Jane Eyre* are steeped in the brooding style and sensibility of film noir. In fact, noir prototypes such as Hitchcock's Gothic thrillers *Rebecca, Suspicion,* and the blackened world Orson Welles embodies in *Jane Eyre,* shift from the stormy milieu of windy moors, steep sea cliffs, and brightly lit "high-key" locations (as in *Rebecca* and *Suspicion* [until its murky finale]) to a darker "low-key" lighting style and brooding, shadowy visual design evocative of film noir in *Jane Eyre.* Hitchcock used expressionistic film noir style in *Suspicion*'s climax as Grant's Gothic homme fatale somberly climbs the stairs shrouded in shadows to potentially murder his innocent wife (Fontaine) with a poisoned glass of milk. In *Jane Eyre* the sinister looking haunted castle Thornfield is cloaked in deep shadow inside and hidden in a blackened fog shrouded night outside as Welles' Rochester suddenly appears out of nowhere like a possessed spirit in a fierce gallop startling and nearly colliding with a stunned Jane (Fontaine) before his horse rears throwing him to the ground. Rochester tells Jane there is an otherworldly quality about her as she appeared in the heavy fog of the moors at night.

As the war intensified, Gothic thrillers grew increasingly dark, adopting film noir style, as in *Jane Eyre.* Welles (albeit uncredited) designed, produced, and directed sequences of the shadowy, chiaroscuro "Gothic noir"-styled setting in the Hollywood film adaptation of Charlotte Brontë's 1847 British Gothic novel *Jane Eyre*, shot from February to April 1943 and released in 1944, which was based on Welles' *Mercury Theater on the Air* radio script. Joan Fontaine insisted Welles was a powerful force of nature taking charge on- and off-screen and confirmed Welles' creative involvement behind-the-scenes (along with July 1943 production memos) in crafting the Gothic design "look and feel" of *Jane Eyre*: From shadowy Gothic spires and eerie towers of haunted Thornfield castle sets to deep focus shot compositions, brooding low-key noir lighting, casting, script, and his performance as Rochester.

Welles nearly received producer credit (it was even reported in Hollywood trades), but Selznick insisted Welles not receive screen credit. Welles' Mercury Theater colleague John Houseman co-adapted the screenplay, and Agnes Moorehead and Erskine Sanford costarred with Welles (Rochester), Fontaine (and young Peggy Ann Garner) as Jane Eyre, and 11-year-old Elizabeth Taylor as an orphan who dies after being abused and mistreated by sadistic fanatically religious schoolmaster Henry Brocklehurst (Henry Daniell). Welles also suggested *Citizen Kane* composer Bernard Hermann (replacing Igor Stravinsky) to score the music. *Jane Eyre* had the striking, undeniable "sights and sounds" of Welles' dark noir style seen in his brilliant 1941 feature film debut, *Citizen Kane* filmed two years earlier.

As a pitch-black night and swirling mists of dense fog enveloped menacing gargoyles and spindly turrets of Thornfield castle and Lowood orphanage was splintered by geometric patterns of barred shadows to cinematically convey its harsh abusive entrapment, Welles' production of *Jane Eyre* was shot during World War II blackouts in Hollywood on dark enclosed soundstages to create an existential abyss of "horrific" crime, "terror" and "sadistic" abuse (resembling Welles" opening of *Citizen Kane* with the ominous *Frankenstein*-like silhouette of Xanadu's gloomy Gothic mansion on a hill [as well as his earlier Mercury Theater stage productions]). Welles got $100,000 and top billing as the movie's star instead of producer (or any design, direction) credit for *Jane Eyre.* Yet, Welles' ironic admission after being denied screen credit: "I do not like being an actor and I don't acknowledge the existence of a job called producer. The only thing I like in films is directing," belied the film's omission of his creative role in *Jane Eyre.*[3]

Such noir styled "dark love" Gothic romance thrillers were so successful that by 1944, as film noir exploded and proliferated—with films like *Double Indemnity, Murder, My Sweet, Laura, Phantom Lady, To Have and Have Not, The Woman in the Window,* and *Gaslight*—the *New York Times* recognized a "psychological" "new horror cycle" of [Gothic noir] films "bulging with screams in the night, supercharged criminal phenomena and esthetic murder." Film industry analyst Fred Stanley observed, "Hollywood Shivers: The Studios Are Busily Stirring Up a Grade A Witches' Brew," referring to *Phantom Lady, Laura, Gaslight, The Woman in the Window* and *Spellbound.* He noted: "Every studio has at least one such picture in production and others coming to a witching boil." A year later, by 1945 industry watchers anticipated that Hollywood studios would "lean toward historical romantic drama for much of its top 'A' productions during 1946."[4]

The legacy and popularity of Gothic noir prototypes (e.g., *Wuthering Heights, Jamaica Inn, Rebecca, Suspicion, Gaslight, Jane Eyre*) inspired later films, including films noir (e.g., *Phantom Lady, Spellbound, Laura*), Gothic noir espionage hybrids (e.g., *Notorious, Gilda, Ministry of Fear, The Stranger*), "color noir" (e.g., *Rear Window, North by Northwest*) and "neo-noir" films, which captured the brooding, atmospheric spirit of Gothic noir thrillers.[4] As "Gothic noir" auteurs Hitchcock and Welles and their (proto) noir-styled films suggest, noir prototypes such as female-centered "crime-

A full-on "Gothic Noir" pose from Hitchcock in *Rebecca*.

horror" "dark romance" *roman noir* Gothic thriller pictures generated a prolific cinematic legacy inspiring and anticipating an array of noir films in the 1940s, as well as "color noir" and "neo-noir" films in later decades.[5]

Notes

1. See Biesen, *Blackout: World War II and the Origins of Film Noir*, 1-5; *Film Censorship; Music in the Shadows.*

2. Hitchcock, *Hitchcock S'Explique* 1965. Set in the Midwest, *North by Northwest* was actually shot in parched fields near Bakersfield, California for its flat, barren landscape. Hitchcock has Cary Grant stand on a bright, stark dusty rural farm road with nothing but crops, sunlight and the occasional passing vehicle...until the crop duster appears in the distance. In a nod to film noir, Hitchcock even plays with viewer expectations by having a black limo sedan drive by (suggesting a noir crime film), followed by an old green car which a man gets out of and waits then catches a bus, as he observes, "that's funny—he's dusting crops where there ain't no crops."

3. Welles; Biesen.

4. Stanley 1944-45; Biesen.

5. The legacy of Gothic noir prototypes (*Wuthering Heights, Gaslight,* Hitchcock's *Jamaica Inn, Rebecca, Suspicion,* Welles' *Jane Eyre*); films noir (e.g., noir Gothic/espionage hybrids *Phantom Lady, Gilda,* Hitchcock's *Spellbound, Notorious,* Welles' *The Stranger* and *The Lady From Shanghai*); and "color noir" films (e.g., Hitchcock's thrillers *Rear Window, North by Northwest*) inspired later "neo-noir" films of the postclassical "new" Hollywood renaissance era. For more on film noir, noir Gothic and espionage thrillers, "color noir" and "neo-noir" films, see Biesen, *Blackout; Music in the Shadows.*

Bibliography

"Alfred Hitchcock Disclaims Art in Mystery Films," *Ogden Standard Examiner.* 5 May 1946.

Biesen, Sheri Chinen. *Blackout: World War II and the Origins of Film Noir,* Baltimore: Johns Hopkins University Press, 2005.

—. *Music in the Shadows: Noir Musical Films,* Baltimore: Johns Hopkins University Press, 2014.

"A Genius of the Films: Alfred Hitchcock and His Work." *The Observer.* 17 November 1935.

Hanson, Helen. *Hollywood Heroines: Women in Film Noir and the Female Gothic Film.* London: I.B. Tauris, 2007.

Hitchcock, Alfred. In "Director Says Women Create Sweater Girls." *New Castle News.* 13 September 1946.

—. *Hitchcock S'Explique*, French documentary, André S. Labarthe, 1965.

Leff, Leonard. *Hitchcock and Selznick.* New York: Weidenfeld and Nicolson, 1987.

—. *The Rich and Strange Collaboration of Alfred Hitchcock and David O. Selznick in Hollywood.* Berkeley: University of California Press, 1999.

"Mr. Hitchcock's New Film, *Notorious*" *The Times.* 14 February 1947.

Schatz, Thomas. *Boom and Bust: American Cinema in the 1940s.* New York: Scribners, 1997.

Spoto, David. *The Dark Side of Genius.* New York: Ballantine, 1983.

Stanley, Fred. "Hollywood Flash: Studios Scrap Many War Stories—The Horror Boys Convene—Other News," *New York Times*, April 16, 1944, B.

—. "Hollywood Shivers: The Studios Are Busily Stirring Up a Grade A Witches" Brew—Other Items," *New York Times*, 28 May 1944.

Truffaut, François. *Hitchcock.* New York: Simon and Schuster, 1985.

Waldman, Diane. "Horror and Domesticity: The Modern Gothic Romance of the 1940s," Unpublished Ph.D. dissertation, Madison: The University of Wisconsin, 1981.

Welles, Orson. In Fred Stanley, "An Old Hollywood Costume," *New York Times*, 21 October 1945, X1, 3.

"Why Thrillers Thrive." *Picturegoer.* 18 January 1936.

Rogue Cop Ed Cornell (Laird Cregar) manhandles handcuffed suspect Frankie Christopher (Victor Mature) in *I Wake Up Screaming*.

The Rogue Cop Film: Theft, Adaptation, and Prototypicality in *Where the Sidewalk Ends*

Robert Miklitsch

I Wake Up Screaming: The Proto-Prototypical "Rogue Cop" Film

The first, if not prototypical, "rogue cop" film of classic American film noir is H. Bruce Humberstone's *I Wake Up Screaming* (1941), which was previewed for the trades only a little over a month after *The Maltese Falcon* (1941). Humberstone had directed a number of Charlie Chan movies in the 1930s, but *I Wake Up Screaming*, which was adapted from an appropriately lurid Steve Fisher novel that was itself an homage to Cornell Woolrich (the investigating detective of both the novel and the film is named Ed Cornell), is a horse of a different color.

The plot of *I Wake Up Screaming* is a mix of *My Fair Lady* and *Peeping Tom*: sports promoter Frankie Christopher (Victor Mature) conspires with a couple of social associates to turn diner waitress Vicky Lynn (Carole Landis) from a "hash slinger" into a "celebrity." However, when she suddenly ends up dead after informing her sponsors that she's going to Hollywood, Frankie becomes the prime suspect. Although Cornell (Laird Cregar) knows that switchboard operator Harry Williams (Elisha Cook Jr.) is the culprit, he's intent on framing Frankie for the murder and for stealing the girl of his dreams. In the meantime Frankie and Vicky's sister, Jill (Betty Grable), become romantically involved as well as amateur detectives à la Nick (William Powell) and Nora Charles (Myrna Loy) in *The Thin Man* series. After the couple extracts a confession from Williams, Frankie goes to Cornell's apartment where he discovers a shrine, complete with pictures and flowers, to the murdered femme.

In *In a Lonely Street* Frank Krutnik proposes that the "contaminated law officer" abuses his position of authority and responsibility for either a woman (*Pushover* [1954]), money (*Rogue Cop* [1954]), or both (*The Prowler* [1951]).[1] Ed Cornell in *I Wake Up Screaming* prefigures the first variation on the "rogue cop" formula. The film also introduces more than a note of "dark perversity" in the form of voyeurism (Cornell "peeps" at Vicky through the front window of the diner like, according to Jill, "the wolf looked at the three little pigs") in addition to "repressed homosexual passion" (see the creepy scene where Frankie wakes up in his apartment to find Cornell seated in a chair at the end of his bed).[2] As the images intimate and as Edward Cronjager's moody, high-contrast lighting attests, *I Wake Up Screaming* is, like *Stranger on the Third Floor* (1940), a seminal proto-noir, but is it a prototypical "rogue cop" film?

I Wake Up Screaming is, I want to argue, a proto-prototypical "rogue cop" film, and the reasons are at once formal, industrial, and historical. If the first, formal reason is something of a quodlibet, it's also one reason why Humberstone's picture is a proto- rather than full-fledged noir: the sound track. I'm referring to the film's recourse to "Over the Rainbow" as Jill's theme. While one might argue that the Harold Arlen music is employed as a whimsical counterpoint to Frankie's big-city motif, Alfred Newman's "Street Scene," the persistent and, ultimately, distracting use of "Over the Rainbow" underscores the film's debt to the 1930s M-G-M musical just as Dwight Taylor's dialogue is more reminiscent of later rather than early Hammett—of, that is to say, *The Thin Man* (1934) rather than *The Maltese Falcon* (1929).[3]

The industrial and historical arguments against Humberstone's film are interrelated. *I Wake Up Screaming* is something of a one-off in that it did not initiate a subsequent cycle or series. As for the historical angle, the cultural-political conditions of possibility for the "rogue cop" film did not

I Wake Up Screaming: Det. Ed Cornell (Laird Cregar) stalks the Lynn sisters, Jill (Betty Grable, left) and Vicky (Carole Landis).

materialize until the late 1940s, a period marked by, among other things, the aftereffects of the war and the rise of anti-communism. In *A Panorama of American Film Noir* Raymond Borde and Étienne Chaumeton succinctly characterize the "demise of the noir series" as the "effacement of the private detective in favor of the official police."[4] Dennis Broe maintains, moreover, that one consequence of what Pierre Kast calls the "liquidation" of the private detective film was the "vigilante cop" picture in which "Hammett's resistant detective transforms into [Mickey] Spillane's fascistic enforcer of the law."[5]

As I argue in more detail elsewhere, the notion that the "vigilante cop" film signals the "end of the line of the noir period" misprizes, however, both the complexity of the historical moment and those dark crime films that emerged out of it.[6] Accordingly, to categorize *Kiss Me Deadly* (1955) as a "vigilante cop" picture, as Broe does, is not only to confuse Robert Aldrich's film with Spillane's novel but to radically slight the performative force of Aldrich and A. I. Bezzerides' détournement of the original, admittedly refractory source material.[7]

Detective Story: In the Name of the Father

> "You think you're on the side of the angels."
>
> —Mary McLeod (Eleanor Parker), *Detective Story* (1952)

Although a case could be made that *The Bribe* (1949) is the prototypical "rogue cop" film—in this M-G-M production, federal agent Rigby (Robert Taylor) abdicates his duty when he falls for a raven-haired siren, Elizabeth Hintten (Ava Gardner)—his abdication, like Elizabeth's blackmail-induced bad turn, is momentary. (Elizabeth agrees to drug Rigby and thereby aid the war-surplus racketeers so that her heart-sick husband won't be arrested and die in prison.) In the final analysis, Robert Z. Leonard's *Bribe* plays more like a noir-inflected melodrama than a classic "rogue cop" film.[8] *The Bribe*'s status as a prototypical "rogue cop" film can be gauged by comparing it to a film that appeared one year later, *Where the Sidewalk Ends* (1950), which benefits from a piratical relation to an acknowledged model of the subgenre, *Detective Story* (1951). Indeed, *Where the Sidewalk Ends* has an unusually complex textual and production history since it's not only based on a "pulp" novel, William Stuart's *Night Cry* (1948), but was substantially revised in light of Sidney Kingsley's Pulitzer Prize-winning Broadway play, *Detective Story* (1949).

The Bribe: Agent Rigby (Robert Taylor) and the wife of his suspect, Elizabeth Hintten (Ava Gardner).

Where the Sidewalk Ends was initially adapted from *Night Cry* by Victor Trivas, Frank P. Rosenberg, and Robert E. Kent, and Ben Hecht was engaged to write the screenplay. Although Hecht submitted a final script in December, 1950, Darryl Zanuck, the head of production at Twentieth Century-Fox, "recommended several ways to mitigate the guilt of the main character,"[9] Mark Dixon, a "rogue cop" who accidentally kills a suspect, then endeavors to cover it up. (The copy for one advertisement reads: "This is the story of Mark Dixon, a tough cop ...who could kill a man with his fists— <u>and one night he did</u>!"), Hecht submitted a revised final script later that month and principal photog-

Detective Story: brutal cop James McLeod (Kirk Douglas) roughs up a suspect in his custody Karl Schneider (George Macready).

raphy commenced on December 27, 1949 in New York City. Shooting concluded in Los Angeles on March 3, 1950, but on March 10, Zanuck, viewing the completed picture, insisted on extensive retakes. "One of Zanuck's motives in demanding the retakes," according to Chris Fujiwara, "may have been to capitalize on the similarity between [*Where the Sidewalk Ends* and *Detective Story*], knowing that *Where the Sidewalk Ends* would reach theatres before *Detective Story* and hoping to steal the competition's thunder."[10]

Detective Story, which Paramount produced and William Wyler directed, is a decidedly faithful adaptation of Kingsley's play. While there are a number of brief exterior scenes, the film is primarily set, like the play, on the second floor of the 21st precinct station in New York City and most of the action takes place either in the main "squad room" or in the lieutenant's office. (Wyler and director of photography Lee Garmes utilize long takes and deep-focus composition to animate what is essentially a stage set.) Jim McLeod (Kirk Douglas) is a detective who's not above violating the constitutional rights of his arrests by using, among other things, a rubber hose. In the course of the film, McLeod's busy booking Arthur (Craig Hill), a young ex-serviceman who has embezzled $480.00 from his employer and helping to question two "cat burglars," Lewis Abbott (Michael Strong) and Charley Gennini (Joseph Wiseman)). However, McLeod's obsessed—a police reporter refers to him at one point as Captain Ahab[11]—with a "black-market baby" doctor, Karl Schneider (George Macready). One of the doctor's patients is currently in critical condition at the hospital. In a police "wagon" on the way to Bellevue where McLeod hopes that she will positively identify Schneider, the detective learns that the girl has died and, after threatening the doctor—"You butcher one more patient and, law or no law, I'll find you and I'll put a bullet in the back of your head and drop your body in the East River"—McLeod punches Schneider in the gut, putting him in the hospital.

Although Schneider, unlike Anderson, lives, his attorney hints that they have something on McLeod, and when Lt. Monaghan (Horace McMahon) interrogates a hood who owns a "creep joint in the Village,"[12] the lieutenant discovers that McLeod's wife, Mary, was impregnated by the "pig" (McLeod's term of abuse), then went to Schneider to farm out the baby. McLeod has idealized his wife—"I thought you were everything good and pure"—but now he thinks she's a "tramp." (In Kingsley's play he calls her a "whore."[13]) The discourse of insanity circulates throughout the film—an "elderly, aristocratic-looking woman" claims that a man's using radar to surveil her from the top of the Empire State Building[14]—and Mary's revelation brings McLeod to the breaking point. Mary, devastated, walks out, but when she returns to the station and informs her husband that she's leaving him (a taxi's waiting outside), McLeod, realizing that he can't live without his wife, tells her that he'd blow his brains out if she wasn't waiting for him every day when he got home.

McLeod, whose moral indignation verges on the messianic, is—as Schneider's attorney remarks—a "law unto himself" or, as Monaghan puts it, "judge and jury." When the police reporter makes a case about the importance of proof, McLeod invokes his ability to sniff out the "stench" of evil, which he learned to do as a child: "Every day of my childhood I saw and heard that father of mine abuse and torment my mother with that criminal mind of his and drive her straight into a lunatic asylum.... Every time I look at one of these babies I see my old man's face!" The word "babies" is ambiguous. Is McLeod referring to the perps in the squad room or those infants who escaped the butcher's knife? Whatever the answer, McLeod's father is the root of the detective's hubris, if not of all evil.

McLeod never does resolve his relationship to his dead father. First, Mary walks out on him when he can't forgive her—in a paranoid spasm, he questions how many other men she's been with—then Charley grabs an officer's revolver and McLeod suicidally tries to take the gun away from him. Although McLeod dies in the line of fire, passing away while reciting the "Act of Contrition" ("In the name of the Father ..."), he does so before he can be redeemed. In the end, it's as if the "justice of the streets" has come back, like a boomerang, to exact its own, violent form of revenge.[15]

Where the Sidewalk Ends: Hate and Theft

> Paine had not stopped living like those thousands who were dead.
> He was beginning to come alive.
>
> —William Stuart, *Night Cry*

Where the Sidewalk Ends, which was the first in a series of noirs that Otto Preminger made in the 1950s, was succeeded by *The Thirteenth Letter* (1951) and *Angel Face* (1953). *Where the Sidewalk Ends* reteamed Preminger with a number of key Fox creative personnel such as art director Lyle Wheeler, set decorator Thomas Little, editor Louis R. Loeffler and, in particular, director of photography Joseph LaShelle; it also re-paired Dana Andrews with Gene Tierney, who had graced *Laura*, a singular picture that put the eponymous heroine, played by the ravishing Tierney, on a pedestal, then brought her back down to earth. When Laura enters her apartment midway through the picture, having ostensibly been murderously disfigured, detective Mark McPherson (Dana Andrews) suddenly wakes up from a dream about the woman in the portrait only to see the dream girl herself, very much alive, standing before his very eyes.

 Where the Sidewalk Ends, as the title indicates, "is set in a gritty, naturalistic milieu far removed from the glamor of *Laura*."[16] The opening credit sequence, in which the film's title is spelled out on a sidewalk with the same sort of white chalk used to outline a dead body, concretizes this difference. A man who's whistling Fox's perennial go-to tune, "Street Scene" (we only see his trousered legs and shoes), steps off a curb where rainwater sluices into a debris-littered gutter.

 The "body" of the film opens with a Times Square process shot of Detective Mark Dixon (Dana Andrews) and his partner, Paul Klein (Bert Freed), driving to the 16th precinct station where Detective Thomas (Karl Malden) is in the process of being promoted to lieutenant. Dixon started out in the department at the same time as Thomas; however, as Inspector Nicholas Foley (Robert Simon) informs him in his office, he's being demoted because of "twelve more citizen complaints against [him] this month for assault and battery." "By who?" Dixon retorts, "Hoods, dusters, mugs, a lotta nickel rats."

```
                    FOLEY
     You've gotta learn what's expected of a
     police officer and what isn't.

                    DIXON
     I'll try to learn not to hate hoods.

                    FOLEY
     You don't hate hoodlums. You like to
     beat them, you get fun out of them...
     Your job is to detect criminals, not
     to punish them.
```

Dixon, it's plain, is a "bad cop," one who's prone not simply to sarcasm but sadism—which is to say he may as well have HATE tattooed on both hands.

 Cut to the 43rd Street Hotel where a floating crap game's in progress. Rich, out-of-town Texan Dick Morrison (Harry von Zell) is winning big to the dismay of Tommy Scalise (Gary Merrill) and the mobster's confederate, Ken Paine (Craig Stevens). However, when "working girl" Morgan Taylor (Gene Tierney)—the "decoy" Paine has used to lure Morrison to the club—tells her estranged husband that it's time to leave, Ken slaps her twice, hard, across the face. For those viewers familiar with *Laura*, it's a shocking scene: Tierney may be beautifully dressed by Oleg Cassini (her husband at the time), but Morgan Taylor is not Laura Hunt, and this is most definitely not the beau monde. Although Morrison gallantly intervenes, in the ensuing fight Paine punches him out like a clock.

Later, when Paine and Klein arrive at the hotel, we learn that Morrison has been knifed to death. Dixon promptly grabs Scalise by the lapels and pulls "Dream Boy" up from a bed on which he's been reclining. The Breen Office, referencing Hecht's stage direction about Scalise speaking in a "dreamy voice," commented that any suggestion that the mobster "is under the influence of narcotics" could not be approved.[17] But despite this caveat, Scalise's constantly putting an inhaler to his nose, and it's not because he has a cold. (It was a common knowledge at the time that soldiers used Benzedrine inhalers during the war to stay alert.)

There's bad blood between Dixon and Scalise: Dixon has been trying to take Scalise down for four years, and two years ago the mobster made a "monkey" out of him by beating a murder rap:

DIXON

You're still a killer.

SCALISE

Why are you always trying to push me
into the gutter, Dixon? I got as much
right to the sidewalk as you have.

Where the Sidewalk Ends:
Det. Mark Dixon (Dana
Andrews) searches mobster
Tommy Scalise (Gary Merrill).

When Scalise proceeds to mention Dixon Sr.—"Your father liked me"—Dixon angrily tells him to shut up. The detective is hot to "handle" Scalise (which, in Dixon's case, means "manhandling" him), but Lt. Thomas, who's just entered the room, orders him to track down Paine.

Paine's address, 58 Pike Street, is an apartment building that sits in the shadow of the Manhattan Bridge. After Dixon pays off the cabbie, he looks through a window where an old woman, Mrs. Tribaum (Grayce Mills), sits asleep at a table on which a radio is playing "Eine kleine Nachtmusik." Once Dixon's inside the building, he opens the door to Paine's apartment and stands there listening. The detective's dressed in a dark fedora and overcoat (the low-angle shot foregrounds the darkness his figure cuts), although Paine's so drunk—he's on the phone trying to locate Morrison—that he remains completely oblivious of the detective. When Dixon finally interrupts him to identify himself, Paine tells him to get lost; when the detective doesn't budge, Paine springs up off the bed and slugs him. Dixon, whose pugilistic instincts have become second nature by now, punches Paine in the stomach, then lands a big uppercut that drops him like a tree.

Dixon bends down to check Paine—he lightly slaps his face and places a hand on his heart—but when Paine doesn't respond, he feels his pulse. As the score steadily rises, the strings trilling, the camera dollies into a medium close-up of Dixon, his face edged with shadow. Cut to a POV shot of a phone. Before Dixon can decide what to do, it rings (it's Klein) and, as the camera tracks in again, he learns that Paine was an ex-syndicated columnist with a "head full of metal and a lot of friends." Dixon slumps against the wall—in the close-up, his eyes are edged again with shadow—and his stunned expression registers the impact of Klein's communication: Dixon hasn't inadvertently killed a "nickel rat," he's killed a "war hero."

The POV shot of Paine's body splayed out on the floor decides the issue: after Dixon retrieves the ex-serviceman's kitbag from the closet, he empties out the dresser, stuffs the contents into the bag, and yanks the overcoat off the dead-heavy corpse. When we next see Dixon, he's dressed in Paine's trench coat, he has a bandage under his left eye, and he's carrying the dead man's bag. (For the noir locus classicus, see Walter Neff [Fred MacMurray] impersonating Mr. Dietrichson [Tom Powers] in *Double Indemnity* [1944].) Dixon's about to get into the cab that he's called when he glances over at the window where Mrs. Tribaum, now awake and wide-eyed, returns his gaze.

In *Film Noir* Andrew Spicer observes that the "maladjusted veteran ceased to be a topical figure by the end of the 1940s, replaced by the rogue cop, another figure trained to kill, skilled in covering up his tracks, and a similarly destabilizing social force."[18] *Where the Sidewalk Ends* literalizes this replacement since, in the above paradigmatic sequence, the "rogue cop" transforms into the "maladjusted veteran." In other words, in impersonating the dead man, Dixon not only effectively becomes Paine but metaphorically assumes his "wound," as if his own distemper, whether occupational or not, were a function of the war. In just this sense, Dixon is a Doppelgänger of Paine, albeit, unlike the ex-service-man, he's engaged in a war against a domestic, not a foreign, enemy.

Although the shot of Dixon-as-Paine standing before a barred ticket counter at Pennsylvania Station does not bode well, suggesting imprisonment, the detective's determined to evade detection at all costs. When he returns to Paine's apartment, Klein's already there and has just checked a closet where the

ex-serviceman's hat and uniform still hang; Dixon, though, gets to the other closet first (inside of which Paine's body is propped up against a wall). Later, Dixon carries the dead man out over his shoulder, momentarily hiding behind a stairwell when Morgan's father, Jiggs (Tom Tully), comes looking for the man who slapped his daughter. (In the wide, low-angle shot where Dixon unloads Paine's body into the backseat of a car, a train on the elevated track above suddenly screeches to a halt.) Still later, at the precinct station, Dixon stands conspicuously in the background of a deep-focus shot—he's centered in the frame to the left of a window, his fedora shading his face—as Lt. Thomas interrogates the taxi driver who drove "Paine" to Penn Station.

Where the Sidewalk Ends: Dixon realizes that his rough interrogation his killed Ken Paine (Craig Stevens).

The same sort of diamond-patterned window in front of which Dixon's perched on a desk also comes to the fore in the following "locker room" scene where Dixon and Klein retire for the night. After the camera pans past an image of a woman taped to a locker, Dixon pauses before the window—the camera's tight on his wasted face—beyond which the "dark city" lies, the windows lit up like little boxes of light. Dixon's face suddenly drops out of the frame and, in a striking time-lapse shot, night turns into day. When the camera pans down to Dixon, past the boxing pictures taped to the wall behind him, he's sitting up in bed smoking, an ashtray full of cigarette stubs on the table next to him.

Both the "girlie" and boxing imagery provide a sub rosa commentary on the next, dressing-room scene (we've just seen Morgan showing an outfit to a department-store buyer and the designer, who's played by Cassini) where another, blonde model lectures her about Ken as she applies "pancake" to Morgan's bruises: "You keep thinking of him as a glamor boy—you won't see him for what he is.... So he won the war and freed the slaves. Does that entitle him to spend the rest of his life drinking barrels of whiskey and punching girls in the nose?" Accordingly, there's no little irony when Dixon—"Mister Tough Guy"[19]—shows up accompanied by Klein to interview Morgan.

Preminger's keen feeling for blocking and choreography—of bodies in repose or moving in space—is amply in evidence in the "interrogation" scene set in a back room where drawings of models, not "dames," decorate the wall: first Dixon's standing in front of and with his back to Morgan, who's seated (Morgan: "Ken and I separated three months ago"), then Dixon's standing to the left and rear of her (Morgan: "Kenneth was drinking and we had a quarrel"/Dixon: "I understand he hit you"), then he's standing in front of a Venetian-blinded window as she sits on a desk (Morgan: "My father went down to Ken's place after he dropped me.... He told me before if Ken ever hit me again he'd beat off his head"), and, finally, Dixon's standing next to Morgan when he informs her that "Morrison was killed last night."

This is the "noir whirlpool": the same moment that Morgan learns that Morrison was murdered, Dixon discovers that the man he killed was married to her and, moreover, that the taxi driver who came to Paine's door as he was hiding in the stairwell was her father.[20] Is this why Dixon stops Morgan on the street as she's leaving for the day and asks her out to dinner? It's no coincidence that this scene—the first exterior, daytime one in the film—features Dixon and Morgan alone together for the first time. When the two return to her apartment so she can change, Jiggs reminds the detective that he received a "diploma" from the mayor "for aiding Mark Dixon in a time of danger." (Jiggs picked up Dixon in his cab when the detective was chasing some "thieves" in Central Park.) The irony, of course, is that while Jiggs's anecdote speaks to Dixon's reputation as a "good cop," Morgan's father, thanks to Dixon, is about to become the prime suspect in Paine's murder. The irony is redoubled when, as Morgan and Dixon are about to leave, Jiggs gives the couple his paternal imprimatur, remarking that at least his daughter is going out with someone who won't, unlike his current son-in-law, "land her up to her neck in crooks."

The film's coupling of Morgan with the man who, unbeknownst to her and Jiggs, killed her husband is reiterated in a "domestic" scene set at a restaurant owned by a middle-aged woman named Martha (Ruth Donnelly). She's obviously fond of Dixon, perhaps because he sent up her "wife beater" husband. The last plot point is not insignificant since it suggests that while Dixon's quick to use his fists, he does not appear to be disposed, like Morgan's estranged husband, to hit women. Martha's affection for Dixon also mirrors Jiggs' unabashed admiration for the detective. In fact, if Jiggs, figuratively speaking, is a positive father figure for Dixon as well as a potential father-in-law, Martha's a surrogate maternal figure who wants Dixon to lay off the "dizzy blondes" with whom he usually consorts and settle down with a "lady" like Morgan: "Fella like him ought to be married to a beautiful girl—have a home, kids...." The fact that Martha relays this advice to Morgan after Dixon has left—Klein has just informed him on the phone that they've discovered Paine's body in the East River—sharpens the contrast between the detective's warring personalities: the "rogue cop" who has never married because he's too busy punishing "crooks" and the policeman who may finally have found something to live for besides trying to exorcise his father's ghost.

Earlier, at Martha's restaurant, Morgan, musing about her estranged husband, laid the blame for their present separation partly on his unemployment in conjunction with pride—"too much pride"—and partly on her inability to understand "what made him so mean and impossible."[21] While the first, economic predicament was not an uncommon one for ex-servicemen returning home after World War II, Morgan's allusion to Ken's meanness and obstinacy arguably applies to both Dixon and Paine: Dixon, not unlike Morgan's husband, doesn't understand why he acts out the way he does and therefore remains wholly subject to his psychic demons.

The doubling of the two men is literalized again—dramatically so—when Morgan and Jiggs are brought to Paine's apartment where Lt. Thomas has summarily concluded that the taxi driver killed the ex-serviceman. The critical moment occurs when Thomas orders Dixon to pretend to be the dead man—to put on the ex-serviceman's hat and raincoat, tape adhesive under his left eye, and carry his traveling bag—so that Mrs. Tribaum can verify the identity of the man who got into the taxi the night Paine was murdered. And, in fact, Mrs. Tribaum remembers that the man did not wave to her as Ken always did, which means that Jiggs, as Foley suspects, killed him. When Foley arrests Morgan's father, Dixon suddenly finds himself on the horns of a dilemma: if he confesses, he'll exonerate Jiggs; he'll also lose Morgan. For Dixon, who's still driven by the desire for self-preservation, there's only one option.

Meeting up with his Klein at a bar, he announces that he's going to make Scalise confess to both murders and, when Klein reminds him of Foley's orders, Dixon, his hand curling into a fist, threatens to hit his partner if he tries to stop him. Cut to a Turkish bath where Steve (Neville Brand) is giving Scalise a massage. Although the Breen Office was concerned about the script's inclusion of a "'pansy' character" in the department-store scene, it evidently did not appear to be troubled by Scalise's "penchant for surrounding himself with young muscular men...his use of a sauna as a hangout, and his habit of receiving visitors lounging in bed" (as in the initial interrogation scene at the 43rd Street Hotel), all of which "carry strong gay connotations."[22] As in the hotel "interrogation" scene, Dixon grabs Scalise, who's wrapped up in a white sheet like a mummy, until Steve stops him. Dixon then slaps Scalise across the face; however, when Steve steps up, Dixon hits him so hard that he staggers backward against the wall. What follows is not especially surprising, so much so that Dixon's aggression appears to mask a deep masochistic desire to be punished: Scalise's goons beat him to a pulp. What is surprising is that before the gang leaves out the back door of the sauna (in a wonderfully atmospheric passage, they're briefly enveloped in a cloud of steam), Scalise's about to smash in Dixon's head with a chair and one of his men has to talk him out of it—twice.

Literally battered senseless, Dixon ends up at the Taylors' apartment where Morgan answers the door in her robe.[23] (The still made bed in the living room indicates her father's out.) As soon as Mark enters, holding a bloodied handkerchief to his chin, he sits down on the bed and says, as if to himself, "Where the devil am I? I keep coming and going." He stands up and is about to leave when he falls back against a wall:

```
                    DIXON
     Why did I come here?  I must have had
     something on my mind.
                    MORGAN
     What happened to you?
                    DIXON
     A run-in with Scalise and his pals.
```

> MORGAN
> Shouldn't I call the police?
>
> DIXON
> Let's leave the police out of this. I
> made a big idiot out of myself
> tonight, bigger than usual...
>
> MORGAN
> I'll fix your head. Come with me.
>
> DIXON
> I suggest you use an axe.

Morgan escorts Dixon to the bathroom where she cleans his wounds, applies a bandage to his jaw, and gives him a wet towel, which he presses against his forehead. The scene is a rich one: Morgan's the nurse and Dixon, like Paine, is suffering from a head wound so severe that he doesn't even know where he is or what he's doing. At the same time, if the bandage on Dixon's jaw is a "visual symbol of [his] inner damage,"[24] the fact that Morgan applies it suggests that if anyone can "fix" him, she can.

Where the Sidewalk Ends: Morgan Taylor (Gene Tieney) tends to an injured Dixon.

Dixon's temporary amnesia evokes certain 1940s "tough" thrillers such as *Somewhere in the Night* (1946), *Crack-Up* (1946), *High Wall* (1947), and *The Crooked Way* (1949) in which the returning veteran's "illness" is a figure for a profound existential crisis.[25] In *Where the Sidewalk Ends* it's also a trope for an equally profound moral one. (In this sense, Scalise's men can be said to have knocked some sense into the detective.) Dixon eventually remembers why he came to the Taylors' apartment—to tell Morgan and Jiggs that they should hire a "big-time lawyer," then confesses (it's obvious that he's talking about himself and Morgan's father), "Innocent people can get unto terrible jams, too. One false move and you're in over your head." Here, Dixon voices both the quintessential noir condition of being and his status as an archetypal noir (anti-) hero, a man "existentially adrift and trapped by circumstance."[26]

Dixon's liminal status—part cop, part killer—is underscored when he returns to the precinct station where Steve has been brought in. After Foley chastises him for going after Scalise and driving him underground, the inspector "invites" him to take one week off out of his annual vacation, "I want you to go someplace and get hold of yourself. Look at you—all bunged up like a barrelhouse vag! First thing you better do is get your head fixed up, inside and out." The scene ends on an ironic, not to say ambiguous, note when Foley instructs Thomas to "try talking to Steve like Dixon would." This directive represents a remarkable about-face on Foley's part—with the proviso that one of the roles of the "rogue cop" in the police procedural is to forcibly remind the authorities that sometimes it's imperative to bend the rules.

Previously, in an exterior scene—only the second, daytime one in which Dixon is shown on the sidewalk—the detective and Morgan have left the café after Martha has "made love" to her because, according to the proprietor, he doesn't know how to. Morgan exclaims, "It's a wonderful day! No job, everybody against me, my poor Dad sitting in cell, and it's a wonderful day!" (Morgan has been fired from her job because of the negative publicity surrounding her father's arrest.) Her sudden optimism is borne, it appears, of the blossoming romance between the two and the fact that she's off to see Ackerman, an expensive defense attorney whom Mark has, in the meantime, raised the necessary down payment for. (The brief but telling scene where he wakes up Klein in the middle of the night for a loan and his partner has to ask his long-suffering wife to pawn her jewelry testifies to the deep bond between the two policemen as well as the scant wages on which they're forced to live.)

Morgan's euphoria is short-lived. The two are returning to Mark's apartment and her earlier romantic enchantment seems to have vanished with the light—Ackerman won't take the case because he says that he's too busy; she knows it's because her father may be found guilty. Now it's her turn to articulate the archetypal noir scenario, "I thought because Dad was innocent nothing could happen to him, but it will." When Mark assures her with a force that startles her that "It won't," her suspicions are immediately aroused, "You know something you haven't told me." Mark turns away—he's about to tell her the truth about Paine's death—when, in the deepening silence, Morgan speaks instead:

```
                    MORGAN
     You don't know what it's like to have
     your father in trouble.
                    DIXON
     My father was a thief. He's dead now.
     He died when I was seventeen trying to
     shoot his way out of jail. I've worked
     all my life to be different from him.
```

True to her post-separation epiphany, Morgan tenderly says his name, then, as he turns to her, "darling," before "Street Scene" swells on the sound track and they kiss.

Although Mark breaks it off—"You'd better go home. You're a sucker for wrong guys like Ken and me." Morgan knows better, "You're not wrong.... I'm glad you told me about your father. You're not like him, I know." Is Morgan right? How different, really, is Dixon from his father? Although Mark may be on the "side of the angels" (as Mary McLeod says to her husband, Jim, in *Detective Story*), he's also crossed the blue line in the past and, having killed Paine and hidden the fact, not to mention allowed an innocent man to go to jail, his behavior has been, strictly speaking, criminal.

The fact is that when push comes to shove, Mark does not and, perhaps, cannot confess to Morgan that he killed her husband. Rather, he confesses to the prime, if largely unconscious, cause of the violence of which Paine's death is an effect. From this perspective, Dixon's crusade against Scalise can be seen for what it is, a displaced act of violence against his father or, in a word, patricide: Dixon doesn't want to avenge his father's death, he symbolically wants to kill him.[27]

While Morgan lies down to sleep, Mark sits at a desk and composes a letter to Inspector Foley "To be opened in case of death":

I didn't have the guts to tell you this when I was alive because I didn't want to end like Sandy Dixon's kid. That's what every hood in New York calls me—Sandy Dixon's kid.... I wanted to end up as a cop and that's what I'm going to do. I killed Kenneth Paine. It was an accident. I went in to pinch him, he slugged me, I hit back. How was I to know he had a silver plate in his head? But I covered it up like a mobster because I couldn't shake loose from what I was. Now I'm shaking loose. I'm going to get Scalise for you. He's a hood like my old man was. You won't have to worry about pinning the Morrison killing on him. You can pull him in for mine.

While Mark's writing, we hear his voice on the sound track and a lamp casts his still bruised and bandaged face, shot in extreme close-up, half in light, half in shadow: the cop who still wants to do good, and the cop who's acted like his old man—like, that is, a hood, like Scalise. In the letter Mark lays bare the root cause of his "rogue" behavior: that, for all his "good" intentions, he hasn't been able to come out of his father's shadow; that, in some profound sense, he's "still Sandy Dixon's kid." Therefore, in his own mind at least, the only way to shake loose of his past, to square his killing of Paine and Scalise's murder of Morrison, is to sacrifice his own life—to die, like McLeod, in the line of fire.

Although Fujiwara claims that Dixon "writes from the perspective of one who is already dead" and it's this foreknowledge that "finally liberates him to act against Scalise,"[28] Dixon, as we've seen, has already acted against Scalise and been severely punished by both the mobster and his superior for doing so. The difference this time is that Dixon knows he may die. At the same time, this knowledge is intimately bound up with another kind of foreknowledge. Before Dixon composes his letter to Foley, he leaves his apartment to meet with a stoolie, Willie (Don Appell), who sets up the rendezvous with Scalise. When he returns, there's a "startlingly erotic" shot of Morgan,[29] a "3rd Avenue Athletics" blanket thrown over her sleeping body. To wit, Dixon's desire for death, his death-wish (to invoke the later, notorious 1974 "rogue cop" film starring Charles Bronson), is tangled up with his equally intense desire for Morgan.

Dixon's waiting under a streetlamp on East River Drive when a car driven by one of Scalise's hoods picks him up. (The shot of the sedan as the elevator ascends to the mobster's hangout at the top of a parking garage with Dixon in the backseat next to one of Scalise's hoods is an inspired one—a frame, as it were, within a frame.) After Dixon turns over his gun and is frisked, he's escorted to Scalise who's reclining, as usual, on a bed. (In what appears to be a sop to the censors, a poster that reads "GIRLS" is plastered to the wall behind him.) Scalise and his men are fixed to leave the next morning—"passports in order and everything." The twist is that Dixon will be left locked inside the room—"sitting [there] for a couple of days desperately trying to attract attention"—an embarrassing situation that, Scalise adds, will give them "something to laugh about": "It will maybe give the department a laugh, too." Dixon, needless to say, is not laughing: when the camera cuts away for the reverse shot, his face is halved in shadow and his eyes are narrowed with hatred.

Dixon stands up (Scalise has previously ordered him to sit down), and the mobster warns him that if he starts "mussing [him] up, [he's] gonna get it": "You'll only throw one punch and they'll let you have it." The audience, though, knows that it's a fait accompli: after Dixon punches Scalise in the face, one of Scalise's hoods shoots him, wounding him in the shoulder. The hood's about to shoot Dixon again when, in a reversal of the sauna scene, Scalise stops him because he suddenly realizes that the detective has come there to frame him. In fact, Scalise orders Kramer (David Wolfe) to fix Dixon up so that he doesn't die.

While Kramer administers to Dixon's wound (in yet another echo—this time, of the bathroom scene at the Taylors' apartment), Scalise, thinks aloud, and it's clear that he understands Dixon better perhaps than the detective understands himself:

"It's a fancy way of trying to frame somebody—getting yourself knocked off. A guy's gotta be out of his head for that. I didn't know a guy could hate that much, not even you, and all because your old man set me up in business. I got it added up now, Dixon.... You found Paine and slugged him and killed him and you took the body to the river... And you've been walking around ever since, half cop and half killer. The man who hates crooks, the law that works by itself, the cop who can't stand to see a killer loose. So what is he? A hood and a mobster like his old man."

The phone suddenly rings. After one of the men reports that the police "beat" the truth about Morrison out of Steve, Scalise and his gang start for the door. Kramer mutters, "What about the bandage?" Scalise's retort is short as a shotgun blast, "Let him bleed."

The moment Scalise and his men are out the door, Dixon tries it—it's locked—then, noticing a staircase, climbs to the roof where he locates the elevator works. While the hand on the elevator "clock" inexorably winds down floor by floor, Dixon pulls the switch on the power, trapping Scalise's getaway car in the lift. A police siren sounds outside. Scalise, looking up, swears "That dirty cop!," an apostrophe that's not, of course, without irony since Dixon's identity as a "clean cop" was predicated on his death and the written "confession" that he's left for Foley.

The coda to *Where the Sidewalk Ends* introduces one final turn of the screw. After the inspector congratulates Dixon, whose arm's in a sling—"Always have to break orders, always have to do things your way"—Morgan walks in with the news that her father's about to be released. There's more good news as well: the inspector is recommending a promotion for Dixon. Foley then hands Mark's letter back to him. When Morgan, shocked, sees the instructions on the envelope ("You expected to die"), Foley explains that Dixon was "pretty sore" at him when he composed the letter and, telling him to tear it up, suggests that he take a rest—"until [his] arm heals." "Dad's waiting," Morgan adds, "Will you come home with us?" A happy ending of the sort that Martha envisioned and that, earlier, Dixon could only have dreamt about now appears to be in the offing.

The camera stays on Mark and Morgan for a pregnant pause (it's a medium two-shot) before he finally asks Foley to read the letter. While the inspector does so, Morgan asks "What is it?" then, when Foley looks up before continuing to read, "Mark?" Her question recalls her earlier, romantic address in Dixon's apartment, one that can be said to have blocked, however unintentionally, his full confession. Yet even now Mark can't look at or answer her; rather, his silence directs her attention to Foley, the embodiment of the law, who declares, "That clears up both cases. You're under arrest."

Morgan can't believe her ears ("No!") and pleads with Mark, "What is it? Please tell me." Since he still can't tell her the truth, he asks Foley if she can read the letter. The inspector hands the letter to Dixon who, turning to face Morgan, hands it to her. After she finishes reading his confession, she looks up and, eyes brimming with tears, says his name. Although he preemptively tells her good-bye, in the reverse shot Morgan's face is lit like an angel's:

MORGAN
Anybody can make a mistake.
DIXON
You mean you're gonna give Sandy
Dixon's kid another chance.
MORGAN
Every chance in the world.
DIXON
That's enough to live for.

Coda: *Night Cry*, or Ringing the Changes

We were born to tread the earth as angels, to seek out heaven this side of the
sky
But they who race alone shall stumble in the dark and fall from grace
Then love alone can make the fallen angel rise
For only two together can enter paradise.

—June Mills (Alice Faye), *Fallen Angel*

In William Stuart's *Night Cry* the detective's name is Mark Deglin and he has a "look of coolness and bitterness and cruelty about him."[30] At the scene of the first crime—a brownstone mansion where Morrison's found dead, knifed in the heart—Deglin complains to the medical examiner that "he's one of the best detectives on the force"[31] and therefore shouldn't have been passed over as captain. In

Where the Sidewalk Ends: Lt. Thomas (Karl Malden, right) puts the arm on Dixon in front of Morgan and his partner Klein (Bert Freed).

other words, the novel draws an explicit connection between Deglin's resentment and his "rogue" propensities: an item in a tabloid opines that "he'll be taking it out on [the seamy side of the underworld] for what he didn't get in the recent Civil Service advances."[32]

In *Where the Sidewalk Ends*, Dixon is, of course, demoted. Moreover, whereas in Preminger's Dixon appears to be single, in the novel he's involved with a "canary," Jane Corby, who sings at a "fashionable and expensive" club called the Flamingo. A key scene in *Night Cry* occurs when Deglin returns to his apartment to find Janie curled up like a cat in an easy chair. However, when she flings herself at him and starts backing him into the bedroom, he slaps her "so hard in the face with his open palm that the impact rang in the apartment."[33] The difference between the novel and film is striking: the fact that in *Where the Sidewalk Ends* it's Paine who slaps Morgan displaces the violence against women from the detective to the husband—from, that is, the explosively violent cop to the separated, ex-serviceman husband. This displacement, together with Martha's reference to her ex-husband as a "wife beater," makes Dixon's character more sympathetic than Deglin's.

Morgan Taylor in *Night Cry* is also substantially different than the character in Preminger's film. In Stuart's novel, she's more reminiscent of the eponymous heroine of *Laura* than the working-class "mannequin" in *Where the Sidewalk Ends*. For example, her "comfortable and respectable parents" live in Greenwich and, after the row with Ken at the private gambling club and before she discovers that he's been murdered, she takes a taxi to her parents' house where, the following morning, she takes a "bay mare" out for a ride at a local stable: "The clouds in the sky were higher and thinner.... A pale sunshine broke through, occasionally touching the trunks and branches of the huge, shedding trees with a hint of gold."[34] This idyllic, autumnal moment has no parallel in Preminger's film, which, set in the guttered environs of the city, studiously avoids any pastoral references. In Stuart's novel, by contrast, the "country" in the guise of nature is employed to mirror the decline of Ken and Morgan's marriage. So, when she comes to Deglin's apartment late at night to talk, she recounts how, throughout the Spring, she had been watching a tree outside the back window of Paine's apartment, and "it was as if it was our tree."[35] In fact, the evening that Ken died Morgan went to his apartment to tell him "maybe she was wrong" and, although he wasn't there, she went to the back of the room: "the light shone from the window full on [the tree], and it seemed as though it was dying."[36]

In *Night Cry* Deglin's fascinated with Morgan—"He had watched her clear, pure profile, the way her eyes lowered, and lifted, the movement of her body in the chair...the sudden trembling of her pale hands."[37] A romance between them never blossoms, however. When she comes to the precinct station with her father to talk to the captain (the DA thinks her former lover, Pete Redfield, killed her husband and that she disposed of the body), Deglin listens to her until she begins explaining why she went to the window ("I—I was watching a tree"), at which point he gets up and walks out. Later, at a bar, Deglin gives the receipt for the incriminating kitbag to the bartender (it's stashed in a cardboard box at a Chelsea storage company) and asks him to give it, in turn, to the captain. In the final scene of *Night Cry,* Deglin returns to his apartment where he borrows some money from Jane, then flees without her. The final words of the novel are: "Run, Deglin. RUN!"[38]

The dénouement of *Night Cry*, in which Deglin goes on the lam, differs considerably—to understate the matter—from the complex, morally complicated "happy ending" of *Where the Sidewalk Ends*. Although Deglin undergoes a moral crisis in the novel and puts into motion an act that will dispel what he calls the "illusion of truth,"[39] he does not turn himself in—he does not submit to the law—and therefore remains an outlaw. In other words, he's still motivated by the desire for self-preservation, a drive that connects up with his earlier, expressed resentment about not being promoted. It's here that the superiority of Hecht's screenplay becomes apparent since Dixon's desire for self-preservation in *Where the Sidewalk Ends* is fueled not by advancement—he's nonplussed when Foley informs him that he's being demoted—but by an overweening desire to punish criminals. More importantly, a minor subplot in the novel—the Scalise brothers' waterfront robberies—becomes, in Preminger's film, a classically antagonistic relation between cop and gangster (this is the "Hecht touch") in which the cop's father can be said to have fathered the gangster. In other words, Dixon and Scalise can be said to be siblings and, when the detective covers up his killing of Paine, brothers in crime.

The elimination of Jane's character and the attendant development of Dixon and Morgan's relationship in *Where the Sidewalk Ends* foregrounds as well the role of the "family romance" in the film. In the novel Deglin's effectively frames Redfield and Morgan, the former of whom he has no real relation to and the latter of whom he keeps a discreet distance from. In Preminger's film the "family romance" compounds Dixon's guilt since he's not only framing a man who admires him, Jiggs Taylor, but the father of the woman with whom he's falling in love. In fact, Deglin's final description of Morgan in *Night Cry*—"It was incredible that someone like Morgan...should be touched by even so much as the edge of violent death"—arguably applies more to the character in the film than the novel. In Stuart's novel, Morgan was formerly an Army nurse—she met Ken while he was convalescing in a hospital—and her ostensible guilt hinges on a "War department photograph, which had been released in the general news pool following the bombardment of an American hospital," and in which Morgan can be seen "carrying a wounded man."[40]

The casting of the "ethereally beautiful" Gene Tierney in *Where the Sidewalk Ends*, paired with Dana Andrews for the final time—they had previously appeared together in *Tobacco Road* (1941), *Belle Starr* (1941), *Laura*, and *The Iron Curtain* (1948)—is notable here.[41] On one hand, Tierney is too beautiful to be true, a being who appears to have been transported from another, alien world ontologically distinct from the "succession of downbeat boarding houses, diners and gangster hide-outs" that everyone in the picture seems to inhabit.[42] On the other hand, Tierney's otherworldly beauty is integral to her character, her open-book face a counter to Andrews' grim, tight-lipped countenance, what one critic has nominated the "face of noir."[43]

Only such a seraphic figure could annul the fatal revenant that is Dixon's dead father and thereby tender a "rogue cop" the promise of redemption. Only a seraph could love someone who's just confessed to killing the ex-"war hero" she married. It defies belief. However, such suspension of disbelief is, pace *I Wake Up Screaming*, just as much a part of film noir as the musical. In *Fallen Angel* a con-man falls in love with the object of his con, and the cop, not the con-man, kills the dark woman who, like Vicky Lynn in *I Wake Up Screaming*, is a waitress at a roadside diner. If Mark Dixon in *Where the Sidewalk Ends* is Mark McPherson five years after *Laura*, the ex-cop who, mad for the girl, goes rogue in *Fallen Angel* is Dixon three more years down the line, the "bad cop" who was not lucky enough to have met a fallen angel who looks just like Gene Tierney.

Notes

1. Frank Krutnik, *In a Lonely Street* (New York: Routledge, 1992), 193.
2. Brian McDonnell, *Encyclopedia of Film Noir*, ed. Geoff Mayer and Brian McDonnell (Westport, CT: Greenwood, 2007), 226; Meredith Brody and Alain Silver, "I Wake Up Screaming," *Film Noir: An Encyclopedic Reference to the American Style,* ed. Alain Silver and Elizabeth Ward (Woodstock, NY: Overlook), 142.
3. On Dashiell Hammett's novels and the various film adaptations, see my "Dashiell Hammett and the Classical Hollywood Cinema," *Literature/Film Quarterly* 43, 3 (2015), 236-240.
4. Raymond Borde and Étienne Chaumeton, *A Panorama of American Film Noir*, trans. Paul Hammond (San Francisco: City Lights), 158.
5. Dennis Broe, *Film Noir, American Workers, and Postwar Hollywood* (Gainesville: University Press of Florida, 2009), 88. For the Kast, see "A Brief Essay on Optimism," trans. R. Barton Palmer, Perspectives on Film Noir, ed. R. Barton Palmer (New York: G. K. Hall, 1996), 48.

6. Broe, *Film Noir*, 88. See my "Preface" to *The Red and the Black: American Film Noir in the 1950s* (Urbana: University of Illinois Press, 2017), xv-xx.

7. On Robert Aldrich and I. A. Bezzerides' détournement of Mickey Spillane's *Kiss Me, Deadly*, see *The Red and the Black*, 144-159.

8. For my reading of *The Bribe*, see *Siren City: Sound and Source Music in Classic American Noir* (New Brunswick, NJ: Rutgers University Press, 2014), 211, 214-216.

9. Chris Fujiwara, *The World and Its Double: The Life and Work of Otto Preminger* (New York: Faber and Faber, 2008), 120.

10. Italics mine. Ibid., 123.

11. Sidney Kingsley, *Detective Story* (New York: Random House, 1949), 15 and 17.

12. Ibid., 63.

13. Ibid., 110.

14. Ibid., 8.

15. Joan Cohen and Elizabeth Ward, "Detective Story," *Film Noir: An Encyclopedic Reference to the American Style*, 89.

16. McDonnell, *Encyclopedia of Film Noir*, 438.

17. Fujiwara, *The World and Its Double*, 121.

18. Andrew Spicer, *Film Noir* (Harlow, UK: Longman, 2002), 86.

19. William Stuart, *Night Cry* (New York: Dial Press, 1948), 33.

20. Foster Hirsch, *Otto Preminger: The Man Who Would Be King* (New York: Knopf, 2007), 169.

21. Gaylyn Studlar, "'The Corpse on Reprieve': Film Noir's Cautionary Tales of 'Tough Guy' Masculinity," *A Companion to Film Noir,* ed. Helen Hanson and Andrew Spicer (Waltham: Wiley-Blackwell, 2013), 376-378.

22. Fujiwara, *The World and Its Double*, 121.

23. In her autobiography, *Self-Portrait*, Gene Tierney recalls that while shooting *Where the Sidewalk Ends* Dana Andrews showed up at her room at five o'clock in the morning—"he had not been to bed [and] ... needed to sober up"—to ask whether she would like to have breakfast ([New York: Wyden, 1979], 164-165).

24. McDonnell, *Encyclopedia of Film Noir*, 438.

25. Krutnik, *In a Lonely Street*, 133.

26. Carl Macek, "Where the Sidewalk Ends," *Film Noir: An Encyclopedic Reference to the American Style*, 310.

27. Fujiwara, *The World and Its Double*, 123.

28. Ibid., 125.

29. McDonnell, *Encyclopedia of Film Noir*, 438.

30. Stuart, *Night Cry,* 14.

31. Ibid., 17.

32. Ibid., 33.

33. Ibid., 84.

34. Ibid., 72.

35. Ibid., 183.

36. Ibid.

37. Ibid., 198.

38. Ibid., 208.

39. Ibid., 198.

40. Ibid., 192.

41. McDonnell, *Encyclopedia of Film Noir*, 257.

42. Alastair Phillips, in Jim Hillier and Alastair Phillips, *100 Film Noirs* (London: BFI, 2009), 257.

43. James McKay, *Dana Andrews: The Face of Noir* (Jefferson, NC: McFarland, 2010), 112.

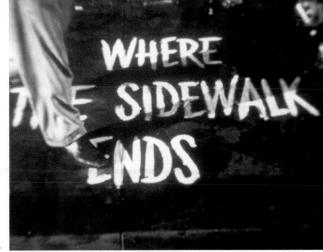

Double Indemnity: after committing murder Neff (Fred MacMurray) and Phyllis (Barbara Stanwyck) meet surreptitiously at a local market

The "House of Death" in Print and On-Screen: *Double Indemnity* as Journalism, Fiction, and Film

Jesse Schlotterbeck

This article reviews *Double Indemnity*'s adaptation to screen, attending to both historical materials and accounts of this process, and to the aesthetic and narrative changes to the story as it moved from one medium to another. I will start with the pre-history of *Double Indemnity* before it was the paradigmatic film noir. Before Paramount released *Double Indemnity* in 1944 (directed by Billy Wilder and starring Barbara Stanwyck, Edward G. Robinson, and Fred MacMurray), the following occurred: first, in 1928, Ruth Snyder is executed by the state of New York for murdering her husband (Albert Snyder) with the aim of collecting insurance money. The Snyder case is a major media event and, by Cain's accounts, a source of inspiration for both *Double Indemnity* and his other most famous work, *The Postman Always Rings Twice*. Second, James M. Cain publishes *Double Indemnity* in 1935 in serial form, in *Liberty* magazine. It is first published as a stand-alone text in 1943. Shortly before this, it appeared along with two other short novels, as part of *Three of a Kind* (along with *Career in C Major* and *The Embezzler*). Third, as can be confirmed in correspondence archived in the "Hollywood, Censorship, and the Motion Picture Production Code, 1927-1968" collection, Metro-Goldwyn-Mayer wrote Joseph Breen (as the head of the Production Code Administration) in 1935 to inquire about the feasibility of producing an adaptation acceptable under the Code. (1-3) Breen discouraged MGM from doing so. The lack of further correspondence suggests that MGM did not pursue the adaptation much beyond this query.

Crime Story to Fiction: First, Ruth Snyder's Murder Trial and Execution (1927-1928); Second, James M. Cain's *The Postman Always Rings Twice* (1934) and *Double Indemnity* (1935)

James M. Cain's *Double Indemnity* and *The Postman Always Rings Twice* both include the standard clarification that they are works of fiction: "The characters, locale, and action of this story are wholly fictitious; they do not represent, and are not intended to represent, actual persons, places or events." Indeed, names, locations, and many specifics of the crime in *Double Indemnity* are unique. On the other hand, Cain himself has clarified that the Snyder case formed the template for *Postman*. Asked by *The Paris Review*, "Do you have any memory of the origins of *The Postman Always Rings Twice*," Cain replied:

> Oh yes, I can remember the beginning of *The Postman*. It was based on the Snyder-Gray case, which was in the papers about then. You ever hear of it? Well. Gray and this woman Snyder killed her husband for the insurance money. Walter Lippmann went to that trial one day and she brushed by him, what was her name? Lee Snyder. Walter said it seemed very odd to be inhaling the perfume or being brushed by the dress of a woman he knew was going to be electrocuted. So the Snyder-Grey case provided the basis" ("The Art of Fiction").

In the same interview, when Cain is asked about *Double Indemnity*, he responds about a story of a double-cross in the publishing industry which led him to reflect on professional ethics:

> I thought about certain traits in human nature. Then out in Hollywood I was trying to think of an idea for a story quick and it flits through my mind; suppose instead of a publisher this had been an insurance agent whose job it was to guard against that one guy who would gyp the company out of money by getting a policy on a barn he intended to burn down and suppose he collaborated with him rather than guarding against him. Wondering about that was how the story came about. ("The Art of Fiction")

Huff's discourse on the same is one of the more eloquent passages of the novel:

> All right, I'm an agent. I'm a croupier in that game. I know all their tricks, I lie awake nights thinking up tricks, so I'll be ready for them when they come at me. And then one night I think up a trick, and get to thinking I could crook the wheel myself if I could only put a plant out there to put down my bet. That's all. When I met Phyllis I met my plant. If that seems funny to you, that I would kill a man just to pick up a stack of chips, it might not seem so funny if you were back of that wheel, instead of out front. I had seen so many houses burned down, so many cars wrecked, so many corpses with blue holes in their temples, so many awful things that people had pulled to crook the wheel, that that stuff didn't seem real to me any more. (23-24)

It is unsurprising, then, that this discourse is also prominently featured in the film:

> You're like the guy behind the roulette wheel, watching the customers to make sure they don't crook the house. And then one night, you get to thinking how you could crook the house yourself. And do it smart. Because you've got that wheel right under your hands. You know every notch in it by heart. … suddenly the doorbell rings and whole set-up is right there in the room with you.

Walter Neff (Fred MacMurray) records this speech on a Dictaphone in a flashback at the moment where he recounts being fully seduced by Phyllis Dietrichsion (Barbara Stanwyck) and committed to their criminal plot. In one of the most compelling sequences (in terms of narrative and aesthetics), this passage is bookended by scenes in Walter's apartment. These cuts are carried by dissolves and brief superimposition moving from Walter's apartment, to the Dictaphone confession, and to Walter's apartment again.

It is interesting, however, that Cain points only to *The Postman Always Rings Twice* as his work inspired by the Snyder case when *Double Indemnity*, also with the wife-who-murders-the-hus-band-with-a-lover plot, is more similar to the Snyder case given the equivalence of the life-insurance-policy rather than the inherited restaurant that the character of Cora stands to inherit in *The Postman*. It stands to reason that *Double Indemnity*, written just a year later, was also greatly influenced by this case. Sheri Chinen Biesen cites a separate interview (with the *Daily News* in 1944) in which Cain point-ed to *Double Indemnity* (not *The Postman Always Rings Twice*) as the novel that took the Snyder case as the inspiration. (43) In "Multiple Indemnity: Film Noir, James M. Cain, and Adaptations of a Tabloid Case," V. Penelope Pelizzon and Nancy Martha West also argue that *Double Indemnity*, more than *The Postman Always Rings Twice*, is the Cain-novel-to-film with greater narrative similarity to the Snyder case. This connection would have still been salient to many mid-1940s viewers of *Double Indemnity* but is something that has been overlooked in film scholarship. Pelizzon and West write, "The signifi-cance of the Snyder-Gray case for Wilder's *Double Indemnity* has been completely obscured in cine-ma scholarship, however. In part this is because, until recently, adaptation studies have focused main-ly on novels translated into film" (212). This article eloquently links *Double Indemnity* to the Snyder murder, citing promotional material circulated by Paramount, comments by Cain himself, and popu-lar press reviews of the film. (233)

Similar to James Naremore in *More Than Night*, Pelizzon and West particularly emphasize the fact that Wilder's planned conclusion to *Double Indemnity* was set in an execution chamber. To con-clude, they write, "[N]oir's penchant for adaptation also implies its debt to the tabloids—a debt not merely for shocking content and narrative strategies but, ultimately, for an attitude toward story-telling itself. It is a stance that regards all material as infinitely recyclable, a stance Cain himself held despite all his claims to novelty. This adaptation-readiness allowed Billy Wilder, so commonly regard-ed as an original auteur, to gesture in his film's original ending toward a tabloid photograph that, by 1944, had itself been reproduced thousands of times" (233). While this photo (easily findable online) is unquestionably the most prominent image associated with the Snyder case, there are other repre-sentations of the case that pre-date both the book and film that suggest a narrative adaptation of this story. Take for example, this six-panel (plus regional map) illustration of the Snyder murder from a

Opposite page: Neff begins to record his confesstion to Keyes. Below, dissolves from Neff on the Dicta-phone to scene of his tryst with Phyllis in his apartment.

Excised Sequence E from the original cut of *Double Indemnity*: Keyes attends Neff's execution. Inset, the front page of *The Daily News* with the photo of Ruth Snyder in the electric chair.

December 1935 issue of the *Chicago Tribune*. The newspaper illustration presents a compelling narrative that is even more intriguing or disturbing when represented through images. As such it anticipates both a fictional and filmic adaptation of this story. Original reviews from the time of the film's release in 1944 were often quick to draw a connection between the film and still-well-known murder trial. For example, the 1944 *Variety* staff review read, "There are unmistakable similarities between the Paramount pic and the famous Snyder-Gray murder . . . Both the fictional and the real murders were for the slain men's insurance. Both were committed by the murdered men's wives and their amours." Having covered the connection between the crime story and the Cain novel, I will now turn my attention to the adaptation of *Double Indemnity* to film. Hollywood had, in fact, showed interest in adapting *Double Indemnity* soon after it had been written, but found the Production Code Administration uncooperative.

MGM's 1935 Inquiry

On October 9, 1935, a representative from MGM wrote to Joseph Breen. The full body of this letter reads, "We are enclosing a copy of DOUBLE INDEMNITY by James M. Cain, and would very much appreciate a report from you at the earliest possible date, as to whether we will be able to make it as it stands or whether you could suggest that would make it possible to get past the censors with it" ("Hollywood, Censorship, and the Motion Picture Production Code, 1927-1968," 1).

Breen writes a detailed, seven-paragraph letter to MGM the day following this initial inquiry. I reproduce the most important passages of that letter here:

> We have received and read with great care the novel, DOUBLE INDEMNITY, by James M. Cain and I regret to inform you that, because of a number of elements inherent in the story in its present form, it is our judgment that the story is in violation of the provisions of the Production Code, and, as such, is almost certain to result in a picture which we would be compelled to reject if, and when, such a picture is presented to us for approval" (2) and "The first part of the story is replete with explicit details of the planning of the murder and the effective of the crime, thus definitely violating the Code provisions which forbid the presentation of 'details of crime.' This part of the story is likewise, seriously questionable, when it is not definitely offensive, because of the cold-blooded fashion in which the murderers proceed to their kill." (2).

MGM appears to have taken Breen's strong recommendation not to adapt *Double Indemnity* as face-value definitive advice, as the Margaret Herrick Library's 50-plus page file on PCA correspondence related to the film contains no further evidence that MGM pursued the adaptation beyond this day-later discouragement. The same archive confirms that both Paramount and Warner Brothers also inquired about the feasibility of adapting this Cain novel. They were told, similarly, that an adaptation of *Double Indemnity* in 1935 was a non-starter and do not appear to have pursued the matter further.

Paramount's 1943 Inquiry

Double Indemnity, as a stand-alone novel, was first published in 1943. As Cain thoroughly explains in the interview with *The Paris Review*, it was published twice before this as well: serialized in *Liberty* magazine in one case and grouped with two other short novels in another. Remarkably, *Double Indemnity* was the last of *Three of a Kind* to be "sold to the pictures":

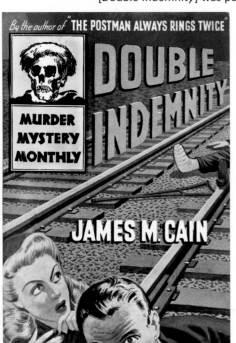

> "[*Double Indemnity*] was published as one of a trilogy of shorter novels. *Three of a Kind* they called it. Two of the stories had already been sold to the pictures by Swanson, my agent, but *Double Indemnity* had not been. So Swanson got some page proofs stitched up and distributed them around. Billy Wilder couldn't find his secretary one day. Around four o'clock in the afternoon he came out of his office to look for her, and she still wasn't there, so he asked the relief girl, "Well, where is she? Every time I come out here she isn't here." "Well I don't know Mr. Wilder, but I think she's still in the ladies room reading that book." "What book?" "Some story Mr. Swanson left here," she said. At which moment the girl came in with the story pressed against her bosom. Wilder took it home to see why the girl couldn't put it down. Next day he wanted to do it as a picture" ("The Art of Fiction").

> Due to other contractual observations, Cain was unavailable to assist with the film adaptation of his novel, which would be adapted by Raymond Chandler and Billy Wilder together.

The Adaptation of Cain's Novel by Paramount (Code-Related Changes)

Interestingly, when Paramount, again, inquired about adapting *Double Indemnity* in 1943, Breen responded the identical text he sent to MGM in 1935, as if it were an original letter. Unlike MGM, however, Paramount (despite some discouragement or reservations from Breen), still attempted an adaptation. Responding the Breen's "copy-pasted" March 15, 1943 letter, Paramount forwarded a nearly-complete script on September 21, writing "we would appreciate receiving your observations and opinion" (12). Breen wrote back promptly on September 24, that the office was "happy to report that the basic story seems to meet the requirements of the Production Code" (13). This correspondence would seem to strongly suggest that—in addition to the request coming eight years later (in 1943 versus 1935)—the fact that Paramount so carefully adapted the Cain novel must also be taken into account as an essential part of the film's being made in the 1940s. Consider, for example, the first two paragraphs of the identical dissuasion letter from 1935 and 1943 (3; 11):

> The second part of the story has to do with the successful efforts of the criminals to avoid arrest and punishment, and culminates in the decision of the man to kill his accomplice. The attempt is frustrated when the woman shoots him, whereupon the wounded man, in love with the stepdaughter of his accomplice, confesses to crime to save the girl he loves, against whom a mass of circumstantial evidence has been piled up.

This story violates the provisions of the Production Code in that:

> The leading characters are murderers who cheat the law and die at their own hands. They avoid successfully the consequences of their crime through a miscarriage of justice, even though, subsequently, they commit suicide. It may be argued, too, that one of these criminals is, in a sense, glorified by his confession to save the girl he loves.

Two additional points (related to an "adulterous sex relationship" and "details of the vicious and cold-blooded murder") are also included, but not discussed with nearly the length of this first point. The 1943 script and eventual film comprehensively follow up on the problems cited by Breen in the identical 1935/1943 letters: in particular, the nature and intensity of Neff/Huff's concern for Nirdlinger's/Dietrichson's daughter, Lola, and the difference between Neff/Huff being apprehended by the state versus committing suicide.

First, Neff/Huff's relationship with Lola is diminished significantly in the film. In the original novel, as emphasized in the comments from Breen above, Huff professes his love for Lola and is motivated out of guilt and obligation from the same to try, in some way, to atone for his devious cooperation with Nirdlinger. Consider, for example, these two passages from the novel, which make the intensity and tenderness of Huff's feeling toward Lola clear:

Opposite, digest-style first printing of the novella alone in 1943.

Right, Neff with Lola (Jean Heather).

She looked different from the last time I had seen her. Then, she looked like a kid. Now, she looked like a woman. Part of that may have been that she was in black, but anybody could see she had been through plenty. I felt like a heel, and yet it did something to me that this girl liked me. (71)

I thought about Lola, how sweet she was, and the awful thing I had done to her. I began subtracting her age from my age. She was nineteen, I'm thirty-four. That made a difference of fifteen years. Then I got to thinking that if she was nearly twenty, that would make a difference of only fourteen years. All of a sudden I sat up and turned on the light. I knew what that meant. I was in love with her. (80)

In the film adaptation, by contrast, Neff is more distant from Lola. While he grows concerned for her, his relationship remains much more distant and paternalistic (and certainly never romantic) in the film. This change clearly addressed Breen's concern that Huff's professed love for Lola in the novel generated unacceptably excessive sympathy for him: "It may be argued, too, that one of these criminals is, in a sense, glorified by his confession to save the girl he loves." Breen's second concern in the above correspondence was the suicide that concludes Cain's *Double Indemnity*.

In a novel that, otherwise, is often terse and dialogue-heavy, the concluding chapter to *Double Indemnity* is unusually poetic. There, Walter and Phyllis are aboard a steamship headed to an uncertain destination. Both are aware that they cannot elude capture for their crime. I will reproduce a large passage of this bold ending in full:

"Somebody moved the elevator..."

We walked around the ship. A sailor was swabbing out the gutter outside the rail. He was nervous, and caught me looking at him. "There's a shark. Following the ship."

I tried not to look, but couldn't help it. I saw a flash of dirty white down in the green. We walked back to the deck chairs.

"Walter, we'll have to wait. Till the moon comes up,"

"I guess we better have a moon."

"I want to see that fin. That black fin. Cutting the water in the moonlight."

The captain knows us. I could tell by his face when he came out of the radio room a little while ago. It will have to be tonight. He's sure to put a guard on us before he puts into Mazatlan.

The bleeding has started again. The internal bleeding, I mean, from the lung where the bullet grazed it. It's not much but I spit blood. I keep thinking about that shark.

I'm writing this in the stateroom. It's about half past nine. She's in her stateroom getting ready. She's made her face chalk white, with black circles under her eyes and red on her lips and cheeks. She's got that red thing on. It's awful-looking. It's just one big square of red silk that she wraps around her, but it's got no armholes, and her hands look like stumps underneath it when she moves them around. She looks like what came aboard the ship to shoot dice for souls in the Rime of the Ancient Mariner.

I didn't hear the stateroom door open, but she's beside me now while I'm writing. I can feel her.

The moon. (114-115)

In the broader context of the criminal story, Breen seems to have interpreted this action as somewhat ethical or even courageous, as the criminal protagonists are determined to punish themselves for the crime committed. In the film, by contrast, we end with the scene in which Keyes (Edward G. Robinson) lights Walter's cigarette as he is, pathetically, slumped in the doorway of the insurance company office (opposite and below). In the film Neff, who had tried to leave the office before collapsing, wryly commenting, "somebody moved the elevator a couple of miles away." He had not submitted to capture; rather, he was physically incapable of fleeing. As with the diminution of Huff's "love" for Lola to more blasé, paternalistic concern, the same character's knowing self-sacrifice (by Breen's interpretation) in the novel, has been reduced to more pathetic physical collapse in the film.

Scholars who have studied the censorship history of Double Indemnity have emphasized other factors as most important to the story of the film's successful adaptation in 1944. Sheri Chinen Biesen, for example, explains the adaptation of the film in the 1940s due to the coalescence of the popularity of "the hard-boiled fiction tradition which flourished in America during the Depression, combined with the equally significant impact of wartime conditions, overrode the Production Code's" (43). Biesen also covers Chandler's writing style, in particular "the use of metaphoric innuendo and verbal wit" as an additional factor that aided in the film's approval. (46) In so doing, the film worked within the Code's parameters while also being unusually thrilling and disturbing. This was not lost on reviewers from the time of the film's release. Commenting on Double Indemnity's successful adaptation, Fred Stanley of the New York Times noted both that "Hollywood, according to present indications, will depend on so-called 'red meat' stories of illicit romance and crime for a major share of its immediate non-war dramatic productions," but was also careful to clarify that, "This renewed interest in certain types of storied sordidness and ultra-sophistication has not prompted any easing of Hays office or State censor-

A towel-clad Phyllis on the balcony. For her entrance the iron balustrade and shadows obscure whether the towel reaches below her knees.

ship regulations. There have been none, and none is expected. It is just that Hollywood is learning to use finesse in dealing with a variety of different plot situations which, if treated objectively or obviously, would be unsuitable." The correspondence in the Herrick Library collection would seem to back-up this view—as MGM's tepid mid-1930s query placed the onus of adaptation almost entirely on Breen. Paramount, by contrast, devoted considerable labor and creative thinking to adapting a film that received the same word-for-word discouraging letter than had been sent to MGM eight years prior.

The changes summarized above directly correspond to the concerns voiced by Breen and cleared the way for an adaptation that was relatively efficient. Biesen's article effectively summarizes a number of smaller changes suggested by Breen following receipt of the full-script, related mostly to

phrases of particular concern and costuming. She concludes, "Wilder complied with most of Breen's requests—with the exception of Stanwyck's towel not being 'below the knees'" (44). While some aspects of the novel-to-film adaptation can be attributed to provisions of the Code or specific requests by Breen there are other aspects of the film (the emphasis on flashback and the use of the Dictaphone, for example) that can be discussed in broader terms, related less directly to the interdiction of the Code.

The Adaptation of Cain's Novel by Paramount (Changes Unrelated to the Code)

In addition to changes made to Cain's story that were prudent if not absolutely necessary given the film's production under the Code, other differences are notable that relate more to the medium-specificity: appropriately, the novel is more textual and the film is more aural. I will explain how more carefully.

An under-analyzed aspect of Cain's original novel is how much the text includes texts-within-texts. Twice, Huff follows the newspaper coverage of his criminal activities. (55; 98) In both cases, capitalization, formatting, and font size are used to capture the story-within-the-story. Further, the exchange of office memoranda is also effectively presented with appropriate formatting on pages 76-77. Finally, though not until the final chapter, Huff reveals the following:

> What you've just read, if you've read it, is the statement. It took me five days to write it, but at last, on Thursday afternoon, I got it done. That was yesterday. I sent it out by the orderly to be registered, and around five o'clock Keyes dropped by for the receipt. It'll be more than he bargained for, but I wanted to put it all down. Maybe she'll [Lola] see it some time, and not think so bad of me after she understands how it all was. Around seven o'clock I put on my clothes. I was weak, but I could walk. (112)

In addition to corroborating Breen's understanding of the prominence of Lola as a love interest of Huff's in the novel, this passage interestingly works with the written-form of the novel—which is repositioned, explicitly, as a first-person written account with this opening to the book's final chapter. While there is a brief clarification much earlier that this is a retrospective account— "All this, what I've been telling you, happened in late winter..." (34)—the later statement is the first that explicitly positions Huff's account (in the imagined "real" version) as one written on paper. This evokes a comparison both with the experience of the reader (ostensibly reading Huff's words in the very format he recorded his story) and, also, the Snyder murder case, which received so much coverage in the popular press. This link is suggested, in particular, when Huff follows the newspaper coverage of his crimes. (55; 98) Thus, the novel contains written documents (memos or news stories) from the world of the story, and the story, itself, is revealed to be a confessional document. While not many critics have emphasized this aspect of the novel, the film adaptation's use of Neff's confession in a medium-specific format has been more widely noted and, even, celebrated.

Here, the written word is replaced by the orality and aurality of the Dictaphone. As Robert Miklitsch writes in *Siren City: Sound and Source Music in Classic American Noir*, "The difference between the novel and film version of *Double Indemnity* is substantial. Whereas in Cain's novel we learn only in the final chapter that what we've just read is Huff's statement, in Wilder's film the [86-87] Dictaphone is introduced near the beginning of the action." Miklitsch notes six total Dictaphone scenes in *Double Indemnity* and identifies this as "a device...to anchor the first-person point of view" (89). The film not only uses a device that emphasizes the aural qualities of the medium, but foregrounds the flashback and confession much more strongly than the novel. According to Chandler biographer Frank MacShane, this shift was deliberately made by both Wilder and Chandler: "[U]nlike most movies of the sort the two criminals were revealed at the very beginning so that, as Wilder said at the premiere, 'we can concentrate on what follows—their efforts to escape, the net closing, closing'" (108). The emphasis on flashback and voiceover would influence the production of numerous subsequent American crime films. As discussed by J.P. Telotte:

> Upon seeing *Double Indemnity* (1944), producer Jerry Wald, who would later make such classic films noir as *Mildred Pierce* (1945), *Dark Passage* (1947), and *Key Largo* (1948), remarked that "from now on, every picture I make will be done in flashback." While he eventually set aside that vow, Wald had quickly and accurately gauged both the popularity and potential of a narrative mechanism that would become fundamentally associated with the film noir form. In fact, today we would typ-

ically begin any list of the basic noir conventions with that narrative combination of voice-over and flashback. (40)

Most critics would agree that *Double Indemnity* is a stronger film than novel. In this respect, it is not surprising the film is the version most remembered today. However, a case could also be made that the strongest aspects of the film are logical translations and extensions of effects already in the novel. The medium-specificity of the written word in the novel is eschewed in favor of the spoken word in the film. The retrospective, confessional aspect of the novel is also clarified and extended in the film adaptation.

Evaluating the Novel Versus the Film and Determining the "Author" of *Double Indemnity*

When an interviewer asked Cain if he watched *Double Indemnity*—"Did you ever go and see the film? What did you think of it?"—he responded, tersely, "I don't go. There are some foods some people just don't like. I just don't like movies. People tell me, don't you care what they've done to your book? I tell them, they haven't done anything to my book. It's right there on the shelf. They paid me and that's the end of it" ("The Art of Fiction"). In another interview Cain described film as generally uninteresting to him, "Moving pictures simply do not excite me intellectually, or aesthetically... I know their technique ... but I don't feel it" (qtd. in Irwin 256). By Frank MacShane's account of the novel's adaptation, he notes that Chandler and Wilder also noted the amount of work needed to translate Cain's compelling story to film.

> Chandler and Wilder first wanted to use as much of the original [dialogue] as possible, but they became aware that something was peculiar about it. It looked all right on paper, but when they got some actors to do a scene right out of the book they discovered that it sounded, as Chandler put it, like a "bad high school play. The dialogue oversaid everything and when spoken sounded quite colorless and tame." Then they had a conference with Cain, who happened to be in Hollywood at the time, and in the end they realized that in the novel the illusion of naturalness was achieved mainly by typographical devices—the elimination of "he said" and "she said." It was written for the eye but not for the ear. They therefore had to write new dialogue that would [107-108] stand up to dramatic presentation. Wilder has acknowledged that Chandler deserves most of the credit for this work (108).

> In her account of the film's adaptation, Biesen writes that "The primary strategy [in scripting a film acceptable under the Code] was to maximize the use of metaphoric innuendo and verbal wit. Rarely had so little been directly stated in a film, yet so much been implied" (46). Biesen, importantly, clarifies that "it was the very restrictions of the Code that made necessary this devious transformation of Cain's gruff material" (47).

> Though Cain was one of many authors, effectively, of the film *Double Indemnity*, upon the film's release he celebrated it as a corroboration of audience demand for his gritty, realistic fiction. Cain took the successful production of *Double Indemnity* as a sign that the industry was "hep to the fact that plenty of real crime takes place every day and that it makes a good movie...The public is fed up with the old-fashioned melodramatic type of hokum" (qtd. in Leff and Simmons 131). Paramount, Wilder, and Chandler had struck a balance in telling Cain's story in a way that preserved the disturbing and realistic qualities of the original, but in a more poetic and allusive way.

Opposite page, "innuendo and verbal wit": in their second meeting Cain's characters talk about iced tea, native Californians, and freckles. Wilder and Chandler lose the freckles, add "a honey of anklet" (see page 23) and this classic exchange:

Walter: "How fast was I going, officer?" Phyllis: "I'd say around ninety." Walter: "Suppose you get down off your motorcycle and give me a ticket." Phyllis: "Suppose I let you off with a warning this time." Walter: "Suppose I bust out crying and put my head on your shoulder." Phyllis: "Suppose you try putting it on my husband's shoulder." Walter: "That tears it."

Sympathy for the Devils: Paramount's *Double Indemnity* as the Subtler and More Disturbing Work

Cain's own discourse about the adaptation of his novel should be clarified by the fact that, despite the necessity of Paramount's working within the parameters of the Production Code, an argument could be made that it is the film that is, incongruously, both subtler and more intense. Though the novel does not contain anything as sensational as the notorious "Bite me! Bite me!" passage of *The Postman Always Rings Twice*, Cain's *Double Indemnity* does contain bold passages that have been toned down in the film. (11) I will focus, in particular, on the lead characters' ethical understanding.

The original novel, to be fair, does have its share of wry, or poetic, or evocative lines; some of which, such as the "red-hot poker," still appear in the film. (13) Along with this, however, are numerous more didactic passages, often resulting in less complex characterization. In many instances, both Nirdlinger and Huff come across as more vulgar, less conflicted characters than they are in the film. Consider this passage of the novel, for example, after Huff and Phyllis have committed the crime:

> She raved like a lunatic. She raved and she kept on raving, about him, about me, about anything that came in her head. Every now and then I'd snap. There we were, after what we had done, snarling at each other like a couple of animals, and neither one of us could stop. It was like somebody had shot us full of some kind of dope. "Phyllis, cut this out. We've got to talk, and it may be our last chance." (52)

Here, Phyllis Nirdlinger evinces a lack of self-control that is never present in Stanwyck's Phyllis Dietrichson in the film. Later, Phyllis of Cain's *Double Indemnity* is also positioned as a self-knowledgeable, devilish-character. She says, "[T]here's something in me, I don't know what. Maybe I'm crazy. But there's something in me that loves Death. I think of myself as Death, sometimes" (18). Wilder's Phyllis Dietrichson is more self-composed, resembling (as compared to Cain's protagonist) Hitchcock's compulsive but less self-aware protagonists. Phyllis is more fascinating in this less transparent form. The same could be said of Walter Neff/Huff. Whereas Walter is more cynical and self-knowing in the novel, he comes across more consistently as overwhelmed and entrapped in the film. Put briefly, Walter and Phyllis in the film are less agentic and, instead, unconscious, psychoanalytic subjects versus subject to drives or compulsions that they, themselves, scarcely understand.

While the novel is defined, often, by didactic self-confidence on the part of the protagonists (absent the dividedness or desperation that is visible on the faces of Stanwyck and MacMurray in the film version), there are passages that anticipate the more nuanced, fatalistic quality of the eventual film. Before Walter's initial meeting with Phyllis, he comments:

In the Wilder-Chandler script's final meeting of the killers, Phyllis echoes the first encounter (when she told Neff, "I think you're rotten."), as she notes: "we're both rotten." Neff's reply is more bitter than ironic: "Only you're a little more rotten."

> I drove out to Glendale to put three new truck drivers on a brewery company bond, and then I remembered this renewal over in Hollywoodland. I decided to run over there. That was how I came to this House of Death, that you've been reading about in the papers. It didn't look like a House of Death when I saw it. It was just a Spanish house, like all the rest of them in California, with white walls, red tile roof, and a patio out to one side. (3)

Here, Cain's novel already anticipates many of the major fascinations of not just *Double Indemnity*, but film noir more generally defined: fatalism and the contrast between apparent prosperity and underlying discontent.

While nearly all critics forced to make the choice between one work or the other as the greater artistic accomplishment would choose Wilder's film, this should not elide the importance of Cain's 1935 story and its containment of some noir themes *avant la lettre*. Hollywood, after all, would not adapt *Double Indemnity* until 1944 and "film noir" would not be prominently defined, as such, until Raymond Borde and Etienne Chaumeton's *A Panorama of American Film Noir* (1941-1953) in 1955.

Sources

Anon. "Review: Double Indemnity." *Variety* staff April 22, 1944. Web.

"The Art of Fiction, no. 69: James M. Cain." Interviewed by David Zinsser. *The Paris Review* 73 (Spring-Summer 1978). Web.

Borde, Raymond and Etienne Chaumeton. *A Panorama of American Film Noir*. 1955. Reprint. San Francisco: City Lights Books, 2002.

Chinen Biesen, Sheri. "Censorship, Film Noir, and Double Indemnity (1944)." *Film & History: An Interdisciplinary Journal of Film and Television Studies* 25.1-2 (1995): 40-52. Print.

Cain, James M. *Double Indemnity*. 1935. Reprint. New York: Random House, 1992. Print.

_____. *The Postman Always Rings Twice*. 1934. Reprint. New York: Random House, 1992. Print.

"Double Indemnity (Paramount Pictures, 1944)." Hollywood, Censorship, and the Motion Picture Production Code, 1927-1968. Archive. Margaret Herrick Library of the Academy of Motion Picture Arts and Sciences. Beverly Hills, California. Reprint. Archives Unbound. Imprint Farmington Hills, MI: Gale, 2012. Web.

Irwin, John T. "Beating the Boss: Cain's *Double Indemnity*." *American Literary History* 14.2 (2002): 255-283. Print.

Leff, Leonard J. and Jerold L. Simmons. *The Dame in the Kimono: Hollywood, Censorship, and the Production Code*. Lexington: University of Kentucky Press, 2001. Print.

MacShane, Frank. *The Life of Raymond Chandler*. New York: Penguin Books, 1978. Print.

Miklitsch, Robert. *Siren City: Sound and Source Music in Classic American Noir*. New Brunswick, NJ: Rutgers University Press, 2011. Print.

Murchie Jr., Guy. "Snyder Murder! Crime of an Insurance Plot." *Chicago Tribune*. Part 7, page9, December 29, 1935. Web.

Naremore, James. *More Than Night: Film Noir in Its Contexts*. Berkeley, CA: University of California Press, 2008. Print.

Pelizzon, V. Penelope and Nancy Martha West. "Multiple Indemnity: Film Noir, James M. Cain, and Adaptations of a Tabloid Case." *Narrative* 13.3 (October 2005): 211-237. Web.

Stanley, Fred. "Hollywood Crime and Romance." *New York Times*. November 19, 1944. XI. Web.

Telotte, J.P. *Voices in the Dark: The Narrative Patterns of Film Noir*. Urbana, IL: University of Illinois Press, 1989. Print.

A posed shot from *Act of Violence*:
Joe Parkson (Robert Ryan) menaces
Frank Enley (Van Heflin).

The Influence of an Émigré Film Noir Auteur: Fred Zinnemann's Social Realism and Cultural Critique in *Act of Violence*

Sheri Chinen Biesen

Influential prototypes to film noir include topical gangster pictures—Mervin Leroy's *Little Caesar* (1930), William Wellman's *The Public Enemy* (1931), Howard Hawks' *Scarface* (1932), and Raoul Walsh's *High Sierra* (1941)—and social realist crime films—LeRoy's *I Am a Fugitive from a Chain Gang* (1932), W. S. Van Dyke's *They Gave Him a Gun* (1937), Michael Curtiz' s *Angels with Dirty Faces* (1938), Busby Berkeley's *They Made Me A Criminal* (1939), and Walsh's *The Roaring Twenties* (1939). Moreover, other forms of social realist cinematic prototypes and auteur directors also influenced film noir. Tapping into real life crime and social concerns, Warner Bros. production chief Darryl Zanuck applauded hard-edged social realism in January 1931. Zanuck argued that *The Public Enemy* and Dashiell Hammett's hard-boiled detective novel *The Maltese Falcon* socially critiqued a growing urban American crime problem (and thus did not violate Hollywood's Production Code censorship), insisting that, "Prohibition did not cause crime, gang violence, or a corrupt environment, but rather Prohibition merely served to bring crime before the public eye" (Zanuck 1931; Biesen 2005). Even overseas, as the Nazis took over Germany (and Germany's UFA filmmaking industry fired Jewish film-makers) in 1933, socially concerned European émigrés—especially Jewish émigrés—flocked to Hollywood seeking political exile and creative opportunity and would have an extraordinary impact on the development of film noir (Biesen 2005; Brook 2009).

I will examine the influence of director Fred Zinnemann's social realism on film noir by exploring the reimagining of Hollywood cinema's social issues and cultural critique in 1940s America as captured in his topical noir film, *Act of Violence*. Zinnemann is typically known for his later 1950s films, such as *The Men* (1950), *High Noon* (1952), and *From Here to Eternity* (1953). Yet, a talented Jewish European émigré born in Vienna, Austria, Zinnemann was an influential auteur director involved in earlier noir prototype films. As early as the silent era, Zinnemann collaborated with other (future) noir auteur directors (and Jewish European émigrés) Robert Siodmak, Edgar Ulmer, and Billy Wilder in 1929 in Germany on *Menschen am Sonntag (People on Sunday)* and worked with documentary film-maker Robert Flaherty, which inspired his social realist directorial style. He also worked with Paul Strand on *Redes (The Wave)*, shot in Mexico in 1934, which earned him an MGM contract. Zinnemann came to Hollywood in December 1934 and worked his way up at MGM. By 1942, Zinnemann directed low budget MGM B mysteries *Kid Glove Killer* and *Eyes in the Night* before directing *The Seventh Cross* (1944) with Spencer Tracy as an escaped fugitive aided by the anti-Nazi Resistance, and also contributed uncredited to directing to *The Clock* (1945). After exploring the destruction and trauma of war in *The Search* (1948), the influence of Zinnemann's social realist concerns on film noir crystallized in his underrated *Act of Violence*.

Zinnemann's under-recognized socially conscious film noir, *Act of Violence* (produced in 1948, released in 1949 by MGM), provides remarkable cultural critique and topical commentary informed by its historical context in the wake of the Second World War. As a European émigré director, Zinnemann's formal aesthetic and social commentary about World War II in *Act of Violence* was informed by the wartime experience, his personal loss, trauma, and influenced by documentary and neorealist technique as in his earlier film shot on location in Europe about displaced refugees from the conflict, *The Search* (1948). It was remarkable that Zinnemann directed *Act of Violence*—his final film at MGM—and Zinnemann's deliberate moments of choice culminated in its extraordinary production, cultural critique and distinctive noir visual style.

In a 1996 interview with Brian Neve for *Cineaste,* Zinnemann recalled, "After I completed *The Search* [in Europe]...When I returned to America I made *Act of Violence*, and I felt that I already knew what I was doing, rather than going by instinct, as before. From *Act of Violence* to the end of *The Men* I was a journeyman, and after that...I felt that I had arrived" (1997: 16). Yet, as a powerful social realist film noir tackling topical issues, Zinnemann's *Act of Violence* transcended the work of a journeyman and suggests the resonance of his later acclaimed socially conscious 1950s films, *The Men, High Noon*, and *From Here to Eternity*.

Act of Violence examined trauma, violence, and conflicted identity in the aftermath of the war, which had particular resonance for Zinnemann, whose family perished in the Holocaust. It revealed postwar tensions such as the Hollywood Blacklist, informing and "naming names" and, like a male melodrama, explored issues of masculinity, honor, loyalty, and betrayal. Zinnemann's visual style and mise-en-scène featured impressive cinematography filmed on location in Los Angeles, Big Bear Lake, and San Bernardino Forest, shifting the noir setting from shadowy "urban jungle" to a sunny, brightly lit rural terrain.

Zinnemann cultivated outstanding performances in his volatile self-destructive noir antiheroes. Troubled World War II veteran Frank Enley (Van Heflin) is celebrated as a war hero, but his dark past is revealed as he's pursued by vengeful former war buddy, Joe (Robert Ryan). Women in *Act of Violence* are nurturing domestic helpmates—wives, girlfriends, and barflies—redeemers of tormented combat veterans.

As Frank flees from Joe and hides in the shadows of his dark home, he tells his young wife, Edith (Janet Leigh), "A lot of things happened in the war that you wouldn't understand. Why should you? I don't understand them myself." Throughout the course of the film, as Frank unravels and tries to hide his mysterious secrets to save his own skin, his fateful words capture the tense mood and disturbing atmosphere that Zinnemann creates in *Act of Violence*, a social conscious film noir scripted by Robert Richards, based on a story by Collier Young, originally called *The Traitor* to be produced at Warner Bros.

Initially, *The Traitor* (*Act of Violence*) project was compared to another socially relevant film noir, Edward Dmytryk's *Crossfire* (1947) at RKO which dealt with anti-Semitism and hate crimes committed by returning combat veterans—commenting on the violence and horror of the war—and other hard-hitting, socially relevant films, including earlier gangster pictures such as Howard Hawks' *Scarface* (1932) and Raoul Walsh's *High Sierra* (1941), Lewis Milestone's social realist antiwar epic *All Quiet on the Western Front* (1930), and John Ford's topical drama *The Informer* (1935).

Early on, Warner Bros., director Don Siegel, and producer Jerry Wald praised *Act of Violence* (aka *The Traitor*) as a film noir project like *Crossfire*, and at one point Raoul Walsh was assigned to direct it. *Crossfire*'s Robert Mitchum, *High Sierra*'s noir icon Humphrey Bogart and *Laura/Best Years of Our Lives* star Dana Andrews were even considered for the lead role.

In October 1947, as Washington's House Committee on Un-American Activities (HUAC) hearings ramped up, Warner executives recommended eliminating night exterior scenes which would have undercut and mitigated against *Act of Violence*'s dark, atmospheric noir style. The Hollywood film industry trade association, the Motion Picture Association of America's (MPAA) chief Eric Johnston insisted in 1947: "We'll have no more films that show the seamy side of American life" (Schumach 1975).

By December, Warner sold the project to independent *Naked City* producer Mark Hellinger, who suddenly died a few weeks later. After several months MGM eventually acquired it in 1948.

"A lot of things happen in war that you wouldn't understand": Frank Enley (Van Heflin) tries to explain himself to his wife Edith (Janet Leigh).

Socially minded executive Dore Schary had backed topical noir *Crossfire* at RKO before moving to MGM and supervising production on *Act of Violence*.

In 1948, recalling *The Search*, Zinnemann explained that he utilized the "raw material of history" to "make a dramatic document" (1948: 12-13, 30; 1997: 15). *Act of Violence* and *The Search* were both realistic 1940s cultural and historical filmic products of their time after the war years—ideal projects for Zinnemann. In *The Search*, Zinnemann movingly portrayed the plight of refugees and families torn apart by war amid the rubble in postwar Europe. After the war, Zinnemann found out his own family had been killed in Nazi concentration camps, like Billy Wilder's and so many others. Zinnemann's experiences informed his insightful realism in *The Search* and *Act of Violence*, his last MGM film. *Act of Violence* is an extraordinary underrated film noir cinematic gem not always considered in critical examinations of Zinnemann's vast, acclaimed body of work such as *The Men, High Noon*, and *From Here to Eternity*. It continues to resonate cultural and historical relevance in its socially conscious themes, taut narrative, and innovative formal-aesthetic style.

Contrary to Warner Bros.' original conception of *The Traitor*, Zinnemann and cinematographer Robert Surtees made deliberate decisions—distinctive moments of choice—to create and emphasize an ominous film noir milieu with night location shots of Los Angeles to visually project its topical social themes and capture the urban jungle's oppressive entrapment vis-à-vis the tormented antihero's subjective point-of-view and cinematically reflect his psychological peril. Zinnemann stressed the importance of fusing documentary realist technique with a darker, moody noir style, as did Surtees who wrote in *American Cinematographer* in 1948 that "reflected lighting, no makeup, natural locations and use of a 28mm lens are some of the new production trends explored in the making of this picture" (1948: 268). Zinnemann recalled his "most vivid memory" of making *Act of Violence* was "the many sleepless nights we spent shooting exteriors in the eerie slums of downtown Los Angeles" (1992: 74). Zinnemann's atmospheric film noir styled night time locales would become an unforgettable highlight of *Act of Violence* with its stark, deep focus, high contrast photography.

Zinnemann establishes a shrouded, chiaroscuro style and menacing mood against the dark silhouette of a nocturnal New York City skyline immediately in the opening of the film with brilliant use of sound as obsessed veteran Joe drags himself across the street. Bronislav Kaper's riveting, atonal minor-key music score, conducted by a young Andre Previn, creates tension and blares an auditory warning.

The noir setting shifts from the New York urban terrain to the quiet (fictitious) town of Santa Lisa, California where World War II veterans march in a Memorial Day parade and happy war-hero family man Frank smiles with his wife and baby in the sunshine as he receives an award from the community. Zinnemann builds suspense in broad daylight and outdoor wilderness as Frank goes fishing on the lake in the mountains with his neighbor. All seems like bliss in this peaceful rural setting until Joe arrives bent on vengeance. Joe rows out on a boat across the lake and crouches, hidden behind a boulder, waiting, then aims his gun to shoot Frank as his boat goes by, but misses the opportunity when the motor turns on and Frank sails to shore.

As Joe appears in the distance behind him, Frank becomes aware he's being stalked and returns home. Frank's entire demeanor changes as he locks the doors, turns out the lights, stands cloaked in shadows, cowers in the blackened corner, apprehensively draws down the blackout shades, and silences his wife in the dark. The kitchen faucet runs as Joe tries to force his way into the house, then waits in his car outside. Frank's home becomes not a domestic sanctuary for he and his wife, but rather a trap imprisoning him as he hides in fear, obsessed with concealing his terrible, guilty lie on which he's built his life. He fears the light will expose him, so he clings to the shadows. Surtees' brooding low-key, deep-focus cinematography shows the expressionistic darkness of Frank's house and Joe lighting his cigarette in the night—from the blackness of his automobile across the street. Sound is used brilliantly to heighten suspense—even the sound of Frank's baby's cry resembles a startling shriek of terror in a noir thriller.

Frank's war hero is hiding a dark, disturbing secret: He betrayed his men to the Nazi enemy which led to their brutal murder. Menacing antagonist Joe is actually his best friend, a disabled victim who barely survived the violence. We witness the transformation and ultimate redemption of both antiheroes as Frank sacrifices his own life to save Joe from assassination by a hit man. Joe, the apparent villain, was in fact a victim of atrocities committed in wartime and enabled by the flawed cowardice of the antihero Frank's betrayal. Frank is ashamed. When Joe tries to kill him, Frank refuses to call the police. He insists to his wife, "You don't know what made him the way he is. I do." Tormented,

afraid, and unable to forgive himself, Frank flees in the night to a convention in Los Angeles.

When his wife tracks him down, Frank pulls her into a dim fire escape stairwell (at left) so they won't be seen. Splintering diagonal patterns of crisscrossing bars and ominous shadows cover him—like the barbed wire chained link fence where his men perished when the Nazis starved, bayoneted and sicced dogs on them, then left them to die. This splicing of the frame, obstructions between camera and subject, and piercing of compositional space in the

The Influence of an Émigré Film Noir Auteur: Fred
Zinnemann's Social Realism and Cultural Critique in
Act of Violence

341

brooding film noir cinematography and mise-en-scène design visually suggests Frank's entrapment as he reveals his horrible betrayal to his wife: "Do I have to spell it out for you? Do I have to draw you a picture? I was an informer." His cold, anguished recounting of events is chilling.

Frank explains to her what he did in Germany, describing how he secretly cut a deal with the Nazi commandant of the prison camp, who lied to him and then ordered his men to be murdered. "It doesn't make any difference why I did it. I betrayed my men. They were dead. The Nazis even paid me a price. They gave me food and I ate it." He shamefully admits:

> I hadn't done it just to save their lives. I talked myself into believing it, that he would keep his word. But in my guts from the start I think I knew he wouldn't. And maybe I didn't even care. They were dead and I was eating, and maybe that's all I did it for, to save one man—me. There were six widows. There were ten men dead. And I couldn't even stop eating.

Zinnemann exposes the shady, seamy side of Los Angeles as Frank runs for his life and walks the skid row streets at night in the howling wind. He is haunted by the voices of his men and the Nazis who killed them. In his guilt ridden, real life nightmare, he runs screaming through a tunnel and tries to commit suicide.

Act of Violence is exceptional for its visual style and cultural critique in its exploration of social issues in World War II's aftermath that tackled issues in a way seldom done during the conflict due to wartime censorship restrictions. Zinnemann's noir artistry in *Act of Violence* is notable in reimagining the Second World War in a distinctly postwar context in the wake of a burgeoning Cold War amid the

The "youthful, innocent and idealistic" Edith (Janet Leigh) meets the embittered and relentless Joe Parkson (Robert Ryan)

scars, cultural tensions, paranoia, and psychological and physical trauma as a result of the conflict's violence, atrocities, death and destruction that destroyed so many lives.

Act of Violence's topical, hard-hitting portrayal of an American serviceman's betrayal leading to the slaying of his U.S. solders who were captured Nazi POW prison camp survivors and the theme of informing resonated with Zinnemann and American culture amid the atrocities and aftermath of the Holocaust and the growing "Red Scare" of HUAC hearings and the Hollywood Blacklist. Such topics as servicemen committing crimes were censored in wartime; the depiction of a US officer betraying men could not be made during the war due to constraints on Hollywood film content by the Production Code Administration and Washington's Office of War Information.

The film suggests veterans Frank and Joe strived to escape the horror and violence of the war and return to the "normalcy" of peacetime prosperity and a middle-class "Main Street, USA" suburban lifestyle, but the scars of the war are buried just below the surface. Thematically, it deals with informing, disloyalty, subversion, and what Frank did in the war to suggest the burgeoning Cold War "Red Scare" paranoia by the late 1940s in an era of HUAC, McCarthy, and the Hollywood Blacklist amid the growing postwar social and cultural tensions about who is secretly a Communist, are Americans betraying us, and the rampant xenophobia concerning who your friends and neighbors are, and who you can trust. Heflin and Ryan amplify suspense and bring the trauma, violence, and psychological scars of the war vividly to life in their flawed, troubled antiheroes.

Frank's wife Edith is so youthful, innocent and idealistic. Yet, she's already married with a baby to a much older man that she has idolized as a larger than life hero, but whom she doesn't really know. He shatters her naïve illusions about him until she dejectedly realizes he has flaws and is "just like everybody else." He's been secretly on the run hiding and trying to escape his past for years, ever since the war ended, perhaps the entire time she has known him. They even packed up suddenly and moved 3,000 miles from Syracuse, New York to California without collecting his last paycheck. She realizes something deeply unsettling is going on as the suburbs are being built and the baby boomers are being born after the war signifying cultural changes in postwar American life. She has married a stranger. Not only has he been living a lie, but he seems to exist in this masculine world of male camaraderie—at work, at a builders convention, at war, even fishing on the lake with the guys—of which

Frank runs down an alleyway adjacent to the popular noir location Angel's Flight. Opposite, Pay (Mary Astor) introduces Frank to hitman Johnny (Berry Kroeger).

The Influence of an Émigré Film Noir Auteur: Fred   343
Zinnemann's Social Realism and Cultural Critique in
Act of Violence

she has no part as she stays in their comfortable middle class home with the baby oblivious to his dark secrets.

Frank stays with a washed up prostitute (Mary Astor) looking to "get kicks," who sets him up with several sleazy, disreputable scam artists and assassins who hustle Frank, and ask him for money, but she regrets the whole dirty business—despite the fact that she and her disreputable cronies are all "on the take." She offers her cheap, simplistic dime philosophy to Frank, insisting that all the problems in the world can be summed up as either "love trouble" or "money trouble." She has no conception of how Frank's grave, complex situation, moral dilemma and suffering have absolutely nothing to do with troubled romance or a shortage of cash.

Women play an important role in humanizing the experience of the men amid the topical cultural critique of *Act of Violence*. Actresses were deglamorized with harsh deep focus photography, high contrast lighting (without softly flattering diffusion), and very little makeup to add to the realism of everyday people. Zinnemann recalled, "It was a special delight to be working with [*Maltese Falcon* femme fatale] Mary Astor, playing an aging streetwalker who picks up the exhausted, desperate Van Heflin running for his life through the creepy, crumbling night time streets" (1992: 74). Moreover, Astor's dress was not from the MGM wardrobe, but rather off the rack at a cheap department store (Astor 1959).

There are several moments of choice evident in the notable differences in Zinnemann's final film version of *Act of Violence* from the original conception of the story at Warner Bros. and initial drafts at MGM which changed the depiction of female characters. In earlier drafts of the script, Joe's girlfriend Ann (Phyllis Thaxter) actually shoots Joe to try to stop his vengeful pursuit of Frank. Then they have a steamy, passionate sexual scene as she comforts him in remorse, suggesting a bit more of a tough, dangerous sexy femme fatale. Also, the hit man Johnny (Barry Kroeger) initially had a larger role and Frank slept at his flat. The sex and brutality were toned down considerably in Zinnemann's final film version of *Act of Violence*. Moreover, originally, in early drafts of the screenplay, Frank goes into a church and sees images of Jesus, the Last Supper, Judas, Christ's crucifixion, and these shots are intermingled with flashbacks of the Nazis to depict his overwhelming guilt and desire to end his own life, but failure to have the courage to do so. However, in the film, Zinnemann dispenses with this

church scene and does not show any religious iconography or images of the Nazis or the prison camp. One early version of the script included a famous LA billboard sign that reads: "Jesus Saves" but this imagery was cut and replaced with a neon sign of *The LA Times* newspaper and dive bars. Instead, in a moment of choice, Zinnemann portrays the most powerful sequences in the film with nocturnal images on the streets of the City of Angels. Ultimately, in this noir universe, life on the street, at the club, and in the big city are presented as undesirable and shown to be a dangerous endeavor.

Zinnemann effectively conveys a treacherous waking nightmare using exterior night location shots of Los Angeles. Surtees' breathtaking cinematography achieves exquisite chiaroscuro film noir style in *Act of Violence* and creates gripping suspense with ominous shadows and disturbing sounds of the city, the long tunnel, and the blaring oncoming train which come vividly to life and conjure images of the antihero's tormented mentality, culminating in an explosive finale. The wind howls and debris blows through the air littering the slick, wet streets as harsh images of the City of Angels become an urban jungle. Zinnemann films the traumatized veteran as a small, diminutive figure on the run dwarfed by huge, imposing, soaring structures in Los Angeles shot from extreme angles to create visual depth and emphasize the deep focus composition and "z axis" of images while suggesting an oppressive, cluttered, chaotic, and claustrophobic noir milieu.

Frank is pressed up against the sides of buildings as he flees for his life, and the surroundings get worse, descending to shabby tenements, neon signs and shady bars. The deteriorating noir environment visually conveys Frank's psychological tumult, crisis and breakdown on the dark streets of Los Angeles past towering edifices through the nocturnal city: a disturbing, bleak abyss. He traverses dark alleys, dodgy street corners, dives, cheap hotels, and ends up in skid row, running down the steep stairs and slopes of Bunker Hill as the Angels Flight funicular railway passes above him.

Parkson's girlfriend Ann (Phyllis Thaxter) begs him to abandon his plan to kill Enley.

The Influence of an Émigré Film Noir Auteur: Fred   345
Zinnemann's Social Realism and Cultural Critique in
Act of Violence

Frank enters the long, claustrophobic Third Street tunnel where he is haunted by memories of his past. Zinnemann conveys the veteran's tortured state of mind and anguished "survivor guilt" by using extraordinary bleak noir visuals and sound design in this climactic scene depicting Frank's crisis and breakdown as he is shown running through the long abyss of the tunnel with its dark passage and stark lights, which brings back horrific nightmare memories of his men dying trapped in the tunnel in the Nazi prison camp during the war after he betrayed them. He hears the sounds and voices of Joe, his men, and the Nazis, then shouts to warn them not to go into the tunnel to try to escape as his hallucinations overwhelm him. He emerges disoriented after fleeing and screaming in the tunnel, then as in a psychotic altered state, gravitates toward the blaring siren of an oncoming train on the railroad tracks in a plume of smoke and stands in its path to end his life. He is overcome by a loss of nerve and jumps out of the way as the train passes, just missing him. In the end, Frank suffers and is punished for his betrayal that led to the death of his men and redeems himself by courageously taking a bullet and doing the right thing to save Joe from the assassin before he dies.

Reviews praised *Act of Violence*, Zinnemann's direction and its performances. The film cost $1,290,000 and earned $703,000 in North America and $426,000 overseas, totaling $1,129,000— albeit a loss of $637,000 for MGM (Mannix 1949). MGM Studio publicity ads clamored: "The Killer...Night and day he stalks his prey. Slowly, surely his shadow of doom darkens the life of his terrified victim." Tapping into the Cold War paranoia of its postwar social climate, Heflin was described as: "The Hunted! What suddenly made him a fugitive?" Ryan was "Menacing...The Hunter! He came from nowhere to avenge!" in "The manhunt no woman could stop!" By December 1948, *Variety* applauded the "realism," "suspense" and "dramatic intensity" in Zinnemann's noir production as a "masterpiece," calling it "stark" "strong meat" and an "excellent" "grim melodrama" (Brog 1948: 6). By January 1949, Bosley Crowther of *The New York Times* insisted that Zinnemann's "smart direction" was the "best thing" about the film (16). Ultimately, as a result of this auteur director's social realist concerns about film noir and these keen moments of choice, Zinnemann's underrated film noir *Act of Violence* is a fascinating cinematic product which articulates cultural tensions in postwar Hollywood by the late 1940s, and anticipates the social realism of his later films *The Men, High Noon*, and *From Here To Eternity*.

Bibliography

Astor, Mary. *A Life on Film*, New York: Doubleday, 1959.

Biesen, Sheri Chinen. *Blackout: World War II and the Origins of Film Noir*, Baltimore: Johns Hopkins University Press, 2005.

Brog., "Act of Violence," *Variety*, 22 December 1948, 6.

Brook, Vincent. *Driven to Darkness: Jewish Émigré Directors and the Rise of Film Noir*, New Brunswick, New Jersey: Rutgers University Press, 2009.

Crowther, Bosley. "Act of Violence (1949)," *New York Times*, 24 January 1949, 16.

Mannix, Eddie. Eddie Mannix Ledger & Fred Zinnemann Collection, Los Angeles: Margaret Herrick Library, Center for Motion Picture Study, 1949.

Neve, Brian. "A Past Master of His Craft: An Interview with Fred Zinnemann," *Cineaste*, 23: 1, (1997), 15-19.

MGM Publicity and Script Files for Act of Violence, MGM & USC Pressbook Collection, Los Angeles: USC Cinematic Arts Library, University of Southern California, 1949.

Schumach, Murray. *The Face on the Cutting Room Floor: The Story of Movie and Television Censorship*, New York: Da Capo Press, 1975.

Surtees, Robert. "The Story of Filming Act of Violence," *American Cinematographer*, 29: 8, (1948), 268-284.

Zanuck, Darryl. MPAA/MPPDA/PCA File, Academy of Motion Picture Arts and Sciences Library, Beverly Hills, California, 6 January 1931.

Zinnemann, Fred. *A Life in the Movies: An Autobiography*, New York: MacMillan Publishing Company, 1992.

_____. "The Story of The Search by Fred Zinnemann," *Screenwriter*, 4: 2, August 1948, 12-13, 30.

Fritz Lang (with megaphone) directs Brigitte Helm (crouching below camera) and the throng of extras in *Metropolis*.

Notes on Contributors

Sheri Chinen Biesen is a professor of Film History and author of *Blackout: World War II and the Origins of Film Noir* (2005) and *Music in the Shadows: Noir Musical Films* (2014) at Johns Hopkins University Press. She received a BA and MA at the University of Southern California School of Cinema, PhD at the University of Texas at Austin, and has taught at USC, University of California, University of Texas, and in England. She has contributed to the BBC documentary *The Rules of Film Noir* and to *Film and History, Film Noir: The Directors, Literature/Film Quarterly, Film Noir Reader 4, Historical Journal of Film, Radio and Television, Film Noir: The Encyclopedia, Quarterly Review of Film and Video, Gangster Film Reader, Popular Culture Review, The Historian, Television and Television History, Film Noir Compendium*, Turner Classic Movies *Public Enemies* for the Warner Bros. Gangster Collection, and edited *The Velvet Light Trap*.

James V. D'Arc recently retired from 41 years as curator of the BYU Motion Picture Archive and the BYU Film Music Archive at Brigham Young University, for which entity he acquired the collections of James Stewart, Cecil B. DeMille, Merian C. Cooper, Howard Hawks, and Max Steiner. In addition to 30 years of teaching courses on film and American culture, D'Arc is the author of *When Hollywood Came to Town: A History of Moviemaking in Utah* (2010). As a youngster he repeatedly saw *The Face Behind the Mask* on Los Angeles television and it left an indelible impression.

Below Robert Florey (leaning over) directs Peter Lorre in *The Face Behind the Mask.*

Alfred Hitchcock watches actors Judith Anderson (left) and Joan Fontaine on the set of *Rebecca.*

Richard L. Edwards is the co-author of *The Maltese Touch of Evil: Film Noir and Potential Criticism* (2011). He is also the co-host of the long-running and popular podcast series, "Out of the Past: Investigating Film Noir." In partnership with Turner Classic Movies, he taught the massive open online course, "Into the Darkness: Investigating Film Noir" (2015) and "TCM Presents The Master of Suspense: 50 Years of Hitchcock" (2017). Currently, he is the Executive Director of iLearn Research at Ball State University.

Todd Erickson coined the term "neo-noir" in the early 1980s during research for his master's thesis, *Film Noir in the Contemporary American Cinema* (Brigham Young University, 1990) under the mentorship of film historian James V. D'Arc and film noir experts Alain Silver and Robert Porfirio. Previous works include "Kill Me Again: Movement Becomes Genre," *Film Noir Reader*, Volume 1 (1996), ten neo-noir essays for *Film Noir: The Encyclopedia* (2010), "Robert Siodmak" in *Film Noir: The Directors* (2012), and "Nothingness and Purpose: Light and Shadow in *It's a Wonderful Life*" for *Film Noir: Light and Shadow* (2016).

Julie Grossman is a Professor of English and Communication and Film Studies at Le Moyne College, USA. Her books include *Rethinking the Femme Fatale in Film Noir* (2009, 2012), *Literature, Film, and Their Hideous Progeny: Adaptation and ElasTEXTity* (2015), and *Ida Lupino, Director: Her Art and Resilience in Times of Transition* (co-authored with Therese Grisham, 2017). With R. Barton Palmer, she is founding co-editor of the book series *Adaptation and Visual Culture* and co-editor of the collection *Adaptation in Visual Culture: Images, Texts, and Their Multiple Worlds* (2017). Forthcoming monographs include *Femme Fatales* (Rutgers UP) and *Major Performers in Hollywood Noir* (co-authored with R. Barton Palmer, Edinburgh UP).

Robert Miklitsch is a Professor in the Department of English Language and Literature at Ohio University. His work on film and television has appeared in *Camera Obscura, Film Quarterly, Journal* *of Film and Video, Journal of Popular Film and Television, New Review of Film and Television Studies,* and *Screen.* He is the editor of *Psycho-Marxism* (1998) and the author of *From Hegel to Madonna* (1998), *Roll Over Adorno* (2006), and *Siren City: Sound and Source Music in Classic American Noir* (2011, which was named a Choice Outstanding Academic Title). His edited collection, *Kiss the Blood Off My Hands: On Classic Noir* (2014), was nominated for an Edgar Allan Poe Award (Criticism) by the Mystery Writers of America and named a Choice Outstanding Academic Title of 2015. His newest book is *The Red and the Black: American Film Noir in the 1950s* (2017).

Homer B. Pettey is Professor of Film and Comparative Literature at the University of Arizona. For Edinburgh University Press, he serves as General/Founding Editor for two series: Global Film Studios and International Film Stars. He also serves as General/Founding Editor for a series for Rutgers University Press: Global Film Directors. With R. Barton Palmer, he co-edited two volumes on film noir, *Film Noir* and *International Noir* (2014). He and Palmer have a collection on *Hitchcock's Moral Gaze* published by SUNY Press (2017), as well as a collection in production at SUNY Press, *Rule Britannia: Biopics and British National Identity* (2017). Palmer and Pettey are assembling a collection on French Literature on Screen for Manchester University Press (2018). Currently, Pettey is completing a forthcoming book on *Cold War Film Genres* for Edinburgh University Press (2018).

Robert G. Porfirio began his ground-breaking work on film noir while in the Master's program at U.C.L.A. and continued with his 1979 dissertation in American Studies, *The Dark Age of American Film: A Study of American Film Noir (1940-1960),* for Yale University where he also did extensive research on comic books. His articles include contributions to *Continuum, Dialog, Literature/Film Quarterly,* and the seminal "No Way Out: Existential Motifs in the Film Noir" for *Sight and Sound.* He is co-editor of *Film Noir Reader 3* and all editions of *Film Noir: An Encyclopedic Reference,* for which he wrote scores of individual entries, and also contributed to *The Noir Style, Film Noir Readers 1, 2,* and *4, The Philosophy of Film Noir, A Companion to Film Noir, Film Noir Compendium,* and *Film Noir Light and Shadow.* He was formerly assistant professor of American Studies at California State University, Fullerton. Our esteemed colleague passed away in 2014.

Tom Ryall is Emeritus Professor of Film History at Sheffield Hallam University. His books include *Anthony Asquith, Britain and the American Cinema,* and *Alfred Hitchcock and the British Cinema.* He has contributed various articles on British and American cinema to collections such as *British Rural Landscapes on Film, Howard Hawks, New Perspectives, The Routledge Companion to British Media History, A Companion to Film Noir, Modern British Drama on Screen, Film Noir The Directors, A Companion to Hitchcock Studies, The British Cinema Book, The Cinema of Britain and Ireland,* and *The Oxford Guide to Film Studies.* He has written for journals such as *Screen, Sight and Sound,* and the *Journal of Popular British Cinema.*

Marlisa Santos is an associate professor and chair of the department of literature and modern languages at Nova Southeastern University in Fort Lauderdale, Florida. Her research focuses on classic film studies and film noir. She is the editor of *Verse, Voice, and Vision: Poetry and the Cinema* (2013) and the author of *The Dark Mirror: Psychiatry and Film Noir* (2010). She has also published numerous articles on various topics such as the James Bond franchise, American mafia cinema, and contemporary southern film, and on directors such as Martin Scorsese, Edgar G. Ulmer, and Joseph Lewis.

Alain Silver wrote and edited the books listed on page 2, the earliest of which was based on his U.C.L.A doctoral dissertation. His articles have appeared in *Film Comment, Movie* (UK*), Wide Angle, Literature/Film Quarterly,* and *Photon* and anthologies on *The Hummer,* Akira Kurosawa, and Crime Fiction, as well as the on-line magazines *Images* and *Senses of Cinema.* His filmed screenplays include *White Nights* (from Dostoyevsky), the Showtime feature *Time at the Top, Nightcomer* (which he also directed), and *Sacred Blood.* He has also produced more than two dozen independent features, ranging from *Cyborg 2* to *Torch* and forty soundtrack albums. His commentaries have been heard and seen on KCET Television, Starz, E! Entertainment Television, Channel Four UK, AMC, Sci-fi Channel, CBC/Ontario and numerous DVDs discussing Raymond Chandler, Robert Aldrich, the gangster film, and the classic period from *Murder My Sweet* to most recently *Ride the Pink Horse*.

Jesse Schlotterbeck is Assistant Professor of Cinema at Denison University. He received his Ph.D. in Film Studies from the University of Iowa and his research focuses on American film genres, in particular, the musical, the biopic, and film noir. He has most recently published articles on *A Hard Day's Night* in *Quarterly Review of Film and Video* and *Sergeant York* in *Howard Hawks: New Perspectives*. His work on film noir appears in *A Companion to Film Noir, Film Noir: The Directors, Journal of Adaptation in Film and Performance*, and *M/C—A Journal of Media and Culture*.

James Ursini wrote and edited the books listed on page 2 and provided text for the Taschen Icon series on Bogart, Dietrich, Elizabeth Taylor, Mae West, and De Niro. His early study of Preston Sturges was reprinted in a bilingual edition by the San Sebastián Film Festival. His film noir DVD commentaries (most often with Alain Silver) include *Out of the Past, The Dark Corner, Nightmare Alley, Lady in the Lake, Kiss of Death, Brute Force, Crossfire, The Lodger, The Street with No Name, Where Danger Lives, Kiss Me Deadly* and such other titles as *Hobson's Choice* and limited edition of *The Egyptian* and *The Wayward Bus*. He has been a producer on features and documentaries, wrote and co-directed the independent neo-noir *Nasty Piece of Work*.

Tony Williams is the co-author of *Italian Western: Opera of Violence* and co-editor of *Vietnam War Films* and *Jack London's The Sea Wolf: A Screenplay by Robert Rossen*. His numerous books include *Jack London: the Movies; Hearths of Darkness: the Family in the American Horror Film; Larry Cohen: Radical Allegories of an American Filmmaker; Structures of Desire: British Cinema 1949-1955; John Woo's Bullet in the Head; The Cinema of George A. Romero: Knight of the Living Dead;* and *Body and Soul: The Cinematic Vision of Robert Aldrich*. His articles have appeared in *Cinema Journal, CineAction, Wide Angle, Jump Cut, Asian Cinema, Creative Filmmaking*, several *Film Noir Readers*, and *The Zombie Film*. He is an Associate Professor and Area Head of Film Studies at Southern Illinois University, Carbondale.

Director Robert Siodmak (center left) and producer Mark Hellinger with actors Charles McGraw and William Conrad on the set of *The Killers*.